THE MAKING OF
MODERN COLOMBIA

THE MAKING OF
MODERN COLOMBIA

A NATION IN SPITE OF ITSELF

DAVID BUSHNELL

University of California Press
Berkeley   Los Angeles   Oxford

University of California Press
Berkeley and Los Angeles, California

University of California Press, Ltd.
Oxford, England

© 1993 by
The Regents of the University of California

Library of Congress Cataloging-in-Publication Data

Bushnell, David, 1923–
    The making of modern Colombia : a nation in spite of itself /
David Bushnell.
        p.   cm.
    Includes bibliographical references and index.
    ISBN 0-520-7802-0 (cloth : alk. paper)
    1. Colombia—History.   I. Title.
F2271.B78   1993
986.1—dc20   91-46038

Printed in the United States of America
9   8   7   6   5   4   3   2   1

The paper used in this publication meets the minimum require-
ments of American National Standard for Information
Sciences—Permanence of Paper for Printed Library Materials,
ANSI Z39.48-1984. ∞

Contents

By Way of Introduction:
Colombia as a Field of Study

Colombia is today the least studied of the major Latin American countries, and probably the least understood. It has attracted the attention
of specialists in Latin American literature, in good part thanks to its
Nobel prize–winning novelist, Gabriel García Márquez; economists
have taken note of its slow but steady economic growth, in a region
better known for sharp (and in recent years mostly downward) fluctuations; and a number of political scientists have been intrigued by
the peculiarities of its traditional two-party system. Nevertheless, in
the papers presented at scholarly meetings and the articles published in
scholarly journals, Colombia is featured far less frequently than Brazil
or Mexico or Argentina or even, say, Chile or Peru. In the field of
history specifically, the only English-language survey is a long-
outdated English translation of a Colombian secondary text,[1] whereas
at least four modern English-language histories are available on Peru.
Meanwhile, at the level of popular impressions—in the United States
and Western Europe—the name *Colombia* suggests mainly drug
trafficking and endemic violence. If anything more positive comes to
mind, it is the familiar Juan Valdez of the Colombian coffee growers'
advertising, whose image is really that of a stereotypical Latin American peasant farmer.

Colombia deserves better than this, if only for reasons of size. It is
the fourth largest Latin American nation, and it is the third most
populous. It had actually been third in population at the time of independence, exceeded only by Mexico and Brazil. Argentina then moved
ahead on the basis of a massive influx of late-nineteenth- and early-
twentieth-century immigration such as Colombia never received, but
in the past year or so Colombia has edged ahead again. In gross production it is only fifth, exceeded also by Venezuela, but it occupies first
place as an exporter of such disparate commodities as emeralds,
books, processed cocaine, and cut flowers.

vii

If, in spite of such claims on the attention of the outside world, Colombia still does not receive its fair share of scholarly attention, one reason undoubtedly is that the pervasive image of violence leads faint-hearted investigators to turn elsewhere. Another, in the view of historian Charles Bergquist, is that Colombia does not fit the stereotypes and "models" conventionally used in discussions of Latin America.[2] After all, what is a Latin Americanist to do with a country where military dictators are almost unknown, the political left has been congenitally weak, and such phenomena as urbanization and industrialization never spawned a "populist" movement of lasting consequence? Actually, for a student of the nineteenth century, Colombia is perhaps the most stereotypical country of all, with its long string of civil wars between Liberals and Conservatives, its retrograde clericalism and radical anticlericalism, all in a context of socioeconomic stagnation. But even scholars who work on the previous century will often choose their country of specialization on the basis of current headlines.

The problem of Colombia's image as a nation is compounded by ambivalent characteristics of the Colombians themselves. Quite apart from their tendency in recent years to take the lead in underscoring negative aspects of the national panorama, they continue to exhibit major differences along the lines of class, region, and in some cases ethnicity. It is thus a commonplace to say (with Colombians often saying first and loudest) that the country lacks a true national identity or a proper spirit of nationalism, at least as compared to most of its Latin American neighbors. Indeed, hyperbolic nationalism is not common in Colombia; and the national character, if such a thing can be said to exist, is a composite of sometimes contradictory traits. However, both the *costeño* (or denizen of the Caribbean coast) and the *cachaco* (from Bogotá or more generally the Andean interior), who profess to have almost nothing in common, make much the same complaints about the country's society and institutions, and do so within a common frame of reference.

For better or worse, Colombia does exist as a nation in the world today. The people and territory known as Colombian have not arrived at this status by an easy path; they have been torn by social, cultural, political, and regional antagonisms and misunderstandings. Yet the story consists of much more than lives lost and opportunities wasted. There have been accomplishments, too, including a remarkably vigorous output of literature and art. Colombians have also shown time and again the ability to recover from terrible predicaments and to continue their daily round of activities under circumstances that to the outside observer might have seemed hopeless. A skill at "muddling through" is certainly one of the traits to be included in any putative model of the national character.

The account that follows, of Colombia's emergence as a modern nation, is the end result of a personal association with Colombia and Colombians that by now goes back almost half a century. It does not pretend to be a wholly objective story. Whether or not full scholarly detachment is even desirable, in practice it is not humanly possible, and I do not claim to be unbiased where Colombia is concerned. I have had my share of bad experiences in that country as elsewhere, and I have seen things that I would rather not have seen; but I have made firm friends there and have come to love the sights and sounds and smells that assault my senses whenever I again set foot on Colombian soil. I have also observed that the great majority of Colombians (trite as it may be to say so) are peaceable, courteous, and not engaged in any kind of violent or criminal activity.

I still do not claim to understand Colombia as well as someone who was born into the culture and has lived there always, though at times my condition as a foreigner may actually help me see a few things more clearly. I have naturally been helped even more by a host of other people, from clerical personnel to distinguished scholars, Colombian and non-Colombian, so numerous that it is better not even to attempt a list of acknowledgments. Either I would inadvertently leave some names out or I would need too many pages. For comparable reasons, of fearing to do too little or too much, I have mostly omitted reference notes, documenting only quotations, statistical data (so that anyone who wishes can check on them), and certain special cases. Some reviewers and other readers will probably object, but the publisher did not, and cutting down on notes does leave more room for text.

I must nevertheless acknowledge at least the help of my immediate family, all of whom have spent time in Colombia with me (one was born there). Above all, I pay a tribute of gratitude to my wife, whom I first dragged off to Colombia in the aftermath of the *Bogotazo*—the explosion of urban rioting that shook the Colombian capital in April 1948—when I was a graduate student setting forth to do Ph.D. research on a wholly inadequate stipend. Her initial exposure proved traumatic, but she kept going back and has come to love the country too; hers have been a second pair of eyes through which I have been able to look at the Colombian scene over the years.

David Bushnell
Gainesville, Florida, 1992

I

Indians and Spaniards

In the beginning there were mountains, plains, and rivers, but especially mountains; no one geographic feature has so molded the history of Colombia as the Andes. They do not attain the same height that they have in Bolivia and Peru, but separated into three principal ranges—the Cordillera Occidental, between the Pacific Ocean and the valley of the Cauca River; the Cordillera Central, between the Cauca and the Magdalena River; and the broad Cordillera Oriental, which branches off toward Venezuela—they give the Colombian landscape its basic structure. They also determine temperature, climate, and ease of human access.

The greatest part of the country's land area is made up of lowland plains. Whether covered with tropical grasses or (as in the Southeast) Amazonian forest, these plains are accurately called *tierra caliente*, "hot land." As one rises in the different Andean ranges, however, average temperature falls and the natural environment changes. In the Cordillera Central and the Oriental, as well as in the isolated mountain outcropping of the Sierra Nevada de Santa Marta along the Caribbean coast, there are even a few snow-covered peaks. But the mountains also contain a string of basins and plateaus some 1,500 to 3,000 meters high that offer moderate temperatures and often the best soils and living conditions. These middle elevations have for centuries held the densest concentrations of human inhabitants; yet the earliest Colombians did not live there, since they first had to cross the lowland plains.

PRE-COLUMBIAN COLOMBIA

No one knows when the first human beings set foot on what is now Colombian soil, but we may assume that they were part of the great migration of Native American peoples who, having crossed over from Asia, spread out through North and then South America. Presumably, they first encountered the present Colombian department of Chocó (adjoining Panama), a hot, densely forested area with some of the world's heaviest yearly rainfall. It was not the most attractive place to settle, but it did become permanently inhabited, by forest groups that made the necessary adaptation to the environment. The rest of the country was ultimately occupied as well, though we have no idea how long the process took, and no physical traces of most of the early occupants have been found.

The first clear evidence of human activity consists of stone chips found at El Abra, a site on the Sabana de Bogotá (the high plain that today contains the nation's capital). These chips have been dated to earlier than 10,000 B.C. On the western edge of the same Sabana, near the Falls of Tequendama (where the Bogotá River suddenly drops 140 meters straight down toward the Magdalena Valley), a similar find has been made. However, we cannot assume that the arts of civilization first developed in the vicinity of Bogotá; and both there and elsewhere, the sequence of developmental stages—the emergence of agriculture, creation of ceramics, and so forth—was exceedingly gradual and generally comparable to that found among other American Indian peoples.

The earliest native culture from which monumental remains have come down to us arose in the upper Magdalena Valley, near the headwaters of the river—in an area of ample rainfall, about 1,800 meters in altitude, and admirably suited for the growing of corn. Commonly referred to as the "San Agustín culture," from the name of the present-day municipality where the principal archeological sites are found, it flourished from at least the middle of the first millennium B.C. until after the coming of the Europeans, although possibly with some interruptions. The most impressive findings are the several hundred stone statues of human or animal figures, some over three meters in height, that apparently stood guard over tombs. Indeed, the archeological record consists mainly of burial sites, since structures for the living were obviously made from perishable materials. It is no less obvious that a society of some complexity and stratification must have existed, to carry out the works.

In other parts of the country, different native peoples, while not equaling those of San Agustín in stone statuary, were perfecting their own crafts, gaining practice in management of the ecology, and gradually creating a more complex social and political organization. One craft that reached high levels of sophistication almost everywhere was goldwork, thanks to the widespread existence of alluvial gold deposits. These were most often found near the western and central cordilleras, but Indians who lacked gold in their own territory had little difficulty obtaining it by trade. Trade and other contact likewise existed with peoples living beyond what is now Colombia—with the Indians of Middle America, for example, and with those of what became the Inca empire to the south. Outside influences do not, however, appear to have been decisive in development of the native civilization; it is worth noting, for example, that the llama, which served as beast of burden as well as source of wool and meat in the central Andes, was not to be found beyond the present northern border of Ecuador. Thus, the native peoples of the present Colombia, like those of North America, were wholly dependent on human power for transport—even on the rivers and few lakes.

The Indian peoples who inhabited the northwest corner of South America belonged variously to the Carib, Arawak, Chibcha, and other groupings, but the greatest number formed part of the larger Chibcha family that extended into Central America and (in various pockets) Ecuador. What Chibchas mainly had in common was the fact that they spoke related languages, so that the term is above all a linguistic designation. Certainly the Chibchas varied widely among themselves in other respects. They did, though, include the two most notable peoples of pre-Columbian Colombia: the Taironas and the Muiscas. The Taironas are the only people who appear to have achieved something like a true urban civilization; the Muiscas had progressed furthest in the direction of political and territorial consolidation by the eve of the Spanish Conquest.

The Taironas lived mainly on the lower slopes (below 1,000 meters) of the Sierra Nevada de Santa Marta, a range that rises abruptly from the Caribbean shore behind the present city of Santa Marta to beyond the snowline (see map 1). Just as the Sierra Nevada itself was cut off from the Andean cordilleras, the Taironas were isolated from other principal centers of Indian civilization, and though their territory was densely inhabited, its limited extent naturally set a limit on their total numbers. Once conquered by the Spanish, they were largely forgotten, and they did not much figure in discussions of Colombian antiquities until the 1970s, when the discovery of "Buritaca 200" (also called "Ciudad Perdida" or "Lost City") and intensified study of other

Map 1. Colonial New Granada, with Areas of Muisca and Tairona Civilizations

Tairona sites suddenly made contemporary Colombians aware of their achievements. These include the most impressive native engineering works found anywhere in the country: roads and bridges made of stone slabs, terracing of mountainsides for the planting of crops, and extensive construction of level platforms on which dwellings or other buildings once stood. The buildings have disappeared, but the system of platforms makes it possible to visualize a form of urban living. In addition, the Taironas produced some statuary, though not on the scale of San Agustín, and a great quantity and variety of other stone objects, goldwork, and fine ceramics. In purely qualitative terms, they were without question the outstanding Amerindian people among the precursors of modern Colombia.

The Muiscas were not equal to the Taironas in technical skill or artistic sophistication, but they were far more numerous (around 600,000,[1] representing the largest concentration of Native Americans between the Inca empire and the Mayas of Middle America) and on that basis alone have tended to mold perceptions of preconquest culture and institutions. They lived in the intermountain basins of the Cordillera Oriental. The altitude of these basins, the largest of which is the Sabana de Bogotá, ranges generally between 2,000 and 3,000 meters, giving them a temperate to cool climate; the land was fertile and well watered; and the surrounding escarpments gave protection from such warlike peoples as the Panches of the upper Magdalena Valley. Apart from ritual anthropophagy, there is no real proof that the Panches were fierce cannibals, as the Spanish later claimed, but they were certainly uncomfortable neighbors.

The Muiscas were a preeminently agricultural people, living chiefly on potatoes and corn and also drinking fermented corn beer, or *chicha*. They were expert at making cotton textiles, from cotton obtained principally through trade; they worked gold, and they did some stone sculpturing. But they had no engineering works comparable to those of the Tairona, nor any settlements that could be described as incipient cities. Like all the other native inhabitants of the present Colombia, they had no form of writing. The Muiscas lived in single-family homes scattered amid the fields, and not just their homes but their "palaces" and temples were made of reed, wood, mud, and similar materials. To be sure, the more important structures might also have thin sheets of hammered gold hanging from the eaves—and these were inevitably among the first things to disappear when the Spaniards arrived on the scene. In some instances small children became con-

struction materials. A child would be placed in the hole dug for one of
the wooden pillars that was to hold up the building; then the pillar
would be set, the child crushed, and construction would proceed. This
was one of a variety of human sacrifices practiced by the Muiscas and
other preconquest inhabitants; but sacrifices were never even remotely
on the Aztec scale.

The Muiscas possessed some salt springs in the vicinity of Zipaquirá (site of the so-called Salt Cathedral that is today a Colombian
tourist attraction), from which they obtained salt for their own use
and for an extensive trade with neighboring peoples. Indeed, most of
their gold came not from their own territory but by way of trade. Even
so, the Muiscas devised the ceremony that is the clearest model for the
legend of El Dorado, literally "The Gilded Man," which the Spaniards
later encountered over much of South America. As part of his installation ceremony, the local chief of one subgroup of the Muiscas would
coat himself with gold dust and then would go out to the middle of
sacred Lake Guatavita (around 50 kilometers northeast of Bogotá)
and plunge into the icy waters. Precious stones and gold objects were
thrown into the lake as offerings to the gods and, together with the
gold dust, settled on the bottom. All this invited the cupidity of the
Spanish once the identity of the lake was established; but their draining efforts were never successful.

Politically, the Muiscas had no overall government, although the
stronger groups among them were gradually extending their rule over
the weaker. At the lowest level, the basic unit of government and society was a clan type of organization, based on kinship ties. The highest-
level political units have been conventionally referred to as kingdoms
or confederations. When the Spanish arrived, two such confederations
predominated: one centered near the present Bogotá and headed by
a figure known as the Zipa; the other located about 100 kilometers
northeast, at Tunja, whose leader bore the title of Zaque. Their respective "capitals," of course, were not cities like the Taironas' but mere
clusters of a few ceremonial or other buildings. Neither the Zipa nor
the Zaque exercised tight control over all those who in some way
owed them allegiance; but they did enjoy positions of great honor and
were surrounded by elaborate court ceremonial. Not even members of
the Indian nobility dared to look at them in the face; and if, say, the
Zipa indicated a need to spit, someone would hold out a piece of rich
cloth for him to spit on, because it would be sacrilegious for anything

so precious as his saliva to touch the ground. Whoever held the cloth (all the while carefully looking the other way) then carried it off to be reverently disposed of.

The Indian leaders, whether local chiefs or heads of whole confederations, normally inherited their positions; but, as with a number of other Native American peoples, inheritance was not patrilineal. Instead, a chief was succeeded by his nephew—the oldest son of his oldest sister. There were exceptions, and the subjects apparently had some say in the matter, if only to confirm the successor in his post. But hereditary succession in the manner indicated was the rule; and, if Europeans had not interfered, it seems reasonable to assume that sooner or later either the Zipa or the Zaque would have absorbed the holdings of the other, along with certain lesser autonomous chiefdoms, thus creating a unified Muisca state. There are also signs that the Muiscas were on the verge of entering a period of more solid building activity and other advances in material civilization. All that, alas, was not to be.

THE COMING OF THE SPANIARDS

One of the numerous Spanish expeditions sent out to explore the Caribbean in the wake of Columbus's initial discovery sighted the Guajira Peninsula of what is now Colombia in 1500. Subsequently, in the early years of the sixteenth century, other expeditions touched on the Colombian coast looking for gold and pearls, Indian slaves, adventure—and the elusive waterway to Asia that Columbus himself had been seeking. Colonization was first attempted along the Gulf of Urabá, near the present border with Panama, where the town of San Sebastián was founded in 1510. From that same stretch of coast, expeditions moved both south into the interior and westward to the Isthmus of Panama, where Balboa, having assumed command of one Spanish band of explorers, happened on the Pacific Ocean in 1513.

Neither San Sebastián nor other settlements on the Gulf of Urabá proved permanent, but lasting footholds did develop elsewhere along the Caribbean coast. Santa Marta, today the oldest Spanish city in Colombia, was founded in 1526. Located on a sheltered bay, somewhat to the east of the mouth of the Magdalena, it was immediately adjacent to the country of the Taironas and also served in due course as point of departure for the conquest of the Muiscas. Cartagena, lying to the west of the Magdalena, was founded in 1533; with an even better harbor, it would eventually eclipse Santa Marta.

Exploration and settlement had likewise been under way in western Venezuela, where Maracaibo, the later oil capital, dates from 1528. The Spanish crown had granted that area to the German banking firm of Welser, to which it owed money, in an arrangement roughly comparable to the proprietary governorships that the English government gave to such entrepreneurs as William Penn. The Germans recruited mostly Spanish soldiers and adventurers, although the commanders were German. Before long they were spilling over into territory to the west that had not been entrusted to them, lured by, among other things, the tales of El Dorado. Ultimately, one of them, Nicolás Federmann, traveled all the way to the territory of the Muiscas, by a most roundabout route; south over the Venezuelan Andes into the Orinoco basin, then westward, and finally climbing the Andes again, to come out on the Sabana de Bogotá—where he ran into other Europeans who had got there first.

Needless to say, the Spanish settlers at Cartagena and Santa Marta had also been hearing about wealthy kingdoms supposed to exist somewhere in the interior and had begun sending expeditions to find out. In April 1536 the expedition that would actually conquer the Muiscas set forth from Santa Marta, under the leadership of Gonzalo Jiménez de Quesada, who had been commissioned by the Spanish governor of Santa Marta to explore the headwaters of the Magdalena River. For that purpose he was given an army of about 800 men—550 foot soldiers, 50 on horseback, and another 200 in seven small boats aiming to sail up the river itself. Jiménez de Quesada was a lawyer by trade. He had come out initially to serve as chief magistrate for Santa Marta, but he proved to be about as tough-minded a commander as any of the professional soldiers of the conquest. And he did not lack opportunities to show his gifts of leadership, since trouble began almost at once. Several of the boats were lost trying to navigate the treacherous mouth of the Magdalena, and the soldiers traveling on foot or horseback (now joined by the shipwreck survivors) had to struggle against swamps, insects, disease, and every kind of annoyance. Worst of all, perhaps, there were few Indians living in the middle stretches of the Magdalena Valley to steal food from; men were reduced to making soup from their leather, and they kept dying of hunger, disease, and exhaustion by the wayside. Yet in March 1537

nearly 200 men from the original party finally got up into the highlands where the Muiscas lived.

Jiménez de Quesada made a good (if misleading) first impression on
the Muiscas by hanging one of his own men who had stolen some
cloth from an Indian. Not until he was approaching Bogotá did he
meet active resistance, from Tisquesusa, the reigning Zipa. The Indians were easily beaten, although Tisquesusa himself managed to
escape and go into hiding—whereupon the invaders hastened northeastward to Tunja, to overcome the Zaque. That, too, was quickly
accomplished, and in Tunja the Spaniards seized a vast amount of gold
as well. They were particularly delighted with those sheets of gold that
the Muiscas would hang from the eaves of their main buildings; as one
chronicler put it, the sound of these sheets as they rustled in the breeze
was "a delicious tinkling" to the Spaniards.[2] Jiménez de Quesada and
his men had been less handsomely rewarded in their initial conquest of
Tisquesusa's realm; so they went next to track down the fugitive Zipa,
defeated him once more, and this time killed him in combat—
inadvertently, because the Spaniards had hoped to take him alive and
torture him until he told them where he had presumably hidden the
rest of his treasure.

Tisquesusa's successor, the next Zipa, then turned around and
made an alliance with the Spaniards, to ward off an attack from the
Muiscas' undesirable neighbors to the west, the Panches of the Magdalena Valley. Although he successfully held off the Panches, he ultimately died under torture administered to him by his new allies in the
vain hope that *he* would tell them where Tisquesusa had buried the
treasure. Nevertheless, within the space of a few months, the conquerors did collect a really impressive amount of gold from all over the
Muisca country. They had established control over a densely settled,
fertile area that offered salt and potatoes, corn and emeralds, as well as
gold artifacts. And they had done all this with just the members of
Jiménez de Quesada's original army. They never received reinforcements from home base—in sharp contrast to the additional armies of
soldiers and adventurers that kept meeting up with Hernán Cortés in
the conquest of Mexico or Francisco Pizarro in the conquest of Peru.
They were completely isolated from other Spaniards for almost three
years, and they probably would not have survived to tell of their
accomplishments if they had met up with anything like the Aztec war
machine. The Muiscas, however, while not lacking in bravery, appear

to have had no special military vocation; and they suffered from the same psychological and technological disadvantages as other Amerindian peoples when faced with the strange appearance and superior weaponry of the Europeans.

In addition to fighting battles, Jiménez de Quesada founded Bogotá as a Spanish city in 1538 and made it the capital of the newly conquered territory, which he named New Granada after his birthplace in Spain. In due course the name would be applied to all of the present Colombia. The city itself was formally named Santa Fe and continued to be known as such until the end of the colonial period (although for convenience it will be better to call it from the start by the name of Bogotá, a Spanish corruption of a nearby Muisca place-name, which the city assumed at the time of independence and retained until in 1991, for reasons not quite clear, it was officially rechristened Santa Fe de Bogotá). But while Jiménez de Quesada was thus attempting to organize his conquest, he was unexpectedly forced to deal with two other streams of explorers, who by odd coincidence arrived on the scene just weeks after the Spanish city was founded. One of these was the expedition commanded by Federmann, coming from Venezuela. The other was a wave coming up from Peru, under one of Pizarro's lieutenants, Sebastián de Belalcázar, who had recently taken Quito—the northernmost city of the Inca empire. Then, seeing new lands to conquer still farther north, Belalcázar set out to conquer them. He had already hit upon what was to become the chief gold-mining area of the Spanish empire, in the Pacific slopes of the Colombian Andes and adjoining lowlands. He founded several cities—most notably, Popayán and Cali in 1536. These two cities became the principal urban centers of southern Colombia from, respectively, the conquest until the middle of the last century and the mid-nineteenth century until the present. He also, in due course, turned eastward, toward the Muisca country—only to encounter the men of Jiménez de Quesada and Federmann, who had arrived before him.

The normal pattern in the Spanish Conquest, when bands of conquistadores converged on the same territory from different directions, would have been for all three groups—the men of Jiménez de Quesada, Belalcázar, and Federmann—to get together in a rip-roaring civil war to determine who should inherit the spoils of the conquered. Remarkably, in New Granada nothing of the sort happened. Instead, in a summit meeting held in early 1539, the three leaders agreed to submit their claims to the government in Spain and to abide by its decision. In the end the Spanish crown quite characteristically refused to give New Granada to any of the three but instead delivered it to a fourth party, the son of the late governor of Santa Marta, who quickly proved to be grasping and abusive. Jiménez de Quesada received numerous honors and lesser rewards, including authorization to conquer huge tracts of land on the *llanos*, or plains stretching east and southeast of the Cordillera Oriental. He had hopes of discovering wealthy empires there, but he did not; without gold and with few Indians who could be made to work, the region remained largely worthless from the Spanish standpoint. Belalcázar was at least confirmed by the king as governor of Popayán. And Federmann (or, more precisely, his employers, the Welser banking firm) was left with just Venezuela, where the Germans proved to be capable explorers and Indian fighters but did little to develop the colony and were eventually relieved of their concession by the Spanish government.

COLONIAL NEW GRANADA:
SOCIETY AND INSTITUTIONS

After years of experimentation with proprietary and other forms of colonial administration, in the second half of the sixteenth century Spain finally established the definitive form of government for New Granada. As in the Spanish empire as a whole, the structure—in principle—was highly centralized. The area was governed by the king and his advisers back in Spain, the most important group of advisers being the Council of the Indies—whose members served as administrative board, fount of legislation, and appeals court all at the same time. At the American end the highest authorities were the Spanish viceroys, each of whom had at his side an Audiencia with functions roughly comparable (on a lesser scale) to those of the Council of the Indies in Spain. For most of the colonial period, present-day Colombia formed part of the Viceroyalty of Peru, but the viceroy at Lima could never expect to wield much real authority over lands so far removed from the Peruvian capital. Hence, a captain-general of New Granada was appointed in 1564. With the aid of his own Audiencia, this officer was to administer all of Venezuela except the Caracas area and all of Colombia except the southwest corner. This portion of Colombia, which included Cali and Popayán, came under the authority of the president of Quito (i.e., Ecuador), who had much the same duties as a captain-general, except in military matters. He, too, had his own Audiencia, as did the president of Panama.

The territorial arrangements just outlined remained basically the same until the eighteenth century, when Spain undertook extensive reforms of colonial administration. In 1717 the Captaincy-General of New Granada was raised to the status of a viceroyalty in its own right, and the ties with Peru were cut. Six years later the previous arrangements were put back in place, because the cost of maintaining a vice-regal court at Bogotá seemed greater than the benefits. But in 1739 the Viceroyalty of New Granada was reestablished for good—largely as a response to heightened colonial rivalry in the Caribbean, which made it desirable to have an official of viceregal rank on the spot in northern South America. The two presidencies of Quito and Panama were attached to the Viceroyalty of New Granada rather than, as before, to that of Peru, although shortly afterward Panama lost its status as a separate presidency. In 1777, finally, Venezuela was made a captaincy-general, having its capital at Caracas and taking in essentially all the territory that comprises Venezuela today. It still formed part of the Viceroyalty of New Granada, but the authorities in Bogotá had little more power over the captain-general and Audiencia now set up in Caracas than the viceroy of Peru had formerly exercised over Bogotá. This lineup of major territorial divisions would exist at the time of independence and would serve as a basis for drawing the eventual boundaries of the new nations.

Below the level of viceroyalties, captaincies-general, and presidencies were smaller territorial divisions that can be generically termed provinces, each with its appointed governor (though this title could also vary). At the very bottom of the political system were the organs of local government, principally the *cabildos*, or town councils. *Cabildo* members were undemocratically chosen, most often by some form of co-optation; but at least they were local residents, whether European-born Spaniards or creoles (i.e., native-born whites). The *cabildo* was thus the one institution of colonial government that did have a certain representative character. The system as a whole, furthermore, though often marked by corruption, inefficiency, and abuse, was neither much worse nor much better than most systems of government in the world at that period. Even what might appear flagrant cases of corruption were often instances where the governing body sensibly ignored a regulation not suited to local conditions or bent the rules (in response to money or influence) in favor of the colonial inhabitants. In that last respect, the "corruptibility" of the system actually made it more representative.

It was gold that had first and most powerfully attracted Spaniards to New Granada, and they found substantial amounts of it. But they were also attracted, as elsewhere in America, to regions that had an Amerindian population sufficiently large and malleable to serve as a labor force, and here again New Granada had much to offer—above all, in the Muisca country and other highland areas of sedentary agriculturalists who were already accustomed to a more than rudimentary form of social and political organization. In such areas the incoming Spaniards established themselves as a dominant upper layer, ruling the conquered peoples through their own local headmen as well as through the new control systems that they themselves instituted. They required labor from the Indians in both mines and fields, though outright enslavement of Indians, widely practiced in the early years in other parts of Spanish America, did not take hold in New Granada. There were less extreme but equally or more effective ways of exploitation. Most important was the system of *encomienda*, whereby groups of Indians were technically entrusted to a Spaniard so that he could help them learn the ways of civilization (naturally including the Christian religion) and in return for such guidance and protection receive tribute from them. The tribute owed by an Indian to the Spaniard (the *encomendero*) could initially be in goods or labor or both. The Spanish government soon made the exaction of tribute in labor illegal, but it continued to be demanded widely in violation of the law. Though eventually the crown ended *encomienda* itself (at which point all tribute went simply to the treasury), even ex-*encomenderos* retained some unofficial authority over their former charges.

Indians could also be legally forced, under certain circumstances, to do paid labor in Spanish-owned mines or estates; and the possibilities for illegal exploitation were even more numerous. One factor that limited the amount of exploitation, however, was the drastic decline in numbers of the Indians themselves. As in other parts of America, including the non-Spanish colonies, the conquered Amerindians suffered a demographic catastrophe in the first two centuries following their contact with the Europeans. Their decimation resulted not only from casualties inflicted during the conquest itself and the repression of postconquest rebellions but also from sheer overwork and mistreatment, the disruption of traditional social relations, and the spread of European diseases such as measles and smallpox. Authorities disagree about the relative importance of the different factors (the new diseases generally being accorded first rank as a cause of death) and about the extent of the decline, which inevitably varied by region. Along the Caribbean coast, one of the regions hardest hit, as much as 95 percent of the population was wiped out in less than a hundred years.[3]

One reason why the rate of decline is difficult to measure and evaluate is that ethnic miscegenation had turned so many descendants of Chibchas into mestizos, of mixed Spanish and Indian ancestry. By the close of the colonial period, less than a quarter of New Granada's estimated 1,400,000 inhabitants were classified as Indians. The rest were either white or mestizo (more of the latter than the former) or else descended from the slaves brought from Africa to work in the Atlantic and Pacific lowlands (and more often by then of mixed than unmixed African ancestry). The total population may have been still somewhat less than that of the preconquest era. It is hard to say how much less; but demographic catastrophe, at least, had been left behind, and the population overall was growing at around 1.6 percent per year.[4]

Even those still counted as Indians had been subject to varying degrees of cultural assimilation, a process that was especially rapid in the principal areas of Spanish settlement. Thus, by the end of the seventeenth century, the language of the Muiscas had virtually disappeared, save in the form of place-names and terms for local plants and fauna that were adopted into Spanish. This situation was repeated in less extreme form elsewhere in the interior highlands. It contrasted with the survival, in such colonies as Mexico and Peru or even highland Ecuador, of whole native peoples who continued to set themselves apart—by means of language, dress, and customs—from the population of Spaniards and mestizos. The extensive assimilation of Amerindians was clearly due in part to their relatively modest numbers and middling level of social and material development as compared to the native peoples of those other regions. Whatever the precise reasons, it sharply reduced, and from an early date, one potential obstacle to national integration, although even culturally assimilated Indians remained near the bottom of a society marked by sharp social and other stratification.

New Granada was one of the less dynamic, economically, of Spain's American colonies. At its center lay the old heartland of the Muiscas—the mountain and plateau country stretching northeastward from the area of Bogotá and corresponding roughly to the present-day Colombian departments of Cundinamarca and Boyacá. This central region was devoted primarily to agriculture and livestock for local consumption. There was no significant demand outside the region for its products; and even if there had been, transportation costs to foreign markets or to other parts of the colony would have been prohibitive. At least the region had been heavily enough inhabited in preconquest times to retain a substantial Indian population even after the usual drastic decline in Indian numbers, and much of its production was carried out by the surviving Indian communities, which—just as before the conquest—owned their lands mainly in common. These common lands (or *resguardos*) were now protected by the law of the conquerors themselves. Much of the best land, however, had come by one means or another into the hands of the conquistadores and their descendants and was formed into haciendas. As in most of Spanish America, these haciendas used extensive methods of cultivation and livestock raising, with little capital investment. For the most part, hacienda workers were technically free subjects, though they might be Indians who had left their own villages for part-time work with a Spanish landowner because they had to earn money to pay their taxes. As time went on, an increasing number of small, separate private plots (incipient *minifundios*) provided a livelihood to the growing mestizo population as well as to poor whites and to a floating element of the Indian masses—i.e., Indians who had become detached from their traditional communities but were not yet reduced to the condition of a landless proletariat.

Assorted small craft industries existed in central New Granada alongside farming and stock raising. Whether practiced by farm families in their spare time or by specialized artisans in the surrounding towns, these, too, were strictly for local consumption. The greatest concentration of artisan shops was naturally to be found in Bogotá itself, which by the eve of independence had grown to a city of about 25,000 people. Simply as the political capital of the colony, it had its inevitable complement of public officials and professional or menial service personnel. But Bogotá's economic role was largely parasitical, and even as a service and marketing center it had to share some of the limelight with Tunja, whose early settlers grew prosperous through the exploitation of nearby *encomienda* Indians.

In the southwestern part of New Granada, the province of Popayán encompassed another highland area of relatively dense Indian population. Socially and culturally, Popayán had much in common with the central core of the colony. However, it also contained some gold-mining territory along the Pacific lowlands. A population of African slaves had been brought in to work the mines, which were controlled mainly by absentee owners in the city of Popayán. This small urban center became a rather wealthy place, with an upper class of definite aristocratic pretensions. Popayán had more Spanish titles of nobility among its leading families than did Bogotá, where the only titled nobleman was the Marqués de San Jorge, who had purchased his title (as was the custom) in the eighteenth century but did not keep up the payments and eventually became enmeshed in a protracted lawsuit over his right to keep on using the title.

Popayán and its hinterland had strong ties with what is now Ecuador, dating from the days of the conquest. It was governed from Quito until the final establishment of the Viceroyalty of New Granada, and even after that Quito retained some shreds of jurisdiction. Pasto, in the far South, sent judicial cases on appeal to the Audiencia of Quito and belonged to the ecclesiastical diocese of Quito until the end of the colonial period. In due course the residents of Pasto, and even some people in Popayán, seriously considered becoming part of the Republic of Ecuador rather than of independent New Granada.

The jurisdiction of Popayán extended northward into the fertile section of the Cauca Valley, whose chief city is Cali. Although today this section is one of the fastest-developing parts of the country, in the colonial era it languished in relative unimportance, chiefly for lack of good transportation—being cut off by the steep Cordillera Central from the Magdalena River artery and from Bogotá, while the nearby Pacific coast did not yet have a Panama Canal through which to ship out goods. Transportation was also difficult for the province of Antioquia, in the Northwest, which lay astride the Cordillera Central itself. However, because Antioquia's leading industry was the mining of gold, it could easily withstand any transport costs. The gold was drawn from placer deposits in the Cauca River and its tributaries, as well as from other deposits scattered throughout the province, and it was exploited both by gangs of slaves in the larger mining operations and by countless individual prospectors. Antioquia consisted mostly of rugged terrain ill suited to the formation of large estates, although some did appear. At the same time, it needed a reliable source of food production to support the mining camps. In part to meet that need, an independent peasant sector composed mainly of poor whites and mestizos came into existence. But the merchants who provided supplies to the mines and handled the export of the ore occupied the dominant position in Antioqueño society.

In the northern part of the colony lay the broad Caribbean coastal plain, whose metropolis was the great port of Cartagena, today the best example of a colonial walled city surviving anywhere in the Americas. Cartagena served as a port of call for convoys passing between Spain and the Isthmus of Panama, from which goods were then transshipped down the west coast of South America; it also handled virtually all the legal import-export trade of New Granada. The exports consisted of almost nothing but gold, for New Granada, though certainly not a one-crop or one-product colony, was without question a one-export colony—thus setting a pattern that would continue in Colombia until quite recent times, with only the substitution of a succession of agricultural commodities for gold as the primary export. This was, indeed, the principal gold-producing colony of the Spanish empire, even if the total yield paled alongside the silver of Mexico and Peru, and even though the mines employed a very small part of the total population.

Besides serving as a gateway to and from the outside world, Cartagena was the chief naval base of the Spanish Main (with Havana, one of the two great centers of Spanish naval power in America) and the principal entry point into Spanish South America for the African slave trade, where newly arrived captives received their first "seasoning" before going on to their ultimate destination. Along with Mexico City and Lima, Cartagena was also one of the three colonial headquarters of the dread Spanish Inquisition, but the local branch was never as busy as the other two centers. Only five (or maybe six) people were burned for heresy at Cartagena in the entire colonial period, as against over a hundred in Mexico and Peru; some 762 were sentenced to lesser penalties.[5]

Among the other coastal settlements, Santa Marta, from which Jiménez de Quesada had set out for the conquest of the Muiscas, also had a good harbor. But it rapidly lost ground, largely because Cartagena was easier to get to from the Magdalena River, the colony's chief artery of internal communication. The ideal might have been a seaport at the very mouth of the river, but the mouth of the Magdalena was difficult to navigate. So a canal was built to connect Cartagena with a small tributary of the river, thus providing direct water transportation all the way from the upper Magdalena Valley to the Caribbean, at Cartagena, and that really precluded a major commercial role for Santa Marta until the nineteenth century. Particularly in the later colonial period, the Caribbean coast acquired additional importance in grazing and agriculture, producing hides, sugar, indigo, and other tropical commodities. But these products never came close to challenging gold as exports for New Granada, and most of the Caribbean lowlands remained very sparsely inhabited.

Although its connection with the rest of New Granada was always somewhat tenuous, the Isthmus of Panama had a number of features in common with the northern coastal region. It played a key role in overseas commerce, while its own internal economy was poorly developed; likewise, there was a noticeable African strain in its general population mixture. It formally became part of New Granada only in the mid-eighteenth century, when it was included in the new viceroyalty. Previously, it had been a dependency of Peru, and Panamanians were not entirely happy with the change. The rule of Lima was at least familiar, and the Peruvian capital was also much easier to get to than Bogotá. All one had to do was climb aboard a coastal vessel and go down the west side of South America to Callao, the port serving Lima. To reach the capital of New Granada, on the other hand, one had to cross the isthmian mountains (if one lived in Panama City on the Pacific side); then take ship to Cartagena, beating against the wind; and from there embark on the excruciatingly uncomfortable month-long trip (usually in a pole boat of some sort) up the Magdalena River to Honda, from which it was still necessary to travel a few more days overland and uphill to Bogotá.

To make things worse, annexation to New Granada was quickly followed by Panama's loss of its status as a separate presidency and, at the same time, by a long era of economic depression, resulting from changes in the Spanish commercial system. The economic importance of Panama, after all, was based on the legal requirement, during most of the colonial period, that all goods to western South America be sent by way of the isthmus, whose people in large part lived from the tran-

sit trade. But in the mid-eighteenth century Spain revamped the imperial commercial regulations in such a way as to discontinue the convoy
system between Cádiz and the isthmus and to make it legally possible
for ships to sail directly from Spain around Cape Horn to the South
American Pacific ports. This change in route was a boon to Chile but a
disaster to Panama, which did not truly recover until the California
gold rush of the next century.

The last major region of New Granada, the Northeast, consisted of
the colonial provinces of Pamplona and Socorro, or modern departments of Norte de Santander and Santander. It was a heterogeneous
area, which to one degree or another exhibited almost all the characteristics of the other regions: it had all the races, all the crops, all the
types of landholding represented. It also had, in the town of Socorro
and surrounding villages, the chief manufacturing center of New Granada. Cotton textiles were the main output, but there was nothing like
a factory system. This was instead a cottage industry that featured
hand spinning and hand weaving, all done in individual family units,
often by the farm families in their spare time or by wives and daugh-
ters while the men were in the field. It was organized according to the
"putting-out system," whereby a single entrepreneur acquired cotton,
handed it out to different households to be made into thread, then
parceled out the thread in the same way to be made into cloth. The end
product was coarse cotton cloth for use both locally and in neighboring provinces. Employment was given to several thousand people, and
while nobody got rich, a lot of people—again mostly poor whites and
mestizos—acquired some added measure of economic independence.

Though not a major region of the colony except in size, the eastern
llanos were at least more important in the colonial period than at any
time before the twentieth century. These were tropical grasslands,
flooded in rainy season and parched in dry season and linked to
Andean population centers by only the most rudimentary trails. The
llanos were home to a limited population of semisettled Indians and to
increasing numbers of wild cattle, to say nothing of mosquitoes and
other such pests. Various expeditions roamed through them in the age
of the conquest, but when no great sources of wealth were found, the
Spanish settlers of New Granada showed little interest in them. The
task of establishing a colonial presence was therefore left to missionary orders—above all, the Jesuits—who strove to gather the Indians
into mission communities so that they could be Christianized and

"civilized." With the help of Indian labor, the Jesuits created not only cattle ranches but plantations of sugar and other commodities. This mission empire passed into the hands of rival religious orders after the Jesuits were expelled from the Spanish empire in 1767. They did not prove equally successful in maintaining it, but the definitive decline of the *llanos* economy came only in the early nineteenth century, when the war of independence decimated the herds of cattle and republican reform legislation dealt the final blow to the mission system.[6]

The use of the frontier mission as a colonizing device was one of the ways in which the Roman Catholic church made itself felt in the life of the colony. It also played an important mediating role between the Hispanic state and society and the settled Indian communities of the Andean highlands, which had been mostly Christianized, at least superficially, soon after the conquest. It took less interest in the population of African slaves, although the Catalan missionary Pedro Claver was ultimately canonized for his work among the newly arrived cargoes of Africans in Cartagena. Among the Spanish and mestizo inhabitants, finally, the church not only ministered to religious needs but provided most of the social services (including education) available during the period. In order to fulfill its functions, it maintained a clergy that by the end of the colonial regime numbered about 1,850, including both male and female, regular and secular. For a population of 1,400,000, this meant a ratio of roughly one to every 750 inhabitants—a much denser clergy-population ratio than the Roman Catholic church can show anywhere in Latin America today.[7] There was, however, a relative overconcentration of clergy of all kinds in Bogotá, Popayán, and a few other urban centers.

The clergy was not only numerous, by present-day standards; it was relatively wealthy, receiving income from parish fees and from the payment of tithes (required by civil and not just ecclesiastical law) and enjoying the income of extensive property holdings that it had accumulated through gifts and investments. The precise extent of its wealth is impossible to estimate with precision; certainly, it was less than nineteenth-century anticlericals would later claim in justification of their attacks on church property. The church may well have owned close to a quarter of the urban property in Bogotá, but for the colony as a whole something like 5 percent of urban and rural real estate (always excluding the vast expanse of unclaimed public domain) would be a better guess.[8] Even so, the church had no serious rival as the principal owner of both urban and rural property. In addition, much of the land not directly under church control was heavily mortgaged *to* the church by way of liens that had been accepted either in return for loans (for church institutions were also the chief moneylenders) or in voluntary support of pious works and endowments.

From its missionary role to its share of property ownership, the church in New Granada conformed to a pattern evident throughout Spanish America, although the church's position was stronger in New Granada than it was in some of the other colonies. Because of its gold and its large population of settled Indians to be converted and exploited, New Granada attracted the close attention of ecclesiastical as well as civil authorities from early in the colonial period. In New Granada the church managed to build the solid institutional base that it never really had in colonies such as Venezuela or Cuba, which became truly important only in the late colonial era, when religious zeal was beginning to flag. To be sure, the church was not as strong in the coastal area as in the Andean interior, a contrast that faithfully reflected its greater interest in creoles and Indians than in the African-Americans who formed a larger proportion of the inhabitants of the tropical lowlands. Even in the highlands the church's hold on the minds of at least the upper social strata began to weaken in the late eighteenth century. But this slight relative shift did not greatly affect the picture of a Roman Catholic church whose position rivaled and in some respects even exceeded that of the state.

Though not exactly a cultural and intellectual backwater, colonial New Granada made far fewer noteworthy contributions to the world of arts and letters than did the two main centers of Spanish power in America, Mexico and Peru. One of the more idiosyncratic, but still valuable, chronicles of the Spanish Conquest itself is the *Elegías de varones ilustres de Indias*, in which the Tunja cleric Juan de Castellanos set out in verse form the great deeds of the first conquerors and explorers. The *Carnero de Bogotá* of Juan Rodríguez Freile is a lively assortment of early colonial gossip, which can be read even today for pleasure and not simply as a historical document. In literature there is not much else to mention. The colony did not even have a printing press until one finally began to function in Bogotá in 1738. In the field of art, aside from much utilitarian and religious folk art, New Granada produced the painter Gregorio Vázquez Arce de Ceballos, whose canvases on religious themes were highly competent even if they lacked the spark of genius. He did not succeed in creating a Bogotá "school" comparable to the Cuzco and Quito "schools," and neither did church architecture attain the same heights of splendor as in those (and a good many other) colonial centers. By far the most notable architectural achievement, in fact, was in military construction: the great fort of San Felipe and associated defense works that guarded Cartagena, completed in the early eighteenth century and never taken by storm.

Facilities for formal education were wholly lacking in rural areas, and everywhere the working class had little access to them. Women, even of the upper social strata, were essentially limited to what instruction they could receive at home. On the other hand, higher education was rather well developed, for sons of the colonial elite. Bogotá had two universities, controlled respectively by the Jesuits and the Dominicans and featuring the basic tracks of law and theology. Moreover, in the last half of the eighteenth century, the capital of New Granada became briefly one of the leading centers of intellectual activity in Spanish America, especially in the field of scientific investigation. An interest in the natural sciences formed part of the intellectual ferment that stirred the entire Western world during the Enlightenment, and not even remote New Granada, it appears, could escape the trends of the time.

The immediate spark for achievements in science was the arrival, in 1760, of José Celestino Mutis, a learned Spanish naturalist who came to Bogotá as personal physician to one of the late colonial viceroys, Pedro Messía de la Cerda. Messía eventually left, after he had expelled the Jesuits; but Mutis stayed on and became increasingly fascinated by the colony's enormous wealth of botanical species, a natural consequence of its topographical diversity. (Colombia is exceeded today only by Brazil among nations of the world in the number of distinct species of flora to which it plays host.) Mutis gained some early notoriety by his frank affirmation of the Copernican thesis that the earth revolves around the sun and not vice versa, which was still a little daring in those Andean fastnesses and got him into trouble with the Inquisition. But, having the sympathy of top civil officials, he was never in serious danger of going off to the Inquisition's dungeons at Cartagena. Instead, he went on to found the Expedición Botánica, an ambitious research project designed to record all the botanical species found in South America north of the equator. That aim was beyond the capacity of anyone to achieve, but with a team of fellow investigators and research assistants, including skilled painters to make drawings of the plants, Mutis did enough to be awarded an honorary membership in the Swedish Academy of Science.

Although Mutis was from the mother country, he drew his collaborators mainly from the creole intelligentsia, and some of them would become leaders of the independence movement early in the next century. That movement would also bring a sudden end to the scientific enlightenment in New Granada, both by dispersing its leading figures (Mutis himself was by then dead) and by opening up a range of new careers for ambitious and intelligent creoles that came to take precedence over scientific pursuits.

Despite its fleeting prominence in science—and its gold—New Granada was not one of the most cherished jewels in Spain's imperial crown. Spanish functionaries were sometimes even unsure where or what it was: the officers of the Cádiz Consulado made reference to the "island" of Santa Marta, as though that oldest of Spanish foundations on the Colombian coast was just another dot somewhere in the middle of the Caribbean.⁹ New Granada was not remotely comparable to New Spain (i.e., Mexico) as a producer of wealth, and it conspicuously lacked the dynamism of such colonies as the Río de la Plata or Venezuela, which in the late colonial period were experiencing rapid economic growth. The picture that emerges from the records is one of a somnolent and largely subsistence economy, presided over by a small upper class descended from either the conquistadores or later Iberian immigrants and distinguished from the mass of the population less by the comforts of their lifestyle (though they did enjoy more amenities) than by their sense of self-importance.

For the rural and urban working classes, among whom mestizos by the eve of independence were already most numerous, the colony's relative stagnation was not an unmixed evil. Even if the obligation to pay tribute forced New Granada's Indians to hire themselves out to creole landowners at least long enough to earn their yearly quota, they faced nothing like the rigors of the Potosí *mita*, the forced labor draft whereby Peruvian and Bolivian villagers were herded to work in the recesses of the great "silver mountain" at Potosí. Fortunately for them, New Granada had no Potosí, and exploitation of any kind of labor was kept within limits, both because the potential returns to the exploiter were modest and because there was still no lack of readily accessible unoccupied land. The gold mines were tended by black slaves, who at least were better off panning gold in New Granada than they would have been cutting cane in Cuba or Brazil. And Bogotá, most isolated of viceregal capitals, was far less of a magnet city—overshadowing lesser cities and draining away their wealth and talents—than, say, Lima or Buenos Aires. Colombia's modern profile as a country of multiple urban centers, each with a vigorous life of its own, goes back to the colonial era. Within those colonial cities and towns, there was already forming a cadre of future leaders—clerks and lawyers, businessmen, absentee landowners, or all those things combined—who would soon set out to form a new nation.

2

Severing the Ties with Spain
(1781–1819)

In colonial New Granada as in the rest of Spanish America, the gradual process of economic and demographic growth inevitably undermined the imperial link with Spain. The colonial people, at least those who gave thought to such matters, had more and more reason to ponder their own importance and to feel less need for the guiding hand of the mother country. By the late eighteenth century, the great majority of whites were American-born creoles rather than peninsular Spaniards; as such, they felt less attachment to the land of their forebears and more to that of their own birth. The mestizos, to say nothing of blacks and Indians, had even more reason for a sense of separate identity. New Granada was different from Spain, not just in its topography and population makeup but in its economic functions and structure and its way of life.

A feeling of local identity obviously did not preclude continued loyalty to the Spanish crown, but it did heighten people's consciousness of any concrete differences of interest with the Spanish monarchy. These differences were again essentially the same as in other parts of the empire, though with variations in relative importance. There was, for example, the standard complaint against Spanish trade restrictions—i.e., the prohibition of any direct trade with ports outside the empire, although temporary and limited exceptions were granted in cases of war emergency. Such permission was granted rather often in the late colonial period, since Spain's involvement in the wars of the French Revolutionary and Napoleonic periods made it impossible for the mother country even to pretend to supply the colonies with what they needed. These exceptions to some extent only whetted the colonial appetite for more, since if direct trade with, say, the United States was a good thing in some temporary emergency, it should be better still on a permanent, regular basis. However, the commercial grievance was less keenly felt in New Granada than in next-door Venezuela, which specialized in the export of bulky raw materials and foodstuffs for which the freight cost was high in relation to the intrinsic value, so that the legal requirement to ship them by way of Spanish ports was a major inconvenience. In New Granada, where commercial activity was more modest and the only significant export was gold, the commercial regulations, while often annoying, were not such a live issue.

The relative lack of dynamism of the New Granadan economy also meant that the colony was less likely to feel the impact of imperial regulations restricting certain industries (e.g., wine making or manufacture of the better grades of cloth) that might conflict with the industries of the mother country. More important was the underlying rivalry between creoles and *peninsulares*, or European Spaniards. The classic historian of Colombian independence, José Manuel Restrepo, assigned this rivalry first place in his listing of the factors that impelled his countrymen to break with Spain.[1] Involving discrimination against creoles in appointments at the top levels of colonial administration, discrimination in economic matters, and all the social slights administered to the American-born by haughty Europeans, the rivalry was a key source of discontent throughout the colonies. But there is no evidence that it presented any special characteristics or assumed unusual intensity in New Granada.

There also was political disaffection, in the sense that some people increasingly came to question the Spanish political system itself, which featured the persistence of absolute monarchy in both colonies and mother country, with no form of political representation save at municipal level, in the *cabildos*. Particularly after the American and French Revolutions, this lack of representation was a glaring anachronism. Those who espoused actual independence were long a tiny minority, but there were others who aspired to at least a greater measure of autonomy within the framework of the Spanish empire. Either way, they were influenced to some degree (it is hard to say exactly how much) by the new ideological currents of the age—subversive currents from the standpoint of the Spanish crown—emanating directly or indirectly from France, England, and the United States. The new ideas had to make their way into the colonies in defiance of censorship and other obstacles, but they did enter, as did news of the English colonies' example of winning independence from the imperial government. This news could hardly have been kept a secret when Spain itself, for reasons of European power rivalry, openly supported the rebellious Anglo-American colonies in their effort, which was favorably publicized by the Spanish press itself. In comparison to Venezuela once again, New Granada was not one of the colonies most easily subject to the influence of ideas from abroad. Thanks to its eighteenth-century cacao boom, its wide commercial contacts abroad, and the sheer geographic proximity of its population centers to the non-Spanish West Indies, Venezuela was in a good position to absorb new intellectual influences. The flourishing of scientific studies promoted by José Celestino Mutis in New Granada could not offset the effects of economic stagnation and geographic isolation. Nevertheless, New Granada in the closing years of the colonial regime did experience a gradual increase in disaffection; and it was also the scene of one of the principal popular rebellions of the late eighteenth century.

ANTECEDENTS AND PRECURSORS OF INDEPENDENCE

The Revolt of the Comuneros of New Granada was one of two major eighteenth-century uprisings in Spanish America (the other was the bloody Indian revolt of Túpac Amaru in Peru, which occurred at exactly the same time). Its precise relationship to the later independence movement is a subject of debate, although it must rank as at least an antecedent of some sort; and it does have a relationship to the independence of the English colonies, since it began as a protest against high taxes, which had just been raised in order to pay for Spain's participation in the American Revolutionary War alongside the *English* American revolutionists. Both revolutions thus had their origin in a protest against the fiscal demands of metropolitan powers seeking to fund their imperial rivalries. In New Granada money was especially needed to support the great naval base of Cartagena, and to get it, the government tobacco monopoly and the very similar government liquor monopoly both raised their prices. These were just two of a series of fiscal monopolies whereby the state took charge of the production and/or sale of specific articles and absorbed the profits into the royal treasury. The tobacco monopoly was easily the most important; together with the customs duties and the *alcabala*, or colonial sales tax, it was one of the three main pillars of the colonial revenue system. But other taxes also were increased; and to make sure they were really collected, the government decreed new and annoying inspection devices at the same time.

The tax decrees went into effect early in 1781, and they put people in a bad mood. In various places angry subjects tore down the tax decrees posted on the walls or even burned government tobacco and spilled government liquor on the ground—just as in the Boston Tea Party. These liquor-and-tobacco parties, so to speak, took place mainly in the province of Socorro, the chief manufacturing center of New Granada, which had been particularly hard hit: among other things, one of the measures had made cotton thread (which was previously exempt) subject to the sales tax. The movement appears to have started as a grass-roots outburst, involving poor and middling creoles and mestizos, who rioted against the new taxes and terrified royal officials on the scene. Members of the local upper class took leadership of the movement after it started, many of them later claiming that they did so only to keep matters from getting too far out of hand and with a view to restoring the authority of the royal government at the earliest opportunity. They no doubt sympathized with the main objective, to reduce taxes, but were better aware than the masses of the possible consequences of rebellion and thus joined in with perfectly sincere hesitation. In any case, in the city of Socorro the inhabitants formed themselves into a popular assembly or commune (in Spanish, *común*, whence the name of the movement) and elected five prominent local creoles, the most important of them Juan Francisco Berbeo, as leaders with the title of captains-general. All five promptly drew up a secret oath stating that they had accepted the job under pressure, and they made sure that word of this secret reservation reached the hands of the authorities.

Elsewhere in Socorro province and in neighboring provinces, the scene was repeated. People would riot, organize themselves into a *común*, and elect their local "captains," who—just as in Socorro— often accepted with reservations. The towns formed a loose alliance under Socorro's leadership, but the ties were very informal; nothing like a unified revolutionary government ever emerged. Once these "communes" were established, they stopped burning tobacco and started selling it, to pay the expenses of the rebellion. They raised armed forces, deposed unpopular officials, and in general took matters into their own hands. The viceroy himself was at Cartagena, attending to defense against the British; and the acting viceroy he left behind in

Bogotá was soon in full flight. That left the Audiencia, the high court of the colony, to function as supreme executive as well as judicial authority. It proved incapable of decisive action, since it was unsure of the loyalty not only of the general population but of the local militia, which—because of the concentration of regular units at Cartagena—was the only military force available.

And so, seeing the way clear, the Comuneros marched on Bogotá, to the cry of "Long Live the King and *Death* to the Bad Government!" This was the conventional slogan of rioters and insurrectionists in all parts of the Spanish empire prior to the final, definitive uprising against the mother country. It did not signify a demand for fundamental changes in the political system but only for the remedying of particular abuses, such as the price of drinks and smokes. Numbering (it is said) as many as 20,000 men,[2] which would be larger than any army in the later independence struggle in this part of Latin America, the Comunero forces finally came to rest at Zipaquirá, not far from the capital. There they entered negotiations with Archbishop Antonio Caballero y Góngora, who had been commissioned by the Audiencia to work out an agreement. The one thing above all that the Audiencia wanted to avoid was the entry of the Comunero army into Bogotá, for fear of what it might do running wild in the city streets. Therefore, while the rebels consented to give up a few lesser demands, and agreed not to enter the city, they in return got pretty much what they wanted. All the additional taxes were repealed, a number of miscellaneous grievances were remedied, and the archbishop even agreed that henceforth creoles should be preferred over *peninsulares* in appointments to office. This last had nothing to do with the financial problems that were the original cause of the movement, but it does show the strength of feeling on the issue.

On the other hand, Berbeo and the top echelon of Comunero leaders were soon having a very bad case of cold feet, especially when they heard that the viceroy had denounced all the agreement terms as soon as he heard of them and that he had finally sent some regular troop reinforcements from the coast to Bogotá. Under these circumstances they meekly accepted the archbishop's suggestion that they voluntarily renounce the concessions they had just obtained. Many of the rank and file were bewildered at this turn of events and, if given firm leadership, might have continued the struggle to keep their gains; they could have made real trouble for the authorities, since the regular force that so frightened the leaders consisted of some 500 men. But the leaders, in effect, refused to lead any longer.

Only a few second-rank figures decided to put on a show of resistance, and they were easily crushed. The most important was José Antonio Galán, a mestizo of relatively humble origin although possessing some education. He and a few others were caught and executed, and their heads were then set on pikes or placed in wooden cages all around central New Granada as a warning to the people. Galán's body was cut in pieces—his head displayed in one place, his right hand in another, and his left hand somewhere else. His house was razed to the ground and the ground sowed with salt, just as the Romans had done at the final defeat of Carthage. Thanks, however, to the intervention of the archbishop, all those who had participated only in the earlier stages of the rebellion did obtain a pardon, and the pardon was honored. Also, while the hated tax measures were put back in force in the short run, the viceroy shortly resigned; his designated successor died soon after taking office; and the next viceroy after that was Archbishop Caballero y Góngora, who proceeded to put things back almost the way they were before the war with England. He also had the dismembered parts of Galán's body finally taken down, after they had been left up a good half year.

Even without the uprising, the tax situation might have reverted to its previous status once the war emergency was over, so one cannot be certain that the Comuneros accomplished anything concrete. Yet the sheer scale on which the revolt had taken place is worth noting. This was no mere street riot, for at its peak the Comunero movement controlled about one third of New Granada, with outcroppings of unrest here and there in the other two thirds and even in Venezuela. Tax officials bore the brunt of it, getting beaten up and sometimes assassinated; but whenever things got started, all kinds of people, with all kinds of grievances, jumped in. Clearly, there was no lack of potentially inflammatory issues in the colony, and any small protest could grow into something bigger.

Moreover, memories of the revolt lingered on, to become part of later Colombian patriotic folklore and, in the meantime, to frighten the Spanish authorities in New Granada, who were never again sure they could trust the local population. As Caballero y Góngora observed, before the revolt the traditional, instinctive loyalty of the people had been enough by itself to maintain order in the colony, but with the revolt of the Comuneros, "the inestimable original innocence was lost."[3] New Granadans, in effect, had tasted the forbidden fruit of revolution, and next time they might have even fewer scruples to overcome. The Spanish authorities accordingly chose to deemphasize the role of the colonial militia in the closing years of the colonial period in favor of a modest buildup of regular army strength, and the later viceroys were insistent that they did not want just any troops stationed in Bogotá: they wanted Spanish-born troops, not local recruits.

At the same time, the authorities were careful not to antagonize the local population unnecessarily. Not only were most of the tax reforms rolled back, but Spain conspicuously refrained from extending to New Granada the intendant system, patterned after French Bourbon procedures, which was used elsewhere in Spanish America to raise the efficiency of administration, and especially of revenue collection, in the late colonial period. Carefully selected and well paid, the intendants superseded an assortment of nonstandardized and often overlapping forms of provincial-level government. In New Granada, which enjoyed generally lower priority from the Spanish perspective, nothing had been done to introduce the new system as of the outbreak of the revolt. Now, for fear of stirring up the inhabitants all over again, the crown simply left the old arrangements in place.

Finally, two questions of interpretation concerning the Comuneros have been much argued about by Colombian historians. One is whether, as some Colombian authors have insisted, the Comuneros really were aiming at independence, even though no such objective was officially proclaimed, only the objective of remedying specific grievances. Since this is an argument about secret intentions, it is hard to prove or to disprove, but most of the evidence advanced in support of it is highly questionable, and certainly it is hard to reconcile with the noteworthy caution displayed by the Comunero high command. More recently the revisionist historian Indalecio Liévano Aguirre argued that the aim of the revolution, at least in the minds of its rank and file, was *social* transformation, and that "oligarchic" leaders such as Berbeo proceeded to betray the movement because they feared its growing radicalization.[4] In fact, there is not much evidence to support this thesis either. There was no difference between "masses" and "oligarchs" as far as opposition to increased taxes was concerned, and the few instances of genuine social-revolutionary protest that occurred in conjunction with the rebellion—e.g., among the Indians of the isolated eastern *llanos*, who rose up against white settlers and attacked the missionary clergy as well—had little to do with the mainstream of the movement.

The end of the rebellion did not, in any event, put an end to unrest; further signs of it continued to appear and came to involve a number of influential people. In this respect the standard example is Antonio Nariño, the New Granadan counterpart of the better-known Venezuelan "Precursor of Independence," Francisco de Miranda. Nariño belonged to the cream of Bogotá society. Only a few members of this select group had been linked in any way to the Comuneros, even though more may well have been sympathizers. Nariño was a prosperous merchant and also an amateur scientist and intellectual, whose library of some 2,000 volumes was one of the largest if not the largest private collection in the colony. In it were numerous works outlawed by civil and religious authorities. Needless to say, the presence of these books in his library does not prove that Nariño had read and absorbed their dangerous teachings, but he had also set up in his home a kind of inner sanctum that he was in the process of decorating with busts and portraits of his most admired ancient and modern heroes. This sanctuary, which was never wholly completed, was to feature thinkers like Socrates and Plato among the ancients—nothing extraordinary—while the moderns were George Washington and Montesquieu, Benjamin Franklin and Jean-Jacques Rousseau, and others of the same ilk. To be placed under the bust of Franklin, who was a particular favorite, Nariño had picked the quotation "He snatched the lightning from the skies, and the scepter from the tyrant's hand."[5] Nariño also could quote substantial portions of Rousseau's writings from memory. Moreover, he used that inner sanctum as a meeting place with a small circle of close friends who came together to ponder the state of the colony and to exchange what, from the standpoint of the authorities, were undoubtedly subversive thoughts. Despite the Franklin inscription, however, it is likely that Nariño hoped at first only for some liberalization of government within the framework of the Spanish empire.

Last but not least, Nariño owned a printing press, on which at the very end of 1793 he committed an act that won him enduring fame. He had obtained a copy of the French Revolutionary Declaration of the Rights of Man—from a captain in the viceroy's palace guard, as a matter of fact—and read it with enthusiasm. He proceeded to translate it and then printed it on his own press, doing the job on a Sunday morning when others had gone to mass. He printed a hundred or more copies, sold one, and gave away another; he then apparently got cold feet, kept the others (and ultimately destroyed them), and tried unsuccessfully to retrieve the ones already distributed. But the deed was eventually found out, and even though Nariño was personally a friend of the viceroy—a rather enlightened official—he was now in serious trouble. His library was raided, and its contents got him into more trouble. When finally brought to trial, Nariño at first tried to deny printing the Rights of Man, and when that defense would not stand, he claimed he had done it only for the money he could earn by selling copies. That was rather unbelievable, too, so in the end he presented still another defense, designed to prove that the Declaration of the Rights of Man was not a subversive document at all—that there was nothing in it for which authority could not be found in St. Thomas Aquinas or other writers of unimpeachable orthodoxy. This argument was quite brilliant and made the whole system of colonial thought control seem foolish, but in the end it was not enough either. Nariño had his property confiscated and was sentenced to ten years' imprisonment at a military post in North Africa and to perpetual exile from America. Even Nariño's defense attorney was sentenced to ten years' imprisonment.

Nariño was shipped off to Spain, en route to North Africa, but managed to escape while the ship was in Cádiz harbor. From there he went straight to Madrid and put out feelers to try to get his sentence revised; when he had no luck, he moved on to Paris and finally England. In London he tried unsuccessfully to see the prime minister but did manage to talk with a member of the British cabinet about the state of the Spanish colonies and the possibility of British aid for their liberation, exactly as the Venezuelan Miranda was accustomed to do as he visited one court after another in his European travels. So, by this time at least, Nariño had been radicalized by his own experiences and was toying with the idea of independence. Ultimately, Nariño went back to New Granada, where he traveled around for a while incognito, observing the state of affairs. He apparently came to the conclusion that people were not yet ready for independence or anything like it; so in 1797 he turned himself in to the viceroy—a new one by then—to whom he gave much good advice, based on firsthand observation, on how to improve the administration of the colony. He spent the next six years in prison. He was later released, then rearrested, and when the definitive independence movement got under way in 1810, Nariño was languishing in the dungeons of the Inquisition at Cartagena.

It must be emphasized that Nariño, though in socioeconomic terms representative of the top layer of the creole aristocracy, was ahead of most of his class in political ideas—not only in his devotion to Franklin and Rousseau but in his readiness, at an early date, to think of outright independence. To be sure, there were kindred spirits who felt the same way, and there were still more who were not yet ready even to contemplate such an extreme solution but were in one degree or another increasingly disaffected toward the colonial regime. The same was true in neighboring colonies, although there was not enough direct contact between them for much reinforcing of revolutionary or simply reformist sentiments to take place.

THE CRISIS OF THE SPANISH MONARCHY

It took an outside stimulus to bring things to a head and, in effect, trigger the outbreak of the independence movement. This stimulus was provided by events in Europe, where in 1808 Napoleon deposed the legitimate king of Spain, Ferdinand VII, took captive the entire Spanish royal family, and attempted to set one of his own brothers on the Spanish throne as Joseph I. Napoleon had successfully established new puppet monarchs in other European countries, but in Spain the result was an outpouring of popular protest and the emergence of a resistance movement—ultimately headed by a Central Junta in Seville—that adamantly rejected Joseph as an intruder and pledged continuing allegiance to Ferdinand. The Spanish junta proposed to rule in his name until he was able to regain his throne, and it proposed to rule the colonies as well as Spain itself. In America royal officials by and large accepted the junta's claims, and so did most of the American population, at least tacitly. But a determined minority insisted that they, the Spanish Americans, had as much right to form juntas and rule the colonies provisionally in the king's name as did any group back in Spain. Moves were soon afoot to create such American juntas, although none would be successfully established until 1810. The fact is simply that, with the turn of events in Spain, Spanish Americans were now forced to choose between competing claims to authority over them, and any who wanted changes in the existing system had a golden opportunity to press their agenda. Even those who truly yearned for separation from Spain could achieve most of the same benefits by organizing their own governments, ostensibly to rule in the name of a king who was the captive of the French. And by invoking his name they could disarm much of the opposition of those who were either too traditionalist or too timid.

A movement of Venezuelan notables to set up a governing junta in Caracas in 1808 was aborted through the decisive measures of the Spanish captain-general of Venezuela. In Quito, in the following year, a junta was actually established, only to be crushed within a few months by forces sent from Peru. In Bogotá as well, there was strong sentiment for creating a junta, especially after Quito set up its own and invited the capital of the viceroyalty to follow suit. Viceroy Antonio Amar y Borbón was unable to prevent the Bogotá city council from holding a debate over the proposal; but with some erratic bursts of intimidation, he succeeding in heading off any final decision. In the end all that the city managed to do was adopt a *Memorial de agravios* (memorial of grievances) to be sent to Spain, and it was never actually sent, though it did circulate in manuscript form. Drafted in November 1809 by Dr. Camilo Torres, who would become one of the leaders and ultimate martyrs of the independence struggle, it not only detailed specific complaints but underscored the basic injustice of Spain's presuming to rule over an American population that was as great as or greater than that of the mother country. He included a distinctly threatening allusion: "The seven millions who made up Great Britain in Europe certainly counted for more than the bare three million who formed English America; and, withal, the weight of justice inclined the balance to their side."[6]

For Torres's threat to become reality, the situation of the mother country had to deteriorate still further. The French never could force all of Spain to accept the rule of Joseph I, but Napoleon's armies eventually took all the principal cities, including Seville, seat of the Central Junta. By early in 1810 the resistance movement was reduced to little more than the port city of Cádiz. In addition, the junta dissolved itself in favor of a newly created Council of Regency, a move that might have seemed a mere technicality but did pose again the question of relations between colonies and mother country, if only because the former were expected to recognize the new Spanish authority. With the very survival of an independent Spain appearing now problematic, the drive to create Spanish American juntas was stronger this time, and the opposition of die-hard Spanish loyalists correspondingly weaker. Hence, the outcome was different: colony after colony came under the control of a native ruling junta, the one major exception in Spanish South America being Peru.

THE PATRIA BOBA (1810–1816)

Caracas this time led the way. On April 19, 1810, the captain-general of Venezuela was deposed in favor of a creole-staffed junta. Cartagena in New Granada was not far behind, setting up its own junta on May 10. Since the news from Spain that set off these events took longer to reach Cartagena, the two juntas were, for all practical purposes, created simultaneously. As the same news traveled through the rest of New Granada, more juntas were created in one province or another, until on July 20 Bogotá, the capital, fell in line. Viceroy Amar y Borbón was initially a member of the Bogotá junta, but there was good reason to doubt his loyalty to the new order, so he was quickly dropped and was in fact placed under arrest. Even his wife was arrested, not so much because she was a threat to the Bogotá junta as to quiet an angry mob of women who wanted to see her humbled.

Exactly as had been done in Caracas (or in Quito the year before), the Bogotá junta swore allegiance to Ferdinand VII even while claiming for itself full authority to rule in his name during his unfortunate captivity. In Venezuela, however, Caracas struck the first blow, and when its junta asserted authority over the whole of the captaincy-general, most of the outlying provinces accepted its claim. In New Granada a number of outlying provinces (such as Cartagena) had acted to create juntas even before the capital city. And when the question arose whether these preexisting juntas (or those that still other provinces began setting up one by one) would accept subordination to the junta in Bogotá, the answer soon came that they would not. At least for the present, each claimed an equal right to take control of affairs in the name of the captive Ferdinand.

This political disunity was to some extent inevitable. Certainly no part of Spanish America had so many natural obstacles to unity—so many obstacles to transportation and communication per square kilometer—as New Granada, with a population scattered in isolated clusters in various Andean ranges, not to mention other settlements along the coast. Geographic separation thus came to reinforce all the basic socioeconomic and cultural differences among major regions, and the result was an intense sectionalism that vastly complicated the first efforts at political organization. In fact, not only did the different provinces prove unable to get together, but some of them began falling apart internally. After all, once you proclaimed the principle that each province should be an independent entity with its own self-governing junta, why stop with just the existing provinces, all holdovers from the previous colonial system? Accordingly, outlying towns began declaring themselves independent of their provincial capitals, with the object of creating still more self-governing provinces; and Cartagena, which was one of those most eager to strike out on its own instead of following the leadership of Bogotá, had a taste of its own medicine when the second largest city of Cartagena province declared itself the head of an independent province, with a junta of its own. This was Mompós, the Magdalena River port where gold for shipment to Spain had traditionally been stored just out of pirates' reach until word came that the fleet to carry it had put in at Cartagena. In the course of bringing Mompós back to obedience in 1811, the forces of Cartagena shed the first blood in civil combat among the patriots of New Granada.

Ultimately, at the end of 1811, a general government of sorts was formed, under the name of United Provinces of New Granada. Its first president was Camilo Torres, author of Bogotá's *Memorial de agravios* (though not himself a native Bogotano). The United Provinces constituted a very loose federation, vaguely comparable to that created by the Articles of Confederation during the English American revolution. Its structural weakness—the federal authorities were wholly dependent on the voluntary cooperation of member provinces—was compounded by the fact that it did not even include all the provinces. In particular, it left out the most important of them all, Bogotá. With one neighboring province, which it in effect annexed, Bogotá drew up a separate constitution of its own under the name of Cundinamarca. This was an Indian name, widely though erroneously thought to have been used for the central area of New Granada before the coming of the Spaniards. Actually, it was a Quechua term, of Peruvian or Ecuadoran origin, whose application to the area of Bogotá rested on a series of misunderstandings.[7] It did, though, symbolize a conscious effort of the revolutionists to distance themselves from Hispanic traditions and emphasize, rhetorically, their American identity.

In the same vein, it was during the years of the independence struggle that the name of Santa Fe, which had always been used in colonial times for the capital of New Granada, was transformed first to Santa Fe de Bogotá and ultimately just plain Bogotá, in honor of the Muisca settlement of more or less that name that had existed on more or less the same spot.

Although Cartagena showed no great haste to release the New Granadan "Precursor," Antonio Nariño, from the prison of the Inquisition, he did eventually regain his freedom, returned to Bogotá, and there plunged into revolutionary politics. He badgered the first president of Cundinamarca to the point that he was forced to step down, whereupon Nariño succeeded to his position. He assumed dictatorial powers, though he used them in moderation. And he kept hammering away at the weakness of the federal type of organization, as embodied in the United Provinces of New Granada, preaching the need for a more centralized government that could exercise real power throughout New Granada.

In view of the dangers faced by the revolutionary movement, Nariño's position clearly made sense. The anti-French rump government holding out against Napoleon in Spain was still unable to do much about the spread of insurrection in the colonies, but Spaniards by and large were under no illusions that their American colonists, once having tasted self-government under the pretense of ruling on behalf of an absent king, would readily return to obedience. Accordingly, Spain's hostility to the new governments being established in America was manifest, and even if Spanish attention was initially directed more to other colonies—such as Venezuela—than to New Granada, this was no assurance of long-term immunity. Indeed, as the European tide slowly turned against Napoleonic France, it became ever more likely that Ferdinand VII would ultimately regain his throne and then attempt, with redoubled resources, to reassert control over the colonies as well.

In addition, the New Granadan patriots faced here and now the hostility of certain pockets of loyalist resistance in their own midst. One such pocket was Santa Marta on the Caribbean coast, which was a traditional (and traditionally unsuccessful) commercial rival of Cartagena. Santa Marta briefly established a revolutionary junta in 1810, but it soon fell victim to a counterrevolutionary reaction that set up a pro-Spanish loyalist government in its place. This reaction was entirely logical, since Cartagena was patriot, and for the next few years the trade rivalry between Santa Marta and Cartagena was sublimated into a loyalist-versus-patriot military conflict. Another trouble spot was Pasto in the far south. Surrounded by high mountains and steep canyons, Pasto was a largely self-contained and deeply conservative community, barely touched by any of the new economic or intellectual currents of the age. (Its people, the Pastusos, are even today the butt of jokes by other Colombians, who dismiss them as ignorant bumpkins. "How many Pastusos does it take to change a light bulb?" and so forth.) They were having none of independence, even if masked by a nominal allegiance to Ferdinand VII; and inconveniently for the patriots they sat astride the main route to Quito, which since 1810 had again established its own ruling junta (and one that this time would last a good two years).

If only for reasons of self-preservation, then, Nariño's recipe of a strong central government to direct the struggle was preferable to a loose league of self-governing provinces, such as the United Provinces of New Granada, which ultimately established its capital at Tunja. But Nariño had no way to compel all the other provinces to accept his ideas; and by keeping his Cundinamarca out of the union because the union did not have a strong enough government, he simply magnified its debility. To make things worse, he intrigued with malcontents in a number of other places to try to overthrow their local authorities and get them to join Cundinamarca. He thereby unleashed a state of civil war between the two sides that began in 1812 and continued sporadically until 1814, when the federal troops of the United Provinces finally conquered Bogotá with the aid of a Venezuelan auxiliary, Simón Bolívar, who had been temporarily thrown out of his own homeland. By that time Nariño himself was already out of the way. He had set off with an army to subdue the loyalists of Pasto in the south, got too far ahead of his own men, and was captured by the enemy. He was then shipped off to prison in Spain and remained there for six years. (If one takes Nariño's whole career from the time of his first arrest for printing the Declaration of the Rights of Man until his final release in 1820, it turns out that approximately two-thirds of all his time was spent in prison.)

Meanwhile, New Granada had also got around to declaring formal independence, just as various other Spanish colonies were also doing, with Venezuela leading the way on July 5, 1811. Only New Granada, thanks to its internal disunity, did so in piecemeal fashion. The province of Cartagena was first to cut all ties with Spain, in November 1811. Cundinamarca did the same, at Nariño's urging, in July 1813. However, by the time independence was declared, it was almost a technicality, because New Granada in practice had been managing or mismanaging its own affairs ever since 1810. July 20, anniversary of the setting up of the original Bogotá junta, rather than any of the dates on which formal independence was proclaimed, would become the principal national holiday of modern Colombia.

Independence was soon cut short by the Spanish "Reconquest" of . New Granada in 1815–16, and the dissension among the patriots themselves over form of government was certainly one factor contributing to that collapse. Another was the sheer inexperience of creole revolutionary leaders, few of whom had previously had much exposure to the work of governing beyond the municipal level. Thanks both to its ultimate failure and to its frequent air of impracticality (of which the adoption of the weakest possible sort of federation by the United Provinces is just one example), the whole period from 1810 to the reconquest was dubbed by later Colombian historians the Patria Boba (Foolish Fatherland). But foolish or not, the earliest independent governments produced a good many worthwhile accomplishments. The terrible Inquisition was abolished, and at Cartagena a bonfire was made not of heretics, as in olden days, but of Inquisitorial paraphernalia. Naturally, discrimination against the native-born in appointment to office was done away with; discrimination was now against European Spaniards instead. And naturally, too, the ports—in reality, *the* port, Cartagena, since Santa Marta was in the hands of the loyalists— became open to the trade of all friendly nations without restrictions.

Particularly interesting were certain socioeconomic reforms that help give the lie to one common interpretation of the Latin American wars of independence—namely, that they were superficial political-military movements devoid of larger significance except that they opened up the region to Anglo-Saxon economic penetration. There was, it is true, no fundamental social transformation, which actually no one as yet was calling for. Nor were any structural reforms carried out on a nationwide basis, because in New Granada there was no effective nationwide government to impose them. Yet some of the separate provinces, by their own action, did carry out noteworthy measures. In 1814, for example, the province of Antioquia (and subsequently one other province) took a first step toward abolition of slavery by granting freedom to every child born to a slave mother in the future. This was the free-birth principle, which after the war was extended to all parts of the country. It was not the first such measure in South America. Chile had done the same thing in 1811 and Argentina in 1813, but Antioquia's action was more significant than that of Chile at least, since Chile had only a few thousand slaves in its entire population, whereas slavery was still widespread in Antioquia's basic gold-mining industry. The slave trade, moreover, for which Cartagena had been the traditional gateway, was formally ended by action of the local revolutionists.

A number of things were also done ostensibly on behalf of the Indians. The tribute—the colonial head tax collected yearly from each adult Indian male—was generally abolished, and a number of provinces (including Bogotá) ordered the distribution of the *resguardos*, or communal lands, among individual Indians as full private property. But these measures, though billed as steps to redeem the native population from its misery, were not quite what they appeared. Abolition of the tribute, which was decreed even by the Spanish rump government holding out in Cádiz, excused the Indians from paying a tax that was symbolically obnoxious, but the corollary was that henceforth they would simply pay all the ordinary taxes from which they had been traditionally exempted *in return* for paying the tribute. As for the liquidation of the *resguardos*, this was not something the Indians themselves (with minor exceptions) had been clamoring for. In fact, dividing the common lands into small private plots would inevitably make it easier for creoles or mestizos to get their hands on them by fair means or foul. It was something that creoles—not Indians—had been lobbying for under Spanish rule, and they had managed to obtain some whittling away of the *resguardos*, but for a clean sweep they had to wait until they had the reins of power directly in their own hands. That they had now achieved, although for the moment the measure in question was virtually impossible to implement, among other reasons for lack of needed administrative machinery.

Another action that creoles had widely sought, abolition of the tobacco monopoly, was carried out in the province of Socorro, which was both an important tobacco-growing area and recently the focus of the Comunero rebellion that had begun in considerable part in protest against the monopoly. That tobacco was the second most important source of government revenue counted for less than the desire of local landowners to grow as much tobacco as they wanted and the desire of other entrepreneurs to manufacture and sell tobacco products freely. The move was in line with the provision in the first provincial constitution of Socorro outlawing any measures contrary to the "sacred right of property"[8] and indeed with the general movement toward a more liberal economy ("liberal" in the nineteenth-century sense), to be based on the free play of individual initiative rather than on regulation of economic activities by the state or by privileged corporate interest groups.

There was no contradiction between economic liberalism—of which the opening of the nation to the trade of the whole world was still another example—and the fact that leaders of the revolutionary movement were predominantly drawn from the creole upper class. Members of that one social group already controlled most of the wealth and factors of production and on the whole had more to gain than to lose by greater economic freedom. They still drew the line at outright abolition of slavery, but the initial moves against that institution are not difficult to understand. As far as the ending of the slave trade was concerned, it was a means of gaining international respectability and possible British favor with minimal impact on the internal economy, since New Granada (unlike Cuba or Brazil) did not have an expanding slave-based plantation economy. Moreover, in the gold-mining districts the existing slave population was already close to reproducing itself by natural means.[9] When they adopted the free-birth principle, therefore, Antioqueños could assume that—along with the growing free black and *pardo* (or "brown") population—enough of the free-born offspring of slaves would be willing to work for pay in the mining industry to meet its labor requirements. The assumption may not have been wholly accurate, but at least there was no reason to expect a critical shortage of workers in either the immediate or the longer-term future.

COLLAPSE AND REVIVAL
OF THE PATRIOT CAUSE

Even though the Patria Boba's reform measures posed no real threat to social or political stability, its factional dissensions—above all, the struggle between Bogotá's centralists and the federalists of the United

Provinces—did clearly undermine its chances of survival. The catastrophe that finally overtook it, however, was by no means unique in Spanish America during the independence period, since only in the Río de la Plata did the patriot regime (first established there as well in 1810) never suffer reconquest at the hands of loyalist forces. And in New Granada the fall of the Patria Boba was closely connected with the course of events in neighboring Venezuela.

As noted already, Venezuela preceded New Granada both in establishing its own junta government and in declaring formal independence. But Venezuela's "First Republic," a close counterpart of the Patria Boba, proved even more short-lived. It adopted a federalist constitution toward the end of 1811, against the advice of the "Precursor," Francisco de Miranda, who had returned from Europe to try to lead his countrymen and was soon enmeshed in local and personal rivalries not unlike those in New Granada. Venezuela, though, with its longer Caribbean coastline and a population concentrated mostly not far from the sea, was more directly vulnerable to the counterattack of loyalist forces assisted from the Spanish Antilles. To make matters worse, Caracas and a number of other key cities were devastated by earthquake during Holy Week of 1812, so that by midyear the First Republic was in collapse and Miranda preceded Nariño to imprisonment in Spain (though unlike Nariño he died in his Spanish jail). Among the leaders who escaped, however, was Simón Bolívar, who ultimately eclipsed all the others and became the object of Latin America's preeminent hero cult. A twentieth-century Colombian priest would address him as a quasi-divinity:

> Our father, Liberator Simón Bolívar, who art in the heaven of American democracy: we wish to invoke your name.[10]

Scion of a wealthy cacao-growing family, Bolívar had acquired some slight military experience as an officer of the colonial militia; but when the Caracas junta was set up, he was only twenty-six years old, and he played a minor role in the defense of the First Republic. He shared Miranda's aversion to federalism but did not trust Miranda as a leader and was one of those who blocked his escape when the First Republic collapsed. Bolívar himself, after some hesitation, took refuge in Curaçao and from there went to Cartagena, where he offered his services to the patriots of New Granada. They were readily accepted, and in 1813 the government of the United Provinces gave him the help he requested to launch an offensive against the restored Spanish regime in Venezuela. In a brilliant, whirlwind campaign, he proceeded to retake Caracas and thereby win for himself the title of "Liberator" that he would proudly wear ever after. Alas, the Second Republic that he created—a de facto military dictatorship rather than a federal republic—collapsed too, in the very next year.

There was no earthquake involved this time, but political dissensions were again a problem. Even more serious was the social and racial backlash stirred up against the patriots by their enemies, taking advantage of the fact that most of the leading revolutionaries, naturally including Bolívar, were associated with the creole landed and slave-owning aristocracy. In the last years of the colonial period, these aristocrats had been both resisting the upward mobility of free *pardos* and moving to convert the open range on the *llanos* of the Orinoco basin into great private estates. The latter development brought them into conflict with the seminomadic and free-living population of *llaneros*, who had previously used the same land to gather and kill the wild cattle of the plains for meat to eat and hides and animal by-products to sell, whenever and wherever they felt the need.

After the independence movement began, the revolutionary government had explicitly repealed all forms of legal discrimination against nonwhites, but the *pardos* either had not heard about this action or did not believe that it was taken in good faith. And the new regime frankly threw its weight behind the attempt of creole landowners to appropriate open range on the *llanos*. Thus, there was an undercurrent of tension between the patriot leadership and the largely nonwhite Venezuelan masses, whether on the *llanos* or elsewhere; and loyalist guerrilla leaders exploited this tension in organizing irregular forces that cruelly harassed and ultimately overthrew the Second Republic. The same social and racial unrest had been present in the First Republic, but that regime was doomed even without it. For that matter, there were similar tensions in New Granada; yet the very fact that New Granada's economy was less dynamic than Venezuela's made the social problem there (apart from certain regional exceptions) less acute. Nonwhite elements of the population first had to be rising economically before their social and legal status could become a major source of friction, and in New Granada there were fewer opportunities to rise. Nor did progress as yet threaten lifestyles on the New Granadan sector of the *llanos*, which was in fact a patriot stronghold.

By the end of 1814, Bolívar found himself again in New Granada, where, as mentioned, he helped the United Provinces finally conquer Bogotá. It was perhaps odd that this declared antifederalist should thus aid the federalist cause in New Granada, but the government of the United Provinces had helped him in 1813. Subsequently, he took part both in the war against the loyalist stronghold of Santa Marta and in a ruinous conflict between the national federal authorities and Cartagena. Such internecine fighting was not to his liking, however, especially since he clearly saw the threat it posed to the very survival of the New Granadan patriots. By this time Ferdinand VII had been restored to his throne, and Spain had prepared a massive expeditionary force, composed of veterans of the national struggle against the French, to crush the colonial rebellion for once and all. Its first destination was Venezuela, where it was expected to mop up remaining pockets of patriot resistance before proceeding on to New Granada. Consequently, Bolívar, in effect, gave up hope for the patriots of New Granada and in mid-1815 moved on once again, to Jamaica and then Haiti, to organize new expeditions for the liberation of his native Venezuela. He departed not long before General Pablo Morillo, commander of the Spanish expedition, arrived in Santa Marta from Venezuela with a force of 5,000 men.

Morillo's initial objective in New Granada was patriot-held Cartagena, a key strategic point that had to be subdued before he could turn his full attention to the revolution in the Andean interior. Once its definitive fortifications were in place, Cartagena had never been taken by force—not even by the powerful British fleet of Admiral Edward Vernon, which sought to take the city in 1742 during the so-called War of Jenkins' Ear. (Vernon won enduring fame instead by virtue of the fact that a member of the English American contingent in his expedition, Laurence Washington, chose to name the family estate after him.) Morillo was not destined to take Cartagena by assault either. However, he did take it, by a 106-day siege in the course of which the city's occupants were reduced to eating rats, burros, and rancid codfish—and died by the hundreds. In one desperate attempt to save the situation, Cartagena formally proclaimed itself part of the British empire, but this offer was politely ignored by British officials in the Caribbean, in line with their government's technical neutrality in the Spanish American conflict.

Morillo made clear almost at once that he did not intend to compromise with rebels. While on one hand restoring the Inquisition, on the other he created a military court to judge leading patriots who had been taken prisoner. Executions began just outside the walls of Cartagena even as separate columns of troops were moving inland to subdue the rest of the colony. The patriots' lack of preparation and growing demoralization made the task of reconquest relatively easy, and in early May 1816 Spanish rule was again established in Bogotá. There, too, and in fact all through New Granada, Morillo and his lieutenants applied a policy of terror designed to liquidate the principal military and political figures of the Patria Boba and, at the same time, impress the population at large with the perils of disobedience. From the fall of Cartagena to the battle of Boyacá in August 1819, which finally doomed Spanish rule, over 300 persons were executed in New Granada, including the former president, Camilo Torres, and the leading creole scientist, Francisco José de Caldas. A fortunate few were merely exiled from New Granada. Another small group of survivors were those who succeeded in escaping to the open spaces of the eastern *llanos* and there stayed just out of reach of their pursuers.

Even as defeat in the form of Morillo's expedition had arrived by way of Venezuela, the final liberation of New Granada came from the same direction. Venezuela had also been largely "pacified" by the beginning of 1816; but before that year was over, Bolívar returned from the West Indies to establish for himself a permanent foothold. This time he succeeded in projecting a more popular image for the patriot cause. He did so by pledging soldier bonuses and the abolition of slavery and by winning the cooperation of other leaders of relatively humble social origin—most notably, José Antonio Páez, a former ranch hand of the Orinoco basin, who even before Bolívar's return had established a base of patriot resistance in the *llanos*. Bolívar still could not make much headway against Morillo's Spanish veterans who held Caracas and the Venezuelan highlands. But toward the middle of 1819 he abruptly turned his sights elsewhere and marched westward, into the heart of New Granada.

He chose New Granada as a target for a number of reasons. First of all, it was more lightly held by the enemy's military forces and was increasingly disaffected toward Spanish rule. The wave of executions had been bad enough; even worse was the fact that taxes were increased to pay the costs of repression. Popular discontent with these measures had encouraged the formation of patriot guerrilla forces, from which an invading army could expect to receive some help. Indirectly, this guerrilla struggle produced the foremost heroine of the Colombian independence movement in Policarpa Salvarrieta, who did not join an irregular band herself but served the guerrillas as contact and informant in the capital city—until she was found out and then took her place in the honor roll of martyrs.

Finally, Bolívar could count on help from a small band of fugitives from the wreck of the Patria Boba who occupied the New Granadan portion of the *llanos*, not far from the foothills of the eastern Andean cordillera, and had managed to turn back all loyalist attempts to retake that thinly populated region. Their key figure was Francisco de Paula Santander, who was destined to become, after Bolívar himself, the foremost national hero of modern Colombia. A law student from Cúcuta on the border between New Granada and Venezuela when the independence struggle got under way, Santander never actually practiced his profession; he joined the patriot armed forces instead and proved to be a competent (even if self-taught) military officer. He was also showing genuine talent as an administrator even at this early stage, in organizing the eastern lowland province of Casanare as a patriot redoubt.

With important help from Santander, Bolívar planned and executed a campaign that was probably the finest of his military achievements. At the head of a mixed army of Venezuelans, New Granadans, and European volunteers, he crossed the *llanos* in rainy season, when vast stretches of the plains were flooded, and then climbed the Andes over a rough trail that rose to a maximum elevation of about 4,000 meters. In the first engagements with the enemy after reaching the highlands, Bolívar suffered one near defeat, but on August 7, 1819, at Boyacá on the road between Tunja and Bogotá, he won a critical victory. As battles go, it was not much of one, with fewer than 3,000 men on either side. However, it virtually destroyed the main Spanish army in the interior of New Granada and opened for Bolívar the road to Bogotá, which he entered unopposed three days later. There he found a treasure of a half million pesos, which the viceroy had left behind in his haste to flee. Thanks to Boyacá, Bolívar gained control of an area with relatively dense population from which to draw both taxes and recruits, not to mention the supplies furnished by its farms and small handcraft industries.

Most of the rest of New Granada fell rapidly into the hands of patriot columns fanning out from Bogotá. Cartagena on the coast was retaken, this time after a siege mounted by the patriots, in October 1821; and Panama, which had remained firmly under Spanish control all during the Patria Boba, staged its own bloodless revolution the following month. That left little more than ever-loyal Pasto under Spanish control, and it too was eventually taken, though only as a by-product of the final liberation of Ecuador. There the port city of Guayaquil rebelled against Spain on its own initiative in October 1820, and Bolívar subsequently dispatched General Antonio José de Sucre to advance from Guayaquil into the Ecuadorian highlands; it was his victory in the battle of Pichincha on the very outskirts of Quito in May 1822 that effectively compelled the Spanish governor of Pasto to seek terms. The definitive subjugation of the Pasto region would take more time, as the Pastusos mounted a bitter guerrilla resistance of their own. Meanwhile, however, troops, money, and matériel from New Granada had helped complete the liberation of Venezuela as well, where the last major battle was won by Páez and Bolívar, at Carabobo, in June 1821.

All things considered, the fight for independence of New Granada was less traumatic than the war in Venezuela—or Mexico—though it was more costly in lives and resources than in Ecuador. In Venezuela, which was fought over almost continually and with unusual ferocity, total population may actually have declined during the independence period; at the very least, military and civilian casualties, including deaths from deprivation and disease and population loss by exile, served to cancel out any natural increase. In New Granada, however, although the creole elite was decimated by the execution squads of the Spanish Reconquest (in a way that the Venezuelan elite, paradoxically, was not), the actual fighting was mainly localized and sporadic. Economically, agriculture in Venezuela was more vulnerable to wartime disruption because the cacao industry, especially, was geared to export markets, while both farming and ranching were hard hit by the continual impressment of workers and seizure of livestock by the contending armies. In New Granada, on the other hand, most trade was purely local, and producers in any one mountain valley were vulnerable mainly to such havoc as might be wreaked in their immediate vicinity. The industry most exposed to disruption was gold mining, whose output appears to have fallen by around 40 percent.[11] Unlike Mexican silver mining, however, where flooding of mine shafts and destruction of equipment caused damage that took many years and heavy new investment to overcome, gold production in New Granada involved not deep mining but mainly exploitation of placer deposits, so that physical destruction of complex installations was not a critical problem. More serious was the loss of slave workers by flight or military conscription. Mining recovery, though, was fairly rapid after the war, despite the continuing decline of slavery. The damage suffered by other sectors of New Granada's basic economy also was quickly repaired.

In many ways the independence struggle had an impact on the social structure itself. Slaves who served in the military were offered freedom as their reward. Still other slaves found the confusion of wartime a good cover for simply running away. For the free population, there were also opportunities to improve one's station in life by military service, a stock example being Venezuela's José Antonio Páez. Páez's lack of education and social standing was offset by his prowess on horseback and gift for leadership; in the end he gained not only high military rank and political power but a vast amount of landed property that had been duly confiscated from supporters of the enemy. Others improved their lot by political intrigues or by financial speculation, but—as exemplified by the property that changed hands through confiscation and then redistribution to deserving patriots—instances of upward mobility as a result of wartime conditions were counterbalanced by other instances of downward mobility, with little net change in the overall pattern. It was, moreover, a pattern that featured a minuscule upper class exercising domination over a vast majority of peasants, cowboys, artisans, and servants, who with the partial exception of the artisans had no access to formal education or political influence and few material comforts—although food, at least, was usually plentiful and cheap.

The dominant groups did appear a shade darker in average skin color than before, because the fortunate few who worked their way up were often mestizos (for example, Páez) or, less frequently, of part African descent (for example, New Granada's leading naval hero of independence, Admiral José Padilla). But the net change in society was, to repeat, limited—and those who rose in status did not necessarily receive *social* recognition commensurate with their political or military or economic accomplishments. Change was also more limited in New Granada than in Venezuela, if only because the total impact of the war there had been less.

3

The Gran Colombian Experiment
(1819–1830)

Immediately after the victory of Boyacá, a Venezuelan congress meeting at Angostura (today Ciudad Bolívar) on the lower Orinoco proclaimed the union of all the territory that comprised the former Viceroyalty of New Granada as a single nation with the name Republic of Colombia. At the time, the present Ecuador was entirely under Spanish rule, and New Granada had only token representation at the congress. Yet, as far as Venezuela and New Granada are concerned, the union was already a virtual fait accompli because of the way in which the military struggle for independence had been waged. Armies indiscriminately composed of Venezuelans and New Granadans had passed back and forth over the boundary between the two, and both of them had accepted the supreme command of the Venezuelan Liberator, Simón Bolívar. He himself, moreover, was a strong supporter of the cause of unity. No definitive organization was adopted at Angostura; that was left for a more representative constituent congress to adopt when the time was ripe. However, the congress at Angostura did set up a provisional government featuring separate administrations for both Venezuela and New Granada, each headed by its own vice-president; it also created a national government consisting of Bolívar as president, a small civilian staff to assist him, and the combined Venezuelan–New Granadan army.

The proclamation of union at Angostura marked the formal establishment of what has become known in history texts as Gran, or Great, Colombia, to distinguish it from the smaller Colombia of today. Under Bolívar's leadership the new nation first eliminated the enemy forces still operating on its own soil and then played a key role in the ultimate liberation of Peru and Bolivia. For a time it would enjoy a degree of stability and international prestige not matched elsewhere in Spanish America. But this state of affairs would last only until the middle of 1826, because certain basic weaknesses could be overcome or ignored for only so long. And at least some of those weaknesses were compounded by the type of constitutional organization devised for the new nation by a constituent congress meeting at Cúcuta in 1821.

THE CONGRESS OF CÚCUTA

The Congress of Cúcuta had been elected by a restricted suffrage that excluded most inhabitants from voting, as was then perfectly normal; since the restrictions were waived for the benefit of soldiers in the revolutionary army itself, in that one respect the election was unusually democratic for the time. When the voting took place, much of Venezuela, including Caracas, and most of Ecuador were still under royalist control and unable to take part. The deputies nevertheless showed few qualms in ratifying the 1819 act of union. Once that was done, however, the old issue of federalism versus centralism, which had plagued earlier patriot regimes in both Venezuela and New Granada, arose again to plague the constituent congress. Moreover, it was a more complex issue now, simply because the area to be centralized or federated was much bigger. Should unitary governments be set up in each of the three major sections—Venezuela, New Granada, Ecuador—but joined in a federal union with each other? Or should each individual province become a separate federal state? Or, finally, should there be no concessions of any sort to demands for federation?

Venezuelan deputies generally took the last of those three positions, if only because they assumed that it was Bolívar's preference. They, and other centralists, tirelessly hammered on the failure of earlier patriot experiments with federalism. The younger liberals of New Granada—already gravitating to the side of Santander, who had been serving as special vice-president for New Granada under the provisional frame of government adopted at Angostura—were mostly centralists too; despite the theoretical appeal of federalism, they could see the tactical advantage of stringing along with the Liberator and hoping for a larger role for themselves in any unitary republic that might be set up. In the end, the sheer practical benefit of having a unified government to fight the war with Spain to its conclusion prompted the "Great Compromise" of the Colombian constituent congress. It adopted a rigidly centralist constitution but with a clause expressly providing for a new convention to reconsider the question after a ten-year trial period. By then, presumably, the war would be over, not just in Colombia but in the rest of South America, and federalism could be safely adopted if the nation wanted it.

The constitution in other respects provided for a conventional republican form of government, with separation of powers and assorted guarantees of individual rights. It retained some property or income limitations on the right to vote and provided that not only the president but also Congress should be chosen indirectly, by an electoral college system; at least no literacy test was to be imposed for nineteen years. To be illiterate in 1821 was seen as an unfortunate legacy of Spanish oppression, for which the individual should not be penalized; after 1840 it would be his own fault. But in order for its handiwork to go into effect immediately, the constituent congress took upon itself the choice of the first constitutional president and vice-president. The choice of Bolívar as president was automatic; and since he was Venezuelan, the vice-president had to be from New Granada. The vice-presidency would be a critically important position, since Bolívar intended to continue at the head of the armies fighting Spain and would leave the vice-president to serve as acting chief executive. The two obvious candidates were Nariño and Santander. Nariño had only recently returned from captivity in Spain and was senior in both years and accomplishments. He had been tapped by Bolívar to serve as provisional vice-president of Colombia while the constituent congress was in session. However, he was burdened by a string of personal and political enmities—in effect, all the unburied grudges of the Patria Boba—and most recently had acted brusquely toward the congress itself. After several ballots, therefore, Santander was chosen, though with some misgivings because his rise to prominence had been so recent and because he was not yet thirty years of age.

The Congress of Cúcuta further enacted a number of basic reforms that it felt could not wait until the first regular Congress met. They were predominantly "liberal" reforms, since a majority of the deputies subscribed in varying degrees to the standard creed of nineteenth-century liberalism, which sought to enlarge the sphere of individual liberty in political, economic, and religious matters and to limit the power not just of the traditional church but also (for some purposes) of the state. And it is no doubt to the credit of the Congress of Cúcuta that its very first enactment, even before the issuance of the new constitution, was a manumission law or, more precisely, a law of free birth. Like the Antioquia law of 1814 on which it was patterned, it provided that all children born of slave mothers in future would go free on reaching a specified age, and it thus reinforced the effect of the war itself in hastening the demise of slavery. Its final passage was marked by scenes of unadulterated romantic emotion, with various deputies rising to declare the immediate freedom of their own human chattel amid tears and acclamation.

The congress also reaffirmed—and made extensive to the entire republic—the earlier move of some New Granadan provinces to liquidate the Indian *resguardos*. As part of an effort to revamp the colonial fiscal system, it did away with the *alcabala* (sales tax) and reiterated the abolition of the Indian tribute, which had been restored during the reconquest. To offset the loss of the *alcabala*, the congress undertook a bold experiment in direct taxation, placing a levy of 10 percent on the income produced by land or capital. To offset the loss of the tribute, it declared the Indians equal citizens and once again made them liable to all the regular taxes from which they were previously exempt. At the same time, the customs system was simplified, and the import tariffs established were generally moderate, designed to generate revenue rather than for the explicit purpose of protecting native producers (save in a few special cases). Even if duties were lower than before, they were all being paid now at South American ports, rather than partly in Spain as before, and this meant a significant increase in the revenues locally collected.

One of the most significant of the reforms was at the same time economic and religious: a law that abolished all monasteries with fewer than eight members and confiscated their assets. Sponsors of this measure decried the immorality, ignorance, and general uselessness of monks and friars, portrayed as outdated relics of the Middle Ages; indeed, even some friends of the monasteries admitted that their standards were generally low. But the religious orders had strong support among the popular classes, and for this reason, as well as from a perfectly sincere desire to promote education, the property taken from the monasteries was earmarked as an endowment for secondary schools throughout Colombia. Education, after all, was also a popular cause. Another law affecting the church, and one considerably less controversial, was the law abolishing the Inquisition, an institution that was dormant but technically alive as a result of its formal restoration during Morillo's reconquest. In a similar vein, all prior censorship of publications on religious or other grounds—except for editions of Holy Scripture—was ended.

Yet it is worth noting some of the things that the deputies at Cúcuta conspicuously did not do. Their legislation on slavery did not free a single slave who was unfortunate enough to have been born before its passage. Although they abolished the *alcabala*, they retained the tobacco monopoly, which was even more objectionable in principle: the government simply needed the money it produced. Likewise, nunneries were spared the fate of monasteries, and suppression of the Inquisition did not in itself usher in religious toleration, a subject on which the constitution cautiously said nothing. Colonial legislation against heresy and heretics thus remained on the books; the law abolishing the Inquisition merely removed one agency that had the special mission of combating heresy. It was no doubt also a signal that heresy should not be combated too vigorously.

In both its achievements and its limitations, the work of the constituent congress had much in common with that of the first independent governments elsewhere in Latin America. All nations abolished the Inquisition, and almost all took at least some action against slavery. All did some tinkering with the fiscal system, and Gran Colombia was not even alone in its seemingly farsighted (though ultimately unsuccessful) effort to introduce direct taxation. Everywhere the ideological thrust of such measures was clearly liberal. But everywhere the net progress made toward revising colonial institutions was limited, either because of the power of vested interests or because of the continuing strength of traditional beliefs and attitudes—*preocupaciones*, as they were referred to by frustrated reformists—among the general population. Thus, in South America only the Brazilian monarchy and the one Argentine province of Buenos Aires dared introduce freedom of public worship as early as the 1820s.

Liberals were normally an influential minority, but a minority nonetheless; and when they pushed their proposals for change beyond the limits of what was acceptable, a more or less violent reaction was almost sure to follow. In Gran Colombia the cause of innovation had some strong supporters among leading merchants and professional people, but these groups were not numerous: there were probably no more than 200 to 300 trained lawyers in the entire country.[1] The military, the clergy, and the landed aristocracy were more liberal than they are often given credit for, but they preferred to take reforms gradually—above all, when their own interests were at stake. The clergy was destined finally to renounce liberalism altogether; and, unlike liberal intellectuals, it had a strong hold on the loyalty of the popular sectors. But these sectors—people mostly engaged in primitive agriculture in the countryside or in menial work in the towns and cities—were in the beginning not even consulted.

THE ADMINISTRATION OF SANTANDER

The official climate of opinion at the outset of Gran Colombia was nevertheless essentially liberal, and Vice-President Santander, who would be running things in the absence of Bolívar, was personally committed to revamping the legal and institutional structure even though pragmatically wary of trying to accomplish everything at once. Santander is a public figure about whom not much exists in the way of human-interest detail and picturesque anecdote.[2] Grave and usually a little distant in manner, he was capable of neither the lighter touches nor the flashes of genius that Bolívar displayed in his personal correspondence and public papers. But Santander was a hard worker with an eye for detail, as indeed he had to be in a system of government so highly centralized that routine appointments in Caracas were acted on in national cabinet sessions. Above all, Santander has become known as "The Man of Laws," a title first bestowed by Bolívar and accurately reflecting both a tendency to harp on legal technicalities and a steadfast devotion to republican and constitutional principles. Nor did he often pass up a chance to instill similar devotion in others. When a military hero of independence was executed for murder in the main plaza of Bogotá, Santander brought a whole body of troops to witness the act; and while the corpse lay bleeding, he issued forth in person to lecture his captive audience on the Majesty of Law and the need to respect civil authority. (That the officer in question may actually have been innocent of the crime for which he was convicted does not detract from the sincerity of the vice-president's sermon to the troops.)

To a surprising extent even if not invariably, Santander practiced what he preached. He was generally respectful of the rights of his opponents, some of whom (and not simply those he hoped to win over) he appointed to government office. To be sure, he was not exactly serene in the face of criticism, and he was given to writing

ill-tempered replies, which then appeared under a thin veneer of ano-
nymity in the progovernment press. But he did not shut down the
opposition press, much less imprison the editors. He was also one
of the somewhat rare nineteenth-century Latin American rulers who
took seriously the prerogatives of the legislative branch—almost too
seriously at times: his favorite excuse for inability to solve some pressing problem was that, by the letter of the constitution, the needed
action could be taken only by Congress. Since he was willing to make
the effort to humor the legislators, however, he usually in the end got
what he wanted from them.

The vice-president and Congress together produced a record of legislation that in many ways supplemented the reforms already adopted
by the constituent congress. There were fiscal reforms further reducing
the import tariff; and the state monopoly of chewing tobacco was abolished, if not the tobacco monopoly as such. Entailed estates were duly
made illegal in 1824, as an outmoded restriction on the free exchange
of landed property, and assorted attempts were made to tighten civilian control over the military. By far the most controversial of the measures adopted were those touching religion. A law of 1824, strongly
supported by Santander, confirmed in the hands of the new republic
the right of *patronato*—i.e., the control traditionally exercised by the
state over the church in clerical appointments and most other matters except doctrine. Gran Colombia thereby rejected the argument
that it could not wield the powers in question without a specific
renewal of authority from the pope. The insistence of administration
leaders and liberals generally on maintaining the *patronato*, a basically
illiberal institution, reflected among other things their distrust of the
use the priests might make of their vast popular prestige if left to their
own devices. Out of habit if nothing else, most of the clergy went
along rather meekly, although a vocal minority protested bitterly,
both on juridical grounds and out of a growing conviction that the
new regime did not always have the interests of the church at heart.

The constituent congress had already planted the seeds of this conviction, and a number of additional acts passed by Congress and
signed by Santander gave further weight to it. Most of these measures
were quite minor, such as those suspending the ecclesiastical *fuero*
(i.e., the traditional exemption of the clergy from the jurisdiction of
lay courts) in a limited number of cases and excusing new plantations
of coffee and cacao from the payment of tithes. But certain steps taken

by the vice-president on his own offended a large sector of the clergy. One was his cosponsorship of the Colombian Bible Society, founded in 1825 by an English missionary whose distribution of cheap testaments was ostensibly harmless but was frankly conceived, by the Englishman at least, as an opening wedge for Protestantism. Even worse, from the standpoint of the orthodox, was Santander's work in education. Despite subsequent liberal propaganda to the contrary, no cleric seriously opposed the founding of new schools and colleges, which the vice-president promoted to the extent that Colombia's limited resources of money and teachers would allow. But putting the works of such heretical authors as the English philosopher of utilitarianism, Jeremy Bentham, on the required curriculum was a different matter. Some militant traditionalists predicted that divine punishment would surely follow, and when Bogotá did in fact suffer a serious earthquake in 1826, they were not surprised.

In general, though, despite the beginning signs of disaffection among the clergy, Gran Colombia in its first few years proved remarkably successful. One source of satisfaction was the leading political-military role it assumed among the Latin American nations, especially those of Spanish South America. The liberation of Quito in May 1822 had been shortly followed by the semivoluntary incorporation of the port of Guayaquil, where strong local factions favored either provincial independence or annexation to Peru. But Bolívar, having taken control of the Ecuadorian highlands, could not permit their outlet to the sea to have an entirely free choice, and so the full territorial claims of Gran Colombia were upheld. The following year Bolívar moved on to Peru, to direct the struggle against Spain in what had been until then the chief bastion of loyalist strength. The war was virtually ended by the victory of his favorite lieutenant, General Sucre, at Ayacucho in December 1824. The army that Sucre commanded was an amalgam of Colombians, Peruvians, Argentines, Chileans, and even a smattering of European volunteers. But the leadership was disproportionately Colombian, and certainly none of the other Latin American liberators came close to matching the stature of Bolívar himself.

Colombia was likewise successful in the diplomatic sphere, obtaining recognition from the United States in 1822 and Great Britain three years later; it was among the first Spanish American nations to be so honored. Another suggestive detail is that the pope, who would not establish formal relations with any Spanish American nation until the

1830s, consented to name bishops for the vacant dioceses of Gran Colombia early in 1827. This gesture was tantamount to informal recognition, especially since the appointees were all men previously approved by Santander—however much the pope also took pains to emphasize that the appointments were made on his own authority and did not imply acceptance of the *patronato* in Colombian hands. The preeminence of Gran Colombia was further attested by its sponsorship of the first inter-American congress, held at Panama in 1826, to which all American nations except Haiti were invited either by Bolívar personally or by Santander. Unfortunately, attendance was spotty and the congress did not accomplish much. Of the two United States delegates, one died on the way and the other reached Panama after the meeting was over. The Spanish American delegates drew up treaties providing for close future cooperation, including military cooperation if needed; but by this time there was no longer any serious danger from Europe, and only Colombia bothered to ratify the agreements.

Even in economic matters there were outward signs of progress. The basic economy still showed the effects of war, but recovery was gradually taking place, and it was hastened in some sectors (e.g., foreign trade) by economic and fiscal policies of the new regime. In addition, for better or worse, the favorable attitude of the authorities toward foreign capital and foreigners in general encouraged European and North American entrepreneurs to descend on Colombia to open trading houses, set up mining and colonization companies, and engage in countless other projects, including one to drain the fabulous lake of El Dorado and recover the gold dust and gold offerings that must have settled on the bottom. Once the gold was cleared away, the idea was to settle industrious Scottish immigrants on the good, rich mud remaining. Yet most of these ventures, which resembled those being launched all over Latin America in the euphoria of the immediate postindependence years, produced little benefit for anyone. The gold of El Dorado was never reclaimed, because the lake was too difficult to drain. Mining companies seldom lived up to the prospectuses by which they offered shares to the public back in Europe, and the number of bona fide immigrants brought to Colombia under various colonization schemes amounted to a mere handful. Even so, a few substantial achievements were registered. Most spectacular was the introduction of steam navigation on the Magdalena River by the German-Colombian Juan Bernardo Elbers. His boats were constantly getting stuck on sandbars, and service was irregular; before long it was indefinitely suspended. But Elbers had made a start, and the attempt was sure to be repeated. Moreover, the influx of foreign promoters, foreign legionaries in the Colombian military, and the first diplomatic agents was stimulating in itself, culturally and socially. The British, for example, brought not only Protestant proselytizing (disguised as mere distribution of Bibles), as already noted, but horse racing as a spectator sport and the example of beer drinking, which was eagerly taken up by some members of the local upper class.

In 1824 Gran Colombia succeeded in raising a loan from English investors for the remarkable sum of thirty million pesos, then worth an equivalent amount in dollars. Much of this money, however, was used merely to consolidate debts contracted abroad by earlier patriot agents or was spent on war supplies that came too late to do much good. For example, two magnificent frigates were purchased in the United States for the Colombian navy, which heretofore had consisted disproportionately of converted schooners and chartered Yankee privateers. The frigates cost over a million dollars, and everyone agreed they were as fine as any ships afloat. The trouble was that Colombia had neither the trained seamen to sail them nor the money to maintain them, nor really anything useful to do with them, since the war with Spain was for all practical purposes over by the time they arrived— although Spain did not formally recognize defeat and sign a treaty until 1837. Colombia briefly considered using the warships in a joint effort with Mexico to liberate Cuba, but the scheme was abandoned on grounds of both impracticality and U.S. and British displeasure. Hence, they were left to deteriorate in Cartagena harbor.

The use of the loan funds to pay off internal creditors—who had also done their part, willingly or not, to finance the winning of independence—was slightly more productive but equally controversial. Unfortunately, many of these creditors' claims were badly inflated or were in the hands of speculators who had bought them up for a fraction of face value. Either way, the money paid to domestic creditors helped finance a binge of imports of European consumer goods that Colombia could not otherwise have afforded, and this spree was positively harmful to many local craftsmen, who were already grumbling over European competition. Such use of the foreign loan money further gave rise to widespread charges of favoritism and corruption, some of which undoubtedly were well founded even though there is no indication that Santander himself was involved in the profiteering. He did show poor judgment in handling of the loan.

A last problem with the 1824 loan was that the Colombian government had borrowed far more than it could repay in the foreseeable future. Here was another flagrant case of overoptimism, since yearly interest and amortization amounted to about one-third of normal government revenue. By mid-1826 Colombia was already in default, as one of the nations involved in Latin America's first, but hardly last, foreign debt crisis. This meant that new foreign loans were not available, which for the present was actually just as well. In fact, even without considering the foreign debt, Colombia was basically insolvent. Customs revenues had risen along with imports, but other revenues did not keep pace; meanwhile, the treasury was saddled with new-fangled burdens that the former viceroys never had to cope with. There were congressmen and diplomats abroad to pay and a swollen military establishment that could not be safely or expediently disbanded overnight. Financial troubles were thus added to the religious disaffection already noted. But there was worse to come, especially in Venezuela.

THE BEGINNING
OF THE END OF UNION

Venezuela had not entirely settled down even after the end of the military struggle there. Sporadic violence and banditry persisted in the back country, complicated by the unrest of unoccupied veterans. Publicists in Caracas, moreover, kept up a steady stream of agitation against the national administration. The fact that the leading malcontents were militant liberals on such questions as the status of the church did not help Vice-President Santander, who was accused of ignoring Venezuelans in his major appointments, putting on the airs of a petty monarch, misappropriating funds, and pretty much anything else that came to mind. Most of the charges were patently unfounded. The complaint about appointments was exaggerated to begin with and overlooked the fact that Venezuelans usually refused to serve in Bogotá even when selected. Also, they made up for a relative lack of high civil office by virtually monopolizing the top military commands—in part because, during the Spanish Reconquest, a disproportionate number of the New Granadans who had held positions of command in the

Patria Boba were physically eliminated; as a result, New Granadan officers in the army of Gran Colombia did not on average equal the Venezuelans in seniority and battlefield experience.

With or without justification, Venezuelans were all too willing to believe that New Granada was somehow absorbing an undue share of the benefits of union. At bottom, they felt lowered in dignity and importance by the mere fact of inclusion in Gran Colombia, especially when the government was centralized to such a degree in Bogotá. Dependence on a king in Madrid had been less galling than dependence on what was until recently just another colonial capital—and Bogotá, perched in the high Andes at the distance of a several weeks' journey over rough mountain trails, seemed as inaccessible as Madrid if not more so. Not all politically conscious Venezuelans wanted the same things, but they were united in opposition to Bogotá. Or, to be precise, most of them were so united; in eastern and western Venezuela local jealousies vis-à-vis Caracas sometimes carried more weight than resentment against Bogotá. Thus, in the national elections of 1826, 41 of Venezuela's 176 electoral votes were actually cast for the reelection of Vice-President Santander. He received not one of these votes from Caracas but did surprisingly well in some of the lesser Venezuelan provinces (as well as obtaining a solid plurality in the nation as a whole).[3]

Shortly after the Gran Colombian Congress confirmed the reelection of both Bolívar and Santander, Venezuela was in revolt and the dissolution of Gran Colombia had in fact started. The immediate occasion was a move in Congress to impeach General José Antonio Páez, who as military commandant of central Venezuela, and with Bolívar still in Peru, was by far the most powerful figure on the Venezuelan scene. He had been accused by the Caracas city council of sending out soldiers to round up peaceable citizens in the streets at gunpoint for militia service, and though the charges were no doubt exaggerated, abuses by the military against civilians were common enough for anyone to believe there must be truth behind them. Congress, moreover, clearly felt that the time had come for a showdown with arbitrary military leaders—to demonstrate once and for all who was boss, the generals or the civil authorities. It was a grievous miscalculation.

When Páez was summoned to Bogotá to stand trial before Congress, he hesitated briefly and then rose in rebellion instead. Among the first who rallied to his side were the same leaders of the Caracas city government who had launched the accusation, since they were even more opposed to the Santander administration than to Páez. Much of the rest of Venezuela likewise joined the movement, even though no one was quite sure what Páez stood for. He and his adherents did demand more regional self-rule, but they were not yet necessarily seeking separation from the union, and all or almost all agreed that nothing drastic should be done until Bolívar returned to act as arbiter.

Santander also hoped at first that Bolívar would somehow peacefully solve the problem and adopted a policy of watchful waiting that was generally supported in New Granada. Ecuador, however, proved to be a different matter. Ecuador was actually the stepchild of the Colombian union: not one Ecuadoran ever held high national office, there was not one Ecuadoran general, and even Ecuadoran colonels were rarities. In economic policy the trend to lower trade barriers, which favored Venezuela as a primarily agricultural and pastoral exporting community, just as clearly hurt Ecuador, the section with the most highly developed domestic textile manufacturing. Ecuadorans were on the whole rather more upset by anticlerical moves than were the Venezuelans, and they had other grievances as well. Accordingly, when Páez made the first move, they too turned upon the regime in Bogotá. There was no outright defiance at first, but a round of improvised assemblies began to call for political and constitutional changes. Federalism (i.e., regional autonomy) was among the changes prominently mentioned. Calls also began to be heard for Bolívar to come home and assume dictatorial powers to cure whatever ailed the republic. Federalism and dictatorship logically did not mix, but in the midst of this growing agitation, an emissary of the Liberator had appeared on the scene and given the impression that a dictatorship was what Bolívar himself wanted. This was enough to rally the military officers of the region, who were mostly non-Ecuadorans, and also the leading members of the Ecuadoran aristocracy, who put more trust in Bolívar than in their fellow citizens.

Bolívar was fully convinced that things had been going badly at home and attributed much of the trouble to the excess haste of Santander and others in pushing liberal reforms. These he considered mostly fine in theory but premature. In fact, of course, reform policies (vis-à-vis the church or otherwise) had little if anything to do with the revolt of Páez, but the discontent they aroused had certainly helped sedition to spread, especially in Ecuador. Bolívar conspicuously failed to condemn Páez, tending to accept his explanation that he was a simple soldier unfairly singled out for persecution by lawyers and intellectuals. Moreover, Bolívar had just finished drafting a constitution for Bolivia that he hoped might offer helpful ideas for Colombia as well. It was a curious document, which featured an awkward three-house legislature and, as its central feature, a president serving for life and naming his successor. The president was to have narrowly defined legal powers, but his life tenure would give him a vast fund of moral influence such as Bolívar felt necessary for stable government in Spanish America. Though often compared with the recent Napoleonic model in Europe, the Bolivian constitution really had more in common with the system devised by Augustus Caesar; it was even decked out with "Tribunes," "Censors," and other trappings of ancient Rome.

Bolívar was inordinately proud of his constitutional handiwork, which he frankly regarded as a panacea for Spanish American ills. And the Venezuelan call for him to act as arbiter, together with the Ecuadoran calls to act as dictator, offered the perfect opportunity to press for adoption of the Bolivian constitution or something like it in Colombia. The Liberator therefore tore himself away at last from Lima, landing in September 1826 at Guayaquil. He did not then openly assume dictatorial powers, but he rewarded those who had offered them. On reaching Bogotá in mid-November, he formally assumed the presidency long enough to issue some emergency decrees and then turned the central administration back over to Santander while he himself moved on to Venezuela and put an end to Páez's rebellion by granting a full pardon to the rebels. However, he did not consider it practical or even desirable to restore constitutional normalcy. Instead, he lingered on in Caracas and issued new decrees and regulations for the Venezuelan provinces without regard to existing national legislation.

Bolívar was no doubt disappointed to observe no groundswell of opinion anywhere in Gran Colombia in favor of his pet invention, the life-presidency constitution. Nevertheless, there was a widespread clamor to hold a national convention for constitutional revision, and to hold it as soon as possible rather than in 1831, the date prescribed by the founding fathers at Cúcuta. Moving up the date was technically illegal, but Bolívar added his weight to the demand. Santander

disagreed, but Congress gave in to the growing demand and summoned a convention to meet early in 1828, at the small city of Ocaña
in northeastern New Granada.

By now Santander and Bolívar had come to the point of open conflict. Santander did not think highly of the Bolivian constitutional
model, which he and most liberal-minded civilians regarded as nothing but monarchy in disguise, a betrayal of the republican principles
they had struggled for against Spain. Santander likewise found Bolívar's recent behavior in Venezuela equivocal to say the least. The vice-
president's close collaborators accordingly launched a bitter campaign
against Bolívar in Congress and the press, for supposedly aiming to
subvert the nation's institutions; and Bolívar was deeply offended by
the criticism, which he blamed on the "perfidious ingratitude" of
Santander.[4] He was even more incensed at Santander's ambivalent
reaction to the mutiny of the Colombian Third Division, which
Bolívar had left behind in Lima. The Third Division overthrew its
appointed commanders in January 1827, returned to Ecuador, and
there proclaimed its intent to punish all those who had just been offering dictatorial power to Bolívar. Santander wishfully chose to consider
the mutinous division more as a potential ally in the cause of consti-
tutionalism than as what it really was—another batch of military
troublemakers—and he scarcely concealed his personal sympathy for
its actions. Under these circumstances Bolívar broke off all personal
correspondence with his vice-president and determined in mid-1827 to
go back to Bogotá, take command once more of the central government, and so put an end to the "subversive" activities of Santander's
political faction.

As Bolívar drew near Bogotá, many of Santander's friends ran for
cover, assuming that the Liberator meant to establish a cruel dictatorship without further delay; but these fears proved ungrounded. At
most a few liberal stalwarts suffered physical abuse in the streets at the
hands of Bolívar's military followers. Moreover, toward the end of the
year Santander himself was able to win a seat in the forthcoming constitutional reform convention and to carry a sizable number of his
adherents to victory with him. The Bolivarian faction apparently had
been overconfident and therefore had failed to exert the pressure that
it might have used on behalf of official candidates. Santander still had
only a minority of the total delegates, but the uncompromising sup-

porters of Bolívar—those committed to revamping the government of Gran Colombia in line with his pet ideas—were a minority also.

It is not easy, at this date, to distinguish the sources of support of the rival political factions. In Colombian historiography it was long customary to look upon the backers of Santander as representing, in embryonic form, the core of the subsequent Liberal Party, and to say the same of Bolívar's following with respect to the Colombian Conservative Party. This once-conventional wisdom contained a grain of truth, as can be seen when the actual circumstances of the birth of the two parties—in the 1840s—are looked at closely (see chapter 4). It is not wholly accurate, however, and neither does it tell us exactly who the backers of the one or the other were in socioeconomic terms. More recently, some revisionist historians have turned the traditional interpretation almost upside down, depicting Bolívar as the more "popular" of the two figures, devoted to the interests of the laboring masses, while Santander is presented as a champion of New Granada's "oligarchy," bent on destroying Bolívar precisely because his vast personal influence stood in the way of assorted vested interests.[5] This view rapidly became an article of faith among members of the Colombian left, which could thereby lay claim to the mantle of the foremost of Latin American national heroes. In reality, though, it has little basis in mere facts.

Santander did enjoy the support of a significant number of business and professional people, most typically from eastern New Granada, his own home region, and from Antioquia. If these were "oligarchs," they were most often second-string oligarchs, seeking to take advantage of any opportunities opened up by the coming of independence to improve their own position. On the other hand, the social and economic elites of Bogotá, Cartagena, and Popayán leaned more to the side of Bolívar. He also had the predominant support of the military, whose top commanders were mostly Venezuelans like himself, and of the church, which was concerned over the association of Santander with incipient anticlericalism. The support of the clergy is in addition the one most obvious linkage between the Bolivarian faction in Gran Colombia and the later Colombian Conservative Party.

It is virtually impossible to say who enjoyed the sympathy of the rural and urban working people. Most of them did not even have the right to vote, and it is unlikely that they were much interested in top-level political rivalries. Yet the backers of Santander apparently had somewhat more success in their efforts to recruit lower-class support. Santander himself took part in these efforts, to the extent of opportunistically adopting the simple dress and unpolished speech of the common people as he mixed with them in political gatherings. He and his collaborators were therefore dismissed as nothing but rabble-rousing demagogues by the Bolivarians, and whether they always had the masses' interests at heart can perhaps be questioned. The reformist programs they were promoting were bound to weaken many of the traditional structures that had (presumably) held the masses down; consequently, these programs may well have struck a responsive chord among any restless members of the popular sectors who were both politically aware and receptive to change. On the other hand, the Santanderistas' commitment to nineteenth-century liberal concepts of individual initiative and economic laissez-faire meant that they did not, by and large, intend for the state to take the masses by the hand and actively help them to rise up. The poor and oppressed were instead to be left to their own devices, to improve their lot as best they could.

It is probably significant, even so, that the few leaders in New Granada who really did have some rapport with the masses were mostly to be found—for whatever reasons—in the camp of Santander, not Bolívar. One of these leaders was Admiral José Padilla, the naval hero who, as a *pardo* himself, easily established a following among the lower-class population of Cartagena, in opposition to its largely pro-Bolívar socioeconomic elite. Another was Colonel José María Obando, related by an illegitimate line to the first families of Popayán. Since his days as an able guerrilla fighter in the war of independence (first on the royalist side, ultimately with the patriots), Obando had built up a strong network of personal followers in the Southwest. His popularity was based in part on personal charisma, in part on the existence of regional rivalries and social resentments that he was able to exploit. He had already clashed with Bolívar during the independence struggle itself, and he was firmly committed now to the cause of Santander. Yet, whatever the exact lineup of forces behind Bolívar or Santander may have been, no one group could claim a working majority at the constitutional convention that finally opened in April of 1828. There were clusters of fence-sitting independents, and there was a band of Venezuelan regionalists who had previously fought Santander but were mainly out to undermine the central administration in any way they could, even though it was now headed by their fellow Venezuelan, Bolívar. Though their real preference may have been separation, they took a position in favor of federalism and on this basis formed a curious alliance with the forces of Santander, who had certainly been no federalist when he was acting chief executive of Gran Colombia. Reduced now to a largely titular role as vice-president and locked in a political struggle with Bolívar, whom he now termed supreme "Perturber" of the republic,[6] he suddenly saw in federalism a means of weakening Bolívar's hold on the nation. This alliance of strange bedfellows succeeded in drawing up a new constitution that was federalist in fact if not in name. At that point the convention broke up: the last-ditch Bolivarians, who had been waging a losing battle to strengthen the national executive power, simply withdrew and made it impossible to muster a quorum for a final vote.

THE DICTATORSHIP OF BOLÍVAR, 1828–1830

When news of the convention's failure reached Bogotá, an impromptu assembly of notables was called to decide what to do next. Legally, the answer was simple; since the move to reform the constitution had failed, the 1821 constitution technically remained in force as originally written. However, the Bolivarian faction was not inclined to give up so easily. The assembly of notables, which it controlled, therefore offered Bolívar dictatorial powers, in June 1828, to "save the republic." Similar meetings rapidly followed throughout the country, and one military commandant frankly stated that he meant to have a proclamation like Bogotá's "even if it costs blood."[7] It did cost blood in a few cases, but not usually.

Probably by this point a majority of those Colombians who gave the matter thought were indeed prepared to let Bolívar "save the republic" by whatever means he saw fit. Regardless of its other drawbacks, dictatorship offered hope of a greater measure of public tranquility than the republic had recently enjoyed, and Bolívar certainly was willing to give it a try. He had become pessimistic about the future, seriously doubting that the union could be held together much longer; at the very least, he felt, it would be necessary to grant some special status to Venezuela and Ecuador. Nevertheless, once he assumed dictatorial powers, he plunged ahead and attempted by military speed and directness to solve the most pressing national problems. One of his chief concerns, in this respect, was to counteract the mistakes that had been made by overzealous reformers since the time of the Congress of Cúcuta.

Dictatorial decrees came forth on every possible subject: restoring monasteries, raising import duties, giving special privileges to the military, even reviving the Indian tribute. This rollback of liberal reforms had started even before the proclamation of dictatorship, with such measures as the restoration of the colonial sales tax, or *alcabala* (enacted by Congress at Bolívar's urging after his return from Lima to Bogotá), and the banning of Bentham from the curriculum (decreed by Bolívar himself early in 1828). But the conservative reaction was not truly sweeping in scope until after Bolívar became dictator. One of the few steps he flatly refused to take in his general appeasement of disgruntled conservatives was to water down the manumission law of 1821, as demanded by a wide array of planters and mine owners. Bolívar may have felt personal distaste for some of the other measures he was taking, but he believed that they were necessary for the consolidation of order, which had clearly become his top priority.

In this reaction against the handiwork of the immediate postindependence years, Bolívar was conforming to a much wider trend in Latin America, where rulers from Mexico to Argentina were scaling down their ambitions for change in the light of greater than expected strains within the body politic and fewer than the originally hoped-for material resources. The dictatorship was, moreover, a generally mild one, even though the dictator's authority inevitably had to be exercised, at the local level, by army officers or civil officials whose main qualification was allegiance to the Liberator rather than executive ability or zeal for the public welfare. Páez was entrusted with broad powers in Venezuela in return for his pledge of undying loyalty, though in practice he acted more as independent potentate than as agent of Bolívar. Opponents of the regime were seldom molested personally for their political beliefs. Yet the liberal press simply went out of existence under official disfavor, and declared partisans of Santander were weeded out of government jobs. Santander found his own position as vice-president abolished at the stroke of a pen, while Bolívar's mistress, Manuela Sáenz, at one point livened up a party by staging a mock execution of Santander—a step hardly calculated to reassure the opposition.

Despite the lack of harsh repression, some people began plotting to destroy the dictatorship; and one group of young hotheads decided to attempt the simplest method of all: assassination of the dictator. They were mostly liberal professional people, but a few army officers joined their ranks, as did Mariano Ospina Rodríguez, who later helped found the Conservative Party and would be elected president of Colombia on the Conservative ticket. On the night of their attempt, September 25, 1828, the would-be assassins stormed the palace and fought their way to the door of Bolívar's bedroom. However, he was alerted in time by the noise, leaped out a window (marked to this day by a plaque commemorating the event), ran through the streets, and hid beneath a bridge until the danger was past.

After the attempt on Bolívar's life, the dictatorship hardened. Fourteen alleged conspirators were executed, including Admiral Padilla, who was totally uninvolved in the plot but conveniently happened to be in prison already on another charge. Numerous friends of Santander who also had no connection with the plot were exiled to distant parts of Colombia or to foreign countries as a precautionary measure. Among the exiles was Santander himself, who at first was sentenced to death, essentially on the ground that as head of the opposition he must have known about the plot and, since he did not report it, must have approved and abetted it. In fact, Santander never denied knowing vaguely that revolutionary plans were afoot, and he did not deny that he felt they might very well be justified. But no evidence was ever produced that linked him directly to the assassination attempt, and it is known that on one previous occasion he had actively discouraged assassination of Bolívar as a means of redress. In the end Bolívar's own cabinet recommended clemency; and with some misgivings Bolívar commuted Santander's penalty to foreign exile.

The flurry of repressive measures still did not end opposition to the dictatorship. One revolt broke out in the Cauca region southwest of Bogotá in October 1828. It was led by José María Obando and another Santanderista military officer, Colonel José Hilario López. Obando and López together proved unable to overthrow or even seriously threaten the government of Bolívar, but they did gain a foothold in the former royalist bastion of Pasto, which welcomed the two liberal colonels not because they were liberals but because they skillfully played up to local grievances and idiosyncrasies. Since Colombia had become engaged in a futile war with Peru, and since Pasto blocked the road to the Peruvian frontier, Bolívar felt compelled to buy off Obando and López with a pardon as full as the one he accorded earlier to Páez.

Relations with Peru had been strained since early in 1827, when a revolt in Lima overthrew the regime established there by Bolívar before his return home. The new Peruvian government had further assisted the mutinous Third Division in its descent on Ecuador, and Bolívar was convinced that Peru was out to stir up trouble, with the precise objective of annexing Guayaquil and possibly even more Ecuadoran territory. There were also concrete disagreements over— among other things—the boundary between the two countries and the debts owed by Peru to Colombia for assistance rendered in the common struggle against Spain. The result was that the two countries drifted into war, by gradual stages, in the latter part of 1828. Peru managed to occupy Guayaquil, but the one major battle of the conflict, fought at Tarqui in the southern Ecuadoran highlands in February 1829, was won by the Colombians under the command of Antonio José de Sucre. Still another revolt in Lima then led to peace negotiations, in which the parties agreed to leave concrete differences over the boundary and debts to be settled later by specially appointed commissioners. Before that could be done, Gran Colombia ceased to exist.

A curious sidelight to the Peruvian war was that it finally gave Gran Colombia something to do with the two fine frigates that had been rotting in Cartagena since their purchase in 1824. After being put in seaworthy condition through untold exertions, they were manned by means of the press gang and similar expedients; and one of them managed to go around the far end of South America with a view to attacking Peru in the Pacific. It arrived only after the war was over, so that the one obvious result of the feat was a further undermining of Colombia's financial solvency. Much the same could be said of the war in general—which was not just expensive but highly unpopular from start to finish.

There was a new domestic revolt to contend with, in Antioquia, in September 1829. It was easily suppressed, but it was soon followed by a far more serious blow, in Venezuela. There most of the underlying factors that made trouble for Santander were still present, and new grievances had been accumulating. The measures Bolívar took to appease the church generally strengthened his position in Ecuador and

New Granada, but they hurt him in Caracas, the most anticlerical of the nation's leading centers. Similarly, by raising tariffs he helped Ecuadoran textile makers but offended Venezuelan agricultural exporters. The final blow was struck when Bolívar's cabinet in Bogotá sounded out the governments of Britain and France about the possibility of establishing a European prince as monarch, on Bolívar's death or retirement. The scheme had been hatched in a mood of despair by men seeking a long-term solution to Colombia's difficulties. Bolívar himself had no direct part in it—he was away directing the Peruvian war when the intrigue began—but his ministers believed they were interpreting his true feelings, and he was caught up along with the rest of his government in the storm of criticism that arose after details of the negotiation seeped out. For monarchy was clearly unpopular. It was especially unpopular in Venezuela, where Páez became the focus of an avowedly separatist movement at the end of 1829. Venezuela did not declare its formal withdrawal from the union until some months later, but in practice Venezuela was already lost.

In view of the situation in Venezuela, the meeting in January 1830 of still another national convention at Bogotá was anticlimactic. It had been summoned originally in the hope that it would replace the dictatorship of Bolívar with a "strong" constitution capable of achieving the same ends by legal means. It did produce a constitution, which strengthened the powers of the national chief executive and lengthened his term of office—from six years to eight, *not* to life. The Constitution of 1830 was signed and formally promulgated, but even while the convention was doing its work, Gran Colombia had continued to disintegrate. A peace commission to Venezuela that was headed by General Sucre, himself a Venezuelan by origin even if now attached through marriage and otherwise more closely to Quito, had no success. Venezuelan troops stationed in the territory of New Granada began deserting to join their fellows; and the local inhabitants were generally delighted to see them go. The separation of Venezuela was not exactly unpopular in New Granada, where union brought to mind not just shared glories but the cost and frequent misbehavior of a military establishment whose top ranks were predominantly Venezuelan; the historian Restrepo, who himself served in Bolívar's cabinet, described this establishment as "the cancer that is devouring the people's substance."[8] Even those who for sentimental or other reasons hoped somehow to revive the union almost invariably opposed the use of force: it was New Granadan opinion as much as anything that permitted Venezuela to break away peaceably.

The repressed followers of Santander also began stirring again, obviously heartened by the news from Venezuela. Bolívar was aware that he could not exclude them indefinitely from political participation, and soon after the constituent convention met, he issued a broad amnesty. But the real comeback of the Santanderistas began when Bolívar himself abandoned the presidency. He had offered countless resignations before to one congress or another, always stressing his desire to return to private life; but no one took these resignations seriously, least of all Bolívar. This time, though, Bolívar reluctantly concluded that his continued presence at the head of government was an obstacle to needed reconciliation. He was also simply worn out from his struggles, indeed physically ill. He therefore took a leave of absence from the presidency in March 1830, and when the time came for the constituent convention to choose a first president to rule under the terms of the new constitution, he insisted that it name someone other than himself. It responded by choosing Joaquín Mosquera, a respected member of the Popayán aristocracy and something of a political independent. Mosquera was absent from Bogotá at the time; so the task of ruling fell momentarily to the newly elected vice-president, General Domingo Caicedo, who, like Mosquera, was a prominent New Granadan aristocrat and political moderate.

Both Caicedo and President Mosquera, who finally assumed office in mid-June, sought to strengthen their government by offering responsible positions to the liberal friends of Santander—a trend highly distasteful to Bolívar. Even more distasteful was the latest news from Venezuela, where a convention called by Páez announced that it would not enter negotiations of any sort with what was left of Gran Colombia as long as Bolívar remained on Colombian soil. The news from Ecuador was more comforting to Bolívar personally but just as fatal for the republic he had founded. As almost had to happen, the Ecuadorans decided to leave the sinking ship and claim their independence too; but instead of proscribing the Liberator, they invited him to come to Quito and rule directly over them. When Bolívar declined the offer, they settled for General Juan José Flores, another Venezuelan-born officer now bound by personal relationships to Ecuador.

Bolívar's refusal to accept Ecuador's invitation to rule was consistent not only with his refusal to stay on as president of Colombia but also with his related decision to go into voluntary exile in Europe. When the invitation reached him, he was heading for the Caribbean coast and intending to take ship from there at the earliest opportunity. Unfortunately, he never did get to Europe. He died at an estate not far from Santa Marta, on December 17, 1830. He had lived just long enough to see the complete disruption of Gran Colombia and to pen one final cry of despair: "He who serves a revolution ploughs the sea."[9]

4

Independent New Granada: A Nation-State, Not Yet a Nation (1830–1849)

The Republic of New Granada lost no time in equipping itself with a formal constitution and a set of liberal political institutions. Up to midcentury—except for the highly confusing War of the Supremes (1839–1842)—it established a record of outward stability superior to that of most of Latin America. Yet the political framework directly touched the lives and affairs of only a small minority of the population. Even among those who were active participants, the nation as an abstract entity usually meant less than the provinces or regions where they lived and in which they conducted their business and professional affairs. But New Granada was not just poorly articulated as a political unit. It was sorely marked by social and economic underdevelopment—or, more precisely, acute poverty and stagnation.

PROLONGATION OF THE COLONIAL ECONOMY

The most obvious of all the obstacles to political and economic integration and development of New Granada was the difficulty and cost of moving from one province to another, and sometimes even within provinces. Actual distances were not great: in a direct line, Bogotá was only about 200 kilometers from Medellín, or 600 from the Caribbean coast at Cartagena. The problem was, instead, that the national territory was broken by a succession of mountains and valleys into isolated compartments, held together by a road network suited for draft animals and human carriers but not for wheeled vehicles, and by a system of river transportation that was also highly primitive for the most part.

Cart roads existed only in the immediate vicinity of Bogotá and various other cities, and they were so poor that they barely deserved the name. There was little incentive to improve or extend them, since the cargo usually would have to be transferred to muleback in any case before it reached its final destination. Freight costs were thus high, running between 20 and 25 centavos (then roughly equivalent to U.S. cents) per ton-kilometer on mule trains covering the 150-kilometer trail from the Magdalena River port of Honda to Bogotá. They were naturally higher for the bulkier items that could not be strapped onto a mule and had to be hauled by teams of human carriers. Travel was also slow, since mules would take five to six days to cover that same stretch between Honda and Bogotá.[1]

New Granada at least had a better river system for internal travel than other Andean nations. The canal linking the Magdalena River with the Caribbean at Cartagena was now almost unusable, and the mouth of the river was still hazardous to navigate; yet the Magdalena itself was navigable as far as Honda, where rapids intervened, and then again above the rapids. The Cauca River, its largest tributary, was also navigable over much of its course. Navigation was not easy, however, since the flow of water was seasonally irregular and much of the land through which the rivers flowed was unhealthy, inhospitable, and very thinly populated. The physical difficulties of navigation, combined with the limited volume of available cargo, delayed the permanent introduction of steam transport on the Magdalena until almost midcentury, even though the first attempts had been made in the 1820s. Meanwhile, the bulk of freight and passenger traffic moved by pole boats of one type or another, the largest being the *champán*, roughly 20 to 25 meters in length. Its roof protected passengers and cargo from the sun and rain and served as a platform for the crew, made up of *bogas*, sturdy and (from the standpoint of foreign visitors and native elite) at most semicivilized dwellers along the river banks, who propelled the boats upstream and helped the current carry them down by thrusting long poles into the river bottom. The trip up to Honda could take as much as a month. The return trip took less time but was almost as uncomfortable, under the combined assault of tropical weather conditions and hordes of mosquitoes, not to mention (according to travelers) the abuse of the *bogas*. River travel, too, was expensive, though significantly less than overland travel.[2]

In most parts of New Granada, even the need for long-distance commerce was not exactly urgent. Precisely because of the country's broken topography, each of the main population clusters of the interior was close to a complete range of ecological zones, in which both tropical and temperate crops were readily available. Basic handicrafts were also widely distributed, even though interregional trade in textiles, for example, had existed since the colonial period. Foreign trade thus seemed to offer the greatest potential for long-distance exchange, but here, too, the obstacles were many. Except for gold, the products of the interior could not easily support the cost of transportation to the coast, and there was no demand for most of them in foreign markets. Some cacao did find its way to export from the interior, though less than before independence; and tobacco, much of it grown along the upper Magdalena River, became an important item in foreign trade in the 1840s. But these were exceptions. As for the Caribbean coastal plain, it could theoretically have developed a significant trade in sugar, cotton, and other such staples, without the handicap of having to pay exorbitant freight rates simply to move the goods to port. However, the coastal region was scantily populated and poorly equipped even with local roads and infrastructure, and it certainly had no obvious advantages over such established competitors as Cuba and the southern United States.

Import trade was affected by many of the same problems. Transport costs made it impossible, except on the coast, to sell any but luxury items, for which the pool of customers was exceedingly restricted. Textile imports were a partial exception, for the progress of the Industrial Revolution in Europe steadily reduced the cost of imported cloth to the extent that all but the coarsest grades could be sold even in interior markets. But the greatest handicap was the lack of sufficient return cargo. As long as New Granada's exports remained anemic, there was no way to pay for a substantial volume of imports, regardless of other considerations. The result was a level of foreign trade that was low even by comparison with other Latin American countries. In the mid-to-late 1830s the value of exports averaged slightly under 3,300,000 pesos a year, which still amounted to a roughly equivalent sum in dollars and was about the same as at the end of the colonial period. Perhaps 75 percent of this total consisted of gold. But, meanwhile, population had been increasing. Thus, in per capita terms, the value of exports—coming to a little less than two pesos a year—had fallen off by one-third from preindependence levels. Moreover, since the country had obtained no new foreign loans such as the 1824 loan and had received no significant foreign capital investment, imports necessarily kept pace with exports, so that they showed a similar pattern of stagnation, at least in monetary terms. Imports increased in volume, thanks principally to the steady decline in the price of imported textiles.[3] Even so, Venezuela with two-thirds the population of New Granada, had a generally higher level of foreign trade, based mainly on the sale of agricultural commodities rather than the monoexport of gold. In per capita terms, the figure was $2.50 (U.S.) in 1831. For Peru, hardly a thriving postindependence economy, it was over $3.00, and for Spanish-held Cuba a remarkable $19.[4]

Initially, for both imports and exports, New Granada's principal trading partner was ostensibly Jamaica in the British West Indies, but only because it served as entrepôt for the commerce of Great Britain and, to a lesser extent, other European countries. The United States had importance as a supplier of foodstuffs, notably flour, to the Caribbean coast, as well as some manufactured goods. Yet neither it nor any other country came close to challenging the leadership of Great Britain, whether as a source of imports or as a purchaser of New Granadan exports and ultimate destination of the country's gold.

A corollary of New Granada's unimpressive performance in the world market was the poverty of public finance, because foreign trade was not only the easiest thing to tax but one of the few potential revenue sources really worth bothering about. Despite the prevalence of contraband, customs duties were the most lucrative single source of government income, accounting for 29 percent of the total collected in the year 1836. The previous failure of the Gran Colombian experiment with direct taxation of property and income had shown that, quite apart from the resistance of wealthier citizens to be taxed, the administrative mechanisms to make such a tax effective just did not exist; and the attempt was not repeated. The internal sales tax, or colonial *alcabala*, reestablished toward the end of Gran Colombia, was reabolished by Congress in 1835, because it was a hindrance to the free exchange of goods and because it was severely regressive, weighing most heavily on those least able to pay. Actually, though, for the *alcabala* to have rivaled the customs duties as a source of income, the rate would have had to be set so high that the majority of the population, living close to subsistence levels, quite literally could not afford to pay it. The only remaining sources of revenue, then, were the government monopolies of tobacco and salt plus assorted nuisance taxes. When all these revenues were added together, they came to about two and a half million pesos, as of the mid-1830s. Even this figure (which, in a population of 1,686,000 according to the 1835 census, would be around one and a half pesos per capita) is highly deceptive, since it includes the gross receipts of the state monopolies and not simply the net profits they turned over to the treasury. There was, needless to say, not a great deal that any government could do with such limited fiscal resources.[5]

Agriculture of one kind or another continued to be the occupation of the great majority of inhabitants, including a good many who worked part time at local handicrafts. In the highlands of the Cordillera Oriental, from Bogotá to Tunja and beyond, the basic crops were potatoes and corn and wheat, just as before independence. Land tenure patterns were mixed, and they have not been carefully studied, although it is reasonably safe to say both that the very best lands (e.g., on the Sabana de Bogotá itself) tended to be held in large estates and that alongside them existed numerous small peasant plots. Indian communities with their respective *resguardos* were still present, despite the legislation calling for their conversion into private holdings. Since the great estates were devoted primarily to livestock raising, the small farmers and Indian communities accounted for most of the production of needed food crops.

The labor force, on the larger properties, was a mix of sharecroppers and renters, day laborers, and others contracted for greater or lesser periods on a variety of terms. Labor arrangements were naturally susceptible to abuses, including—in rare instances—forms of debt peonage. But slavery was almost nonexistent, and any overt coercion of rural labor certainly was not typical of the region. Indeed, it was not necessary. Centuries of subordination to the Spanish state and church as well as to the small upper class of European descent had instilled in the Indian and mestizo peasantry an instinctive deference that caused them to address an employer as "mi amo" ("master") and those of higher social standing as "su merced" ("your mercy," a form of address that has not wholly died out in the hinterland of Tunja even today). This sociocultural pattern was obviously not favorable to the emergence of a vital political democracy—not that one was even attempted. As the French chargé observed in 1840, "What is one to expect from a republic where every man calls 'master' any individual whiter or better dressed than himself?"[6]

In the provinces of Popayán and Pasto to the southwest, a quite similar rural society prevailed, except for the much larger proportion of surviving Indian *resguardos*. North of Popayán, in the Valle del Cauca (the broadest portion of the valley of the Cauca River), a more tropical climate favored the production of sugarcane as another major crop. An appreciable population of black slaves was here in evidence, employed on large estates that also raised cattle and food crops. The Valle del Cauca, with Cali as its leading center, had rich soil and was adequately watered. However, the mountain ranges that cut it off from the Pacific and from central New Granada as yet condemned it to a marginal economic role.

The northwestern province of Antioquia was home to numerous small and middling family farms, entirely dedicated to the production of foodstuffs. Demographically, the high fertility rates in this area reflected a tendency to early and stable marriages, which was associated in turn with the region's higher than usual degree of adherence to formal Catholicism. Because of the rapid population growth—at a rate approaching 2.5 percent a year, as against a national average more like 1.5 percent[7]—and the steady subdivision of peasant farms through inheritance, suitable farmland was becoming scarce in parts of Antioquia. The resulting population pressure triggered a process of internal migration to previously unoccupied lands on adjoining slopes of the Cordillera Central and to a lesser extent the Cordillera Occidental. This process did not lack antecedents even in the late colonial period, but it steadily gathered momentum after independence, in the form of both individual homesteading and settlement by organized groups. Both types of colonists were protected in their claims to land in the public domain and given tax exemptions and other privileges by legislation passed in 1834. They still had to contend, however, with the rival claims of powerful individuals who came forth with ancient, often highly dubious, titles to the same lands, once colonization got under way. Protracted litigation and intermittent bursts of physical violence were the result, just as they would be features of all subsequent movements of frontier settlement in Colombia. Antioqueño colonization, even so, moved steadily forward. Manizales, destined later to become a principal center of the coffee industry, was founded in the second half of the 1840s. Not until the early twentieth century did the process come more or less to a halt, with the exhaustion of readily available and suitable lands, by which time the settlers were approaching the area of Cali in the southwest and that of Ibagué on the other side of the Cordillera Central.

Frontier colonization was only one facet of the dynamism displayed by Antioquia amid the overall stagnation of the early postindependence period. Antioquia also expanded its relative share of gold mining, at the expense of the Pacific lowlands. One reason for this expansion was that mining in Antioquia—much of it by small-scale prospectors—had been less dependent on slave labor and was thus less affected by the decline of slavery as an institution. In addition, Antioquia witnessed a notable increase in the exploitation of vein deposits, as distinct from the alluvial placers that were still the mainstay of the mining industry. Foreign investors and technicians, mainly British, played a key role in this development, but in association with local entrepreneurs. The yields did not necessarily live up to expectations, and as late as midcentury New Granadan gold production still had not returned to late colonial levels.[8] Nevertheless, the earnings from gold, even if not distributed equally, assured Antioquia of what by the very modest standards of the country as a whole may be called a faint glow of prosperity.

Socially, the northeastern provinces of Socorro and Pamplona had much in common with Antioquia, in particular a high proportion of small peasant landowners. Like the Antioqueños, their people were stereotypically hard-working and independent-minded. Unlike Antioquia, the region did not form a true exception to the general picture of poverty and stagnation. The land was often eroded, the roads invariably bad, and though Socorro still had substantial handicraft industries—with straw hats increasingly important alongside the coarse cottons for which it was known in the colonial period—these industries did not generate the same wealth as Antioqueño gold mines. Textile production, in fact, held its own against factory-made imports only by virtue of the high cost of transportation from the ports and the ability of rural and small-town spinners and weavers to subsist on minimal cash income.

The Caribbean coast was also experiencing socioeconomic stagnation. Plantation agriculture was hurt by the decline of slavery, and the port cities of Cartagena and Santa Marta could hardly thrive while the general level of foreign trade remained so low. Panama, to be sure, began to emerge from its secular depression when the California gold rush of the 1840s caused a sharp increase in the number of travelers to the North American Pacific coast and made them even less eager to take the slow all-water route around Cape Horn. The sudden influx of foreign travelers on the Panama route, not to mention all those who came after them to minister to their various needs, provided an economic stimulus but also created social and cultural tensions.[9] At the same time, these developments—which would be massively reinforced by the building of the Panama Railroad in the following decade—further tightened economic and other relations between the isthmus and the outside world, while sharpening the contrasts and lack of understanding that already existed with respect to the rest of New Granada.

Even on the isthmus, away from the transit zone itself, life was not radically different from what it had been for three centuries. In New Granada generally, the rural population, which accounted for at least 90 percent of the total, continued to live under material conditions that to foreign observers often appeared infrahuman. Hunger, however, was less widespread than in the industrializing nations of the North Atlantic world, for such essentials of the national cuisine as potatoes, corn, and plantains were abundant and inexpensive. The diet might not meet all nutritional requirements (in some regions the average consumption of proteins was almost certainly inadequate), but total caloric intake was not a problem. Especially at the lower elevations, with their warmer climate, housing and clothing requirements were also easily met, although the dwellings of mud and wattle or similar materials offered few comforts. It was, in any case, a common complaint of elite and foreign commentators that members of the lower orders were unreliable as workers precisely because they could meet their minimum needs with so little effort. That complaint was made less often about the peasants and townspeople at higher altitudes, where more substantial housing and garments (including a woolen ruana or poncho) were essential for protection against the cold Andean air. Their houses, though, were notorious for giving protection to innumerable insects along with family members, and the furnishings and utensils of wood and clay were rudimentary at best.

Another standard observation of foreign visitors was that the middle sectors (clerks, small tradesmen, and independent artisans) and the well-to-do did not really live much better than members of the working class—at least not in the Andean interior. One difference in lifestyle, however, as far as the country's upper class was concerned, was that its members were overwhelmingly urban, preferring to live in the cities even if they owned extensive rural properties. Bogotá itself had slightly over 40,000 people, according to the census of 1843,[10] although this figure includes those living in nearby rural districts as well as the urban core. It had paved streets, which also functioned as open sewers; the highest offices of state and church; a broad central plaza, which served as meeting place, site of executions, and weekly market; and a theater and a museum. Yet only the homes of the wealthy were of more than one story, and not even all of them boasted such refinements as glass for the windows and rugs (rather than just straw mats) to cover the floors. As of the mid-1830s the city boasted only three enclosed carriages, one of them belonging to the president himself. In many respects the local elite lived in conditions more modest than those of the French or English middle class; and in Bogotá society the equivalent of ten thousand dollars (of that era) per year was a princely income. Nor would one of the capital's leading merchants consider it demeaning to wait on retail customers himself in his shop.

There might have been more aristocratic pretensions in Popayán, and Cartagena had better facilities for hosting foreign travelers than did Bogotá. But none of the country's other "cities" had much over 10,000 people, and most were little more than overgrown villages. Overall, in the lack of any appreciable commercial stimulus, the urban population since independence was growing more slowly than the population as a whole and was thus declining as a percentage of the total. The minuscule urban centers, nevertheless, kept a strong consciousness of their separate identities; and welding them and their respective hinterlands into a true nation would not be at all an easy task.

THE FIRST STEPS OF NATION BUILDING

Given the scarcity of resources and lack of articulation of one region with another, the task of maintaining political order and a minimum level of public services in independent New Granada was inevitably daunting. It was not even clear at first how large a territory was to be governed. For a time the authorities at Bogotá continued to use the name of Colombia and ruled, in theory, according to the Constitution of 1830, which was supposed to have solved the problems that were tearing apart the Gran Colombian union. In practice, by the time it was promulgated, Venezuela was already lost; Ecuador would soon follow; and the government of President Joaquín Mosquera and Vice-President Domingo Caicedo, which assumed power when Bolívar finally stepped aside, was a strictly New Granadan affair. But the dissolution of the larger union was still not quite etched in stone.

In August 1830 a brief military uprising deposed Mosquera in favor of General Rafael Urdaneta. The revolt was in part the result of friction and distrust between the civil authorities and the Bogotá garrison, largely composed of Venezuelans. However, it received active support from a faction of civilians, including members of the lower clergy, who looked askance at the Mosquera-Caicedo administration because of its working alliance with the liberal followers of the exiled Santander, some of whom were perceived as dangerous enemies of religion. The fact that Urdaneta himself was of Venezuelan origin, furthermore, made it all the more necessary for him to express his aims in broadly Colombian terms. Indeed, another assembly of notables in Bogotá now called on Bolívar to reassume command and save Colombia, merely entrusting Urdaneta with dictatorial power until such time as Bolívar did return. The ailing Liberator did not accept the invitation, but neither did he repudiate Urdaneta; and until his death at the end of 1830, his supporters could and did join others with various kinds of personal interest at stake to press for a restoration of union.

Among those calling for Bolívar to take power again was a secessionist government established on the Isthmus of Panama, which claimed that it would not return to the fold under any other circumstances. Secession was also proclaimed by the province of Casanare in the eastern *llanos*, but this province voted to join the virulently anti-Bolivarian government then taking shape in Venezuela. There was good reason for Casanare to consider such a move, because it had far more in common with the adjoining *llanos* of Venezuela than with Andean New Granada. Possible separation was likewise seriously discussed in the far South, where Pasto was mindful of its historic connections with Ecuador and was subject to ardent wooing by the new government of Ecuador headed by Juan José Flores. There were even those as far north as Popayán who toyed with the idea of joining Ecuador—particularly after their native son Mosquera was so rudely dislodged from the presidency in Bogotá.

The Venezuelan government itself ended the threat of secession by Casanare when it gallantly refused to take advantage of New Granada's distress and rejected the offer. The other threats were ended, too, but only after the intrusive Urdaneta government was disposed of. It did not last long: arbitrary and ineffective, it soon antagonized just about everybody and in the process discredited the Bolivarian party that was its main political support. Generals José María Obando and José Hilario López, who had risen against the Liberator in 1828, took the lead in organizing a military countermovement, and early in 1831 Urdaneta bowed to the inevitable and departed without a struggle. The victors then called elections for a constituent convention that met later in the year, formally restored the name of New Granada, and elected Santander, still in absentia, to the presidency.

The convention drafted New Granada's first constitution, which went into effect in 1832. It was generally unremarkable, quite similar to the original Gran Colombian constitution. Though clearly liberal and republican, it was not strictly democratic; the right to vote was again limited by economic requirements (a minimum amount of property or yearly income) that excluded the great majority. At least the effective date of the literacy requirement, which in 1821 had been set at 1840, was changed to 1850, in recognition of the scant progress made to date in teaching citizens to read. The new constitution also tempered the extreme centralism of the earlier document. The elected assemblies at the provincial level, which in Gran Colombia served only to draw up petitions and act as electoral colleges, now received the right to enact ordinances on schools and roads and similar matters of local concern. The measures could be annulled by the national authorities, and provincial governors were once again appointed agents of the national executive, but a small step had been taken in the direction of greater local autonomy.

In addition to framing a constitution, the New Granadan convention restored some of the Gran Colombian reform measures that Bolívar had repealed or suspended in his final dictatorship. The suppression of the smaller monasteries was reaffirmed, with the significant exception of those in the province of Pasto, whose ultraconservative inhabitants would have regarded such suppression as one more reason to join Ecuador instead of New Granada. In the text of the constitution itself, the convention incorporated one reform that liberals of the previous decade had not felt quite up to: the elimination of the military *fuero*, the special privilege exempting members of the armed forces from the jurisdiction of the ordinary courts. Again significantly, this reform was not extended to the similar *fuero* enjoyed by the clergy, whose political strength was just too great. The image of the military, by contrast, had already suffered during the years of Gran Colombia from too close an association with Venezuelan influence. With the defeat of the Urdaneta dictatorship, most of the remaining Venezuelan military men on New Granada's soil did at last go home, and the Bolivarian group of New Granadan officers had been discredited by their own association with that regime. Those officers like López and Obando, finally, who had overthrown Urdaneta in close alliance with liberal civilians, were not inclined to take a stand in favor of military privileges such as the *fuero*, now seen as a relic of colonialism incompatible with notions of republican equality before the law.

In addition, the provisional government carried out a general purge of officers who had served Urdaneta, thus further diminishing the size of the military institution and setting the stage for serious unrest over the next few years among the purge victims. Meanwhile, though, the remaining threats of secession were laid to rest. In Panama military officers sympathetic to the New Granadan liberals came to power by their own efforts and restored obedience to Bogotá. In the far Southwest, sentiment for joining Ecuador had been reinforced by the presence of Ecuadoran troops, but a mixture of political diplomacy and military maneuvers culminated in the peaceful reincorporation of Pasto in September 1832.

In the same month, Santander was installed as president at Bogotá. He served initially on a provisional basis but in 1833 began a regular four-year term, to which he was popularly elected by overwhelming majority under the Constitution of 1832. (See Appendix B.) The lack of serious challenge to his candidacy revealed the extent to which all those in New Granada who had backed the causes of Bolívar and Urdaneta were disheartened by defeat. They also feared, not without reason, that the candidacy of one of themselves would have faced various kinds of official obstruction. Nonetheless, a majority of active citizens undoubtedly believed that Santander was the person with the best chance of getting their fragile new republic off to a good start. His followers had demonstrated their military and organizational capability, and he himself was remembered as a skilled administrator. The fact that he had been absent from the country during the recent strife was another obvious asset.

As president of New Granada, Santander displayed most of the traits that he had already been known for as vice-president of Gran Colombia. He showed the same interest in administrative detail, the same high regard for the letter (if not always equally high regard for the spirit) of the law and the constitution, the same tendency to let off steam against his critics through anonymous articles in the progovernment press. He also showed a streak of vindictiveness that precluded any serious effort to conciliate the Bolivarians. They were not physically harmed, unless charged with conspiracy, but they were treated with evident coolness and remained generally excluded from civil and military positions and political influence.

Governmental exclusivism and denial of patronage added to the unhappiness of military malcontents, whose subversive thoughts from time to time spilled over into active plotting. For the most part, Santander was able to ward off trouble by shuffling of military commands and shows of force, but he did face one major crisis in the conspiracy of the Catalan-born general José Sardá, a victim of the recent military purges. With a network of conspirators that extended into several parts of the country, Sardá had prepared an uprising for the middle of 1833. The conspirators were discovered before it was time to start, whereupon the affair resolved itself into a long effort to catch and punish the offenders. Sardá was caught, tried, and condemned to death, but he escaped and with the help of influential sympathizers remained hidden in the capital itself. Finally, he was tracked down by loyal officers who were admitted to his hideaway on the pretense of wanting to join his movement—and instead shot him in cold blood. Since Sardá could have been taken alive and then dispatched by firing squad in accord with the existing sentence, Santander's enemies raised a hue and cry over the unnecessary cruelty used, but Santander refused to reprimand his subordinates. By that time seventeen others had already been shot in the main square of Bogotá, as Santander (who rejected the court's recommendation of clemency in seven of the cases) watched through an office window. Another of the conspirators, Bolívar's former mistress, Manuela Sáenz, was merely sent into exile.[11]

Uncompromising firmness against conspirators was only part of Santander's formula for stability. Careful management of government finances and avoidance of radical innovations were no less important. As vice-president of Gran Colombia, he had the task of administering the brief bonanza of the 1824 English loan. As president of New Granada he fell heir to an impoverished treasury, the inevitable corollary of an impoverished nation. Total revenues, as already noted, amounted to something like a peso and a half per inhabitant. But somehow President Santander was able to manage with the money on hand: he might run a slight deficit one year but would have a surplus the next, and during his administration as a whole, the government was basically solvent. Since the largest item in the budget was always the armed forces, he had to keep a tight rein on military outlays, which fluctuated within the fairly narrow range of 46 to 51 percent of total expenditures.[12] The size of the military establishment was kept under strict control, with the authorized force level hovering around 3,300 men,[13] or one for every 500 inhabitants, more or less.

Since the Constitution of 1832 provided for the strength of the armed forces to be set by act of Congress, the latter shared credit for holding down military expenses. In this respect it was moved by fiscal considerations; by the continuing distrust of Santanderistas toward former Bolivarian officers; and by a certain disdain of the New Granadan upper classes for military men, who were seen as lacking the qualities of birth and education necessary for social and political prominence.[14] There were, of course, a few officers who combined military rank with inherited social prestige; but the most prominent of these officers, such as General Tomás Cipriano de Mosquera, tended to be committed Bolivarians and therefore were denied an active role as long as Santander and his people were in power.

Even if there was no serious disagreement between Congress and Santander on holding down the cost of the military, they did not always see eye to eye on other financial issues. When Congress definitively abolished the *alcabala*, it had to do so over the president's veto. He did not object to the aim of removing this burdensome impost, but he believed that the national treasury was not yet in a position to do without it. For similar reasons, and this time with success, he fought off a strong move in Congress to abolish the state tobacco monopoly. In both instances Santander showed a retreat from theoretical liberal objectives, and the same can be said of his stand on tariff policy. During the years of Gran Colombia he had stood for a basically revenue tariff, showing scant sympathy for protectionist demands. But by the 1830s he had grown more skeptical of the notion that economic progress would come about automatically through the operation of natural market forces. He therefore showed a greater willingness to meet at least part way the demands for higher tariffs put forth by local producers. He further approved the granting of special privileges to a number of mostly Bogotano entrepreneurs, who sought with limited success to establish factories for the making of glass, chinaware, paper, and cotton textiles. He made his personal statement in favor of domestic industry by ostentatiously wearing locally made cloth—although he furnished his house in Bogotá with chairs imported from the United States and rugs from Belgium. At least he could afford the cost of bringing these things up the Magdalena and over the mountainsides to the New Granadan capital. Most others could not, and so for many articles the cost of transportation continued to provide a more important measure of protection than the customs tariff.

Neither the tariff increases (actually rather moderate) nor the granting of special privileges had much effect in promoting domestic industry. And Santander's insistence on opposing tax cuts even while keeping a tight lid on the government payroll (civil as well as military) and other official expenses can only have had some deflationary impact, accentuating the country's long-term stagnation. The president was also a bit naive in the pride he took in balancing the budget when his government was operating at such a minimal level of per capita expenditures. However, Santander was willing to loosen the official purse strings somewhat for public investment in education, to which he was deeply committed, just as in the days of Gran Colombia. While Santander was in office as president, the number of children attending public primary schools rose from 17,000 to more than 20,000. Even including private school enrollment, the rate of schooling came to less than 15 percent of the primary-age population, still a not very impressive record.[15] But it was better than Venezuela, with a more dynamic economy, was then doing;[16] and if the rate of progress had been maintained (which of course did not happen), New Granada would have become one of the leaders in Latin America.

Santander did more than just encourage basic primary education. He saw to it that new secondary schools were opened, and he showed a special interest in them, often attending their public exercises in person. He also reinstated the controversial Plan of Studies of Gran Colombia, so that Jeremy Bentham and other writers of questionable orthodoxy went back into the curriculum. The same howls of protest were heard, but again Santander stood his ground. He was willing to hold off on most other reforms because—like Bolívar, in the last analysis—he had essentially come to feel that people were not ready for them. When a newspaper published by a close political ally set off a firestorm of controversy by calling for the suppression of all monasteries and the introduction of religious toleration, Santander put pressure on him to discontinue the newspaper, even though it was one of those to which the president himself had contributed articles. But the least Santander could do was make sure that the next generation *would* be ready for freedom of worship and for the whole gamut of liberal reform measures.

Although much of the clergy was unhappy over Bentham and the Plan of Studies, the government of New Granada became the first in Spanish America to achieve formal diplomatic relations with the papacy. This was a tribute to the country's relative stability in a continent wracked with disorder and also a result of skillful and persistent diplomacy going back to the days of Gran Colombia. The first papal nuncio presented his credentials just weeks before the end of Santander's term. In his welcoming remarks, Santander included a pointed reminder that relations with the church must be in conformity with the laws of the nation—meaning specifically the *patronato*, which gave the state a voice in such things as ecclesiastical appointments. There would be friction with the nuncio over the *patronato* and other matters, but the task of dealing with him was left to Santander's successor, and church-state relations were in general harmonious—especially as compared to the midcentury period that was to come.

The election of that successor, in 1837, stands out in the wider context of nineteenth-century Latin America for the mere fact that the candidate favored by the outgoing administration went down to defeat and that his defeat was peacefully accepted. Santander's own choice had been José María Obando, whose credentials as an able fighter for liberal causes were abundantly evident. In addition, Obando had a loyal personal following throughout the southwestern provinces. There was, though, a large cloud over his candidacy, in the form of existing suspicion that he had somehow engineered the assassination in 1830 of General Antonio José de Sucre, Bolívar's most trusted helper and one of the acclaimed heroes of the independence struggle. This allegation (still a topic of heated controversy in the Gran Colombian republics)[17] was never proved but was widely believed and was sure to hurt Obando even among people who espoused the same objectives. To Santander it was simply outweighed by his proven record of service—and by his military rank, since Santander believed that New Granada was not yet ready for a civilian chief executive.

That was just one of the reasons why Santander opposed the candidacy of the eventual winner, Dr. José Ignacio de Márquez. Márquez had worked with Santander in the government of Gran Colombia and most recently had served as vice-president of New Granada, but the two had been steadily drifting apart. One version attributed the coolness between them to an incident in which Santander took offense at Márquez for advances to his longtime mistress, Nicolasa Ibáñez.[18] Mainly, however, the two men had different political temperaments. Márquez had moderated his position on questions of policy even more than Santander had, and he did not share Santander's extreme antipathy toward anyone who had been associated with the dictatorship of Bolívar. He thus received the overwhelming support of the Bolivarian faction, which still did not try to mount a serious candidacy on its own. In effect, Márquez became the opposition candidate, even if his differences with Santander were basically differences of degree and emphasis. But the combined votes of moderates like Márquez himself and of all those who flatly opposed the administration for any reason gave Márquez the largest number of electoral votes. Because no candidate had an outright majority, Congress made the final choice, confirming his victory. Santander then delivered his office to someone he had opposed—taking pains to point out, in a proclamation, that he had thus respected the will of the people and the law of the land.

Márquez, at least initially, represented a change more of style than of substance. He sought to promote an atmosphere of national conciliation and good feeling by taking several of his predecessor's sworn enemies, the Bolivarians, into his government, but he also had quite a few holdovers from the Santander administration. In a sense, he was a holdover himself. He made no move to throw Bentham or other heterodox authors out of the curriculum; he just did not show the same degree of enthusiasm for them. During the first half of his term, he continued to balance the budget and to preside over a gradual reduction in size of the armed forces. He saw to the formal ratification of the agreement that Santander had negotiated with Venezuela and Ecuador for division of the Gran Colombian foreign debt, which was still in default; and he took one further step in the direction of consolidating the new regime: he established diplomatic relations with the former mother country. New Granada was not the first Spanish American republic to exchange ministers with Spain, but it was one of the first.

THE WAR OF THE SUPREMES AND
EMERGENCE OF PARTY ALIGNMENTS

In the middle of his term of office, Márquez had to face a revolutionary outbreak that was confusing and in some ways highly contradictory but had major importance for the country's political system. The
unlikely spark that ignited it was the decision of Congress to suppress
the smaller monasteries in Pasto, which had been exempted from the
suppression decreed by New Granada's constitutional convention.
The bishop of Popayán accepted the measure, but the people of Pasto
chose to view it as a blow against religion itself; and unquestionably
there was a strong element of regional protest against outside meddling in Pasto affairs. So the Pastusos rose in rebellion and were suppressed. Then, early in 1840, José María Obando came to their support and revived the movement. He was a figure closely aligned with
liberal political factions and certainly no proclerical reactionary, but
the Pasto area was one of his own bases of support, and clearly in this
case the leader saw fit to adopt the cause of those he led. The move, in
addition, was related to political developments at the national level,
where the Márquez administration was coming under increasing
attack from hard-core Santanderistas (who called themselves "Progresistas," or "Progressives") for its working alliance with the former
president's foes. Santander himself, who after leaving the presidency
had won election to the Chamber of Representatives (exactly as had
John Quincy Adams in the United States), was now a leader of congressional opposition to Márquez. He did not favor the use of revolutionary violence, but not all his fellow partisans were as devoted to
legal methods; and Santander's death in May 1840 put an end to his
personal restraining influence.

Obando declared himself "Supreme Director of the War in Pasto,
General in Chief of the Restoring Army, and Protector of the Religion
of Christ Crucified."[19] He also called for national reorganization
along federalist lines, thus illustrating once again the particular appeal
of federalism for factions out of power. Santander and his friends had
dabbled in federalism in 1828, in opposition to Bolívar's dictatorship,
but were quite content with the centralist Constitution of 1832 as long
as they were in control of the government at Bogotá. Now, following a
change of administration, more and more of the Progresistas redis-

covered the theoretical advantages of federalism, to say nothing of its tactical advantages as a banner with which to rally regionalist sentiment (as in Pasto). Indeed, various military officers in the rest of New Granada began rising up against the Márquez government, just as Obando had done, and to one extent or another proclaiming federalism as an objective. The movement came to be known as the *Guerra de los Supremos* (War of the Supremes), from the tendency of local chieftains to dub themselves *jefe supremo* of this or that. There was never any effective nationwide revolutionary leadership; rather, the struggle took place in numerous poorly coordinated regional theaters, with the revolutionists' greatest strength along the Caribbean coast.

Early in 1842 government forces finally prevailed. By then the antagonism between President Márquez and his critics had been fanned to a point of no return, even among those Progresistas who stayed aloof from the armed struggle. To suppress the rebellion, moreover, Márquez was compelled to reinforce his ties with the Bolivarian faction— in particular its chief military figures, such as Tomás C. Mosquera and Pedro Alcántara Herrán. In the midst of the military struggle, Herrán won election to the presidency as Márquez's successor, thus in effect completing the rapprochement between moderate liberals of the Márquez variety and the former backers of Bolívar. Since they were the ones who held office (both civil and military), they received the name of Ministeriales, or Ministerial Party; but they constituted in embryo the party that in 1849 would formally adopt the title of Conservative. Their opponents, on the other hand, now began to abandon the Progresista label in order to claim for themselves that of Liberal. To all intents and purposes, Colombia's two traditional parties had been born.

Formal party organizations evolved only in the second half of the nineteenth century, and only in the present century have they existed on a permanent, year-round basis. Likewise, even before the War of the Supremes, political activists had formed ad hoc organizations and correspondence networks for particular elections. The civil war of 1839–1842 was thus a watershed merely because it was then that alignments first truly solidified in the patterns that were to last. Those patterns, however, are not easy to define. As mentioned, the feud between Bolívar and Santander and their respective supporters in the decade of Gran Colombia to some extent anticipated the later division between the parties. The surviving adherents of Bolívar, with insignificant exceptions, ended up in the Ministerial/Conservative camp; but the situation is more complex as far as Santander's original followers are concerned. Márquez himself, after all, had been one of them. More striking still is the case of Mariano Ospina Rodríguez, one of the would-be assassins of the Liberator in September 1828, who ended up as an ally of Márquez and then became secretary of the interior in the administration of his one-time enemy Herrán.

Neither were there clear social and economic differences between the two groups. Some authors once claimed that the Liberal-Conservative dichotomy originated in a conflict between *tienda* (store) and hacienda, with Liberals representing commercial and professional interests and Conservatives the large landholders. But, as Frank Safford pointed out in what is still the most insightful analysis of the initial party alignments, the occupational differences in party membership were slight, among other reasons because the same individual was often landowner, merchant, and lawyer rolled into one; or, if he wasn't, he had family members involved in all these lines of activity. Moreover, as we shall see, there were few questions on which the specific interests of merchants and landowners would lead them to take opposite sides politically. Safford thus suggests a scheme in which the Conservatives were strongest in those areas (especially Bogotá, Popayán, and Cartagena) that—at the end of the colonial era and the beginning of the republican era—were politically and economically most important, and Liberals were strongest in more peripheral areas (such as the eastern provinces that became modern Santander and Norte de Santander departments). Safford's analysis points to a difference in social prestige and family connections between the leaders of the two sides, and also a regional difference. It does not suggest any clear difference in economic occupation, although it does not exclude the possibility that Conservative merchants or landowners may have been more powerful than Liberal counterparts. Safford's scheme also replicates the slightly more aristocratic flavor of the Bolivarian faction as against that of Santander in the days of Gran Colombia, even if he readily admits that it is a rough model and that it cannot account, say, for the predominantly Conservative leaning of Antioquia, which in some ways (socially and geographically if not economically) should be classed with the peripheral regions.[20]

In any case, both parties were multiclass and nationwide. Despite all differences in *relative* strength from one region to another, and despite the havoc they sometimes caused with their squabbles, the parties were among the few unifying forces in a nation sorely fragmented geographically and culturally. Not only were the parties present in all areas of the country, but they were destined to promote collaboration across class lines, or—to put it a bit differently—to serve as one more mechanism of social control whereby upper-class leaders manipulated lower-class followers. At the time that the parties were taking shape, most men and all women were legally excluded from active participation in electoral politics, although urban artisans generally met the requirements for voting, and so did many (not necessarily all) rural smallholders. But political leaders had reason to seek out even the support of nonvoters, for staging rallies, intimidating rivals, and fighting civil wars. In the formative stages of the party system, it is hard to say how widespread a sense of identification with one or the other really was, even among the enfranchised. Nevertheless, to the extent that it did take hold, such loyalty to a multiclass partisan cause could not help but take some of the edge off of conflict between classes.

Among nonelite groups urban artisans were the most inclined to approach party politics with a specific agenda of their own to press. Tariff protection of their crafts was a major part of that agenda, although they were also interested in such issues as training in industrial arts and more responsible local government.[21] Since the artisans had both votes and skills to offer, politicians often bid for their support by promising to act on their demands (and just as often failed to carry through once elected). It has been generally assumed, on the other hand, that in rural areas peasants ended up in a particular political camp by the irresistible influence of some powerful local boss, or *cacique*, who at times was also the dominant landowner of the district. The notion that the partisan affiliations of the rural masses were imposed upon them rather than consciously chosen may well be overdrawn. Yet it is significant that from the beginning rural communities tended to lean overwhelmingly to either one side or the other, whereas in the cities a greater number of competing forces were always represented.

In both rural and urban jurisdictions, priests often acted as political organizers, almost invariably on the Ministerial/Conservative side. The clergy's attitude was rooted, of course, in the same fear of anticlerical reform measures and education à la Bentham that caused much of the clergy to rally to the side of Bolívar against Santander in the 1820s. Despite the caution shown on most religious issues by Santander as president of New Granada, he and his close adherents—in effect, the fledgling Liberal Party—still aroused feelings among the priesthood that ranged from mild distrust to fanatic hostility. It was far easier, moreover, for the clergy than for lay opinion-makers to stir the populace into action—as evidenced, say, by the minor tumult that erupted in Medellín in 1836 in an attempt to free one trouble-making priest from jail.

The tactical advantage of having the clergy on one's side was not lost on the forerunners and founders of the Conservative Party; and for the rest of the nineteenth century, the one consistent difference between the parties had to do precisely with the status of the church. Liberals still aimed to reduce its power and influence as obstacles to the nation's material and intellectual progress—even if, like Santander, they came to realize that the general population was not yet ready for major changes. The emerging Conservative Party had no desire to bring back the Inquisition, however much Liberal propagandists might sometimes imply just that; but its adherents did propose to go even more slowly in ecclesiastical innovation, and not just for the short-range benefit of having the clergy as an ally. Given the uncertain state of public order and what seemed to many a dangerous loss of social discipline, they saw in the Roman Catholic religion an essential support for both political and social stability. Catholicism was, after all, one of the few things that served, at least nominally, to link all members of the society and polity with one another. For that very reason, its institutions were not to be tampered with lightly.

The harrowing experience that the country had just gone through in the War of the Supremes was added reason, from the Ministerial standpoint, to strengthen the position of the church and the values associated with it. This attitude was neatly symbolized when the victors in that civil war issued a new constitution in 1843 and changed the wording of the preamble from "In the name of God, Author and Supreme Legislator of the Universe"—the formula of the 1832 constitution—to "In the name of God the Father, Son, and Holy Spirit."[22] The earlier wording, with its nuances of eighteenth-century deism, thus gave way to an expression of traditional orthodoxy. In addition, the Herrán administration saw fit to roll back one notorious act of Spanish enlightened despotism by inviting the Jesuits, expelled

from the empire in 1767, to return to New Granada. It was anticipated that they would serve as skilled, thoroughly orthodox teachers
and in addition resume the frontier mission work that had been in
sharp decline since the end of the colonial period. In practice they
would have little opportunity except to establish secondary schools for
upper-class youth before being expelled again in 1850.

In a related move, Herrán's secretary of interior, Mariano Ospina
Rodríguez, now launched a general educational counterreform that
removed Bentham and others once more from the approved curriculum. The intention, however, was not simply to replace heterodox
writings with a heavier dose of old-time religion but to downplay
theoretical in favor of more useful studies, such as the natural sciences.
These, it was hoped, would divert the young from idle and possibly
dangerous philosophical speculation and steer them in the direction of
practical undertakings for the good of the country. In addition, especially when Herrán left the presidency and became minister to the
United States, New Granadan students were encouraged to seek advanced technical training abroad. The program was logically conceived,
but the underdeveloped state of the economy, which provided few
career opportunities for professional engineers, meant that the results
fell far short of expectations.[23]

Politically, the principal changes embodied in the 1843 constitution
served to strengthen the national executive as against both Congress
and the provincial assemblies. These changes, too, were made in reaction to the recent outburst of civil disorder, and Liberal critics
assailed the increase in presidential powers as creating a veritable
autocracy. Their accusations, though, were vastly exaggerated: the
changes made were only of degree. Herrán himself had been a loyal
servant of Bolívar's dictatorship, but neither he nor any other of the
ex-Bolivarians proposed to reestablish it now. Much less did they
seek to exhume such panaceas as life presidency and constitutional
monarchy, which members of their faction had tried to foist on the
Gran Colombian union in its later days. They had by now come to
accept a quite conventional sort of liberal republicanism, in which
they scarcely differed from such ex-Santanderistas as Márquez and
Ospina. In the last analysis, the political thinking of the Ministerial/
Conservative camp really owed more to Santander than to Bolívar. It
rejected the federalist tendencies that were now making headway

among the Liberals; but Santander himself, as ruler, had been no federalist.

A rough consensus thus existed on the fundamentals of political structure even if not on such technical details as what leader or faction should be in charge of running the system. The dominant sectors of New Granadan society wanted a government of limited powers and limited popular participation, operating in a predictable legal framework, and that is exactly what the 1832 and 1843 constitutions provided. Those dominant sectors did not, as a rule, have reason to fear the popular sectors; hence, they did not feel any need for a strong military or other hand to keep the lower orders in line; rather, they themselves might become threatened by an authoritarian regime, because of its inherent uncontrollability. Not all of them, of course, were prepared to play the game of politics by the legal rules; if they had been, neither a Sardá conspiracy nor a War of the Supremes would have arisen. The use of force or fraud to try to gain more than one's fair share of power was to be an all too common phenomenon throughout the nineteenth century. However, the monopolization of power by any one group would never be tolerated for long, and usually a decent level of civility between political adversaries prevailed. After all, the actors on both sides generally knew each other and had many interests in common.

The existence of shared interests makes it particularly hard to discern clear-cut differences between the parties in their approach to economic matters. Government fiscal policy inevitably gave rise to disagreements and debate, but seldom to heated controversy until just before midcentury, when a battle flared over tariff protectionism. However, that battle, and most other arguments over economic issues, did not pit Liberals against Ministerials/Conservatives but, rather, cut across party lines. Neither were there obvious conflicts of economic interest among the merchants, landowners, and professional groups who provided most of the leadership of both parties. One partial exception concerned the question of slavery. The Liberals and no doubt most of their adversaries as well were content to maintain the principle of gradual abolition by the free-birth method, as adopted in 1821 by the Congress of Cúcuta. But the largest slaveholders of the Cauca Valley, Popayán, and the Southwest, overwhelmingly aligned with the Ministerials, were still unhappy with the law. Among other concerns, they felt that the requirement for the technically free children of slaves to serve their mothers' masters until age eighteen was insufficient compensation. Their experience in the War of the Supremes, when Obando and other Liberal chieftains appealed with considerable success to slaves and free blacks to back the revolutionary forces, only increased their resentment. They saw a need for stricter control of the region's blacks; and their lobbying bore fruit in a law of 1842 that authorized the extension of the free-born offspring's compulsory service to age twenty-five. Even more striking was a law passed the following year that permitted the exportation of slaves to neighboring countries. A number of powerful slave owners thereby rid themselves of apparent troublemakers, selling them to Peru. Such revival of the slave trade, even on a limited scale, brought diplomatic remonstrances from the British yet may even have hastened the eventual extinction of slavery, by focusing attention on its abuses.[24]

If the handling of slavery revealed the less enlightened side of the Ministerial (or proto-Conservative) regime, its more progressive tendencies came to the fore during the administration of Tomás Cipriano de Mosquera, who in 1845 succeeded Herrán in the presidency. Mosquera belonged to one of the aristocratic clans of Popayán that had earnestly striven to water down the manumission law, and he had been a fanatical admirer of Bolívar. He was noted for his vanity, claiming among other things to be a direct descendant of Charlemagne, and he had a streak of vengeful cruelty, which he demonstrated in the execution of prisoners during the War of the Supremes. After the war Herrán (who happened to be his Bogotano son-in-law) sent him on a diplomatic mission to southern South America, which he gladly accepted—in part because it gave him the opportunity to continue harassing his recent foe and regional rival General Obando, whose extradition from Peruvian exile he vainly sought. At the same time, however, Mosquera was not burdened with doctrinaire preconceptions and was refreshingly unpredictable, not to mention sincerely devoted to the advancement of his country. To the despair of many of the fellow Ministerials who had made him president, it was really he who initiated the period of frantic innovation of all sorts that would mark New Granada at midcentury.

Mosquera's general activism found expression in a wide range of public works and technical improvements. He increased spending on

roads and began construction of the present Colombian capitol building, whose impressive neoclassic design and yellow-gray stonework
grace the south side of Bogotá's central Plaza Bolívar (although the
building was not completed until well into the present century). His
government introduced the metric system of weights and measures
and modern techniques of official bookkeeping, and it removed depreciated coinage from circulation. With the help of government subsidies, steam navigation on the Magdalena River finally took hold on a
permanent basis. In addition, the Mosquera administration negotiated
the Mallarino-Bidlack Treaty of 1846, whereby the United States
guaranteed to protect both New Granadan sovereignty and the safety
of transit over the Isthmus of Panama. It is the same treaty that Theodore Roosevelt later invoked to prevent Colombia from putting down
the Panama Revolution of 1903, but at the time it appeared a necessary step toward the construction of either a railroad or a canal across
Panama, to the immediate benefit of the Panamanians and the country
as a whole. The treaty promptly led to the signing of a contract, with
U.S. entrepreneurs, for the construction of the nation's first railroad
across the isthmus, although the final approval of the contract and
laying of the rails would come only after Mosquera left office.

The treaty and the Panama railroad contract were clear indications
of a commitment to seek closer economic relations with the North
Atlantic world. Indeed, the most striking single aspect of Mosquera's
policy was his embrace of a liberal economic program designed to free
private initiative from obsolete restrictions and thereby lay the basis
for an aggressively outward-oriented development strategy. The policy
shift was in considerable part the work of Florentino González, a man
of liberal Santanderista credentials but of an independence of mind to
match Mosquera's. González accepted appointment as secretary of
finance in the Mosquera cabinet and in that capacity set in motion a
series of steps that would lead to the final abolition of the tobacco
monopoly by 1850. By then, a gradual privatization of the tobacco
business had already resulted in substantial increases of production
and export sales. More controversial was the tariff reform of 1847,
which brought a general 25 percent reduction in duties, much to the
consternation of domestic artisans. There was consternation also over
these and other moves in some sectors of the president's own party,
but not so much for doctrinal reasons—as already noted, economic

policy was not an area of clear-cut differences between the parties—as because they were a product of collaboration with the Liberal adversary.

In the last analysis, Mosquera's whole approach to governing raised doubts about his political orthodoxy and caused a deep split in Ministerial/Conservative ranks. That split persisted into the battle for the presidential succession of 1849, with the government party divided between two major and some minor candidates. The result was victory for the Liberal candidate, José Hilario López, who took up where Mosquera had left off and carried the process of innovation to even greater extremes.

5

The Nineteenth-Century Liberal
Revolution (1849–1885)

At no point in its history has Colombia (as the Republic of New Granada rechristened itself in 1863) more clearly exemplified developments on the larger Latin American scene than in the third quarter of the nineteenth century. Despite a moderate burst of outward-oriented economic growth, it remained one of the countries most poorly articulated with the North Atlantic market; but the state of its domestic economy was not far from the norm. In the political realm, it exemplified the struggle between "liberals" and "conservatives," church and anticlericals, that currently raged in country after country. As elsewhere, liberals generally had the upper hand during the years in question and imposed their program on the country.

THE MIDCENTURY CONJUNCTURE

Both in New Granada and in such countries as Mexico (with the "Reforma" of Benito Juárez and others) and Argentina (which underwent reorganization on liberal lines following the overthrow of the long dictatorship of Juan Manuel de Rosas), the ascendancy of liberalism at or soon after midcentury was in part an inevitable reaction against the real or perceived shortcomings of previous national leaders. Neither the rule of the Ministerial faction in New Granada nor the earlier presidential administration of a Santander who had grown more cautious through hard experience remotely matched the sheer irresponsibility of Mexico's Santa Anna or the brutality of Rosas in Buenos Aires; but both Santander and the Ministerials had been wary of radical departures from established practice, and they represented the continued domination of the same people who had fought the war of independence and then crafted the first republican institutions. From the standpoint of those who had come of age since freedom from Spain was won, it was time for others to have a chance. The midcentury generation did not seek to bar the heroes of independence from public life; but they wanted a major share of responsibility, and they wanted to impose their own agenda.

The generational change entailed the emergence of the first national leaders who had been trained wholly in republican, not colonial, schools and who had been more directly exposed to a wider range of ideas from abroad than was possible before independence, when intellectual or other contact with the outside world, though never lacking, was always more complicated. Bolívar in his final dictatorship and the Ministerials in the 1840s sought to purify the school system of the teachings of Bentham and other heterodox authors, but such works were still readily available for anyone who wanted to read them. Moreover, all but a tiny obscurantist minority among the country's ruling groups felt the influence of the liberal currents—political and social and economic—that were increasingly ascendant in the Western world. An illustrative detail is the fact that when news of the French Revolution of 1848 finally reached far-off Bogotá, none other than Mariano Ospina Rodríguez, the same who as minister had proscribed Jeremy Bentham, called for church bells to be rung in celebration.[1]

Just as the strength of liberalism in Western Europe and the United States is conventionally associated with the consolidation of the capitalist order and rise of the bourgeoisie, economic developments created a more favorable atmosphere for the reception of liberal ideas in New Granada. The economy was still a mix of capitalist and pre-capitalist elements (their relative proportions depending on one's definition of capitalism), and nothing quite like the French or British bourgeoisie was in evidence. Nevertheless, the economy began to emerge from its long-term stagnation. Like the appearance of a new generation, this economic change resulted in part from the mere passage of time. Most of whatever damage the economy suffered in the independence struggle had been overcome, while population had been slowly expanding—all of which increased the potential for economic growth. There had likewise been some improvements made in basic infrastructure, of which the most notable instance was the definitive introduction of steam navigation on the Magdalena. More important still, however, were the continuing growth of the North Atlantic market and the movement of the terms of trade in a direction favorable to producers of primary commodities, as world prices of manufactured goods steadily declined. In the judgment of New Granada's political and business leaders, this was an opportunity not to be wasted.

Midcentury thus saw a rebirth of the economic optimism that had prevailed, without much real foundation, in the immediate aftermath of independence and then collapsed, reinforcing the generally more conservative mood of the next two decades. The sudden prospect that greater resources and opportunities would be available made people more willing to think again of trying new approaches. In particular, the moment seemed right for a systematic pursuit of outward-oriented economic growth. The timid protectionist moves of the 1830s had failed to produce the desired results, and in addition it now seemed that the laissez-faire dogmas of economic liberalism were becoming universally accepted. They permeated the latest books and reviews that crossed the Atlantic, whether the writers were English economists or French romantic novelists or even early utopian socialists such as Proudhon and Saint-Simon, who were read in Bogotá as exalted defenders of individual liberties rather than precursors of collectivism. Fittingly, too, the century's leading economic power, Great Britain, after years of preaching free trade to others while practicing protectionism itself, had finally decided to set a proper example by repealing the last of the so-called corn laws in 1846 and dismantling its own protective tariffs.

It is easy enough to see how those who favored the promotion of import-export trade would have further assumed that the best way to do so was to give private entrepreneurs a free hand, so that they might rapidly respond to market incentives. In turn, the partial reorientation of the economy in that direction during roughly the third quarter of the century strengthened the hand of groups that had a vested interest in liberal policies, while the apparent success of the strategy in question heightened the appeal of still other aspects of the liberal program. Hence, it was not only free-trade liberalism that now came to the fore in New Granada. The ideas of free trade and economic laissez-faire, on one hand, and the aims of liberalism in political and cultural and even religious affairs, on the other, were fundamentally congruent and mutually reinforcing, because in each instance the guiding impulse was to diminish the control of government or other corporate bodies over individual decisions and actions. Liberal tenets thus came to be accepted quite widely in New Granadan society. Some drew the line at liberal anticlericalism, and artisans fought a losing rearguard action against opening to the world economy, but liberalism was not the monopoly of any one economic sector, nor of the Liberal Party either, although that party would assume the reins of power in 1849 and keep them for most of the years from then until the mid-1880s.

THE FIRST ROUND
OF LIBERAL REFORMISM

As noted in the previous chapter, the Tomás Mosquera administration had already given the country a foretaste of reform activism; but the floodgates did not open until after the 1849 election, which brought the Liberal Party candidate, José Hilario López, to the presidency. López did not win a majority of the electoral votes cast, but he outdistanced both of the men who split the backing of the divided Ministerial faction, which was now beginning to call itself the Conservative Party. The Liberals, moreover, though they had failed to carry Bogotá, had important blocs of supporters in the capital city among young intellectuals and organized artisans. The artisans were furious at the party in power for having sharply cut tariff rates on imported manufactures, and they threw their support to López in the hope that he would somehow remedy their grievances. That hope eventually proved mistaken, but meanwhile artisans as well as students and liberal professionals massively packed the Church of Santo Domingo when Congress met there to make the final choice of president from among the most-voted contestants. On the last ballot the Conservative Mariano Ospina threw his vote to López, claiming that if he were not elected, the congressmen would not get out of the building alive.[2] There was little real basis for the allegation, but it reflects the emotionally charged atmosphere in which López finally won.

The continuity from the Mosquera administration to that of López was mainly evident in economic policy, where the new government and Congress did raise customs duties somewhat but not enough to satisfy artisan demands for effective tariff protectionism and in addition completed the process of releasing tobacco growers and traders from the shackles of the state monopoly. The production and sale of tobacco had been partly privatized already; in May 1850 they became completely free of state control. By happy coincidence all this occurred at a time when the world demand for tobacco was steadily increasing

and was undergoing certain changes, with snuff and pipe tobacco losing ground (the first of them absolutely, the second relatively) vis-à-vis
the consumption of cigars. The result was a sudden opportunity for
new producers to come forth with just what the market was now demanding; and Colombia, whose share in the world tobacco trade until
the late 1840s was minimal, became for the first time a significant
exporter. By the middle of the next decade, tobacco represented more
than a quarter of total exports, close behind gold; and in the 1860s it
actually took first place, accounting for over one-third of the total.

The tobacco success story was a turning point in the very structure
of Colombian foreign commerce, because it marked the first time that
an agricultural export had even approached precious metals in importance. The tobacco boom was not destined to last, because Colombian
growers failed to keep up with competitors (e.g., in the Dutch East
Indies) in quality control, processing, and packaging of tobacco. In the
1870s, therefore, gold briefly regained first place among Colombian
exports, with tobacco falling to fourth place behind coffee and
quinine. Even then, however, the combined value of agricultural exports far exceeded that of gold, so that the change in the nature of
foreign trade was lasting even if the tobacco bonanza was short-lived.[3]

At least while it did last, the surge in tobacco exports was inevitably
seen as the clearest vindication of liberal economic policies. Later
scholars have been less sure, not only because it proved to rest on
weak foundations but also because the organization of production in
tobacco-growing zones was inimical to small producers. The former
state monopoly, from its founding in the colonial period, had typically
contracted directly with small farmers to buy their tobacco crops. In
the 1850s, however, a different pattern took hold in the Ambalema
region, located along the Magdalena River above Honda, which was
now the most important single growing area. Here the best tobacco
land was concentrated in large estates, where the direct producers
worked under a combined rental and piecework system that was clearly less advantageous. To a lesser extent, similar patterns could be
found in other growing areas. When one further takes account of the
large share of the proceeds from tobacco sales that accrued to commercial middlemen—who also reaped profits from the increased
mechandise importing made possible by the foreign exchange tobacco
generated—it can be plausibly argued that the tobacco boom served to
heighten socioeconomic inequality. Not all the benefits, however,

accrued to merchants and large landowners. Quite apart from the persistence of independent small-scale tobacco farmers in some places,
even those who lacked such status may often have been marginally
better off than they were before. After all, we also read of peasants
from the uplands of the Cordillera Oriental streaming to the Magdalena Valley for work in the tobacco plantations, lured by the prospect of a cash income (when they had been living mostly outside the
money economy) and by the possibility of acquiring such unaccus-
tomed small luxuries as meat in their diet.[4]

Another reform whose socioeconomic impact has drawn mixed reviews concerned the status of the Indian common lands, or *resguardos*, whose distribution among individual Indian families had been
ordered repeatedly since the beginning of the independence movement
without ever being fully implemented. Moreover, to protect the
Indians themselves against the wiles of creoles or mestizos intent on
usurping their land, legislation on this matter specified that Indians
who received a parcel of former *resguardo* land as private property
could not legally alienate it for a number of years. In 1850, however,
with a view to freeing the Indians once and for all from this vestige of
traditional collectivism, Congress authorized the provincial assemblies
to regulate the distribution of *resguardo* land and explicitly revoked
the limitations on alienation of the parcels distributed. This law led to
the final liquidation of the *resguardos* in the eastern highlands and
most other parts of the country, though not in the Southwest, where
most of the Indian communities were located and where the provincial
authorities hesitated to abolish the *resguardos* at one stroke. Where
the division did take place, the result, according to one interpretation,
was the rapid despoiling of the Indians and their reduction to the status of a landless proletariat. But that picture is no doubt a little overdrawn, since not all of the former community land passed into the
possession of non-Indians, and in some cases members of the Indian
communities themselves were among those pressing to make the distribution effective. Such Indians may have ended up taking advantage
of their fellow Indians, but at least they were not just grasping
creoles.[5]

While the Liberals' policy on Indian lands may not really have benefited those whom it was supposed to help, their treatment of another
depressed racial minority—the black slaves—is harder to quarrel
with. By a law of May 1851, all remaining slaves in New Granada

received their freedom on January 1 of the following year. There were only about 20,000,[6] because the free-birth principle had been at work since 1821; and their material conditions of life did not necessarily change, since little was done to help the newly freed blacks improve their situation, whereas the former owners did receive compensation in the form of government debt warrants (of admittedly questionable value). On the other hand, there is no evidence that any former slaves asked to return to slave status; and enough of them moved horizontally if not vertically, abandoning the mining camps or plantations where they had been working, to create problems for a good many former owners in the western provinces. Fear of just that outcome was a minor contributing factor behind an abortive Conservative revolt of 1851. At the same time, the mere fact that final emancipation had come under Liberal auspices helped the Liberal Party to capture and maintain the overwhelming allegiance of the nation's blacks.

Underlying the measures on slaves and Indians was a concerted effort to eliminate restrictions on the free movement and allocation of property and labor. Numerous other reforms were adopted to the same effect during López's four-year presidential term. One law facilitated the redemption of ecclesiastical *censos* (i.e., church liens or mortgages), which were perceived as an unproductive drain on the income of landowners and a hindrance to the sale and transfer of landed property. Another ended the academic degree requirements for the exercise of the professions, other than pharmacy: adopted in the name of "freedom of education," the measure left each citizen free to obtain in any way at all either as much or as little training as that citizen desired, and it implicitly enshrined *caveat emptor* as the guiding principle for potential consumers of professional services. Still another law extended this principle to the marketplace of ideas, by abolishing libel laws and any other limitations on the printed word. Tax burdens, too, fell right and left, with such levies as the tithes and the *quinto* (or percentage levy on precious metals mined) turned over by the national government to the provinces and then more often than not abolished. Other such examples could easily be added.

In all of the foregoing, New Granada seemed intent on ushering in without more delay the absolute reign of human liberty. In the process the state itself seemed intent on withering away, in line with the dictum "that government is best which governs least." There were indeed some Liberals who believed just that, but the state did not disappear.

The loss of assorted revenues (and in this regard abolition of the tobacco monopoly was far more important than the loss of any of the others) was offset in considerable part, as Liberal ideologues predicted, by an increase in customs receipts; and a number of functions besides distribution of the *resguardos* were simply transferred from the national government to provincial authorities. Yet the Liberals stopped short of outright federalism. In a new constitution that took effect in 1853, they made provincial governors locally elective, and this measure (in conjunction with increased provincial revenues and responsibilities) represented a move in the federalist direction; but the elected governors were still to be in some sense agents of the national executive, and the apportioning of specific functions was still weighted on the side of the central authorities.

The Constitution of 1853 incorporated most of the reforms already adopted and added some more. One of these reforms was universal male suffrage, concerning which many Liberals still had strong mental reservations. Over and above any doubts about the intrinsic ability of the common man to make an intelligent choice of candidates, there was the danger that the newly enfranchised—peasants especially— would be easily manipulated by priests, landowners, or other bosses, rather than voting independently. However, the combination of democratic theory and the always revered example of France (which had adopted universal male suffrage following the Revolution of 1848) overcame the Liberals' own doubts. What is more, they went on to institute direct elections in place of the electoral college system previously in effect and to provide for a remarkable list of public officials, including not just provincial governors but the national attorney-general and Supreme Court judges, to be chosen by popular vote.

The provincial legislature of Vélez, in eastern New Granada, went still further and voted to extend the suffrage to women, with the added specification that women be duly represented along with men in local electoral boards, to make sure that their participation was really effective. This remarkable measure—adopted in 1853, sixteen years before Wyoming became the first state of the United States to do the same— was sponsored by a Liberal governor of radically doctrinaire leanings, who also appears to have had a politically forceful wife. Yet obviously it was not the work of a single couple. There had even been a kind of precedent in 1852, in the presidential voting to choose López's successor, when one elector for Bogotá cast his ballot for Sixta Pontón de

Santander, the former president's widow. Unfortunately, adherents of the formal political emancipation of women were still a small minority. Not only did Doña Sixta not become the world's first woman president but the national Supreme Court proceeded to annul the provincial ordinance of Vélez on the ground that no province could give anyone more rights than those granted by the national constitution—and apparently nullification came even before any Veleña was able to make use of the suffrage.[7]

On another front the new constitution established full religious toleration in New Granada by including freedom of worship among the rights guaranteed to all citizens. Together with the abolition of religious censorship, as provided in the previous law granting absolute freedom of the press, this provision opened the way for the first avowed Protestant missionary activity to be undertaken, before the decade was out, by Presbyterians from the United States. Toleration no longer was a reform that aroused violent opposition—and the first missionaries were careful not to stir up trouble by indiscreetly aggressive proselytizing. The Roman Catholic church was considerably less happy with the formal separation of church and state—implicitly, by the omission of any reference to church-state relations in the 1853 constitution; and explicitly, by a law passed later the same year. It was glad to be free from government interference with clerical appointments but objected to the withdrawal of any kind of special privilege or protection. The church and more devout Catholic laity were offended, too, by such unwelcome corollaries of toleration and disestablishment as the introduction of civil marriage and (worse yet) of legalized divorce.

Actually, relations between the Liberal administration and the church had got off to a bad start with López's decree, in May 1850, for the reexpulsion of the Jesuits from New Granada. This glaring violation of the principles of religious and other liberty that the Liberals presumed to stand for was rationalized, somewhat vaguely, on the ground that the Jesuits were an international organization dedicated to undermining those very principles. In the words of José María Samper, at the time a young Liberal zealot, they were a "scourge of all humanity, a vampire raised in the dark dungeons of crime, ready to suck the blood of the unwary man."[8] The Jesuits' acknowledged skill as educators, and the fact that they maintained generally higher standards of conduct than the clergy as a whole, made them all the more dangerous in the eyes of their enemies. President López himself, who was no Liberal ideologue and knew that the Jesuits had a wide circle of friends and admirers, hesitated to order the expulsion but in the end yielded to pressure from his associates. Since there was no valid legal basis for the measure, the government simply declared that the pragmatic sanction of 1767, whereby the Jesuits were first expelled from the Spanish empire, had not been repealed in New Granada and therefore was still in force.

The church was subject to other, generally minor, annoyances, although as yet there was no generalized assault on its property holdings or on the religious orders (other than Jesuits). Even so, the protests of the hierarchy against Liberal policy as it affected the church led to the exiling of the archbishop of Bogotá, Manuel José Mosquera, and two other prelates. On their part, anticlerical Liberals were generally careful to portray themselves as faithful believers in church doctrine who merely wished to prune away certain civil powers and prerogatives of the clergy, which had no basis anyway in apostolic Christianity. They thus claimed an ideological kinship with Jesus Christ, who had waged battle against the ecclesiastical establishment of his own day. That claim did not, however, convince many members of the clergy in mid-nineteenth-century New Granada. And neither did it convince the leaders of the Conservative Party, who rallied to the support of the church hierarchy and found in the religious question both a useful tool for attacking their Liberal opponents and the one issue on which they could trace a clear dividing line between the Liberals and themselves.

Some Conservatives, as already noted, took offense at the abolition of slavery, but that was hardly a position shared by Conservatives in general. Likewise, both parties insisted that they favored popular sovereignty and individual freedoms, political and economic. As a result, Conservative criticism of the party in power centered on its violation of its own principles, in a matter such as the Jesuits, and on the extremism that it allegedly displayed even in pursuit of otherwise admirable goals. Conservative publicists such as José Eusebio Caro— who was coauthor with Mariano Ospina Rodríguez of the manifesto that served as the Conservative Party's declaration of principles and was personally the spearhead of a reaction against the vogue of Bentham in New Granada—likewise deplored Liberals' fondness for heterodox European writers as against traditional Catholic thinking. But the conclusions that Conservatives drew from their own sources of inspiration were not radically different, save as regards the treatment of the church.

The disaffection of church and Conservatives was not a major threat to the Liberal regime, particularly after the premature Conservative rebellion of 1851, which was easily repressed and left even those Conservatives who had nothing to do with it in an awkward position. Assuming that they would not be allowed to take power even if they won, the Conservatives made no effort to contest the presidential election of 1853—despite the fact that the Liberals this time were rallying behind the candidacy of José María Obando, a figure cordially detested and feared by many Conservatives. Obando became the first candidate since Santander to receive an outright majority of electoral votes. However, the overwhelming victory of Obando merely papered over divisions among the Liberals that were ultimately more serious than the opposition of the other party.

One Liberal faction was made up of radical reformers, who were anxious to move ahead rapidly with the dismantling of all governmental and corporate restrictions on individual liberty. Their approach was doctrinaire, often contemptuous of both inherited custom and practical difficulties, and they came to be known as "Gólgotas" because of an impassioned oratorical appeal that one of them made to "the martyr of Golgotha" (i.e., Jesus Christ). The name was at first bestowed satirically, but this was in fact the dominant group among Liberal publicists and top officials, including members of Congress. It was also typically made up of educated civilians, of higher social origin than most of their intraparty rivals.

A quite different group of Liberal activists was composed of the organized artisans whom future Gólgotas had helped to recruit in support of the presidential campaign of José Hilario López, only to come later to a parting of the ways. The artisans, of course, were interested above all in rolling back the tariff reform adopted under Mosquera. Yet for a time they accepted the collaboration of young upper-class Liberals in the Sociedad Democrática of Bogotá, an organization that was an outgrowth of an earlier artisan society and devoted itself to supporting the Liberal administration and agitating for a wide range of reform causes, many of which (e.g., expulsion of the Jesuits) had nothing to do with the artisans' immediate interests. Failure to achieve the tariff protection they most wanted, along with a growing sense that they were being used for purposes not their own, led to disenchantment with the Gólgota wing of the party and finally to an open break, though not before the Sociedad Democrática of Bogotá had helped create a network of similar societies elsewhere in the country. These societies almost always became deeply involved in politics; in the Valle del Cauca, in particular, their adherents joined in fomenting a wave of violent attacks on local Conservatives. In Cali and surrounding towns the artisan sector was less important than in Bogotá, but there was widespread popular resentment against the great landowners who had been encroaching on the *ejidos,* or commons, which had always been available to the inhabitants generally for pasturing animals or other uses. One objective of the Liberal regime was precisely to eliminate collective in favor of individual forms of property ownership, but it so happened that the Valle's hacendados were overwhelmingly Conservative, while the local "democrats" were less concerned than the Gólgotas about fine points of economic theory. The result was an explosive combination of partisan and class conflict that contributed to the outbreak of the 1851 Conservative rebellion as well as to growing tensions within the Liberal camp, some of whose members were made uneasy by the inciting of social resentments.

The last major faction of Liberals was that known as the Draconianos, who took a stand of pragmatic moderation on most policy matters and feared that the Gólgotas, in their frantic quest for greater individual liberties, were sacrificing social order. One issue on which they differed (and which actually earned them the "Draconian" label) was the death penalty, which the Gólgotas sought to abolish and the Draconianos defended; they defended it successfully, thus far, except for its abolition in the case of "political" offenses. They also looked askance at the further reduction in size of the standing army, set at a mere 1,500 men by Congress in 1853.[9] Indeed, military men were more in evidence among the leaders of the Draconianos than among the Gólgotas—particularly officers of other than aristocratic background. The Draconiano faction as a whole can safely be described as having a more popular social flavor. Certainly it had greater popular appeal, not least because its preeminent figure was José María Obando, with his firm hold on the admiration of the Liberal rank and file. It is hardly surprising, then, that as internal divisions among the Liberals deepened, the artisans and, in general, the network of Sociedades Democráticas aligned themselves ever more decisively on the side of the Draconianos.

Things came to a head only after the election of Obando as president. The Gólgotas had opposed his election, although they had no serious expectation of preventing it. Despite his own lack of enthusiasm for various aspects of the 1853 constitution, Obando dutifully put it into effect; but distrust steadily mounted between his administration and a Congress that was controlled by his adversaries, both Gólgotas and Conservatives. In April 1854, finally, congressional moves to reduce the size and influence of the armed forces (including the national guard, in which artisans had come to play an important role) provoked a coup by General José María Melo, commander of the Bogotá garrison. Melo's hope was that Obando would accept the coup as an expression of the popular will, suspend the 1853 constitution and Congress, and stay on as president. When Obando failed to go along, Melo assumed the presidency himself and established a short-lived military dictatorship.

Melo's coup was repudiated not only by Obando but by ex-president López (who had maintained generally good relations with all Liberal factions) and several of the top civilian Draconianos. His only sure supporters were the troops he commanded personally—and the Bogotá artisans, who demonstrated in the streets against scheming Gólgotas and grasping merchants and enthusiastically served in the national guard or otherwise in defense of the new government. But this support was not enough. Except in areas fairly close to Bogotá, most military and civilian officials refused to accept Melo as president and gave recognition instead to the "Constitutionalist" rump government that was soon set up by his Gólgota and Conservative opponents. These men gradually retook the territory under Melo's control and in early December fought their way into Bogotá. General Melo (having first killed his two favorite horses with his own hand in the reception rooms of the presidential palace, lest they fall into the hands of his tormentors) surrendered and was ultimately sent into exile. Another 300 to 400 Melo supporters, many of them from the artisans' movement, ended up in internal exile, sentenced from the cool Sabana de Bogotá to the hot, humid, and rather less healthy Isthmus of Panama. A significant number of them would never come back.[10]

CONSERVATIVE HIATUS

The alliance of Gólgotas and Conservatives against Draconianos and artisans was perfectly logical, since the leaders of the first two groups had similar social origins and—except in matters involving the church—no unbridgeable differences on national policy. The alliance worked well until Melo was overcome, and even for a time longer. The Conservatives, however, had clearly contributed more to the joint victory. They had greater nationwide support to draw on, and even if they may have had less impressive reserves of some kinds of talent—thinkers and publicists, perhaps—they had more experienced generals and colonels to put into battle. Of three military ex-presidents who took leading roles in repressing the Melistas, Mosquera and Herrán were Conservatives, only López a Liberal; and he was not strictly speaking a Gólgota. It is thus hardly surprising that the former opposition party steadily expanded its own role in government until, in effect, the roles were reversed.

Obando never returned to the presidency, since the victors in the brief civil war accused him of having been at worst an accomplice of the very people who deposed him and at best guilty of irresponsible negligence in not preventing the coup. He was impeached by the restored Congress and in that way removed from office formally and for good. Obando's vice-president, José de Obaldía, who had escaped from the Melistas after first taking refuge in the U.S. legation, headed the provisional Constitutionalist government; but his term (which did not coincide with that of the president) expired early in 1855. In the election held to choose his successor, the winner was a Conservative, Manuel María Mallarino, who thus in effect completed Obando's term. Mallarino continued to head a coalition regime, with two Liberals in his cabinet, but in April 1857 he was succeeded by another Conservative, Mariano Ospina Rodríguez, winner of the first strictly presidential election held since the introduction of universal male suffrage; and Ospina Rodríguez then organized an all-Conservative administration.

The president also brought back the Jesuits; and already under Mallarino Congress had repealed the legalization of divorce, which was one of the more scandalous measures of the previous Liberal regime. Otherwise, little was done, or even attempted, in the way of rolling back the reform breakthroughs of 1849–1853. Moreover, in one area the Conservatives actually took the Liberal program a step further, for it was under their auspices that the nation adopted in 1858 its first overtly federalist constitution, under the name of Granadine Confederation.

The formal adoption of federalism was, to be sure, a less radical step in practice than it might appear. The Constitution of 1853, though centralist in principle, had been gradually transformed by successive acts of Congress creating quasi-autonomous regional governments bound to the rest of New Granada through a federative link. The first of these was created in early 1855 for Panama, where autonomist sentiment was rife and many of the problems that government had to deal with were in fact unique. Subsequently, other parts of the country demanded similar privileges for themselves, and one after another additional federated "states" took their place alongside Panama. Hence, there was much to be said for issuing a frankly federalist frame of government, incorporating a single set of rules for these separate regional entities. The step was made easier because many leading Conservatives had now come to the support of federalism as a form of political organization—whether moved by theoretical arguments, by the successful example of federalism in the United States, or by the tactical consideration that under a federal system they could always expect to enjoy solid control of at least those regions where they were strongest. If Liberal ideologues should regain power in Bogotá, Conservatives could still do in Antioquia, say, whatever they wanted.

Even more fundamentally, creeping federalization attested to the continued weakness of the various ties holding the regions of New Granada together. The national state, never strong, had been further restricted by many of the midcentury reforms. The church, with its unifying role, also had been weakened, though not yet grievously. Economic growth had accelerated, but with the emphasis on seeking ties to foreign markets, interregional trade was relatively more neglected than ever. If there was an added impetus for national unity from any source at all, it came from the further development of the country's party system—even though the parties were at the same time a source of national discord. The 1850s were in any case a crucial period for the consolidation of the Colombian parties, thanks both to the broadening of political participation and to the highly competitive nature of politics over most of the decade.

The introduction of universal male suffrage, above all, contributed to the broadening of participation. Now it became advantageous for political leaders to recruit rank-and-file adherents, and the more the better, not merely to exert pressure on opponents and in extreme cases to bear arms for the party but to vote in elections. And vote they did, in large numbers. In the one instance where a rough estimate of actual voter participation exists, the presidential election of 1856, 40 percent of adult males supposedly went to the polls. The total is remarkably, even suspiciously, high for any country in the mid-nineteenth century, and especially for a country where the great majority of people were still rural and often living at substantial distances (over very bad roads) from the polling places. In a few districts the apparent participation rate approached 100 percent, which strongly suggests either that outright fraud was perpetrated or that people were herded en masse to vote as directed by local bosses. However, the overall pattern that emerges is not implausible: very high turnouts were typical in areas of entrenched sociopolitical clientelism (such as the province of Tunja, with 71 percent), whereas the rates were lower in areas with a more independent peasantry (such as Antioquia, with 32 percent) or where linkages to the national political system were weak (as they were in Panama, with a mere 21 percent).[11] Even if one makes the necessary allowances for electoral malpractice, it is clear that political leaders had been largely successful in getting their countrymen involved in the electoral process.

Those leaders had an obvious incentive to seek popular involvement on their behalf, in that the political game was closely contested and no one party or faction was assured of mastery. In the immediate aftermath of the Conservatives' defeat in the 1851 civil war, things had been different; for the moment, Liberals faced no effective opposition. Yet, even then, the rival factions of Gólgotas and Draconianos felt the need to keep recruiting followers for their internecine struggle. And already by the end of 1853, when the first nationwide election by universal male suffrage was held, to choose an attorney-general and three Supreme Court judges, Conservative-backed candidates (one of them Mosquera's former Liberal minister of finance, Florentino González) made a clean sweep. Throughout the rest of the decade, except for the Melo interlude, the country was engaged in spirited and almost constant interparty competition, since voting for different national and provincial or state offices was usually conducted at different times—even president and vice-president being elected in different years for staggered terms. There was always a campaign in progress somewhere, and most often in several parts of the country simultaneously. This in turn entailed constant cajoling and recruitment, as well as indoctrination of those recruited with the slogans and symbols of a partisan cause.

Despite the Gólgota-Draconiano split and other factional divisions repeatedly suffered by both parties, the emerging party system was essentially bipolar, Conservative versus Liberal. This pattern did undergo one serious challenge, when ex-president Mosquera, increasingly estranged from his fellow Conservatives, launched his own candidacy in the 1857 presidential election. For this purpose he improvised a separate National Party, and in the end he polled about 15 percent of the total vote. That was not enough for him to win, and it is unlikely that the votes he drained away from the other candidates influenced the final outcome. Like the other third parties that appeared from time to time, Mosquera's new grouping did not last. Rather, it proved a stepping-stone in his own evolution from Conservative to member of the Liberals, whom he subsequently led to victory in the civil war that toppled the election victor, Ospina Rodríguez.

This tendency toward a two-party system was not, of course, unique for nineteenth-century Latin America; the same pattern appeared in Mexico, Central America, Ecuador, and a number of other countries. But modern Colombia is unique in that the Liberal-Conservative dichotomy survived from the mid-nineteenth century to almost the end of the twentieth. No consensus has emerged on the reasons for its remarkable staying power, though the religious question, with its simple polarization of anticlerical versus proclerical, no doubt reinforced any other factors favoring a bipartisan system and thus had at least something to do with the end result. Religious controversy was not unique with Colombia either, but it was longer lasting and harder fought, if only because the two sides were more or less evenly matched: a nucleus of doctrinaire anticlerical reformers, who held the reins of the Liberal Party, facing a strong institutional church with powerful lay allies. In Venezuela, by contrast, the church was too weak to put up a good fight against the anticlericals, while in Ecuador Liberalism was too weak, at least until the very end of the nineteenth century. In Mexico, where the balance of strength more closely approximated that in New Granada/Colombia, the church and the Conservatives were hopelessly discredited by their alliance with the intrusive empire of Maximilian in the 1860s.

Whatever the precise reasons for enduring bipartisanship may be, the commanding position of the two major parties was already evident in New Granada at midcentury. In the 1857 presidential election, with over 200,000 votes cast, only 75 were recorded for candidates other than the Liberal and Conservative standard-bearers or General Mosquera, whose following would soon be reabsorbed into the other two camps.[12] The regional patterns of party strength were clearly fixed as well. Conservativism was preponderant, for example, in Pasto, Antioquia, and the area of Tunja; Liberalism was preponderant on the coast; and many small towns (including hard-pressed Liberal enclaves in Conservative areas and vice versa) were already exhibiting an overwhelming (sometimes even unanimous) allegiance to their own party that would be repeated in election after election until quite recent times.

The intensity of party competition created a potentially unstable situation; petty outbreaks of violence at the local level were a normal accompaniment of election campaigns, and from time to time general civil war broke out. Interparty violence of any kind naturally intensified rival allegiances, as followers of one side and the other closed ranks in self-defense against the foe. Another paradox of Colombian history, however, is that political violence, frequent as it may have been, has proved generally ineffective in causing anything but death and destruction, for governments have almost never been overthrown by force. Political scientist James Payne aptly explained this phenomenon on the basis of the very breadth and depth of popular identification with the traditional parties: when to all the natural advantages of incumbency there was added the instinctive support of those loyalists who would back the devil himself if only he was wearing the right party colors, governments became almost impossible to overturn.[13] Even so, a few presidents have fallen victim to a coup, including José María Obando (whether one considers him to have been removed by Melo or by the victorious Constitutionalists). And one—just one—president has gone down to defeat in a full-fledged revolution, Mariano Ospina Rodríguez.

Ospina did not lack attractive character traits. Even as president, he would walk the streets of Bogotá without guards or official entourage; and he continued to teach a law class, in which he was always alert to warn his students against corrosive doctrines. He was also so committed to the bourgeois values of orderliness, practicality, and hard work, which he saw exemplified in the United States, that he actually requested his minister in Washington to explore the possibility of annexing New Granada to the North American union.[14] This request did not become widely known at the time or even later; neither did it produce any result. On the other hand, Ospina's setting up of a one-party government after the coalition rule of Mallarino soon brought friction with the Liberals, and he faced the particular hostility of ex-president Mosquera, now the elected governor of the state of Cauca. Mosquera's antipathy to Ospina was part personal dislike, part political rivalry, but it further reflected the fact that Mosquera as governor was very much concerned with defending and enhancing his state's autonomy, whereas Ospina, though he had embraced federalism, took a generous interpretation of the powers still vested in the central authorities. Ospina therefore backed a group of laws adopted by Congress in 1859 that gave those central authorities a greater role in such things as the supervision of elections for president and congressional seats. The measures were adopted against bitter Liberal opposition, and a majority of state governments rejected them as unconstitutional.

A series of local revolutions, against the governments of particular states, proved to be forerunners of general civil war. These revolutions began in the state of Santander, which had been formed out of the earlier provinces of Socorro and Pamplona and was a stronghold of the Radical faction of the Liberal Party, most of whose leaders had been Gólgotas a few years back. In the government of Santander they had resumed the hyperactive reformism of 1849–1853, abolishing the death penalty, decreeing that henceforth anyone at all was free to coin money, turning over road building and education to private initiative, and replacing most other taxes with a single direct levy on personal wealth. Some of these measures were quickly rescinded or modified, but Santander still gained a national reputation for utopian experimentation.[15] From the standpoint of local Conservatives, who were wholly excluded from state power by the electoral system, it all added up to a climate of lawless anarchy. They rose in rebellion and, when repressed, rebelled again. With similar outbreaks occurring elsewhere, the Ospina administration in the latter part of 1859 declared a public-order emergency, to justify the use of national forces in restoring stability.

In May of the following year, finally, Mosquera rose in open rebellion and assumed the leadership of Liberal forces dedicated to the overthrow of Ospina. The struggle then engulfed almost the entire country, and losses were heavy on both sides. But the Liberals did come out on top: in July 1861 Mosquera took Bogotá, and though fighting continued for over a year after that, the result was no longer in doubt. Ex-president Ospina (whose term had expired in the middle of the war, at which point he handed over his office to an interim successor) was among those taken prisoner in the fall of the nation's capital, and Mosquera's first instinct had been to shoot him. In the end he was merely exiled and spent the next nine years in Guatemala, where he studied that country's burgeoning coffee industry for lessons to be applied at home once he returned.

THE RADICAL REPUBLIC

The Liberal civil war victory ushered in a period of active reformism even more radical than that of 1849–1853. The first target was the church. In the earlier round of reforms, it had been cut off from the traditional protection of the state but, except for the loss of compulsory tithes and the Jesuits, emerged with its basic structures intact. Those structures now came under assault by General Mosquera in his capacity as provisional head of state, even before the fighting ceased. Not long after his occupation of Bogotá in July 1861, Mosquera issued a series of decrees that assigned to the government a right of "tutelage" over the church (*tuición de cultos* was the Spanish formula), again expelled the Jesuits, and expropriated most church assets other than the buildings actually in use for religious purposes. The bulk of church real estate holdings and mortgage investments passed into the hands of the state, which promised in return to pay the church the yearly equivalent of 6 percent of the value of what was seized. Subsequent decrees rounded out the package of anticlerical measures with the legal abolition of the other religious orders of both monks and nuns (albeit with a loophole that allowed them still to exist in certain regions). For objecting too vigorously to all this, the archbishop of Bogotá (now Antonio Herrán, brother of ex-president Herrán) was placed under arrest; Mosquera was excommunicated by the pope.

This more sweeping offensive against the institutional church reflected not just Liberal triumphalism in the wake of military victory but the feelings of anger and revenge inspired by the clergy's close collaboration with the defeated Conservatives. Not surprisingly, in light of the earlier round of religious reforms, both priests and bishops had urged the faithful to support the government of Ospina Rodríguez, and often their services went beyond the mere use of moral suasion. The example of the sweeping disamortization of church property and related measures just enacted by the Mexican Liberals under Benito Juárez also played a part.[16] The underlying motives, however, were largely economic: the longstanding conviction of Liberals that church assets, if placed in circulation, would give a powerful stimulus to the economy and meet the pressing short-term need for funds to pay government debts, including the cost of the late revolution.

Both economic objectives could be satisfied if the former church assets were sold to new owners, although there was soon disagreement among the Liberals themselves concerning the procedures to be followed. Mosquera expressed hope that the liquidation of church holdings, with special facilities for their division and sale in small lots, would produce a wider distribution of landed property in the country. Since such a program would take time to implement and the need for money in the treasury was immediate, he proposed to issue treasury bills with the real estate as backing, aiming to redeem the bills when the property was finally disposed of. The scheme was coherent and well intentioned, but, because of the widespread lack of confidence in government obligations, it probably would not produce as much revenue as could be obtained from outright sale; and it further conflicted with the ambitions of those wealthy citizens (some of them influential Liberal politicians) who were eager to obtain for themselves a share of what the church had lost.

The procedural conflict was resolved largely in favor of those who wanted a quick sale of properties—and it still produced no more than a fraction of the real worth of the church assets, particularly since payment was chiefly made in depreciated government obligations. Neither did the total value of church holdings turn out to be as great as Liberals had hoped: about ten million pesos (or roughly four pesos per capita), including both the real estate seized and the *censos* (ecclesiastical mortgages) that buyers "redeemed" by depositing their face value in the treasury.[17] The net benefit to the treasury was thus short-lived and generally disappointing. Liberal theorists still found justification for the measure in the presumed benefits to the economy at large when so much property was released from the *manos muertas*, or "dead hands" of the church; but there is little evidence that the new owners made more productive use of it than the former ecclesiastical owners.

To be sure, there also is not much evidence to support the notion that lay purchasers of former church estates raised the rates charged peasant renters or simply evicted them to bring in cattle instead (likely as not, the cattle had already been put there by the clergy). Except for the further enrichment of certain large-scale purchasers, the economic effects of disamortization do not appear to have been great, although the church did lose an important source of income. The amount of its net loss is impossible to determine, but certainly the clergy became even less able to maintain their traditional welfare and educational services—and at a time when the state was not yet prepared to take up the slack.

The next target of Liberal reformers was the central state itself. In 1863 a constituent convention meeting at R'onegro in Antioquia produced a new constitution, which took the concept of federalism to the greatest extremes of any American fundamental law. The name of the country was now changed to Estados Unidos de Colombia, but the states received much more sweeping powers than in the Anglo-American model. The states were nine in number: Antioquia, Bolívar (comprising Cartagena and the major part of the Caribbean coast), Boyacá (Tunja and its hinterland), Cauca, Cundinamarca, Magdalena (the part of the coastal plain lying east of the river, its capital Santa Marta), Panama, Santander, and Tolima (formed out of the old provinces of Neiva and Mariquita in the upper Magdalena Valley). (See map 2.) These states retained all powers not expressly delegated to the central authorities, and the specified national functions were closely circumscribed. Thus, for example, the national government had responsibility only for "interoceanic" transportation routes. The states received the concurrent right to establish their own postal systems, and several did in fact proceed to issue their own stamps. The upper house of the national Congress was aptly termed Senado de Plenipotenciarios, as if its members were the emissaries of sovereign nations. The president was chosen on a basis of one state, one vote; and the states were free to establish the requirements for voting in national as well as local elections. (A majority took this opportunity to retreat from universal male suffrage, whose results had not been wholly satisfactory from the Liberal standpoint, and to reinstate literacy or

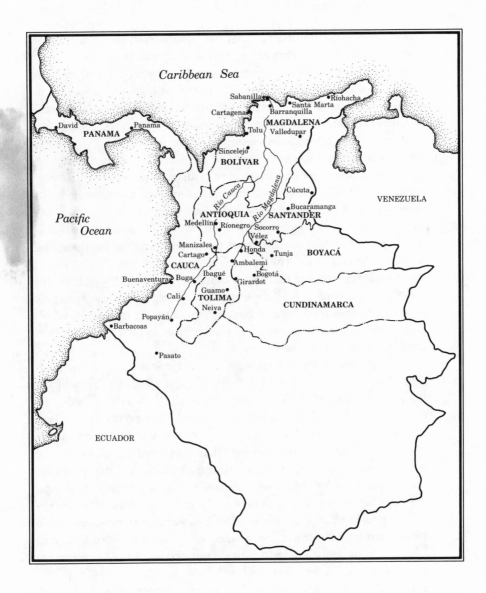

Map 2. The United States of Colombia (1863–1885) (Reprinted by permission of Louisiana State University Press from *Rafael Núñez and the Politics of Colombian Regionalism, 1863–1886* by James William Park. Copyright 1985 by Louisiana State University Press.)

socioeconomic qualifications.) Last but hardly least, any amendment to the constitution required the approval of all nine states.

The new constitution further limited the effectiveness of the national administration by allowing the president only a two-year term, without the possibility of immediate reelection. This provision resulted not so much from theoretical principles as from the distrust felt by many of the Liberals themselves for their new leader, Mosquera, who was obviously going to serve as president under the charter. A rigorously doctrinaire liberalism was evident, however, in the treatment of individual liberties, which were defined in as sweeping terms as possible. The absolute press freedom of the 1850s was now extended to the spoken word as well: citizens could make false accusations, call for violent overthrow of the government, or anything else they took a mind to and enjoy constitutional protection. The constitution further guaranteed the inviolability of human life, which meant that the death penalty was abolished for all offenses; yet at the same time, with some theoretical inconsistency perhaps, it guaranteed all citizens the right to keep arms and ammunition and to engage freely in the arms trade in times of peace.

A critical test of the federalist spirit and letter of the new constitution came soon after Manuel Murillo Toro, the leading figure of the Radical Liberals and the first president actually to be elected under the new system, succeeded Mosquera as federal chief executive in 1864. One side effect of the Liberals' victory in civil war had been the replacement of all state governments that supported the Conservative national administration of Ospina Rodríguez, including that of Antioquia. However, Antioquia was a strongly Conservative region; and Antioqueño Conservatives, chafing under imposed minority rule, overthrew their Liberal state rulers to establish one of themselves, Pedro Justo Berrío, as governor. It was then up to Murillo Toro to decide whether to accept the Conservatives' fait accompli or—as a pretext for rolling back what they had done—to invoke the vague power vested in the federal president by the 1863 constitution to "watch over" the maintenance of order.

When Murillo Toro agreed to deal with Berrío as governor of Antioquia, he signaled that the self-determination of the federated states was indeed going to be meaningful. Berrío and his party then proceeded to turn Antioquia's state government into something of a model, favored by the region's social homogeneity and the cohesiveness of its commercial bourgeoisie. There were modest but steady advances in education and public works and quite high standards of administrative honesty and efficiency. Schooling for girls received commendable attention, so that by 1880 Antioquia had more girls than boys in primary school, although the situation was quite different at secondary level and the education imparted to the girls heavily stressed domestic and religious training.[18] In fact, the Antioqueño Conservatives worked closely in almost everything with the powerful local clergy—all the while conspicuously failing to cooperate in the implementation of national measures against church property.

Conservatives later managed to gain control of two other states, Tolima and Cundinamarca; but since the state of Cundinamarca contained the national capital itself, they were not long allowed to remain in control there. Elsewhere, the reins of power at state level remained in Liberal hands for the life of the 1863 constitution, the Conservatives being kept at bay if necessary through any combination of electoral gerrymandering, outright fraud, and intimidation. Thus, when a state government was overturned, either at the ballot box or by armed force (as was not infrequent), it usually meant that one Liberal faction had ousted another. The national authorities themselves were not above meddling at times in political conflicts within the states. They did so even after the passage of an 1867 law (repealed in 1876) that expressly prohibited the national president from taking sides in a state civil war.

In these generally intra-Liberal squabbles electoral irregularities were regrettably common: from the federal era came the Colombian aphorism "El que escruta elige" (roughly translatable as "He who counts elects"). One extreme example occurred in the state of Bolívar, in 1875, when 44,112 votes for national president were recorded in favor of Rafael Núñez against a mere 7 for the rival Liberal candidate, Aquileo Parra, who was the eventual winner because he had more states in his column and that is what counted in the end—not popular votes, whether fraudulent or fair.[19] The fact that Núñez was a native son of Bolívar would explain a lopsided vote in his favor, and this was not one of the states that had abandoned universal male suffrage; but the official results would still have represented a thoroughly implausible turnout of approximately 90 percent of the adult male population.

Even though their electoral practices left much to be desired, and though the national authorities sometimes intervened in their affairs in violation of the letter or spirit of the constitution, the federal states really did enjoy a large degree of autonomy. A few of them made good use of it to take care of things that had been either neglected or less well handled by officials in Bogotá. Most of the states, however, lacked the resources to do very much for either good or ill, particularly since the national government retained possession of the one most lucrative revenue source, the customs. As of 1873–74, according to the calculations of Malcolm Deas, state revenues per capita ranged from 24 centavos in Boyacá to 1.08 pesos in Antioquia and 1.42 in Panama (where costs were not really comparable). The median, corresponding to the state of Bolívar, was 83 centavos.[20] The devolution of governmental functions to the states therefore meant, among other things, a reinforcement of the existing inequality in levels of development between regions of the country, since a few states successfully brought government closer to the governed, as federalism was supposed to do, and the greater number did barely more than meet a minuscule state payroll. Almost unavoidably, subventions began to be paid to the states from the national treasury on one pretext or another. Together with the national government's taking over of some functions that belonged to it only by the loosest interpretation of the constitution, this practice might have undermined the federal system itself, except that the process still had not gone far when the federalist experiment was abruptly ended.

At both state and national levels, the Liberals (and the Conservatives in their state strongholds) showed a generally high level of respect for press freedom and other individual liberties. And though state governors were sometimes overthrown, presidents of the federation— with one exception—peacefully succeeded one another at the constitutional two-year intervals. The exception occurred in 1867, after Tomás Cipriano de Mosquera had been elected one more time to the nation's highest office. The distrust between Mosquera and the leaders of the Radical faction had not disappeared, and it was heightened by a number of his actions after taking office. For instance, he now called for a review of all sales of confiscated church property made during Murillo Toro's administration, with a view to correcting possible irregularities. Quite apart from the implicit aspersion on Murillo Toro's handling of the matter, Mosquera's move upset all the people who had obtained the properties in question. Mosquera had to backtrack on this issue; but other quarrels kept coming up.

Things finally came to a head with the discovery that behind Congress's back the president had been attempting to purchase a warship in New York, so that Peru could use it in a new conflict that had arisen between Peru and the former mother country, Spain. Mosquera's objective was noble, but irregularities had been committed, and his enemies in Congress seized upon them. Faced with this uproar, Mosquera dissolved the Congress, assumed dictatorial powers, and called on the military and working classes to rally to his support in a reedition of the artisan-Draconiano alliance. But the strategy was even less successful for Mosquera than for Melo. He was quickly overthrown by Constitutionalist military officers, who—just as in 1854—had the strong support of Radicals and Conservatives. So ended one more abortive attempt to interrupt constitutional normalcy. It was the last such attempt by anyone holding power at the national level until President Rafael Núñez in 1885 declared that the federal constitution itself had been superseded by events.

From the standpoint of Mosquera himself and certain later revisionists—most notably, Indalecio Liévano Aguirre[21]—the root cause of his overthrow was the inability of the Radical "oligarchy" to tolerate his efforts to rule in the interest of the nation as a whole. Nor is there any denying that the Radical leaders, though for the most part high-minded and capable, were narrowly sectarian in their approach to politics and wedded to specific economic interests. Many were involved in aspects of the export economy (as were, to be sure, quite a few of their rivals); they included a number of the "parvenus and litterati" (in the words of Marco Palacios)[22] who had been rising in society through politics and political connections; and they came disproportionately from the three central and eastern states of Cundinamarca, Boyacá, and Santander. They believed that the strategy of outward-directed economic growth, officially favored since the late 1840s, would eventually bring greater well-being to all Colombians; they also felt that government measures expressly designed to assist the poorer elements of society were usually counterproductive. Indeed, the Radicals had a distinctly modest view of the role of government as such. President Eustorgio Salgar put it well in his 1870 inaugural address, in which he expressly warned the nation that "it should not expect from my government the realization of great undertakings."[23] Nevertheless, they were true to the legacy of Santander in that they did take a particular interest in education. As Gólgotas in the 1850s, the senior members of the Radical faction had generally backed measures tending toward the privatization of education; but over the next two decades, they made an important contribution to the development of public education in Colombia.

One accomplishment was the founding in 1867 of the Universidad Nacional de Colombia in Bogotá. This measure undid one part of the educational reform of 1850, which had simply abolished as unnecessary the universities then existing and integrated their programs into the system of secondary-level *colegios*. The new university included the traditional disciplines of law, medicine, and philosophy, but in addition it placed a major emphasis on technical studies, reflecting the earnest desire of Colombian leaders for their country to come to terms with the new age of railroads and mechanization generally. In this respect its program of studies brings to mind that of Mariano Ospina Rodríguez in the 1840s, although most Liberals would have resented the comparison. But the university was remarkably free of petty partisanship. The roster of professors was a virtual who's who of the capital's intellectual elite; it included the Conservative ideologue and humanist scholar Miguel Antonio Caro (as professor of Latin) alongside adherents of both classical liberalism and the rising school of positivism, not to mention others more difficult to label. The creation of the university, moreover, formed part of a wider cultural florescence also marked by vigorous political journalism, by much *costumbrista* fiction recording picturesque regional folkways, and by the appearance of one enduring Latin American classic, the romantic novel *María* (1867), in which Jorge Isaacs offered a powerfully nostalgic evocation of hacienda life in the Cauca Valley.

None of the developments just mentioned had much meaning for the average Colombian, who could not even read. Nevertheless, the Liberal regime did make a laudable effort to revitalize primary education, which had progressed very little since the 1830s. Here the key measure was the decree of 1870, issued by President Salgar and his interior secretary, Felipe Zapata, that declared primary instruction free and obligatory throughout the nation and further provided for it to be religiously neutral. Secretary Zapata, who more than any other one figure designed the program, thus ranks as the Colombian counterpart of the great Argentine educator-president Domingo F. Sarmiento. As in Argentina, normal schools were founded to prepare the necessary teachers, and foreign experts were brought in to impart the latest advances in pedagogical theory and practice. Unlike Sarmiento, who invited U.S. educationists to Argentina, the Colombians imported a German mission. An even greater difference between the two countries, however, had to do with the level of financial resources available. Argentina during Sarmiento's presidency (1868–1874) was just on the verge of its economic takeoff, whereas the growth of the Colombian economy was far more modest. The national government earmarked 4 percent of its budget for education, and that amounted to a mere 200,000 pesos, of which one-fifth went to the Universidad Nacional.[24]

Education was a responsibility legally shared by the national government with the states and municipalities, but most of them were equally or more strapped for funds and therefore were simply unable to contribute much money. They also were jealous of their own autonomy. But the biggest problem of all was the hostility of the church and the Conservative Party. The 1870 decree did not exclude all religion from the public schools; it simply stated that religion should be taught by representatives of the churches, in designated hours, to students whose parents requested it. Some of the more moderate churchmen were satisfied with this formula, but Catholic and Conservative activists claimed to see in the measure the first step toward a wholly godless school system and called on families, local authorities, and anyone else who would lend an ear to have nothing to do with the official schools. A few states insisted that religious education be obligatory, contrary to the terms of the decree. The fact that some members of the German pedagogical mission were Protestants fanned the flames still higher. And mounting agitation over this one issue, more than any other factor, triggered the outbreak of a Conservative revolution in 1876 that was by far the most serious disruption of public order since the close of the 1859–1862 civil war. Under such circumstances it is all the more noteworthy that an advance in primary education did take place, with the number of students in primary schools rising from 60,155 in 1870 to almost 84,000 four years later. Three percent of the total population was now enrolled, as against 1.2 percent in 1835.[25] Unfortunately, this spurt of educational progress was sharply curtailed during the 1876 civil war and in its aftermath, when the Liberals chose to put less emphasis on this part of their program.

The 1876 uprising was prompted by other grievances besides the perceived threat to religion in official education. That is what mobilized ardent churchmen and the Conservative masses, but the party's leadership was also frustrated by its exclusion from a meaningful share of power, except in Antioquia and Tolima; and it was encouraged by signs of increasing dissension within the Liberal camp itself, where the old rivalry between Radicals and Mosqueristas was now replaced by an even more threatening split between the Radical "oligarchy" and a new faction that called itself Independent. Most of the surviving backers of Mosquera—who after a brief exile in Peru returned to become governor of his home state of Cauca and once again a power in regional politics—joined the Independents. This new faction also capitalized on regional disaffection along the Caribbean coast, whose Liberal politicians tended to feel (as the Conservatives did everywhere) that they had less influence than they deserved. They did not, of course, object to Liberal hegemony as such, but they resented the domination of the federal executive branch by Radical leaders from the Cordillera Oriental, who had provided every one of the presidents since Mosquera's overthrow.

Independents further accused the eastern Radicals of concentrating national resources on projects of special interest to their own region. As a prime example, they cited the Ferrocarril del Norte, or Northern Railroad, an overambitious project designed to link Bogotá with the Magdalena River by a route crossing the states of Cundinamarca, Boyacá, and Santander. For this scheme to receive any national financing at all was a bit irregular in view of the constitutional article authorizing the general government to concern itself only with "interoceanic" routes, by which was clearly meant such things as the Panama Railroad; but by a bold, if not ludicrous, leap of interpretation, the Ferrocarril del Norte became a potential link in a combined rail-highway-riverboat corridor from Pacific to Atlantic by way of the Colombian capital. The railroad was never built, but some federal money was spent in preparation for it, and to Independent Liberals it became a symbol of the Radical leadership's narrow devotion to regional interests. When Independents put forward the candidacy of Rafael Núñez in the presidential election of 1876, their appeal had little to do with doctrinal matters: their aim was to end the monopolization of federal power by Radical politicians predominantly beholden to a single region.

After Núñez lost, in a bitter contest, Conservative revolutionists hoped that his Independent faction would not rally to the support of his successful Radical opponent, Aquileo Parra. They made their move three months after Parra's inauguration—and they were disappointed. In part, at least, because of the seeming fanaticism of clerical elements backing the rebellion, most Independents stuck with the Radical administration, as a lesser evil. The struggle was hard-fought and destructive of both lives and resources, but before the end of the year the government had prevailed. In doing so, it deposed the Conservative governors of Antioquia and Tolima, who had joined the uprising (Antioquia's with obvious reluctance, in view of the comfortable modus vivendi that Antioqueño Conservatives had arrived at with the Liberal regime). For the Radicals a troublesome result was the prestige won by the leading Liberal general in the struggle, Julián Trujillo, himself aligned with the Independents, who went on to be elected the next president (and would be succeeded by Núñez in 1880). However, while the Liberals were fighting the Conservatives and quarreling with each other, the cycle of export expansion that set in at midcentury was beginning to run out of steam. In the long run, economic frustration was to prove even more threatening to their survival in power.

APOGEE OF
THE OUTWARD-GROWTH MODEL

The growth of commodity exporting did persist through most of the Liberal era, inevitable with fluctuations and with changes in the mix of commodities exported. The value of annual exports, in gold pesos, which had risen from 3.3 million in the first half of the 1840s to 6.4 million in the period 1854–1858, stood at almost 10 million in the early 1870s and then peaked at nearly 15.5 million in 1881–1883. In per capita terms the record was less impressive, showing only a return to and then a modest improvement on late colonial levels. However, the prices of imported manufactures—especially textiles—continued to fall, so that export earnings paid for a much sharper increase in the volume, if not the value, of imports. The *purchasing power* of Colombian exports multiplied almost nine times in that same period.[26]

The tobacco boom, which had led the way, proved transitory for reasons already noted, but tobacco remained an important item of export sales through the 1870s and then finally collapsed early in the following decade. Its one serious rival, for the Liberal era as a whole, was quinine, or more precisely cinchona bark, which had widespread medicinal use, especially in the treatment of malaria. Quinine was already a minor export of colonial New Granada. It languished in the early postindependence years, during which Bolivia became the main source of supply; but favorable market conditions about midcentury induced Colombian entrepreneurs to reenter the quinine trade on a large scale, and for roughly the next thirty years they decisively dominated the business. It was a typical extractive industry, in which teams of gatherers, usually working for merchant speculators, swept through ever larger stands of forest in Santander and other regions, stripping the bark off the cinchona trees. In the early 1880s quinine briefly became the most important single export, accounting for 31 percent of total value, only to collapse even more rapidly and completely than tobacco by the end of that same decade. The immediate cause was competition from quinine plantations recently created in India and Southeast Asia. Unfortunately, the method of exploitation in Colombia was such that production could only keep up with rising world demand by continuously destroying the resource itself; and though a few producers attempted to cultivate quinine on a plantation basis in Colombia as well, they were unable to withstand the competition of Asian producers.

Two even more short-lived bonanzas were cotton and indigo. There were colonial antecedents for the export production of cotton on the Caribbean coastal plain, but it was not an important export of republican New Granada. The U.S. Civil War, however, created a sudden scarcity and sharp price increases on the world market, which Colombian producers rushed to take advantage of. But since their product was of generally poor quality, it could not compete successfully once normal conditions in the cotton trade returned. Indigo also had a long history of production, for mainly local use as a dye. As cotton receded once again into unimportance, indigo briefly became a major export crop—as a result of disturbances in the growing areas of India, which had been the principal supplier. Plantations were organized in various parts of Colombia to take advantage of this latest sudden opportunity, and in the early 1880s indigo represented almost 7 percent of total exports. Yet local producers never saw fit to make the investments in irrigation and fertilizers or scientific management that would have been necessary to establish the industry on a permanent basis, and it, too, soon declined. It thus became one more instance where Colombians succeeded in detecting favorable market conditions and moved to exploit them but failed to take the steps that might have given the industry long-term significance in the Colombian economy. The economist José Antonio Ocampo has argued, to be sure, that the speculative mentality revealed by this pattern was not wholly irrational.[27] With their high transport costs and inadequacies of almost every sort of infrastructure, to say nothing of mere political uncertainties, they may well have had good reason to hold back from larger commitments.

There were two areas, furthermore, in which some basis was laid for lasting expansion. One was livestock raising. Large landowners introduced artificial pastures and barbed wire and other technical improvements, which led to a major increase in numbers of livestock over the second half of the century and had some impact also on export trade, through foreign sales of hides and of live cattle (mainly to Venezuela). Even more important was coffee, whose cultivation expanded steadily. By the end of the 1870s, it had moved into first place among agricultural exports, though it was still not far ahead of quinine and tobacco. Cultivation for export first became important in northeastern Santander (or what is today Norte de Santander department), from which the product was shipped over the Zulia River route to the Venezuelan port of Maracaibo. Later, Cundinamarca became a major producer. In both states the pioneers of coffee exporting were large landowners, who generally relied on some combination of wage labor with tenancy or sharecropping to operate their plantations; but especially in Santander smaller family farms also were involved in coffee growing, anticipating the pattern that would eventually become dominant in the Colombian coffee industry.

In spite of the emergence of agricultural commodity exporting, precious metals remained a major item in export trade. They represented a declining proportion (by the late nineteenth century slightly under 25 percent) only because the value of total exports was growing faster. As already mentioned, however, the growth of exports per capita was not particularly impressive: from a depressed level of $1.88 (U.S.) in the mid-1830s to $3.28 in 1855 and $4.77 in 1880. Nor was this record at all noteworthy in a wider Latin American perspective, for in 1880 Venezuela was exporting $6.38 per capita; Brazil, $8.53; Argentina, $31.69—and in 1884 the Spanish colony of Cuba, $45.91.[28] The apparent success of the country's export-led growth strategy must therefore be described as shallow at best. The export economy was also fragile, undergoing a recession in the mid-1870s, with the 1876 civil war as an aggravating factor, and then "severe depression" (in Ocampo's terminology) starting in 1883. The depression reflected a temporary leveling off of coffee expansion, together with the definitive collapse of quinine exports and a deterioration of the international terms of trade.[29] Coming on top of the stop/go, boom/bust performance of many individual commodities, these developments made some Colombians increasingly skeptical of the chosen economic strategy and of the political framework within which it was being implemented.

Such success as export promotion did achieve was both cause and effect of modest and overdue improvements in the country's infrastructure. The most obvious example is the construction of railroads. The Panama Railroad was completed in 1856, and no less than nine more were at least begun during the period of Liberal rule from the 1860s to 1885 (see table).

These railroads shared a number of characteristics. They all were short, either in total length (e.g., 27 kilometers for the Barranquilla-Sabanilla route) or in the part actually finished by 1885 (e.g., 38 kilometers westward from the Magdalena for the Antioquia Railroad). Almost all were built by some combination of foreign and native enterprise, the most important foreign promoter being the Cuban-born U.S. citizen Francisco J. Cisneros; and they were financed through a varying mix of subsidies and privileges granted by the states or the federal authorities. They were unconnected one with another, although the Girardot Railroad and the Sabana Railroad from Bogotá to Facatativá would eventually merge. Most of them were conceived as auxiliary to Magdalena River transport, although the Santa Marta Railroad never actually got that far. And, to one degree or another, they were all designed to serve the expansion of external trade. The Barranquilla-Sabanilla line, in fact, had almost no other reason for existence.

Colombia's bits and pieces of railroad were almost insignificant as compared to the networks that countries like Mexico and Argentina were building in the same period. The difficulty of the terrain through which most of them had to pass made construction inevitably expensive—above all, in relation to the actual or potential cargo to be carried. Not surprisingly, the Barranquilla-Sabanilla and the La Dorada Railroads, which climbed no mountains and directly complemented

Railroad Construction, 1869–1885

Name of Line	Dates of Construction[a]	Kilometers Built by 1885	Route
Barranquilla-Sabanilla	1869–1871	27	Barranquilla to Sabanilla (on the Caribbean) bypassing dangerous river entrance
Antioquia	1874–1929	38	Medellín to Puerto Berrío (on Magdalena River)
Pacific	1878–1915	26	Buenaventura (on Pacific coast) to Cali
Cúcuta-Zulia	1878–1888	54	Cúcuta to Zulia River
Girardot	1881–1910	31	Girardot (on Magdalena River) to Bogotá
La Dorada	1881–1882	15	Rail bypass around Magdalena River rapids
Puerto Wilches	1881–[b]	4	Puerto Wilches (on Magdalena) to Bucaramanga
Sabana	1882–1889	18	Bogotá to Facatativá (chief town of western Sabana)
Santa Marta	1882–[c]	12	Santa Marta to Magdalena River

[a] Ending date is that of completion of principal section.
[b] Never completed.
[c] Never completed as originally planned, but incorporated in Atlantic Railroad from Bogotá to Santa Marta, finished in 1961.
Source: Alfredo Ortega, *Ferrocarriles colombianos*, 4 vols. (Bogotá, 1920–1949), 1:27, 2: passim.

the existing Magdalena River system, were the two most profitable. Yet Colombia, like most of the rest of the world in the second half of the nineteenth century, was swept up in the romance and excitement of railroad building, to the extent that the country's leaders took it for granted that railroads were the key to Colombia's becoming genuinely a part of the modern world. As a consequence, highway construction was still relatively neglected. A road suitable for wheeled vehicles was built during the 1870s from Medellín to Barbosa, a point farther down the Aburrá Valley; and the cart road from Bogotá to Facatativá was by 1885 extended to Cambao on the Magdalena, although it was not really very adequate. Not much else could be shown in the way of transport infrastructure. Telegraphy, fortunately, was easier to introduce than a proper road or railroad network, because wires could climb peaks and span chasms with relative ease. The first telegraph message was received in Bogotá in 1865, and the service was soon extended to other main cities. Two years later, an underwater cable connection was completed with New York.

Progress also was made toward overcoming the deficiencies of financial infrastructure. Until the middle of the nineteenth century Colombia was a country without a formal banking system. Some religious institutions made mortgage loans, and merchant speculators would lend money at high interest, but banks as known in more developed economies simply did not exist. The scarcity of liquid capital, the low volume of commercial transactions, and political uncertainties all conspired against the establishment of banking institutions. One early attempt to create a bank in Bogotá had failed in the aftermath of the War of the Supremes, following a flurry of speculative operations. Savings banks, primarily intended to serve the urban artisans, appeared in several cities in the 1840s and proved relatively successful, but they did not meet the needs of commerce and industry, and the attempt in 1864 to launch a branch of the Bank of London, Mexico, and South America ended in failure. But in 1870 the nation's first permanent banking institution came into existence: the Banco de Bogotá, whose founders included men closely associated with commodity exporting. Among its original depositors was one distrustful soul who every week stopped by to have a cashier count out his deposited money, to make sure it was still there. Such lack of confidence in the banking system was understandable, in view of its novelty, but was soon overcome, with other financial institutions soon joining the Banco de Bogotá, and not just in the national capital.

The development of commodity production for the world market was again an important contributing factor, though certainly not the only one, behind a continuing movement of population (as even earlier in Antioquia) from the highlands into medium-altitude slopes or in certain cases the hot-country lowlands. Coffee, which grew best at altitudes between 800 and 1,800 meters, clearly exemplified the process, but the same could be said of the other leading export commodities. It could also be said of the expansion of cattle raising, much of which occurred in lower or medium elevations, often in conjunction with the spread of new crops. Whatever the incentive in any given case, the movement of settlers to occupy what had been thinly inhabited mountain slopes had as one incidental result the gradual constriction of the internal frontier that served as outlet for population growth and an alternative to hacienda labor for the rural working class. In fact, large landowners often appropriated, legally or illegally, greater stretches of the public domain than they needed for production, at least in part for the very purpose of assuring themselves a supply of labor.

None of the new export commodities was produced on a purely capitalistic, wage-labor basis: both seasonal fluctuations in the need for labor and the continuing unreliability of labor supply dictated the combination of wage labor with other methods. This is just one of the reasons why it becomes almost impossible to determine whether or to what extent the average standard of living of the rural masses may have been affected by the economic changes taking place; but the best guess is that probably it was not affected very much. There was some relative expansion of the large-estate system, and the remuneration of labor in any form at all was seldom generous. Even so, when the growth of population and constant subdivision of small peasant plots in older settled areas induced people to move, say, from Boyacá to the Magdalena Valley in search of opportunities, they were most likely better off than they would have been if they had stayed.

Despite the succession of export booms, production for internal consumption continued to be vastly greater than production for foreign markets; yet it was far from having the same importance as a motor of change in the general economy. The population also continued to be overwhelmingly more rural than urban. Nevertheless, the second half of the century did see some slight quickening of urban expansion. Between the censuses of 1851 and 1870, the population of Medellín more than doubled, and Bogotá (which in 1876 received gas lighting and early in the next decade horse-drawn streetcars) by the end of the century had passed the 100,000 population mark. Elsewhere the increase was usually less spectacular, but urban growth was at least keeping up with that of the population as a whole, which it had not done in the quarter century following independence; and probably it exceeded the overall increase by a slight margin.

The quickening of export-import trade gave impetus to the growth of such commercial crossroads as Bucaramanga and Cúcuta, both benefiting from Santander's coffee trade, not to mention Barranquilla at the northern terminus of Magdalena navigation. Foreign trade also contributed to the growth of Medellín and Bogotá, although the heyday of Medellín as a coffee center would come only in the early twentieth century and the immediate vicinity of Bogotá was more important as a market for imports than as point of origin of exports. What mainly propelled Bogotá's growth, of course, was its role as a provider of governmental and other services. A few small factories—of chocolate, matches, and the like—did make their appearance in the nation's capital, drawing heavily on female labor, but there as elsewhere most manufacturing was still of the artisan or handicraft variety.

Domestic artisans, both urban and rural, held their own, albeit with difficulty, against competing imports—thanks to the continuing high cost of transportation and to their own ability to support themselves partly through other occupations. Moreover, despite appearances to the contrary, they still enjoyed a certain amount of de facto tariff protection. Until almost the end of the Liberal era, governments were committed to a low-tariff policy and to the promotion of foreign trade as a primary engine of growth. But some tariffs were always needed for revenue purposes, and though rates were generally moderate, they could appreciably affect the cost of certain imports. In particular, the decision to tax broad categories of imported merchandise by weight rather than declared value—adopted in 1861 as a means of simplifying collection and discouraging fraud—tended to place a proportionately higher burden of customs duties on the cheaper grades of textiles and other goods of wide popular consumption. This method of taxation admirably suited the consumers of imported luxuries, but it also gave some protection to the artisans whose output was concentrated in those cheaper grades. Domestic textile production thus did not diminish; imports merely covered the increase in demand that came with growing population and changing consumer tastes.

After the election of Rafael Núñez as president in 1880, the vestigial protectionism of the 1860s and 1870s would become overt, as part of a new official activism in economic matters. This change in policy, to be sure, had somewhat more of form than of substance, as will be seen in the next chapter. For that matter, the Radical Liberals who controlled the national administration during most of the life of the 1863 constitution did not practice the hands-off doctrines of classic economic liberalism with absolute consistency. Not only did they give artisans that trace of tariff protection, but they subsidized railroad building and tried to build up a national public education system, and they collaborated with their archrival Mosquera in despoiling the church. At the same time, they practiced a style of administration—at the national level anyway—that was generally orderly and well meaning. They made little progress, unfortunately, toward creating a truly unified nation in a land still marked by great regional and social differences.

6

The Regeneration and Its Aftermath: A Positivist-Conservative Reaction (1885–1904)

The period of Liberal ascendancy in Colombia finally came to an end in the next-to-last decade of the nineteenth century. The excesses of Liberal administrations toward the church, the ultrafederalism that weakened maintenance of public order, and growing doubts concerning the Liberals' economic policy all contributed to setting off the inevitable reaction. Squabbling with the clergy was no way to win the heartfelt allegiance of an overwhelmingly Roman Catholic population, while federalism, though as much a result as a cause of the national government's pitiful weakness, had seemingly made a bad situation even worse. In economic matters the Liberal regime had frankly looked to closer integration between the Colombian economy and world markets as the key to continued growth and had assumed that private enterprise would spontaneously produce this growth if individuals were freed from arbitrary restrictions. As long as commodity exports were doing well, the approach seemed to be vindicated. But when, eventually, there was a weakening in foreign demand for Colombian primary commodities, the result appears to have been some loss of confidence among Liberal leaders themselves as well as an increase in vigor on the part of their critics. The crisis of foreign trade may not have been the most important cause of discontent, but it was in a sense the final straw.

THE PROGRAM OF NÚÑEZ AND CARO: ORDER, PROGRESS, TRADITION

The man who eventually put together a successful coalition in opposition to the Liberal establishment was Dr. Rafael Núñez. In the 1850s Núñez had been something of a doctrinaire Liberal himself, but his thinking steadily evolved until at the height of his career he came to represent a Colombian manifestation of the "positivist" school of thought that exerted such strong influence in Latin America in the late nineteenth century and early twentieth. He was not a positivist in any strict philosophical sense, although he was certainly attracted to the British positivists and social Darwinists, notably Herbert Spencer. Mainly, he is to be classed with positivists in the broad sense of rejecting abstract ideologies (be they Liberal or Conservative or something else) in favor of *practical* concentration on the goals of order and progress. He showed the influence of Spencer in particular in his concern with society as a complex, evolving organism that can be manipulated up to a point but cannot be transformed overnight.[1]

Núñez sought to reform the Constitution of 1863 because he felt it had so strengthened the states and weakened the national executive that effective administration was impossible: it was an ideal creation out of touch with Colombian reality. Though personally a religious freethinker, he was no less convinced that an amicable settlement must be worked out between state and church. Since the Roman Catholic church for better or worse formed an integral part of the Colombian social organism, Núñez reasoned that the only practical course was to accept its presence and grant it a special position of power and influence. Indeed, it should be intelligently *used*, to promote morality and social discipline. Finally, Núñez called for changes in economic policy, all involving a greater sphere of activity for the state. Probably the clearest example is his belief that the government should promote domestic industry through tariff (and other) protection. Critics saw in his call for higher tariffs a mere political tactic to win the votes of the artisans, and they found similar explanations for Núñez's other departures from the strict creed of economic laissez-faire. But whatever his precise motives, his departure from that creed is one more indication of the pragmatism and lack of doctrinaire preconceptions that made him a "positivist" in the loose sense employed above.

It has often been said that Núñez ultimately "turned Conservative." Among Colombian Liberals this was for many years another way of saying that he betrayed his own party, a charge that lay at the very heart of the partisan polemics that swirled up concerning his role. The charge is not, however, technically correct, even though he was a largely unintentional contributor to the Conservative Party's domination in Colombia from the late nineteenth century until 1930. In the

1870s, as a publicist and an active politician with a strong following on the Caribbean coast, his native region, Núñez emerged as leader of the Liberal Party faction known as Independents—in contrast to the Radicals, who stood for doctrinal purity (not that they always practiced it) and generally controlled the national government. As noted in the previous chapter, there was an element of regional conflict in this intraparty split, since the bastion of Radical strength was in the states of Cundinamarca, Boyacá, and Santander, while Independents were strongest on the coast and in Cauca, in the latter case thanks to their virtual coalescence with the followers of ex-president Mosquera.

Núñez failed on his first try for the presidency in 1875, but he finally won election for the 1880–1882 term with the combined votes of Independent Liberals and the Conservatives, to whom he was at the very least a lesser evil. He then managed to put through a few measures enlarging the authority of the national executive, as well as to raise tariffs, since artisans of both parties had joined his coalition. Yet full implementation of the changes he proposed, which in his view amounted to the "Regeneration" of Colombia—as in his slogan "Regeneration or Catastrophe!"—required the reform of the existing constitution. To amend it, unanimous consent of all the states was needed. Thus, the Radicals could block his plans as long as they controlled a single state; and they controlled more than that. They recognized that many of Núñez's criticisms of the current state of affairs were valid, but they sorely distrusted Núñez—in part simply because of his alliance with the Conservatives—and this distrust made them obstructionist.

After the two-year waiting period stipulated by the constitution, Núñez returned to the presidency in 1884. This time he had his stroke of luck. In 1885, fearing that Núñez planned to enact reforms in defiance of the constitution, the Radicals launched a revolt against him, which was quickly suppressed—with massive Conservative help. This turn of events gave Núñez the pretext he needed to announce flatly, "The Constitution of 1863 has ceased to exist."[2] It also increased his dependence on Conservative support, but he still did not join the Conservative Party. Instead, he tried to form a new party, called National, from his own Independent Liberals plus like-minded Conservatives. The bulk of Colombian Liberals hardened their opposition to Núñez and all he stood for rather than joining the new party, whose formerly Liberal members were as a result increasingly overshadowed by their ex-Conservative associates. After Núñez's death in 1894, the National Party as such would become little more than one particular faction of the Conservatives.

Though his third party proved abortive, like other such attempts in Colombia, Núñez did accomplish most of his objectives. His political settlement was basically contained in the new Constitution of 1886, which remained in effect (even if much amended) until 1991. The immediate author of the constitution was one of Núñez's Conservative collaborators, Miguel Antonio Caro, a classical scholar, inflexible defender of traditional Catholic values, and unabashed admirer of the Spanish colonial heritage. But there is no indication of substantive disagreement between the two over the new frame of government. It was rigidly centralist: the states, renamed "departments," retained elected assemblies with limited power to adopt local ordinances, but their governors were named by the national president, and the governors in turn named all the mayors. The party that controlled the presidency could thus wield an absolute monopoly of executive power at all levels. These arrangements were not wholly unlike those established by the first New Granadan Constitution of 1832, but at that time the party system was only embryonic, so that the implications were different. Now the lines were much more clearly drawn, and the total exclusion of one of the nationwide parties from a share of patronage and power could only exacerbate political sectarianism and (indirectly) increase the likelihood of partisan violence. The new constitution further strengthened the national presidency by extending the term to six years and by authorizing immediate reelection. The suffrage was limited once again on a nationwide basis, by the imposition of a literacy requirement for national (not local) elections, and guarantees of civil liberties were couched in less sweeping language than in 1863. The death penalty, finally, was restored.

Núñez's contribution to the cause of national unification went beyond the adoption of a new constitution with a strong central executive and the creation (admittedly ephemeral) of a party that was intended to rise above Liberal-Conservative feuding. He made a further symbolic contribution by composing what became his country's national anthem. That Colombia still did not have such a musical rallying point as late as the 1880s was perhaps one more sign of the relative weakness of national sentiment; Venezuela's anthem, by contrast, dated back to the period of independence itself. Núñez, who was among other things a minor poet, wrote the words; an Italian music teacher in Bogotá contributed the music. The anthem's opening chorus was stirring even if somewhat abstract:

> ¡O gloria inmarcesible!
> ¡o júbilo inmortal!
> En surcos de dolores
> el bien germina ya.

Or, roughly translated:

> Oh, ineffable glory!
> Oh, immortal jubilation!
> In furrows of sorrows
> Well-being now germinates.

In the first verse of the anthem, by way of celebrating independence from Spain, Núñez included the lines "And all humanity, which groans in chains, understands the words of Him who died on the cross." This effort to associate the birth of the Colombian nation with the teachings of Christ may have been historically far-fetched, but no more so than the midcentury appeal of radical reformers to the "Martyr of Golgotha," and what the "Regenerator" appealed to was a more orthodox version of Roman Catholic Christianity. Even more than his political arrangements, the religious settlement that Núñez proceeded to carry out represented a sharp reaction against what had just gone before. Some of its terms were written into the constitution itself; others formed part of a concordat signed with the Vatican in 1887. Religious toleration stayed in effect, and there was no return of compulsory tithing; otherwise, virtually all the enactments of Liberal anticlericals were rolled back. Property seized from the church that was still in government hands was returned, and the church was offered an indemnity for what had passed into the hands of private third parties and could not readily be given back. Religious orders were again legal—even Jesuits. A limited version of the ecclesiastical *fuero* was reinstituted. The constitution also contained the provision that public education must henceforth be conducted in accordance with the teachings of the Roman Catholic religion; that provision would be interpreted in practice in such a way as to give the clergy a veto power over school texts, curricula, and even teacher appointments. Most intriguing of all was the article of the concordat that declared the past and present validity of all Catholic marriages without exception. The original marriage of President Núñez himself was thereby reinstated and his subsequent divorce and civil remarriage invalidated; his present wife—Colombia's First Lady—became legally converted into a mere concubine. Such was the price that Núñez was willing to pay in return for religious tranquility. Fortunately for the presidential couple, the original Señora de Núñez died not long after, allowing them to regularize their situation with church blessing.

In hemispheric perspective the religious policy of Núñez inevitably brings to mind that of the positivist-influenced dictatorship of Porfirio Díaz in Mexico, which similarly called a halt to the anticlerical reforms launched in that country by Benito Juárez and other Mexican Liberals at midcentury. In Mexico, though, the reforms were not repealed but simply became more and more a dead letter as the dictatorship forged its own rapprochement with the church. The objective of removing religious controversy from politics so as to concentrate on other matters was equally clear in both cases, but only Núñez entered into a full-scale alliance with his country's Conservatives, who could thus obtain the formal reinstatement of powers and privileges to the Catholic church. Mexico's Conservatives had been too discredited by their association with the French-backed empire of Maximilian; Colombia's had committed no similar betrayal.

Although his economic policies and programs were not as wide-ranging as those of the Díaz dictatorship, Núñez carried out a number of innovations in this area, too (starting in his first presidency, as already noted). Their significance is less clear than that of his political and religious reforms. Increased tariffs no doubt gave some help to the artisans, but official protectionism was not systematic enough to spur real industrialization. Creation of the official Banco Nacional, also dating back to Núñez's 1880–1882 term, led to the issuing of the Colombian national government's first paper money, which in due course replaced that issued by private financial institutions. Starting in the mid-1880s, as a matter of fact, the Banco Nacional issued too much paper currency, with inevitable inflationary effects. Both the Liberal opposition and dissident Conservatives assailed the loose-money practices of the Regeneration as a departure from theoretical orthodoxy and as a threat to the nation's international credit standing (not that it was very high to begin with). In addition, some people were obviously hurt by these practices, since wages tended as usual to lag behind the rise in prices, and creditors did not like accepting depreciated paper in payment of debts. At the same time, by causing a decline in the exchange value of the peso vis-à-vis foreign currencies, domestic inflation made imports more expensive, thereby angering import merchants although giving some additional relief to the artisans. But the process of currency depreciation tended to improve the competitive position of Colombian exports in the world market and, some scholars have argued, thus contributed to a sharp increase in export sales of coffee, which in the late nineteenth century consolidated its position as the country's dominant export crop. Evidence on this point is inconclusive, however;[3] and even now Colombia did not achieve a position of leadership in the world coffee market. That would happen only in the second decade of the following century.

As a fiscal corollary of political centralization, the government of the Regeneration regained control of some of the revenues previously levied by the states. It also devised a number of new imposts, including an export tax on coffee, which was bitterly assailed as an unwarranted stumbling block in the way of closer integration with the North Atlantic economy. The coffee export tax came only after the death of Núñez; but he was as intent as any of his collaborators on generating new revenues, among other reasons because he saw for the national government an enlarged role in the promotion of railroads and public works, with a view to remedying the woeful inadequacy of the country's economic infrastructure. However, the new regime could never generate enough resources to accomplish much in this regard. One small achievement was the completion in 1889 of the first railroad into Bogotá, but it was the one that stretched a mere 40 kilometers across the Sabana, linking the capital with the small town of Facatativá. The equipment for it, including rails and disassembled locomotives, had been brought with great difficulty over a primitive cart trail up from the Magdalena River. Various other railroad lines begun earlier inched forward, and the Cúcuta-Zulia line, for instance, had been completed in 1888. Yet, aside from monetary policy, and despite Núñez's rhetorical commitment to a more activist state, there was no really sharp break—economically—from the preceding Liberal era. World market conditions and the basic features of Colombian topography and physical resources continued to have far more to do with the state of production and commerce than anything the government did or did not do.

Even if scant progress was made toward modernizing the basic transportation system, some conveniences were making their appearance in the larger towns and cities—generally as a result of private initiative, though with the encouragement of municipal authorities. The changes could be seen most clearly in Bogotá, which obtained its first telephones in 1884 and electric lighting (to supplement the gas introduced earlier) some six years later. During the same period a municipally chartered private company built a modern aqueduct with metal pipes to replace the badly deteriorated colonial-era water system, which had supplied only public fountains and a few public or private buildings. These and similar innovations, however, still served mainly government offices located in the city center and upper-class dwellings nearby. The great majority of Bogotanos continued to draw water from open ditches running through the city or from fountains in the streets and plazas. They certainly did not yet have telephones; nor did they patronize the racetrack that opened for the entertainment of the elite in 1898. Indeed, "progress" of this sort served to highlight the class distinctions that had always existed but had been less glaring as long as even the more wealthy inhabitants adhered, for sheer lack of alternatives, to a lifestyle of relative simplicity.

Increasing social inequality could not be fairly blamed on specific Regeneration policies, and certainly it is not what chiefly bothered opposition spokesmen. The Liberal Party, in particular, was far more concerned with political excesses, which did occur, whether or not Núñez personally was to blame for them. Though titular president until his death in 1894, Núñez spent most of his time in his native Cartagena while someone else took immediate charge of the government in Bogotá. Toward the end, that someone was Miguel Antonio Caro, who as vice-president was also Núñez's successor to fill out his final term of 1892–1898. These were years of continual repression, in any case, from the standpoint of the Liberals, who found themselves totally denied executive office at all levels and thus even more thoroughly excluded from power than the Conservatives in the period 1863–1885, when under the federal system they at least had a chance to control individual states. Liberals similarly complained that they were cheated out of their fair share of elective positions in the national Congress, departmental assemblies, and municipal councils. Between 1896 and 1904 the Liberals were able to elect only two members of the Chamber of Representatives; and though their party undoubtedly enjoyed only minority support in the nation at large, there were many election districts where it could still have won under conditions of fair competition. A number of Liberals were sent into exile, and some opposition newspapers were silenced—although the pattern was more one of intermittent crackdowns than of systematic harassment.

The Liberals were not the only targets of official repression. Among other victims were the Bogotá artisans, who had been favorably impressed by Núñez's tariff policy but inconvenienced by rising prices. In January 1893 the artisans were goaded into mass rioting by an article in a progovernment newspaper that cast aspersions on their moral character; between forty and forty-five persons were killed in this remote precursor of the 1948 *Bogotazo*. In its aftermath intermittent restrictions were placed on artisan political activity, and artisans were subjected to intensified surveillance by a Bogotá police force in the process of being professionalized under an imported French technical expert.[4] The grievances of the Liberal Party, even so, posed the greatest threat to political stability. Liberal depictions of the Regeneration as a full-fledged dictatorship were overdrawn, but things were bad enough to goad the Liberals more than once into armed rebellion, in which they invariably lost. One such instance was a short-lived Liberal uprising in 1895. Far more serious was the War of a Thousand Days, fought from 1899 to 1902.

TWIN CALAMITIES: THE THOUSAND DAYS' WAR AND LOSS OF PANAMA

Rafael Núñez had insisted that his "Regeneration" was the alternative to national catastrophe, but the achievement of his program did not prevent, and in some ways even abetted, two separate catastrophes that struck Colombia about the turn of the century: the most lethal of all the country's civil wars and the dismemberment of its territory. The first of these calamities immediately followed another disputed election, in which, according to the Liberals, the outgoing Caro administration had arbitrarily imposed its own choice as president, thereby trampling on the rights of Liberals and dissident Conservatives. Since the administration's choice was Manuel A. Sanclemente, over eighty years of age and more than a little feeble, the Liberals assumed that Caro meant to continue ruling from behind the scenes and that consequently there was small likelihood of any real improvement in the political situation.

A good case can be made that the outbreak of civil war was also triggered, at least in part (as argued most forcefully by the historian Charles Bergquist),[5] by another round of economic crisis. The downturn in commodity exports associated with the demise of the previous Liberal hegemony had given way to a surge of coffee exports in the early years of the Regeneration; but rapidly increasing production, in Colombia and other coffee-growing countries, led to a sharp fall in the world price in the latter half of the 1890s—a fall whose impact on Colombia was severely aggravated, according to the government's critics, by official economic policies. Here they had in mind not just its alleged monetary mismanagement but the imposition in 1895 of the export tax on coffee. It is hard to say exactly how much truth the charges contained, but at a minimum the country's economic distress intensified opposition to the regime among Liberals and Conservative dissidents, of whom the latter had their greatest stronghold precisely in Antioquia, a major coffee-growing region. The dissidents—taking the name of Históricos, or Historical Conservatives, in opposition to Caro's Nationalists, who were the direct heirs of Núñez and his National Party—never entered into formal alliance with the Liberals; but their disaffection gave the Liberals encouragement and necessarily weakened the government in Bogotá. Thus, few were surprised when, in late 1899, militant Liberals unleashed the new round of civil warfare that was to last roughly three years and contribute, indirectly, to the loss of Panama. Within the Liberal Party there was a faction of moderates who foresaw, if not the loss of Panama, some of the other ill effects the war was sure to bring, but the party's frustrations were by this point simply too great to allow for temporizing.

The Liberals were disappointed to discover that the Historical Conservatives, when the chips were down, would stand with their intraparty rivals and support the government in power rather than give aid and comfort to the other party. In this respect their behavior exactly replicated that of the Independent Liberals who so disappointed rebellious Conservatives in 1876. The Liberals nevertheless managed almost at once to put both an army and a Magdalena River flotilla into action. The river fleet was soon destroyed by government forces, but the fortunes of the war on land—fought principally in the eastern department of Santander, which had been a stronghold of Radical Liberals during the federal era—proved fickle.

A Liberal defeat at Bucaramanga on November 13, 1899, was followed in December by a decisive Liberal victory when forces under

Generals Rafael Uribe Uribe and Benjamín Herrera prevailed over a larger government army in the battle of Peralonso. The Liberals did not follow up this victory by pursuing their enemy to the gates of Bogotá, as they might well have tried to do. Instead, lulled by success into overconfidence, they lost time while awaiting government concessions that never came. What came instead was a decisive Conservative victory in the battle of Palonegro, fought from May 11 to May 26, 1900. During the two weeks that the battle lasted without letup, the two armies, numbering some 25,000 men between them, suffered over 4,000 casualties—the Liberals suffering most. The stench from decomposing bodies of men and animals that littered the field became almost unbearable. Doctors and nurses, especially on the revolutionary side, were unable to cope with the number of wounded, many of whom were left to die in excruciating pain; and the pollution of water supplies compounded the ravages of disease, which in the war generally were even more lethal than the shots fired in combat. In the end the Liberals lost not only the battle but great quantities of arms and equipment that they could never replace, and a momentum that they never truly recovered.

After Palonegro the Liberals were unable to wage conventional warfare—except on the Isthmus of Panama and, intermittently, the Caribbean coast—and were reduced to an irregular war of guerrilla fighting in the vain hope of wearing down the government in power. This variety of warfare was most prevalent in the upper Magdalena Valley and adjoining Andean slopes, west and south of Bogotá, an area of rapidly expanding settlement (attracted by the recent surge in coffee production) in which traditional institutions were relatively weak. Before long, the guerrilla struggle came to be marked by outbreaks of brutality and banditry on both sides, to the point where alarmed upper-class Liberals—who had little real control over the rural bands nominally affiliated with their party—grew more and more anxious for a negotiated settlement to the civil war.

Prospects for such a settlement had briefly seemed favorable in the latter part of 1900, after Historical Conservatives promoted a coup that deposed the aged and ailing President Sanclemente in favor of his vice-president, the only slightly younger José Manuel Marroquín. Once in office, however, Marroquín proved equally obdurate, and it was not until almost the end of 1902 that the war did in fact come to a close. Sheer exhaustion helped force the issue. The conventional estimate of fatalities from the conflict is the remarkably high figure of one hundred thousand, which in a population of around four million at the time works out to 2.5 percent of all Colombians (and naturally a much higher proportion of adult males). This is a statistic repeated from one text to another, without anybody's knowing exactly how it was originally arrived at, and it is probably too high. Still, the bloodletting was bad enough to underscore demands for peace, and economic costs of the war had the same effect. Not only were production and trade intermittently disrupted in much of the country, but Liberals and Conservatives alike were called upon to pay for the mayhem. Liberals paid the most, since they were hit by the government with punitive forced loans, but government supporters could not avoid bearing part of the burden.

No one, certainly, could escape the impact of the runaway inflation that resulted from the government's increasing reliance on the printing press to pay its military and other expenses. When more suitable paper stock was not available at the government printing office, paper that had been prepared for chocolate wrappers at a local factory was fed into the presses, with the brand name still clearly visible on the resulting currency.[6] The value of the peso, which had been on the order of four to the dollar at the start of the conflict, was more than one hundred to the dollar by November 1902.[7] Even with the help of unbacked paper currency, the government was so hard-pressed that—to cite just one example—it could no longer maintain the country's three leper colonies, whose patients were turned loose to wander through the nearby towns and byways, fending for themselves.

Still another incentive for peace was the critical state of negotiations with the United States for a concession to build a canal across the Isthmus of Panama. The fact that Panama itself was one of the main battle theaters in the late stages of the struggle was more than a little awkward in this regard, though it did not actually disturb isthmian transit: the government in Bogotá had no choice but to agree to the landing of U.S. forces to protect the transit route. (And their presence incidentally protected the terminal cities of Panama and Colón from falling into the hands of the revolutionists.) More serious was the government's inability to give concerted attention to the canal negotiations as long as the country was torn apart in civil war, to say nothing of the potential weakening of Colombia's bargaining position vis-à-vis the attractions of the rival Nicaraguan canal route. Appropriately enough, the agreement that finally ended the war was the so-called Treaty of the *Wisconsin*, signed aboard a U.S. warship off the Panamanian coast in November 1902. Like a preliminary peace treaty signed one month earlier by Liberal forces in the Caribbean coastal region of northern Colombia, it offered guarantees of personal protection to the ex-revolutionaries but no explicit promises of political or other reforms. The Liberals' resort to violence to achieve their objectives had, once again, proved counterproductive.

The disastrous denouement of the isthmian canal question came a year later, with the successful separation of Panama from Colombia, although the historical roots of that secession can be traced back to the time when Panama first became a part of Colombia, or more precisely of colonial New Granada. As noted in a preceding chapter, the relationship got off to a poor start because the Spanish authorities shifted Panama from Peruvian to New Granadan jurisdiction at the very time the isthmus was entering a period of difficult economic readjustment. After independence, Panamanian leaders looked on the customs regulations and the civil disturbances of Colombia as factors inhibiting what they considered to be the natural mission of the isthmus, to serve as a world emporium of free trade; and more than once Panama declared at least temporary independence of Bogotá. It always returned to the fold before long, but politically it showed a consistent preference for federalism, as a means of maximizing Panamanian regional autonomy; and in this last respect the ultracentralism of the Regeneration's political settlement proved a crushing setback to Panamanian aspirations.

Among the complaints of Panamanians was that—through taxes generated by the transit trade, annuities paid by the Panama Railroad Company, and other special funding sources—Panama produced far more revenue for the treasury in Bogotá than it ever got back in services rendered. They would no doubt have put up with this discrimination and with their subordinate status indefinitely, however, provided they could continue to profit from the transit business; and it was on this last point that Panama's relationship with the rest of Colombia finally broke down. The failure of the French to construct a sea-level canal had at least left Panama with the freight and passenger traffic that used the existing railroad, even while discussions proceeded concerning a possible new canal to be built by the United States. From the Panamanian standpoint the one thing to be avoided at all costs was construction of a canal somewhere else. For this reason the mere chance that the United States would eventually choose to build a canal in Nicaragua, if negotiations with Colombia failed, caused Panamanian merchants and politicians to follow those negotiations, even amid the Thousand Days' War, with a sense of urgency that other Colombians seldom displayed.

In September 1902, in the closing weeks of the war, the Colombian chargé in Washington, Tomás Herrán, did finally sign a treaty with the U.S. secretary of state, John Hay, for the construction of a canal through the isthmus. The treaty gave the United States permanent control of a narrow strip in which the canal was to be built; and in other ways, too, the terms of the agreement accurately reflected the weak bargaining position of the Colombian negotiator. But the precise terms were less important to Panama's leading families and to the international assortment of canal promoters interested in the Panama route than the mere fact of the agreement. Even though some in Bogotá firmly believed that U.S. spokesmen were bluffing when they suggested that failure of Colombia to ratify the treaty would cause their country to look to Nicaragua instead, in Panama there was no disposition to put the United States to that test. The danger that Panama would secede if the treaty was rejected was perfectly evident even before the Colombian Senate began its deliberations on whether to ratify the agreement.

In the rest of Colombia as well, there were people who believed that a canal on less than optimum terms was better than no Panama Canal at all—or at least no Panama Canal under Colombian joint auspices. These pragmatic voices were lost, however, in the debate that developed. Led by former president Miguel Antonio Caro, whose inability to compromise in domestic matters had helped bring on the Thousand Days' War, opponents of the agreement correctly pointed out that the granting to the United States of permanent, direct control over the proposed canal zone was incompatible with Colombian sovereignty; it was therefore unacceptable. Whether truly convinced by Caro's arguments or fearful for political reasons of showing weakness in defense of national honor, at a time when the rival Nationalist and Historical Conservative factions were jockeying for influence in the postwar scene, the senators in early August 1903 unanimously rejected the Hay-Herrán Treaty. Significantly, this unanimity was possible only because a senator from Panama had withdrawn before the vote.

Three months later, on November 3, the Panamanian revolution

occurred; the evident complicity of the United States added to the out-
rage in Colombia but made the adoption of effective countermeasures
more difficult. There were demonstrations against the United States in
some Colombian cities, and there was bold talk of subjugating Panama by force. But the United States, citing the same treaty obligations
originally assumed for the defense of New Granadan sovereignty on
the isthmus, made clear that Colombian troops would not be allowed
to land, lest they disturb the free transit of goods from ocean to ocean,
as also guaranteed by the treaty terms. That was really all the U.S.
"intervention" that was needed. Moreover, the movement's leaders
(among them the French canal promoter Philippe Bunau-Varilla, who
hoped to be liberally compensated for his investments in the previous
French enterprise) managed to obtain the passivity of the few Colombian forces stationed on the isthmus through bribes and personal
or social influence. They had no massive popular support, but neither
was there any sign of grass-roots opposition to the coup. U.S. diplomatic recognition of the new Panamanian government followed in a
few days, with seemingly indecent haste. So, too, did that of most
other governments, including, to Colombia's distress, other Latin
American governments.

If anything made the loss of Panama easier to bear, it was the fact
that—just as Panamanians had never felt much solidarity with the rest
of Colombia—Colombians felt no deep cultural or other ties to the
people of the isthmus. Indeed, the sense of national unity in Colombia
as a whole continued weak, and scattered voices in other regions of the
country even suggested that maybe the Panamanian example was not
so much to be deplored as imitated. In a longer view, however, the loss
of Panama became one more step in the slow and painful emergence of
a Colombian national identity. It made what was left of Colombia a
little more homogeneous, and it gave Colombians an external target
that most of them, at least, could agree to react against. Above all,
together with the War of a Thousand Days that it so closely followed,
it acted as a wholesome shock to the nation's political class, demonstrating the need to rise above traditional partisanship and work
together for a while on the unfinished business of nation building.

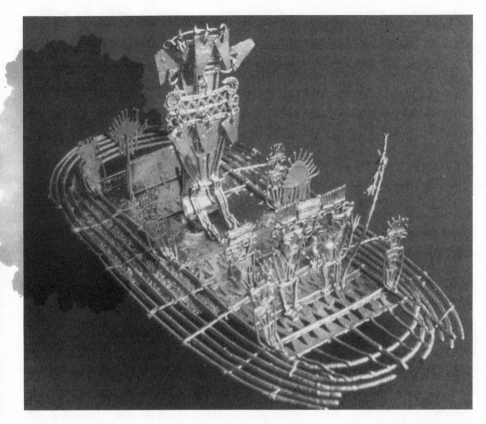

Masterpiece of Muisca goldwork: the raft of El Dorado. Courtesy of Museo de Oro, Bogotá.

Cathedral, Tunja, Boyacá. Author's collection.

Colonial Fortifications, Cartagena. Courtesy of George Scheffer.

Simón Bolívar with Native American allegorical figure. Courtesy of Quinta y Museo de Bolívar, Bogotá.

Francisco de Paula Santander as civil ruler. Courtesy of Fundación Francisco de Paula Santander, Bogotá.

Passenger travel, Indian-back. Lithographie A. Delarue, Paris, 1878.

Champán: Magdalena River pole boat. Lithographie A. Delarue, Paris, 1878.

Peasants in typical apparel, Santander region, mid-nineteenth century. Collection of Comisión Corográfica de la Nueva Granada.

Patio of wealthy merchant's home, Bogotá, mid-nineteenth century. Author's collection.

Philatelic federalism: stamp issues of the sovereign states. Author's collection.

Birthplaces of Colombian presidents. Above: Marco Fidel Suárez, Bello, Antioquia. Below: Eduardo Santos, Barrio La Candelaria, Bogotá. Author's collection.

Plaza Bolívar, Bogotá, with Colombian capitol building in background.
Above: Before *El nueve de abril*. Below: Today. Author's collection.

The martyred Jorge Eliécer Gaitán on 1949 "Liberal Almanac." Author's collection.

Gustavo Rojas Pinilla and María Eugenia (ANAPO poster). Author's collection.

Headquarters of Medellín's leading industry: Coltejer Building. Author's collection.

7

The New Age of Peace and Coffee
(1904–1930)

From the loss of Panama to the worldwide economic depression, Colombia experienced the longest period of internal political stability of its independent history. The two traditional parties displayed a capacity for civilized debate and peaceful competition that provided a heartening contrast with their recent behavior; by 1930 Colombia was on the verge of being acclaimed as an exemplary Latin American democracy. The economy, meanwhile, was setting records in its pace of growth. The expansion of coffee production and exporting was the most notable feature, but bananas, petroleum, and manufacturing industry were other poles of development. Not everything was going as well beneath as on the surface of society, but certainly within the Latin American context Colombia's leaders had much ground for satisfaction. And, needless to say, the political settling down and the economic growth were intimately related phenomena: each one was a principal cause—and effect—of the other.

CORRECTING THE EXCESSES OF THE REGENERATION:
RAFAEL REYES AND HIS LEGACY

Even though the Liberals had lost the War of a Thousand Days and thus failed in their attempt to annul the key features of Núñez's Regeneration, they had at least demonstrated that Colombia could not be governed peacefully when one of the two parties was totally excluded from power and subjected to intermittent harassment. The Historical Conservatives had maintained this position all along, and they found in the loss of Panama additional reason to seek national reconciliation. By no means were all the victorious Conservatives inclined even then to make significant concessions. By a narrow margin, however, one of the foremost champions of interparty collaboration, General Rafael

Reyes, won the first postwar presidential election and took office in Bogotá in August 1904.

Reyes was a man of provincial upper-class background, originally from the eastern department of Boyacá. He first made a name for himself, and a fortune, in the southwestern Cauca region, as a successful entrepreneur in the quinine boom of the 1870s. He lost part of that same fortune in subsequent efforts to colonize the fringes of Colombia's Amazonia. He was also a talented military commander in the civil wars of 1885 and 1895, fighting on the side of the Conservatives, but he had no taste for either fiery partisanship or ideological rigidity. On the contrary, Reyes was wholly convinced of the need for Colombians to rise above their empty party struggles and concentrate on material progress. As he stated in one passage that is automatically quoted in any discussion of his program and outlook, "In past times it was the Cross or the Koran, the sword or the book, that made the conquests of civilization; at present it is the powerful locomotive, flying along the shiny rail, breathing like a volcano, that awakens peoples to progress, to well-being, and to freedom. . . . And those who are resistant to progress are crushed under its wheels."[1]

Reyes delivered that pronouncement while serving as Colombian delegate to the Pan American Conference that met in Mexico City in 1901, during the War of a Thousand Days. Indeed, he contrived to be away from Colombia for most of the struggle; after it was finished, he became a spokesman both for Liberal-Conservative reconciliation and for approval of the Hay-Herrán Treaty, both of which he saw as prerequisites for the entry of Colombia into the locomotive age. He lost the fight for the treaty, but he won the presidency the following year with the predominant support of the Historicals and other Conservative moderates, plus the votes of whatever Liberals did in fact participate in the election. (The Liberal Party did not even try to run a slate of its own.) He likewise had the help of one local boss in the Guajira Peninsula, who threw the vote of his district's electors to Reyes by some transparent chicanery. In the end this particular instance of fraud gave Reyes his margin of victory, but it was a beneficent fraud that assured the victory of the more popular candidate: had Liberals everywhere been in a position to vote freely, Reyes would have defeated his principal rival, a less flexible Conservative, overwhelmingly.

Reyes immediately demonstrated that he meant what he said about national reconciliation by naming two Liberals to his five-man cabinet. He named members of the opposition party to lesser positions as well, and in due course he introduced the principle of guaranteed minority representation in the makeup of deliberative bodies, from municipal councils to the national Congress. Equally important, he carried out a military reform designed to convert the armed forces into a purely professional organization, above partisanship, that would both defend the nation's borders against foreign attack and unquestioningly uphold constitutional order at home. This program entailed the reorganization of military education under the auspices of a Chilean military mission, whose members passed on to Colombian officers the lessons that the Chileans themselves had been learning from a succession of German military training missions. One side effect of the Chilean presence and of the German influence that came with it was the adoption of Prussian-style dress uniforms (of which a surviving vestige in Colombia today is the use of Prussian spiked helmets by the presidential guard).

Still another aspect of the military reform was Reyes's personal effort to induce Liberal families to send their sons to military school, with a view to obtaining a more even balance of party strength in the officers' corps. Since the reformed military were supposed to be rigorously nonpartisan, the prior civilian party affiliation of officers should in principle have made no difference, but Reyes was realistically aware that party loyalties could not be simply rooted out. For that very reason among others, the military reform was not wholly to the liking of the existing Colombian army, which Reyes had inherited on taking office and which was in effect the victorious Conservative army of the late civil war. Many officers were simply politicians in uniform, not much interested in learning the latest German-Chilean military techniques and more than a little suspicious of the president's rapprochement with the Liberal enemy. Nevertheless, the reform did increasingly take hold over the following years. Though individual officers might dabble in partisan intrigues and otherwise ignore professional standards, the army as a whole compiled a record of subservience to civil authority that was not broken until 1953, in the midst of the epidemic of mostly irregular clashes between Liberals and Conservatives known to Colombians simply as *La Violencia*.

Military officers of the traditional variety were not the only ones who made the work of Reyes more difficult. He also had trouble with civilian politicians, in Congress and elsewhere, who failed to share the president's sense of urgency about what was needed to get Colombia on the right course. Soon after taking office, he began asking Congress to grant him special authorizations to revise the tax system, let railroad contracts, and take other steps for economic reconstruction and development by presidential decree. Congress did not flatly refuse to cooperate but on one pretext or another failed to vote the powers requested. Reyes therefore decided to do without Congress altogether and in early 1905 convoked in its place a national assembly, whose members were to be named directly by departmental administrators, for the purpose of reforming the constitution and adopting other emergency measures. The method of choosing the assembly produced a substantial contingent of Liberal delegates, whereas few Liberals would have won seats if back-country Conservative bosses had been free to manipulate the electoral process in the accustomed manner.

The national assembly formally adopted the principle of guaranteed minority representation for future elections. In addition, at Reyes's behest, it re-formed the nation's territorial organization, creating a number of new departments out of the former ones (which were nothing but the old states of the federal period), in the hope of diminishing the strength of traditional regional attachments and making administration more efficient. The national assembly naturally gave the president the powers he wanted in economic and fiscal matters. In fact, its eagerness to please Reyes led it even to vote an extension of his presidential term, from six years to ten.

That last feature was indicative of the increasing personalism of Reyes's rule, as was his tendency to ignore or else induce the compliant national assembly to override inconvenient legal restrictions. Before he stepped down, some individual critics had also been subject to arrest or other arbitrary treatment, so that the Reyes administration—which in practice was to last five years, not ten, and thus became known as the *quinquenio*—is generally regarded as at least a mild dictatorship. But its harshest act was the summary execution, as ordered by a purely ad hoc tribunal, of four men involved in a failed attempt to assassinate the president in 1906. This was the last assassination attempt that any Colombian president has suffered, though other public figures, notably including presidential candidates, unfortunately have not been as lucky.

High-handed though it may sometimes have been, the Reyes regime was definitely a constructive one, and not merely in its successful effort to bring the Liberals back into the mainstream of political life. Above all, Reyes is remembered for his efforts to promote economic and technological modernization in a manner that brings to mind the example of Mexico's Díaz dictatorship, which Reyes had seen at first hand and much admired. In Colombia as in Mexico, moreover, one of the strongman's primary concerns was to encourage railroad construction. The results, though, were a bit different in the two countries. Whereas Mexico already had 14,000 kilometers of track by the beginning of the twentieth century, Colombia increased the network of lines in operation from just 565 to 901 kilometers in the years 1904–1909, roughly corresponding to the Reyes presidency.[2] Even that much was accomplished at great cost in subsidies and concessions to railroad companies; but the accomplishments were still considerable. Bogotá was finally linked to the Magdalena River by rail when the Girardot Railroad, winding up the mountainsides from that river port, made connection with the route that crossed the Sabana from the capital to Facatativá. Significant progress also was made on other key routes, including the Antioquia Railroad, which would link Medellín with the Magdalena River, and the Pacific Railroad, which would link Cali with the Pacific port of Buenaventura.

Railroads, in any case, were only the most visible form of infrastructural development. Reyes is the president who gave Colombia a Ministry of Public Works; and he strove both to improve river navigation on the Magdalena and to expand the nation's wholly inadequate road system. When he became president, there were still almost no roads suitable for wheeled vehicles outside the towns and cities; when he left office, one could reach even his birthplace in Boyacá, over 200 kilometers from the capital, by cart or carriage—or by automobile. Reyes himself, while president, put his seal of approval on the automobile by taking a ride in the first one to reach Bogotá.

Reyes also was eager to create the conditions for economic recovery and development by placing Colombia's currency again on a sound footing. His most important measure in this regard was a monetary reform whereby he issued new pesos equivalent in value to one hundred of the depreciated units then in circulation. The new currency not only helped lighten people's pockets of excess paper money but simplified business transactions and had an important psychological effect, since the peso was returned to approximate parity with the U.S. dollar. By adhering to generally orthodox fiscal policies, Reyes was able to maintain the value of the new currency even though he did not make much progress toward retiring the nearly worthless previous currency from circulation. In a related move Reyes reached an agreement with foreign creditors for the resumption of service on the Colombian foreign debt—thus reestablishing (for the first time since well before the War of a Thousand Days) Colombia's credit rating in international money markets. To accomplish this objective as quickly as possible, he accepted most of the creditors' demands with little quibbling, but he thereby achieved the further result that most interested him: a climate more conducive to foreign investment in Colombia, which he considered essential for national development.

Certain other official actions gave help to specific industries. There were tax benefits and subsidies for export agriculture as well as for various lines of manufacturing, while the Reyes tariff of 1905 and subsequent measures provided a more effective level of protection for "infant industries" (and some not so infant) than had the earlier tariff increases of Rafael Núñez. Some of the results of these efforts are discussed in more detail below. It must be emphasized, however, that— just as his accomplishments in railway building were impressive only by Colombian standards—Reyes's activism in other areas of economic policy was always circumscribed by the nation's continuing scarcity of capital and infrastructure and by the government's own lack of financial resources. As of 1909 the Colombian state was operating on annual revenues of around sixteen million pesos, or not quite four dollars per capita.[3] Reyes had a coherent vision, and he set some important precedents, but the return of peace meant more for the growth of the economy than anything the national administration was capable of doing.

The president's own realization of the limits imposed by material underdevelopment—to say nothing of the lack of sufficient trained personnel—undoubtedly contributed to his impatience with all those who in his view were set on making his work even more difficult through needless harping on legal technicalities. Nevertheless, his own development programs, even if on the whole well received, exposed him to additional criticism because of the instances of graft and favoritism (some undeniable, others merely rumored) in the awarding of contracts and the like. Thus, the level of opposition to Reyes steadily increased as time went on. What then brought it to a final crescendo was his attempted settlement of Colombian differences with the

United States that resulted from U.S. involvement in the loss of Panama.

Both as a growing market for Colombian exports and as a potential source of investment capital, the United States had an important role to play in Reyes's plans for a stronger, more prosperous Colombia; and one essential step was to restore normal relations between the two countries. Relations had never technically been broken, but they were certainly strained. Reyes accordingly negotiated an agreement in which the United States granted Colombia a modest indemnity and preferential treatment in the use of the future canal, while Colombia formally recognized Panamanian independence. The terms generally anticipated those of the Urrutia-Thomson Treaty, which was finally ratified between the two countries in 1922; but when Reyes entered into negotiations, the time was not yet ripe. There is no indication that Boyacá peasants or cowboys on the eastern plains were much exercised over the issue, but political opinion makers, students and intellectuals, and people who opposed Reyes on any other ground spared no effort in depicting the agreement as a betrayal of national interests and honor. The result was a hardening of anti-Reyes sentiment, as reflected in serious public disturbances in Bogotá in March 1909, which led to a shelving of the proposed agreement and, by the middle of the year, the quiet departure of Reyes himself from Colombia.

THE LAST TWO DECADES
OF CONSERVATIVE HEGEMONY

Although the Panama question brought matters to a head, a more fundamental reason for the fall of Reyes was the fact that dictatorship of any kind—even a mild and generally constructive one—rubbed the members of Colombia's *clase política*, Conservative and Liberal, the wrong way. It limited their own opportunities to cut a fancy figure on the political stage, and it was inherently less predictable than the workings of a properly constitutional government, thus posing at least a potential threat to the socioeconomic interests that both traditional parties, directly or indirectly, represented. But the political system devised by Reyes, insofar as it involved a peaceful modus vivendi between the parties, managed to survive him. A constitutional reform in 1910 made permanent the principle of guaranteed minority representation in Congress and other deliberative bodies; at the same time it reduced the presidential term to four years, with prohibition of immediate reelection. (The vice-presidency was abolished for good measure.) Moreover, although Conservatives remained in control of government until 1930 (even Carlos E. Restrepo, made president by the 1910 constituent assembly and nominally head of a new third party known as Republican Union, was in reality a Conservative), they continued Reyes's practice of sharing administrative appointments with the Liberals. Unlike Reyes, they avoided dictatorial tactics; and the successive Conservative presidents scrupulously stepped down at the end of their terms—except one, who left sooner by voluntary resignation.

Liberals, of course, did not feel they were getting their fair share of either executive offices or elected legislative positions. Indeed, elections, though regularly held, were almost always marked by scattered incidents of violence in the back country and by charges of fraud that were often well founded. Liberal voters might suffer intimidation on election day, while Conservative strongholds often produced suspiciously high voter turnouts. In the presidential election of 1914, for example, the ultra-Conservative small town of Guasca, Cundinamarca, cast roughly 20 percent as many votes as Bogotá, though it had at most 5 percent of Bogotá's population;[4] and the disproportion in number of literate adults would have been even greater, at a time when literacy was still required for voting in national elections. As in the southern United States at the same period, where it was used at the expense of blacks, arbitrary implementation or nonimplementation of a literacy test was one handy means of controlling access to the polls. At least the Liberals were not wholly shut out, as they had been from Núñez to Reyes—and they now stopped making revolutions.

Actually, the old issues that had divided the parties in the nineteenth century—the sacred principles of constitutional organization and church-state relations—were becoming less and less important. As far as the church question was concerned, Liberals remained unhappy with the religious settlement of the Regeneration, but they were learning to live with it. Where possible, they established non-church private institutions of higher education, to minimize the effects of church control on their children's education. The Liberals were also coming to recognize that some strengthening of central authority, as carried out by Núñez, had in fact been necessary. They were accordingly losing interest in federalism and instead hoping to increase their own power and influence at national level. Rafael Uribe Uribe, who had been a leading Liberal general in the late war and then one of the strongest Liberal supporters of Reyes, even went so far as to espouse what he called "state socialism," although what it really amounted to was only a mild flirtation with social-democratic reformism. That in itself, to be sure, represented a break with the doctrinaire laissez-faire position of the former Radical Liberalism. Uribe Uribe was assassinated in 1914 without ever having a chance to put his ideas in practice; but other Liberals began talking of social and labor reforms, at least to the extent needed to blunt the potential challenge posed by small socialist and other radical groups that began appearing, especially in the 1920s. These groups were inevitably influenced in some degree by such outside developments as the Mexican and Russian Revolutions; their roots and leadership were almost wholly Colombian, with their main strength coming from urban artisans, transportation workers, and disaffected professionals.

The incipient leftist movement in politics and labor was reflected on the intellectual scene in the appearance of ephemeral radical publications and in the formation of small socialist discussion groups in Bogotá and other cities. These developments, however, were overshadowed by the continued flowering of more traditional forms of cultural activity, which in the late nineteenth century had won Bogotá the name of "Athens of South America." Men of letters produced learned essays and clever conversation on almost any subject except the deprivations suffered by the Colombian masses, and they excelled above all in the writing and recitation of poetry on every conceivable occasion. An exception was the novelist José Eustacio Rivera, whose *La vorágine*, published in 1924, was a realistic tale of the exploitation of rubber workers in the Amazon forests. More typical was Guillermo Valencia, scion of an aristocratic Popayán family and author of poetry in the "modernist" style, making much display of superficial erudition and quite out of touch with Colombian reality. He was lionized in his own time as a poet of classic stature; unlike Rivera's masterpiece, his compositions are seldom read today.

Valencia was in addition an active Conservative politician and unsuccessful presidential candidate in 1918 and again in 1930, defeated the first time by the candidate of a rival faction of his own party and the second time by the first Liberal to become president in almost fifty years. Had he won, he would have taken his place among a series of generally well-meaning and conscientious Conservative chief executives, adorned with numerous good qualities although not always the particular good qualities called for by the times. As José Vicente Concha (1914–1918) later observed concerning his own administration, in words recalling those of the Radical Eustorgio Salgar (when in his inaugural address he disclaimed any intention of high achievement): "I should not be judged for the new bricks that I laid, but for the tremendous ruins that I avoided."[5] Concha indeed was no bricklayer in the manner of Rafael Reyes, but among other things he successfully maintained Colombian neutrality in World War I. The last in the series of Conservative presidents, Miguel Abadía Méndez (1926–1930), was a professor of constitutional law at the time of his election; like Mariano Ospina Rodríguez in the 1850s, he continued teaching his courses even after taking office: the one change was that students now had to come to class in the presidential palace. The president's approachability was no doubt an attractive character trait; yet when the same president was faced with a major banana workers' strike in 1928, he could come up with no better solution than to send in the army to repress the strikers by force.

The most interesting of the presidents from Reyes to Abadía Méndez, even if not for any great accomplishments while in office, is the one who resigned before completing his term, Marco Fidel Suárez (1918–1921). He is noteworthy for his social background, or lack of it, being the illegitimate son of an Antioquia peasant girl. He has therefore been cited as an example by those who would deny that a narrow oligarchic caste has historically dominated Colombian life, as is often alleged. The peasant hut in which Suárez was born is the Colombian equivalent of a Kentucky log cabin; fittingly, it is preserved today as a tourist attraction, wholly enclosed in a glass-and-concrete monument constructed by the giant textile company Fabricato, which has its main plant in Suárez's home town of Bello. The company no doubt wished to drive home to its workers the point that any of them, by working hard enough, could become president, too. But Suárez, by the time he reached the presidency, was a religious mystic, literary dilettante, and long-time Conservative functionary who did very little for his fellow peasants. In fact, during the Suárez presidency the working class received what one labor historian has called its "baptism of blood."[6] A demonstration instigated by Bogotá tailors against an announced plan to buy military uniforms and other equipment abroad degenerated into violence, with seven rioters killed and others wounded by shots from the presidential guard. By the time of the incident, the uniform proposal had been canceled, so the demonstration itself was uncalled for. The official response was even more uncalled for.

Suárez was at the same time an ardent admirer of the United States; Abraham Lincoln, not surprisingly, was his special hero. Because of his own antecedents, he felt an obvious attraction to the land that made a fetish of the self-made man, and he translated his admiration into a guiding principle for Colombian foreign policy, which he termed the "Doctrine of the Polar Star." He meant that Colombia must look northward, toward the pole (the United States), to find a model of social and political democracy and a natural collaborator in political and economic affairs. In line with this concept, Suárez was deeply committed to achieving ratification of the Urrutia-Thomson Treaty, which finally settled the Panama question. The treaty provided for the payment of an indemnity of twenty-five million dollars for the U.S. role in the loss of the isthmus and otherwise regularized Colombian relations with the United States and the new Republic of Panama. When he became convinced that opposition to him personally was obstructing ratification of the treaty in the Colombian Congress, Suárez resigned the presidency and left to his interim successor the task of guiding the treaty to a successful conclusion.

It was certainly appropriate that the president elected in 1922 for the next complete term, Pedro Nel Ospina, was a figure with the same enthusiasm for building economic infrastructure as Rafael Reyes. Thanks to the U.S. indemnity as well as the loans that were plentifully available from Wall Street bankers in the boom years of the 1920s, he had far more resources at his disposal, and these were used for a veritable binge of railroad construction and other public works. Departmental governments, busily raising their own foreign loans, took part in the frenzy, which resulted in valuable extensions of the Pacific and Antioquia Railroads along with such ostentatious projects as the construction of a gubernatorial palace in Medellín designed to look like a medieval cathedral, replete with flying buttresses and other exotic features. The total length of the railway network increased from 1,481 kilometers in 1922 to 2,434 in 1929, and new highways were filling at least some of the gaps between the railway lines.

At Barranquilla in 1919 the air age arrived as well, with the establishment of the Sociedad Colombo-Alemana de Transportes Aéreos, or SCADTA. Despite its name—Colombo-German Society of Air Transport—SCADTA was a Colombian corporation, founded by members of the local German community. Reorganized during World War II as Avianca, it is the oldest commercial airline in the Americas and generally accounted to be second oldest in the entire world. It was an immediate success, because—despite recent advances—the nation's land transportation routes remained sorely inadequate. Magdalena River steamboats were still the standard means of travel between the Caribbean coast and the interior when SCADTA inaugurated its air service, which did not even wait for the construction of landing fields but used hydroplanes that landed on the river itself. The initial "airport" serving the Colombian capital was thus the waters of the Magdalena at the river port of Girardot, from which train service was available the rest of the way.

Pedro Nel Ospina became the first chief executive in active service anywhere in the world to ride in a commercial airliner. At least such is the claim made by Avianca public relations people, and though it might be hard to prove, there is no denying the president's keen interest in transportation improvements of all sorts. Ospina showed a similarly keen interest in financial infrastructure, playing host to the Kemmerer Mission of U.S. fiscal experts, on whose recommendation the Banco de la República was created in 1923 as a modern central bank of issue with broad responsibility to regulate the money supply and exchange rate. One immediate result was a sharp drop in interest rates, as the bank's operations brought currency demand and supply more nearly into balance. Private financial interests, however, received a major role in the setting of central bank policy, in keeping with the general tenor of economic policy throughout the period: the functions of the state were increasing, but the ruling Conservatives (and for that matter most Liberals) still believed that the state's main function was to create the conditions for private enterprise to prosper. Although attempts were made to regulate the private sector in the interests of the workers or of society at large (a workers' accident compensation law was enacted as early as 1915), they were not extensive or consistently enforced. And though a modest income tax had been introduced in 1919, customs duties continued to provide the bulk of government revenue, quite painlessly as far as wealthy Colombians were concerned.

There was little interest in using revenues for programs of education and welfare aimed at the popular classes. In the field of education, a first woman doctor was graduated at university level in 1925, but only slow progress was made toward the goal of spreading basic literacy—something that a majority of Colombians still lacked in 1930.[7] In that year the figure for average life expectancy, as good an indicator as any of general health conditions, stood at thirty-four years; compared with thirty and a half years in 1910,[8] this figure reflected modest improvement but certainly no high level of emphasis on public health programs. Indeed, the one area of significantly increased emphasis remained public works: the respective ministry's share of the national budget rose from 3.6 percent in 1911 to 20.1 percent in 1920 and 35 percent in 1929.[9] These, of course, were expenditures with more direct economic payoff than investments in health or education, and with the further advantage of being paid for in large part out of the indemnity funds and foreign credit (to say nothing of the comfortable benefits that accrued to public works contractors).

Public works likewise received far more emphasis than military expenditures. The budget of the war ministry, which had stood at 30 percent of the total in 1911, fell to 14 percent in 1920 and continued falling until it was only 8.8 percent in 1929. This decline accurately reflected the inner logic of the Conservative ascendancy itself, which was thoroughly civilian in spirit and even somewhat wary of military power. Colombian Conservatives preferred to base their rule on the strength of social and religious tradition—on the natural deference of the lower orders toward their social betters and, above all, on the pervasive influence of the Roman Catholic church. Not since the colonial era had state-church relations been as close as they became in the closing years of the nineteenth century and would remain through the 1920s.

The alliance was not so much between the church and the state per se as between the church and the Conservative Party that controlled the state. Folkloric instances of the activism of local Catholic clergy on behalf of the Conservative cause abound during these years. As an Antioqueño priest advised his flock in 1913, "Men and women who listen to me, bear in mind that parricide, infanticide, theft, crime, adultery, incest, etc., are lesser evils than to be liberal, especially as far as women are concerned."[10] Another such priest, in reporting election results in his locality, gave the score as "Catholics, 435; rebels against

God and His Holy Church, 217."[11] Spiritual penalties might be threatened from the pulpit for parishioners who dared to read the Liberal press. It was not just uneducated back-country priests who took such positions. The diocesan authorities of Pamplona not only joined in the anathematizing of Liberal newspapers but once imposed the pain of excommunication on anyone who even supported a dissident Conservative candidate.

To the extent that the faithful took seriously all the injunctions of the clergy (and many of them did), they would have been far too preoccupied with the struggle against impious, freethinking Liberalism to be concerned with mere social and economic injustices; but, in addition, the general tenor of church teaching continued to encourage automatic acceptance of the existing order that God in His wisdom had provided. Even the relatively few priests who by the 1920s were showing an interest in labor problems and promoting the establishment of Catholic unions thus put their emphasis on bread-and-butter issues and goals of individual improvement, as distinct from the advocacy of structural changes.

In some parts of Colombia, marked by a lower degree of popular religiosity and lower clergy-population ratio, the political and social influence of the church was measurably less. The Caribbean coastal region is the most obvious example. But in small towns of the Andean interior, much of life continued to revolve around the parish church, whose festivals were a release from community boredom and whose resident priest was the final arbiter of behavior. This was a pattern perfectly suited to the persistence of Conservative rule, and the Conservatives in return did what they could to undergird the church's position short of actually abolishing constitutional religious toleration. Symptomatic in this regard was the marriage legislation adopted in 1924 (the Ley Concha). Ostensibly designed to regulate the institution of civil marriage, which had not technically been abolished in the Regeneration but was surrounded with many practical difficulties, the new legislation simply codified those difficulties. Under its terms anyone baptized as a Roman Catholic could marry in a civil ceremony only after first making a public abjuration of the Catholic faith. In Bogotá or Barranquilla this was not, perhaps, an impossible condition. In smaller cities and rural villages, where the pressures for religious conformity and unofficial penalties for defying them were great, it certainly was.

THE TAKEOFF
OF THE COFFEE INDUSTRY

Up to a point, the relative tranquility of the post-Reyes years resulted from the mere fact that both Liberals and Conservatives were finding substitute outlets for their aggressive energies in economic pursuits— most notably, in the country's coffee industry, which finally came into its own in the second and third decades of the present century. From 1910 to 1920 total Colombian exports grew at a rate of more than 10 percent a year, and the greatest part of that growth was accounted for by coffee. Annual exports, which were one million 60-kilo bags in 1913, reached two million in 1921 and stood at three million by 1930.[12] Colombia had emerged as the world's second leading coffee producer, displacing Venezuela and now exceeded only by Brazil. It is hard to say precisely when Colombia attained this ranking, because some of the coffee classified as Venezuelan had all along been of Colombian origin, exported via Maracaibo. But the ranking would remain constant, at least until 1990, when Colombia actually led Brazil in value if not in volume of coffee exported.[13]

This explosion of coffee production was the culmination of a long and slow process. The first coffee seems to have been exported from Colombia at least as early as 1835; but the growth of production and exports was for many years unimpressive, so that only in the late nineteenth century did coffee emerge as the principal Colombian export commodity. In 1898 it accounted for almost half of the nation's export trade; but that was half of a fairly unimpressive amount, and there soon followed a decline in both coffee exports and total foreign trade under the combined impact of the War of a Thousand Days and depressed world coffee prices. The Reyes *quinquenio*, however, brought an end to political and military disruptions, and in 1909 prices began to rise sharply; they faltered again during World War I (with shipping uncertainties and temporary loss of the German market) but recovered nicely in the 1920s. In 1924 coffee came to represent almost 80 percent of the nation's export value, which in turn was then six times the 1898 total.

The conditions of world demand obviously had much to do with the rise of coffee production and sales. Spurred by innovations in processing and marketing, the custom of drinking coffee in North America and much of Europe had spread by the early twentieth century from the middle and upper strata of society to broad segments of the working class. In the United States in particular, coffee was now a standard item of popular consumption. Another positive external circumstance was the off-and-on Brazilian campaign, starting in 1906, to support the international price by holding excess stocks of coffee off the market. Other producers such as Colombia, in effect, enjoyed a free ride at Brazilian expense.

Domestic factors, however, contributed to Colombia's growing success in the world coffee market. Inflationary issues of paper money, which led to exchange-rate depreciation, may have played a role in the earlier stages of coffee expansion (according to a thesis noted in the previous chapter); but they can hardly have been a factor during the years of most rapid growth in the present century, which were a time of relative monetary stability. Transportation improvements, on the other hand, unquestionably played an important role, and more so in the early twentieth than in the late nineteenth century. The extension of the railway system measurably reduced the freight costs for coffee grown in much of the Colombian interior, as did the gradual improvement of mule trails that fed into the rail network. In particular, by 1914 the Antioquia Railroad, running from Medellín to Puerto Berrío on the Magdalena, was completed (except for one small link in its middle portion); and in 1915 the Pacific Railroad succeeded in connecting Cali and the central Cauca Valley with the Pacific coast at Buenaventura. Buenaventura thus became the first Colombian port with a direct rail link to the interior, and it was soon handling the greatest amount of cargo, coffee in particular. It did so not only because of the railroad but also because of the Panama Canal, which had opened one year before, in 1914, greatly reducing the cost and time of transportation from Colombia's Pacific coast to world markets. Colombia, paradoxically, was perhaps the South American country to derive greatest economic benefit from the building of the canal through territory that had just been wrested from it.

The critical importance of the Antioquia and Pacific Railroads and of the Panama Canal for the expansion of coffee cultivation was closely related to a westward shift in the center of gravity of the coffee industry itself. Though coffee is grown to some extent in almost every section of Colombia (see map 3), export production was originally centered in the present department of Norte de Santander; by the late nineteenth century, the area south and west of Bogotá going toward

Map 3. Contemporary Colombia: Political Divisions and the Coffee Industry

the Magdalena River was also becoming covered with coffee plantations. However, in the first third of the present century, these older
coffee-growing regions were eclipsed by Antioquia and the areas
directly south of Antioquia in the Cordillera Central and Cauca Valley
(present-day departments of Caldas, Quindío, Risaralda, and parts of
Tolima and Valle del Cauca), which since the mid-nineteenth century
had been receiving a steady stream of Antioqueño colonization. As the
colonists cleared the forest and founded new towns, they planted
mainly subsistence crops for a livelihood—until, around the turn of
the century, they began turning more and more to coffee. The coffee
trees (or "bushes," as they are also called) were readily adaptable to
the broken topography characteristic of the entire area of Antioqueño
colonization. Furthermore, coffee was a crop well suited to production
in the small family-sized units that were another characteristic of this
stream of internal migration.

The geographic shift in the coffee industry thus entailed a social
change as well, although in either case the difference was relative, not
absolute. There had always been small properties in the coffee industry
of the eastern cordillera alongside the larger plantations, especially in
Norte de Santander but also in the coffee-growing districts southwest
of Bogotá; and there was large-estate coffee in Antioquia and the areas
of Antioqueño colonization. Yet in these newer areas the most prevalent pattern was that represented by the stereotypical figure Juan Valdez of the Colombian coffee growers' television commercials: the sturdy, independent farmer who tends his own coffee trees with loving
care and the help of family members, picking each individual coffee
bean just as it reaches the point of perfect ripeness—which is why
consumers are expected to pay a slight premium to be sure of getting
the 100 percent Colombian product.

The commercials, of course, do not show the actual living and
working conditions of the Valdez family. The smallholder mode of
production proved ultimately more successful in Colombia than large-
estate production precisely because it solved a problem of labor costs
and availability that had from the start bedeviled estate owners, and it
did so by bringing to bear a vast amount of human labor that on an
hourly basis was insignificantly requited. Coffee production everywhere was labor-intensive rather than mechanized, and it was even
more so on the steep slopes of the Andes. Labor was by far the greatest
expense of large-estate owners, who experimented with different kinds

of tenancy and sharecropping arrangements alongside permanent and seasonal wage labor but could never get enough dependable help at an affordable cost—and so were at a competitive disadvantage vis-à-vis the small producer. The latter, except perhaps at harvest time, relied on his immediate family members, who received no pay at all but merely shared his food and shelter. Fortunately, the food, much of it grown between the coffee trees themselves, was generally adequate in quantity even if it may not have been well balanced nutritionally; and the housing did give minimal protection against the elements. But amenities were few. Moreover, coffee tended to be grown on the middle-altitude slopes, most often between 1,000 and 2,000 meters, where scenery is magnificent but the warm climate favors the multi-plication of insects and parasites and tropical diseases; and until recently governments had done little to offset these conditions by extending public health and medical services into rural areas.

It also goes without saying that suppliers, middlemen, and coffee exporters were more generously rewarded than the small growers. The establishment in 1927 of the Federación Nacional de Cafeteros (or FEDECAFE) gave the coffee industry a national trade association that has worked with commendable efficiency to regulate internal prices, assure supplies of credit, control the quality of the Colombian prod-uct, and much else besides; and all those involved in growing and selling coffee were invited to belong. In practice, the federation was dominated by the larger growers and the coffee merchants, who natu-rally derived the principal benefit from its services. At the same time, though, the mere fact that the small grower was himself an indepen-dent operator did give him a sense of having a stake, even if a modest one, in the existing system; and it certainly limited the extent to which he could identify with the rural (much less urban) proletariat. Rather, the landless rural workers sought to identify with *him*, aspiring to become smallholders in their own right. The tendency of tenants and sharecroppers to act like peasant proprietors—e.g., growing and sell-ing coffee on their own account even when forbidden to do so by the terms of their contracts—led to serious agrarian conflicts on the upper Magdalena Valley coffee estates during the 1920s and 1930s. Those conflicts provided the opening for a fledgling Communist movement to gain a rural foothold in the same years—paradoxically, in defense of the peasantry's petit-bourgeois aspirations.

In the country as a whole, the coffee industry had a decidedly conservatizing effect on society, making the rural masses more willing to accept not just the capitalist socioeconomic order but the traditional Liberal-Conservative political order that supported and was supported by it. And the mere fact that the country's leading industry was almost entirely in Colombian hands—foreign participation being important only in export marketing—deprived economic nationalism in Colombia of a key target. Thereby it also delayed the emergence of nationalism generally as an aggressive force.

TEXTILES, OIL, BANANAS

Though coffee came into its own in the early twentieth century as the one economic activity that affected the greatest number of people and generated the bulk of Colombia's foreign earnings, the same years brought important economic advances in other areas as well. One that had a close symbiotic relationship with coffee was the rise of industrialization. In the beginning, manufacturing industry—like the coffee industry—was almost entirely in native hands, and the growth of coffee production and sales added to the available stock of investment capital while increasing the size of the domestic market for manufactured consumer goods. It was no accident that the capital of Antioquia, Medellín, became the early industrial capital of the country.

After a string of mostly unsuccessful attempts to bring factory production to Colombia, a number of generally small enterprises had taken root in different cities by the late nineteenth century, turning out light consumer goods, such as textiles, along with processed foods and beverages. One model of successful entrepreneurship was the brewery Bavaria, founded in Bogotá by a German immigrant in 1889, which also started its own bottle factory and before long was the largest employer in the national capital apart from the government itself. However, the beginnings of serious industrialization are best dated from the administration of Rafael Reyes, who provided not only a propitious political climate but tariff protection for industrial development.

The tariff of 1905, though still primarily a revenue tariff, raised duties somewhat on imported textiles; more important, it offered a reduction in the duty on imported textile yarn and fibers. This differential between the tariff charged on semifinished and finished goods was to provide the basis and incentive for the creation of a modern manufacturing industry. Or, to put it differently, Colombians were encouraged to import textiles in unassembled form, performing only the last stage of the process locally, thanks to that tariff differential. Cotton grown in Mississippi would cross the Atlantic to England to be made into yarn, and the yarn would come back across the Atlantic to Colombia for assembly into cloth. This was perhaps a curious way to go about it, and indeed textile manufacturers did try to encourage domestic cotton production. But in the beginning it was not adequate to meet the needs of the industry. Hence, the method chosen—to import even the yarn that was needed—was the fastest and easiest way to get started.

Textile factories began springing up—especially in Medellín and its surrounding area, to a lesser extent in other cities. Coltejer, today Colombia's leading textile firm, whose office skyscraper towers over downtown Medellín, was launched in 1907. Total output grew steadily, at the expense of both domestic artisanal production and textile imports; much of the labor was provided by young women from rural villages or urban working-class homes, who toiled for wages on the order of thirty cents (U.S.) per day. In addition, they received highly protective treatment from their employers, including carefully chaperoned dormitories for those who came from towns away from Medellín and did not live at home, company chapels, and spare-time courses for personal improvement. One firm carried its paternalism to the point of requiring the young girls who tended its looms to work barefoot, so as to avoid invidious comparisons between those who could and could not afford shoes. As in the early textile industry in other countries, where women workers were also widely used, the more skilled and better-paid positions were given to men, who over time would increase their share of the textile work force. Even so, women textile workers found their meager pay an attractive alternative to such more traditional options for working-class women as domestic service and prostitution—or to having no cash income at all.

Tariffs were not the only form of official protection for new industries; tax concessions and the giving of preference in government purchases also figured among the techniques used. Nor was official protectionism focused solely on textiles. To promote Colombian flour milling, for example, the same tariff of 1905 that established the differential between imported yarn and finished cloth set a high duty on flour while letting in wheat at a purely nominal tariff rate. This measure was designed to assist the milling industry on the Caribbean coast and did not really hurt the wheat growers of the cool Andean high country, whose market was essentially regional: it was directed against imported flour. Yet the fact remains that the textile industry registered the most impressive growth. By 1915 it represented roughly a quarter of the total capital invested in manufacturing, and 70 percent of this capital was concentrated in and around Medellín.

The leading role of textiles in a newly industrializing country was natural enough, in view of the relatively simple technology required and the presence of a large potential domestic market for the end product. The reasons for the leadership of Antioquia are less obvious. It had no clear advantage from the standpoint of availability of raw materials and was isolated from other population centers by a difficult terrain and wholly inadequate transportation (at least until the completion of the Antioquia Railroad to the Magdalena River). Antioquia did, on the other hand, have a supply of commercial capital readily available for investment in new enterprises, much of it resulting from the region's long prominence in gold mining but supplemented lately by coffee export earnings. Antioquia's coffee industry also provided rural families with a new source of cash income, to be spent on the products of the textile mills, and within the Medellín River valley there was water power and hydroelectric potential. Finally, the Antioqueños themselves seemed to possess an entrepreneurial spirit that in some hard-to-define way set them apart from the people of other Colombian regions.

One hoary explanation for that last trait of regional character—which seems to have begun circulating in the mid-nineteenth century—would have it that the original settlers of Antioquia included a disproportionate number of converted Spanish Jews, who supposedly bequeathed their fabled commercial expertise to their Colombian descendants. The fact that Antioquia was also noted for its high level of popular Catholic religiosity never fazed the adherents of this thesis; they insisted that the converts often put on a display of fervor precisely to deflect suspicions that their conversion was insincere. There is, of course, no evidence whatever for this particular explanation of Antioqueño business skill.[14] More plausible interpretations have centered on the region's tradition of adventurous prospecting for gold; the active role of Antioqueño merchants and middlemen serving the mining industry, which at the same time allowed for the accumulation of capital in their hands; and a slightly more even distribution of landed property, which allowed for the development of something like a rural middle class. Whatever the precise reasons, Antioqueños did display uncommon energy and acumen in business pursuits—and not just in manufacturing but in commerce and finance as well.

Two quite different areas of economic growth in the first third of the twentieth century were petroleum and bananas—which, unlike coffee or manufacturing, became enclaves of foreign capital penetration. Exploration for oil reserves began at the turn of the century, at first with indifferent success. But foreign as well as Colombian interests took part in the search; and it was generally assumed that both the interest of U.S. oil firms in Colombia and the Colombian government's desire to spur petroleum investment were among the reasons for the final ratification by both countries of the Urrutia-Thomson Treaty. By the 1920s the Tropical Oil Company (a subsidiary of Jersey Standard) was producing ever larger quantities from fields it controlled in the central Magdalena Valley. It developed a refinery complex at Barrancabermeja, to supply the Colombian domestic market; and after completion of a pipeline to the Caribbean at Cartagena in 1926, it began exporting on what compared to Venezuela was a modest scale but soon amounted to seventeen percent of Colombia's export trade. The one other major firm involved in the petroleum industry was Colombian Petroleum, which despite its name was actually a jointly owned subsidiary of Gulf and Socony. It had acquired the so-called Barco Concession in Norte de Santander, which was in effect an extension of the Venezuelan oil fields around Lake Maracaibo. Colombian Petroleum, however, found its concession rights under almost continual legal attack and did not begin production on a significant scale until the 1930s.

The problems faced by Colombian Petroleum were not unique. For one thing, the basic Colombian subsoil legislation was unusually complex, thus practically guaranteeing an endless round of legal claims and counterclaims. During the Liberal heyday of the third quarter of the last century, Colombia had briefly abandoned the traditional Spanish legal doctrine that separated ownership of the surface from that of the subsoil (which thus remained part of the public domain unless expressly alienated). A subsequent measure of 1873 restored the earlier system, but the courts ruled that it could not be applied retroactively. Therefore, if a given property was privately owned *be-*

fore 1873, the present owner held title to subsoil as well as surface. In view of the often chaotic state of land records, the result was a rush to discover—or, if necessary, manufacture—pre-1873 land titles, covering properties that were suspected to contain oil reserves; and lawyers had a field day working both to validate their clients' titles and to challenge those of others. As one oil engineer later expressed the matter, with an envious side glance at Colombia's eastern neighbor, "While in Colombia they litigate, in Venezuela they drill."[15]

The amount of litigation was also related to regulatory practices. Venezuela, under the tight dictatorship of Juan Vicente Gómez, had arrived at a mutually profitable relationship with the international oil companies and was anxious to avoid any petty interference with their activities. In Colombia the Conservative regime was anxious to encourage oil production; but, in a more open and competitive political system such as Colombia's, government officials did not wish to be perceived as negligent in defending national interests. Therefore, regulation was closer—as well as (it seemed) almost constantly changing.

Apart from lawyers and government regulators, the oil companies had to contend with serious labor unrest, which was one more disadvantage of doing business in Colombia as compared to its neighbor Venezuela. The wages that the companies paid were higher than the national average, if only because they operated in sparsely settled areas with limited amenities and had to offer pay levels sufficient to attract workers from other parts of the country. On the other hand, the native workers had to endure generally poor living conditions, alongside which the premium pay and special fringe benefits enjoyed by foreign employees formed a galling contrast. Moreover, the very fact that the employer was a foreign company made it easier for agitators to mobilize worker sentiment against it and to obtain the sympathy of the general population. Hence, Tropical Oil in 1924 and again in 1927 was faced with massive strike actions, in which some of the country's early Communists as well as other leftist leaders took part. In both cases, in the face of actual or threatened violence, the government intervened by force to help suppress the strikers. The workers did, even so, obtain some improvements—while the government lost prestige for its handling of the situation.

The government lost far more prestige in the great banana workers' strike of 1928. The commercial export of bananas had begun in Colombia around the turn of the century, and by the 1920s it was a major industry, providing 6 percent of Colombian exports toward the end of the decade. The industry was wholly controlled by the United Fruit Company of Boston, Massachusetts, whose extensive holdings in Central America and the Caribbean and intricate shipping and marketing network made it a model of successful horizontal and vertical integration. In Colombia it did not generally own the banana plantations themselves, preferring to buy fruit from Colombian growers. But it also controlled the Santa Marta Railroad, which carried the bananas to port; it managed the distribution of irrigation water in the banana zone; and it had a string of local and national politicians on its payroll as "legal representatives" or something comparable. Wage levels in the banana industry were higher than in agricultural employment generally; for, just as in the petroleum industry, the company had to attract workers from other parts of the country to an area of relatively sparse prior population. However, again as in the petroleum industry, local workers' living conditions were poor and were made to seem even worse by contrast with the privileged status of foreign employees. A further grievance was the refusal of United Fruit to provide even the rather modest fringe benefits (such as accident insurance) called for by Colombian law, on the technical ground that the workers were not its own direct employees but were hired either by its Colombian suppliers or by the private labor contractors that the firm also used.

The 1928 banana strike was the culmination of years of rising labor tension. A number of foreign anarchists—whose influence in Colombia generally was minimal—had been active in the banana zone, and so was the Partido Socialista Revolucionario (PSR), which was founded in the mid-1920s and would in 1930 become the Colombian Communist Party. The PSR sent several of its key figures—including María Cano, the "Revolutionary Red Flower" and a pioneer in the struggle for women's rights as well as labor demands—to help organize the banana workers. The workers had wide support even among such strictly nonrevolutionary elements as the independent merchants of the banana zone, who resented the competition of United Fruit's company stores.

When the strike began, in October 1928, the workers' demands ranged from wage increases and improvements in working conditions to formal recognition of the union they had formed. The company proved unyielding, and the government of President Abadía Méndez backed it up, in part because of an exaggerated concern over the presence of radical agitators. Matters came to a head on December 6, when in the town of Ciénaga soldiers fired into a mass of strikers, killing by official admission some thirteen people. This proved to be just the start of an all-out campaign of repression that led to an indeterminate number of deaths and to the arrest of the principal strike leaders. The fate of the strikers became immortalized in one of the chapters of Gabriel García Márquez's *One Hundred Years of Solitude*, where one reads of thousands of victims and of bodies being loaded onto railroad flatcars to be taken and dumped in the sea so as to obliterate all evidence of the atrocity committed. The novelist's account need not be taken as literal truth: from sixty to seventy-five seems to be the most authoritative estimate of the death toll.[16] That was certainly bad enough.

Regardless of the statistical exactness of any one casualty figure, the episode caused a backlash of sentiment against the Conservative administration, not least because the fruit company had neglected to cultivate the opposition Liberals as carefully as it had the ruling party. The rising Liberal politician Jorge Eliécer Gaitán, one of those who attacked the government most relentlessly for its handling of the strike, first attracted national prominence by his exploitation of the issue on the floor of the Chamber of Representatives. The massacre of the banana workers was thus one of the factors contributing to the final collapse of the Conservative hegemony. Yet it was hardly the decisive factor. More important than either the banana strike or the natural attrition resulting from too long a hold on power was the impact of the world economic depression, whose first effects were being felt in Colombia even before the October 1929 Wall Street crash. A sharp decline in the value of Colombian exports brought a slowing of the economy generally, as well as a corresponding drop in government revenue; and conditions in world financial markets ruled out the obtaining of new foreign loans either to weather the immediate crisis or to continue the ambitious spending programs of the last few years. It is little wonder that the Conservatives' will to hold on to power was perceptibly less as the elections of 1930 approached. If an economic downturn a half century earlier under Liberal rule helped bring the Conservatives to power, there was a certain logic in another and more serious downturn heralding the end of their hegemony.

8

The Liberal Republic
(1930–1946)

Colombia was one of the handful of Latin American countries that did not undergo a revolutionary change of government during the depression years. Instead, the Conservative government then in power went down to defeat in a free election and handed over power peacefully to a Liberal president. Thus began a period marked by quickening social change and political controversy that would last until 1946, when Conservatives again took control in Bogotá.

The immediate cause of the change of party in power in 1930 was that the ruling Conservatives had split their votes between two different candidates, so that the Liberal, Enrique Olaya Herrera, was able to win even though he polled a mere plurality of the votes cast. Previously, when the Conservatives had been thus divided, they called on the archbishop of Bogotá to arbitrate and then backed his choice. In 1930, however, the archbishop had trouble making up his mind, backing first one candidate and then the other—with the result that the Liberals returned to power after almost fifty years in opposition. To be sure, more was involved than a cleric's indecision. The deepening economic crisis and the backlash against the Conservative regime for its heavy-handed reaction to the banana workers' strike of 1928, as well as other accumulated errors and omissions, emboldened the enemies of the government and sapped the morale of its supporters. But Olaya Herrera himself was a decidedly moderate Liberal, who had most recently been serving, under the Conservatives, as Colombian minister to Washington; hence, few sharp changes in official policy were to be expected in the short run.

The most immediate change was instead a sudden deterioration of public order in much of the country. This outburst of violence contrasted with the apparent tranquility of Colombian political life (apart from labor strikes and agitation) all through the latter part of the Conservative hegemony. During that period the government had seemed to be running smoothly and according to the constitution, an atmosphere of civility prevailed between the high commands of the two parties, speech and press remained unfettered, and Colombia seemed to be emerging as one of Latin America's select circle of model democracies. However, those appearances had been in some respects misleading. The average Liberal or Conservative had never truly understood what the party slogans and principles were about, and perhaps for that very reason never fully grasped the fact that the issues that once divided the parties—federalism, the church question, and so forth—were no longer really important. Indeed, the Colombian two-party system, though superficially taken as evidence of the country's political stability, was a handy way of keeping alive old grudges and passing them on from father to son to grandson: as one Conservative statesman well put it, the Colombian parties were in effect two "hereditary hatreds."[1] And though the religious question had declined in intensity in Bogotá, it had not declined in the back hills, where the parish priest might still be a man who refused to give communion to someone known to vote the Liberal ticket. It was safe to say that the Liberals had mellowed more toward the church than vice versa; the clergy, especially the lower clergy, had still not forgiven what the Liberals did to them in the anticlerical reforms of the mid-nineteenth century.

In 1930 one problem was simply that the Liberals had been out of power for roughly a half century. At most, they had held whatever minor share of jobs and spoils the Conservatives saw fit to give them. Conservatives had grown used to having the public payroll almost as their private possession, whereas hordes of good Liberals had been waiting all that time for their fair share. In addition to their unsatisfied bureaucratic ambitions, Liberals had an accumulation of grudges resulting from injuries received at the hands of the other party during the long Conservative hegemony. The transition was thus bound to be ticklish in some respects, and Olaya Herrera sought to ease the process by setting up a formal coalition government, with Conservatives serving in the cabinet and elsewhere. As far as top-level relations between the parties were concerned, the coalition held. But scattered outbreaks of violence occurred in a number of departments. In some instances trouble began when jubilant Liberals set out to settle old scores, to take revenge for real or imaginary injustices received under the rule of their adversaries; in other instances local Conservatives were not prepared to hand over power gracefully. The toll of dead and wounded seems rather insignificant compared with that of the late 1940s and early 1950s, the period known by Colombians as *La Violencia*; and in fact the situation attracted little attention outside Colombia at the time. It was just a few peasants getting killed, so these rustic tragedies were overshadowed by Colombia's spectacular success in staging the peaceful transfer of power at Bogotá.

The wave of violence was ultimately brought under control, and the only other really dramatic occurrence of Olaya Herrera's four-year term was a petty Amazon border conflict, the Leticia affair. This conflict began when a band of Peruvian adventurers seized the narrow salient of Colombian territory that reached the Amazon River at the town of Leticia. Though they were not officially licensed by the Peruvian government to do what they did, the popular enthusiasm aroused by their recovery of what most Peruvians still considered rightfully Peruvian territory (despite a border treaty of 1922, which assigned it to Colombia) made it politically impossible for Peru to disown them. The upshot was a brief armed conflict. In order to fall on the Peruvians and finally vanquish them, Colombia, lacking any passable overland communications with Leticia, had to commandeer a United Fruit Company banana boat to carry troops from the Caribbean coast down the eastern side of South America, then up the Amazon for a distance of some 3,000 kilometers through Brazilian territory. Meanwhile, the League of Nations had also been brought into the affair for purposes of mediation, and the matter was later solved for good by a treaty between Peru and Colombia that confirmed Colombia's possession of Leticia. The conflict did have one positive side effect in that it triggered a wave of patriotic sentiment in Colombia in protest against the Peruvian violation of Colombian territory; it is thus one of the reasons why the outbreak of interparty strife that followed the Liberals' return to power did finally subside.

Another positive side effect of the Leticia affair was a burst of government military spending whose pump-priming effect helped Colombia recover from the world depression more rapidly than might otherwise have been the case. The military spending was not, of course, undertaken as an economic recovery measure. Nor were the effects of the depression quite as traumatic in Colombia as might have been feared. The rural population still mostly combined subsistence farming with production for market, and the existing peasant society was able to absorb a return flow of workers who had lost jobs in the cities or on public works projects. In the coffee industry the fall in prices was partly compensated by an increase in the volume sold. As for those policies that were consciously adopted to deal with the economic crisis, they took two slightly contradictory approaches. On the one hand, Colombia, like most Latin American countries in the same years, devalued the currency, imposed exchange controls, and adjusted tariff rates upward, with a view to making exports more competitive in the world market and imports scarcer and more expensive. Defensive measures such as these tended to encourage import-substitution industrialization and had obvious implications of economic nationalism. Yet, on the other hand, Olaya Herrera went out of his way to try to please the U.S. government and business community, in the vain hope that the United States with its vastly superior resources would somehow help Colombia weather the depression.

To demonstrate Colombia's fiscal responsibility, Olaya Herrera maintained service on the foreign debt long after most Latin American nations had gone into default, even at the cost of cutting domestic programs and the income of government employees. He likewise took pains to settle outstanding controversies over the status of U.S. companies in Colombia—essentially on the companies' terms. Most striking of all (though not publicly known at the time), when he came to choose a new minister of industries, whose cabinet position had to do with both oil and bananas, the Colombian president first checked with the U.S. minister to Colombia to make sure the man he had in mind was acceptable. The U.S. minister replied that the suggested candidate looked all right to him, but he noted that United Fruit had had trouble with him in the past; so the president of Colombia then asked the U.S. minister to check with the local manager of United Fruit, who in turn consulted his home office in Boston, and only when approval of the authorities in Boston was relayed back to Bogotá did Olaya Herrera make the formal appointment.[2] All this reflected in part the mere fact that Olaya Herrera really liked and trusted the United States; but he was also inspired by the notion that if he leaned over backward to favor U.S. interests, then Wall Street bankers would bail Colombia out of the difficulties of the great depression with a new round of loans— something that, as it turned out, they still refused to do.

Between the depression, Leticia, and the initial wave of partisan violence in the countryside, Olaya Herrera did not have much time to think of fundamental reforms, even if he had been so inclined. During his term the Liberals did, though, adopt a few forward-looking measures. For workers there was the enactment of the eight-hour day and a reform giving explicit legal recognition to the right of labor to organize in unions. Another accomplishment, remarkable only because it had not happened sooner, was a decree granting to secondary schools for female students the right to award the *bachillerato* degree, a standard requirement for admission to university. (As a result, by 1938 some 6 of the 284 students graduating from all Colombian universities in that year were women.)[3] One more advance in women's rights was a revision of the civil code that gave married women the legal right to own and dispose of property on the same terms as their husbands—an overdue correction that aroused a storm of protests from those who felt it threatened family stability and traditional values. The controversy over these reforms was quite minor, however, compared to the storms stirred up by the policy innovations of Olaya Herrera's successor, Alfonso López Pumarejo, who became president unopposed in 1934. The Conservatives, who had still not resolved their own internal dissensions, and insisted that the Liberals would not allow a fair contest in any case, chose not to put up a candidate.

"LA REVOLUCIÓN EN MARCHA"

Alfonso López Pumarejo was to play, in Colombia, a role comparable to that of his contemporary Franklin D. Roosevelt in the United States, and in some respects he was undoubtedly influenced by Roosevelt's "New Deal." It was he who brought social and labor issues into the very center of political debate for the first time, and in the process he stirred up intense opposition from traditional-minded political and business leaders; but, after López, Colombia would not be the same again. Like Roosevelt, he was a wealthy man; in fact, he was a banker. Yet he was well aware that Colombia could not go on indefinitely ignoring the needs and problems of what he once described as "that vast and miserable economic class that does not read, that does not write, that does not dress, that does not wear shoes, that barely eats, that remains . . . on the margin of [national life]."[4] In his opinion, such neglect was not only wrong but also dangerous, because the masses would sooner or later demand a larger share of the amenities of life.

He believed that his own Liberal Party should take the initiative and channel such demands to a peaceful resolution.

There had already been some signs of popular unrest over socioeconomic grievances, as distinct from the conventional outbreaks of political violence between Liberals and Conservatives. The most obvious example was the banana strike of 1928. Elsewhere in the country there were additional signs, for those who cared to look, of agrarian unrest, in the form of disputes over land titles, tenant struggles against payment of rent, and movements by peasant squatters to occupy unused or underused portions of large private estates. Serious agrarian unrest was still limited to a few areas, but it reflected the pressure of a growing rural population whose needs were not being met by the existing patterns of land tenure: at one extreme, huge latifundios that were often not fully cultivated or were being devoted to cattle when the land could have been more productively used in crop farming; at the other extreme, a much larger number of small peasant plots that were held on precarious terms of occupancy or were simply too small to provide a proper livelihood.

Urban unrest was appearing, too, along with the growth of cities themselves. Bogotá, which had barely over a hundred thousand inhabitants at the beginning of the century, had a third of a million by the mid-1930s. This increase reflected an accelerating pace of urbanization that could also be seen in Medellín, which lagged not far behind the nation's capital, and in Barranquilla, which was both industrial center and chief Caribbean port. Urban growth was based on the expansion of service and construction trades and manufacturing as well, especially in Medellín. Industrial output in Colombia almost doubled its share of total domestic product in just the years from 1929 to 1945.[5] It derived considerable stimulus from the impact of the depression, which had caused a sharp decline in the price of Colombian exports and therefore had made the cost of foreign manufactures simply out of range for many Colombian consumers, while setting off the defensive reaction of economic nationalism already mentioned. Textile production, in particular, was increasing during the 1930s at a faster annual rate than in Great Britain during the "takeoff" phase of the Industrial Revolution. Unfortunately, the textile industry did not trigger a lasting, self-sustaining process of economic growth in Colombia as it did in eighteenth-century England. Since technology and machinery were mostly imported, the expansion did not have the same wide-ranging secondary effects on the rest of the economy, and the lack of purchasing power of the Colombian masses imposed certain constraints that were less noticeable in England (particularly since the early textile industry there, unlike the industry in Colombia, was also producing for export). In Colombia factories were not the main focus of urban labor militancy; it was more pronounced among transportation workers. However, progress of industrialization virtually ensured that industrial labor problems would in due course have to be dealt with.

As president, then, López saw the beginnings of potentially serious social problems. He wanted to do something about them before they got out of hand, and he therefore adopted a program that he grandly called "La Revolución en Marcha" ("The Revolution on the March"). Despite his use of the term *revolution*—which in Latin America tends to be a cliché meaning all things to all people—López had nothing violent in mind, and certainly no desire to scrap the existing social and economic system. He desired only to help the poorer Colombians obtain a larger share of the system's benefits, just as Roosevelt was doing in the United States and just as Lázaro Cárdenas was doing in Mexico. The Mexican Revolution—which was more truly revolutionary than López's program, though scarcely Marxist in orientation—was then going through its most radical stage as a movement for socioeconomic change; and it, too, served as a model for at least some of the things that would be done in Colombia.

Something that had Mexican, but certainly not U.S., precedents was agrarian reform. In order, he hoped, to forestall peasant unrest, López sponsored Colombia's first agrarian reform law, adopted in 1936. It was a moderate measure that did not cause any landowners to lose land that they were actively exploiting, but it established possession as nine-tenths of the law for landless peasants who had simply moved in on the unused outer fringes of large private estates. In some instances this approach would prove counterproductive, encouraging landlords to replace human tenants with cattle, lest the tenants conceive the idea of applying for title to the land they were occupying. But the government also imposed higher taxes on land that was not being efficiently used for productive purposes, and in some areas it moved to purchase private properties for subdivision and distribution among peasant farmers. Actually, this last tactic did not originate with López; Olaya Herrera had used it to defuse tensions in particular agrarian trouble spots. Because it was expensive, it could not be applied very widely, but it was undoubtedly the most effective single method of overcoming rural discontent. Whatever may have been the precise reasons (and economic recovery was certainly one of them), agrarian unrest visibly diminished in the years following the 1936 agrarian reform law.

In general, the López administration made its mark as protector of the working class not so much through specific social legislation as through something López conspicuously did *not* do—namely, put the state and its agencies at the service of employers in either rural or urban labor disputes, as Conservative governments had consistently done. If employers could not count on the help of state coercion, López believed, they would be more amenable to just worker demands. And in those special cases where he did personally take a hand in resolving labor disputes, López typically sided with the workers.[6] At the same time, official protection and encouragement were given to the formation of labor unions, which roughly doubled in number and size during López's four-year term. In 1936 the first true nationwide labor confederation was established: the Confederación de Trabajadores Colombianos (CTC). It was to a great extent the labor arm of the Liberal Party—or at least the more activist wing of the party— though Communists also played an influential part. There were not many Communists in Colombia, in part because the very nature of the country's party system, with its two sets of hereditary allegiances blanketing the population, left little room for other groups to gain a foothold; but a small Communist Party did exist, and López, though obviously no Communist himself, did not necessarily reject its cooperation. In fact, one Communist leader—during that same year, 1936—addressed the people of Bogotá from the balcony of the presidential palace, much to the consternation of both the Conservatives and a good many Liberals.

López modestly increased spending on schools and rural road construction; and in order to pay for these and other initiatives, he sought to reform the tax system. Colombia already had a moderate income tax, enacted during the latter part of the long Conservative hegemony, but López now raised the rates while tightening up collection, even if he never managed to stamp out all tax dodging by the wealthier citizens. He raised rates and tightened collections especially against large foreign-owned firms, such as the U.S.-owned Tropical Oil Company, which in just one year under López paid almost as much to the government in taxes as during the eight years before he took office (yet somehow continued to make profits). The United Fruit Company was hit with more than just higher taxes, since the Liberals had never quite forgiven its earlier close relationship with the Conservative regime, or forgotten the great banana strike. They now not only used their control of government to favor the workers in disputes with the company but subjected the local manager of United Fruit to off-and-on harassment—even holding him in jail for a few days on charges subsequently dismissed by the Colombian courts.

Finally, López capped off his reform program with a series of amendments to the constitution, adopted in 1936, which did three main things. First of all, they specifically increased the powers of the state in economic matters, spelling out—in terms that inevitably brought to mind the Mexican Constitution of 1917—the doctrine that property rights must be limited by social rights and obligations. This provision gave an express constitutional basis for whatever innovations the Liberals had already adopted in socioeconomic matters and smoothed the way for more of the same in years to come. In the second place, the 1936 constitutional reform removed the previous article that required public education to be conducted in accord with the Roman Catholic religion. López had no interest in removing all religious teaching from the schools, but he did want to make clear that the state, not the church, had final authority in the educational field. The clergy, however, as well as many devout laypeople, feared the worst, particularly because López's Ministry of Education had meanwhile been giving discreet encouragement to coeducation (still a bit daring in Colombia) in official institutions of learning and had invited several European scholars of a liberal humanist bent to come to Colombia as educational specialists. It thus seemed that the Liberal administration was out to rekindle the nineteenth-century church-state conflict with a new assault on the position of the Catholic church and on traditional moral and religious values. The result was a storm somewhat comparable to that stirred up in the United States by the Supreme Court decision banning prayer from the public schools.

Last as well as least, the constitutional reform eliminated the literacy requirement for voting. Universal male suffrage, which had been first enacted in the 1850s and then repealed, was at last in place for good. The move should not be overestimated. Although it affected a large number of people, the country being still about half illiterate in the mid-1930s, it made little difference in the relative standing of the two parties, simply because they were not class-based parties, and there were about as many illiterate Conservatives as Liberals to be benefited by the reform. Proportionately, more Conservatives may have benefited, since the Liberals tended to be stronger in the cities, where public education was more widely available than in rural areas. The reform also did not give women the vote at this time. There was some support for enfranchisement of Colombian women on the left of the political spectrum and here and there among mainstream Liberals and Conservatives. In general, though, the Liberals were still too fearful of clerical influence over the country's women, which might incline them to vote for the other party; and the Conservatives themselves, who presumably would have been the beneficiaries if that were in fact the case, were with honorable exceptions still too committed to the view that women had been intended by their creator to cultivate domestic virtues and not venture forth into the rough-and-tumble of political action.

Extension of the suffrage was mainly important for its symbolic content, as the sign of a national commitment to make the lower classes more active participants in the political system, just as López's other reforms were designed to make them fuller participants in the benefits of the social and economic system. Up to a point, however, the López reforms had even served to increase inequality, since they improved the status of an ambitious upper segment of the peasant population and of skilled or organized urban workers but did not usually reach the great majority. The persistence of stark social differences was itself nicely symbolized by another development of the mid-1930s: the disappearance of second-class coaches from most Colombian railroads, leaving third class and first class and nothing in between. One official explained that the railroads were attempting to "adapt the service to the modalities of the public and simplify the formation of trains."[7] In other words, the popular majority could afford only the hard, wooden seats of third-class coaches, while members of the upwardly striving middle sectors did not wish to be seen traveling in less than first class; hence, second class was discontinued for lack of sufficient patrons.

In the last analysis, López's greatest contribution was not so much anything he delivered in the way of benefits to the masses as the mere fact that he made Colombia truly face up for the first time to its social question. Even those who did not like his policies and methods could no longer ignore the problems involved. For this reason he can be considered, in the words of one leading Conservative, "the most important Colombian of the twentieth century."[8] As part of the same contribution, he made broad segments of the working population conscious for the first time of the fact that they need not go on forever eking out a bare existence. In the process he clearly expanded the Liberals' constituency. The trouble was, however, that he had been awakening hopes faster than he or his party could satisfy them. Hence, frustrations began to accumulate. At the same time, simply by putting across his generally reasonable and moderate program, he was also arousing the bitter opposition of a great majority of Conservatives and the more standpat elements in his own Liberal Party.

An aggravating political circumstance was the growing influence of what may be called the "radical right," primarily within the ranks of the Conservative Party. Until the 1930s, although neither the Conservatives nor the Liberals always practiced what they preached, both parties had adhered to a theoretical belief in political democracy. For a while, starting in the mid-1930s, there came to be a difference between the parties in this respect, though to just what extent is debatable. Liberals did not change their political faith, and neither did many Conservatives; but at least some Conservatives began to question the underlying principles of democratic government. There was no doubt an element of foreign influence here, as Liberals liked to charge, because quite a few Colombian Conservatives, like rightists elsewhere in Latin America, took a tolerant view of Hitler and Mussolini, and all were rabid supporters of Franco and his Nationalists in the Spanish Civil War of 1936–1939. But the question was more complex, and one of the most complicated cases—as well as most important—was that of Dr. Laureano Gómez, who had emerged as the unquestioned leader of the Conservative Party.

An engineer turned politician who had made a good record as minister of public works in the last decade of the Conservative hegemony, Gómez had been an outspoken critic of the Nazi-Fascist dictatorships in the early 1930s. Although his criticisms of them may have become less vehement with time, there is no basis for the allegations of Colombian Liberals and some foreign commentators that Gómez simply went over to their side. He did, however, agree with the Nazi-

Fascists on some points and was no doubt influenced by them. He shared their hatred of Bolsheviks, he was grateful to them for helping Franco, he was blatantly anti-Semitic, and, finally, he agreed that Western-style liberal democracy was in some way decadent. There were of course a few Conservatives, on the farthest lunatic fringe of their party, who did go all the way and call for a totalitarian dictatorship on the German or Italian model, just as there were Colombian Liberals on the outer fringes of their party who were virtual fellow travelers of the Communists. Gómez himself had no such thing in mind. He was just aware, realistically, that liberal democracy as practiced in Colombia had its shortcomings—particularly, in his view, with the Liberals in power—and he was beginning to question whether the gap between Colombian practice and conventional democratic theory could or even should be fully closed. Apparently, he had not yet figured out just how he would fundamentally change the rules of the game if given a chance; but he was clearly considering such a possibility. Meanwhile, Gómez had perfected a confrontational style of politics in which he and his newspaper, *El Siglo*, automatically denounced any Liberal policy as something outrageous, and blew up every small misstep by the government in power into a national scandal. For his vitriolic negativism Gómez came to be known, among the Liberals, as "El Monstruo" ("The Monster").

RETRENCHMENT AT HOME
AND WAR ABROAD

Amid the increasing polarization of political debate, López's presidential term drew to a close. In the struggle for the Liberal nomination in the next election, the outgoing president's own choice lost out to the favorite of the more moderate Liberals. This was Dr. Eduardo Santos—publisher of the nation's leading newspaper, *El Tiempo* of Bogotá—who in 1938 won the presidency unopposed, since the Conservatives again failed to put up a candidate of their own. They still claimed that they could not count on a fair election, and they also assumed that the absence of a Conservative candidate would encourage the Liberals to continue squabbling among themselves; for that matter, they were initially rather well disposed toward Santos, who frankly intended to give the country a four-year breathing spell. He did not undo any of López's measures, and he actually enlarged the role of the state in promoting national development through the creation of the Instituto de Fomento Industrial (IFI), whose mission was to assist in the establishment of new industries by granting subsidized credit and other assistance. But Santos did not show the same interest in the problems of labor and the peasant as he did in helping the industrialists, and his style was definitely less combative than that of López. All things considered, his was a rather passive administration in domestic affairs—the "Great Pause of Eduardo Santos," in the words of one left-leaning history.[9] Paradoxically, somewhat the same can be said of the government of his immediate successor—Alfonso López Pumarejo, back for a second term.

López had been returned to the presidency in 1942 after a bitter election that the Conservatives did contest, to the extent of openly supporting a dissident Liberal candidate; and many Colombians either hoped or feared that López would now resume the work of reform left unfinished at the close of his first term. Alas, by 1942 the world was at war, and the repercussions of that struggle on Colombia would absorb the president's attention and create less than favorable conditions for a resurrection of the "Revolución en Marcha." A 1944 revision of the 1936 agrarian reform law actually made it more difficult for peasants to establish a claim to hacienda land; and new labor legislation in 1945, while increasing a number of worker benefits, broadened the definition of "public service" industries where strikes were prohibited. This provision was used before the year was out to put down a strike launched by the Magdalena riverworkers' union, which happened to be a Communist stronghold, and largely crush the union in the process.

The last years leading up to World War II and the war years themselves were a period of considerable importance from the standpoint of Colombia's international relations. During the first López administration, foreign affairs were greatly overshadowed by domestic concerns, and López himself never displayed the same intimate cordiality toward the United States that his predecessor, Olaya Herrera, had shown. López had allowed the nation's foreign debt (mainly owed to U.S. banks) to go into default, while concentrating resources on domestic programs, although he did at least sign a reciprocal trade treaty eagerly sought by the U.S. State Department. But when Santos succeeded him, the pendulum swung back in the direction of closer relations. Santos brought the first U.S. military missions to Colombia and renewed service on the foreign debt, thereby enabling Colombia to receive new credits from the U.S. government through the Export-Import Bank. The beginnings of U.S. technical assistance programs in Colombia also date from the Santos administration; and all Colombian governments since, however different they may have been in some respects, have maintained an array of bilateral programs with the United States, whether out of earnest conviction or from a feeling that pure self-interest required staying on close terms with the leading hemispheric political and economic power.

Santos himself was less ardently pro–United States than Olaya Herrera had been. In fact, Santos had once been regarded as anti-American; but he was a fanatic Francophile and actually spent a good part of his adult life in Paris. He came to office on the eve of World War II, was wholeheartedly on the side of the democracies against the Axis, and looked to the United States to help support both France and Colombia and the rest of the world against Adolf Hitler. The United States, on its part, as it first prepared for and then entered the war, was anxious to assist reliable friends on its southern flank. Hence, the tightening of formal U.S.-Colombian relations—while reflecting the growth of economic and cultural ties and even a sort of ideological affinity between Colombian Liberals and U.S. Democrats—also had much to do with developments on the larger world scene. Once the war actually began, Colombia gave full cooperation to the United States both before and after Pearl Harbor. The Santos administration never declared war, but it expedited the supply of strategic materials and supported all proposals for hemispheric defense collaboration made at inter-American gatherings.

A good example of wartime cooperation was the way in which Santos helped to eliminate German influence from Colombian civil aviation. SCADTA, the domestic airline founded just after World War I by members of the Colombo-German community at Barranquilla, had over the years compiled an outstanding record of service. It was so successful that it began showing interest in international routes to other Latin American republics. At that point it suddenly aroused the concern of Pan American Airways, which quietly bought up a controlling share of SCADTA stock. Pan Am left the existing Colombo-German management in control, in view of its proven efficiency, and did not seem worried when SCADTA continued to bring pilots from Germany, some of them in training for future service with the *Luft-*

waffe. All that mattered to the U.S. firm was that its newly acquired Colombian subsidiary should not venture out onto the international airways in competition. On the other hand, the U.S. government and press were increasingly alarmed, as world tensions mounted, at the thought of German pilots flying so close to the Panama Canal. Hence, pressure was applied on Pan Am to divest itself of its German helpers and on the Colombian government to expedite the transformation of SCADTA into something that would seem less threatening to hemispheric security. The upshot was the creation of Avianca, the present Colombian national airline, which took over the planes and assets of SCADTA but not its pilots and was placed under a safely Colombian management, though with Pan Am continuing at first as an important stockholder.

The war also brought economic dislocations in the form of shortages of needed goods that were previously imported; scarcity of transport for Colombian exports; and fiscal stringency for the government, because there was less trade to levy taxes on. The resumption of lending to Colombia by the United States was designed in large part to lessen the impact of these problems. As in other Latin American countries, efforts were made to encourage local production of goods now in short supply. Thus, a first Colombian tire plant was established by one of the major U.S. tire manufacturers in collaboration with the Colombian government's IFI. At the same time, the war brought a virtual collapse of the once-important banana industry. The immediate cause was the spread of Sigatoka disease on plantations supplying the United Fruit Company in the Santa Marta banana zone. The plant disease in question could perfectly well have been checked, but only through a heavy investment in control measures. United Fruit flatly refused to make such an investment, despite the pleas of the Colombian government and the U.S. Embassy in Bogotá, partly because it knew that bananas were bound to enjoy a low priority for wartime shipping but also because it had serious doubts about its own long-term prospects in Colombia. It had not forgotten the strike of 1928 and the continuing hostility of many Colombians, Liberals especially, toward the company. It therefore saw fit to concentrate its efforts elsewhere; and when bananas again won a secure place among the leading Colombian exports, in the 1960s and 1970s, the industry was in mainly Colombian hands and was also based in a different part of the country.

Wartime collaboration with the United States eventually reached the point of an outright declaration of war on the Axis, made after Alfonso López Pumarejo had returned to the presidency and technically in retaliation for German attacks on Colombian shipping in the Caribbean. The basic policy had the support of all sectors of the ruling Liberal Party and of many individual Conservatives. Nevertheless, it led to difficulties with the nation's "radical right"—in particular, all those Conservatives who faithfully followed the leadership of Dr. Laureano Gómez. Once a brief honeymoon with Santos came to an end (as a result of an incident in which Liberal police fired on a group of Conservative peasants), Gómez had resumed his obstructionist tactics; and in foreign affairs he came to find fault with almost everything that Santos and subsequently López did, while implying that Colombia had been reduced to the status of an abject satellite of the United States. Liberal spokesmen, as well as some foreign observers, attributed the attitude of Gómez and his followers to supposedly pro-Axis sympathies. Yet only a small minority of Colombians truly supported the Axis powers in World War II, and, despite what his enemies alleged, the Conservative leader was not one of them. Whatever he may have thought about Adolf Hitler (and for the most part it was not favorable), Laureano Gómez had not forgiven Germany for having also produced Martin Luther. His real preference would have been for Colombia to adhere as closely as possible to a policy of neutrality—or "nonalignment," as it would be termed today; but the practical effect of Gómez's neutralism was inevitably anti–United States, as well as anti-Liberal in the Colombian context. The one thing that kept Gómez's antagonism toward the United States at least partly in check was the dependence of his newspaper, *El Siglo*, on U.S. supplies of newsprint and on revenue from the advertising of U.S. business firms. At one point a concerted withdrawal of advertising by those firms, orchestrated by the U.S. Embassy, produced an overnight change in *El Siglo*'s editorial policy in favor of greater friendliness, although the effect of one such application of pressure would eventually wear off and have to be supplemented by another.

THE END OF THE LIBERAL REPUBLIC

Gómez's responsiveness to overt U.S. pressure nicely illustrates the sheer tactical opportunism that was as much a part of his approach to politics as was the ideological rigidity that generally attracted more attention. The combination of these two qualities made him a brilliant oppositionist, and the second López administration—marked by unfulfilled expectations, wartime economic problems, and assorted instances of petty misconduct by Liberals grown careless in office—was made to order for his talents. Among other things, Gómez played on discontent among the military, a majority of whom had Conservative sympathies underneath their official posture of nonpartisanship. Aware of these sympathies, López as president tended to build up the police forces at the regular army's expense. In July 1944 there was an abortive coup attempt, in the course of which the president was briefly taken prisoner. The movement was easily suppressed, but it was a disturbing sign: Colombia had not seen anything of the sort for a very long time. Some months later, López resigned in sheer discouragement, allowing a trusted associate, Alberto Lleras Camargo, to complete his term.

The greatest threat to the survival of the Liberal regime was deepening dissension in the Liberals' own ranks—not between Lopista reformers and Liberal moderates, as in the first López administration, but between the official party hierarchy and a rapidly growing movement of populist rebels led by Jorge Eliécer Gaitán. To Gaitán and his followers, Alfonso López was just one more representative of an oppressive establishment. Gaitán was certainly a quite different character from López: whereas the latter was an elegant, polished gentleman, with a fondness for London-tailored suits and Scotch whiskey (which he helped popularize in Colombian upper-class circles), Gaitán came from distinctly lower-middle economic background. He had been described in the mid-1930s by the British minister to Colombia as a "mulatto of humble origins" who was not likely to go far in Colombian politics.[10] The description was wrong on both counts (Gaitán being of mestizo rather than mulatto racial background), but it does nicely capture the disdain with which he was viewed by the Colombian social elite and by foreigners who associated with it. His father had been a small-time Liberal politician who ran a second-hand bookshop in Bogotá. He was a domineering father, too, so that amateur psychoanalysts have been able to find childhood complexes to explain pretty much everything in Gaitán's later career. More important was the mere fact that the family had a constant struggle to make ends meet. Thus, Gaitán was a strictly self-made figure—something that was by no means unheard of in Colombian public life but still was not common in his day. Yet he was clearly a man of talent, who took up the study of law, received a scholarship for advanced work in his field in Italy, and became a brilliant criminal lawyer. After entering politics, he first attracted nationwide notice—as mentioned in the previous chapter—for his denunciations of the Conservative regime's handling of the 1928 banana strike.

As a gifted orator and phrase maker, Gaitán was the man who made the term *oligarchy* a household word in Colombia, and a bad word at that. It designated the small, wealthy, educated elite that supposedly ran the government, the church, the army, business, everything, including the two traditional parties. According to Gaitán, Liberal oligarchs and Conservative oligarchs competed for the spoils and prestige of office while ignoring the needs of the people and were in fact bound to each other in an unwritten, unholy alliance precisely to head off meaningful change. He thus sounded a good bit like his Argentine contemporary Juan Domingo Perón, or even in some respects Benito Mussolini in Italy, whose oratorical style seems to have made an impression on young Gaitán while he was a student there. To what extent he shared the objectives of either Perón or Mussolini is a quite different matter; it is hard to say, because unlike them he never obtained control of government.

In reality, Gaitán never got around to articulating a clear-cut program. He talked vaguely about socialism but was no Marxist, even if influenced in some respects by Marxism. He certainly proposed to go further than López had gone in the way of state intervention in the economy and promotion of labor and welfare reform, but here the differences were essentially of degree. The major difference between Gaitán and López had to do with style: López, the public-spirited aristocrat, presumed to speak *for* the masses but remained a bit distant from them; Gaitán, who identified himself with the common people, made an explicit appeal to class resentments with his continual tirade against the "oligarchy." According to Herbert Braun, the most perceptive student of Gaitán's career, he was at heart a "petit-bourgeois" reformist.[11] Nothing he had to say was really threatening to the existing socioeconomic order or political system; but the way he said it, seeking to establish a direct relationship with the underprivileged classes as he appealed to them over the heads of traditional party leaders, aroused bitter resentment. It also marked him as a classic example of the twentieth-century Latin American "populist."

Since the end of the Conservative hegemony, Gaitán had alternated between efforts to create his own independent left-wing movement and attempts to gain his objectives by collaborating with the Liberal Party leadership. He had served as mayor of Bogotá and as national minister of education in the decidedly centrist Santos administration; and he did not last long in either position. He proved to be an able administrator, but as mayor he stirred up an explosion of protest from taxi drivers for trying to make them wear uniforms, and as education minister he was resented for trying to increase direct national control over departmental and municipal school authorities. What gave him his great opportunity, in any case, was the second López administration, whose real and alleged shortcomings generally shook the prestige of the Liberal branch of the Colombian ruling class.

Accordingly, Gaitán offered himself as candidate for the Liberal nomination for president in the elections of 1946. The party machine would not take him, nominating instead an able but colorless moderate, Gabriel Turbay. The Conservatives chose not to put forward the name of their maximum leader, Laureano Gómez, fearful that the Liberals' loathing of him was the one thing that might cause them to end their feuding. They therefore chose instead Mariano Ospina Pérez, a mild-mannered millionaire long active in the coffee industry as well as other lines of business and with an engineering degree from Louisiana State University. He was the grandson of one previous Conservative president and nephew of another, and with his interlocking economic, social, and political distinctions he was an oligarch if ever there was one.

The two Liberal candidates between them garnered substantially more than half the votes cast, in keeping with the fact that since 1930 the Liberals had unquestionably displaced the Conservatives as Colombia's majority party. In view of the traditionally hereditary nature of party allegiances, this shift (which the Conservatives refused to acknowledge) at first glance poses a problem. There is no indication that Liberals were simply outreproducing their rivals. But there were always exceptions to the pattern of hereditary partisan affiliation, and in recent years the exceptions had generally favored the Liberals—in part as a natural consequence of their success in identifying themselves with the cause of socioeconomic reform. They were also helped by the continuing process of urbanization, which concentrated more and more people in the larger cities, where the Liberal Party tended to be strongest. And there were no doubt some petty frauds committed here and there on election day at Conservative expense—though hardly enough to affect the outcome.

Among the two Liberals, Turbay came out ahead on election day, because he was the official candidate and in most small-town and rural Liberal strongholds the party machine delivered the vote solidly to him. The Communist high command also backed Turbay, as did most leaders of organized labor, whose own interests—whether they themselves happened to be Communists or Liberals—had been closely tied in with those of the Liberal administrations. But the labor bosses were less able than the back-country party bosses to deliver the vote of their followers, so that Gaitán was able to carry not just Bogotá but several other large cities. He did well even outside the big cities in the Caribbean coastal region, the one part of the country where he had significant support even within the Liberal Party machine. Nevertheless, with the Liberals divided, Ospina Pérez, with a minority of the total votes cast, was the one who ended up the winner. The 1946 election thus proved to be an almost exact repetition of the 1930 election, which had brought an end to Conservative rule; only the names of the parties were reversed.

9

The Era of the *Violencia*
(1946–1957)

The Conservative president who took office in Bogotá in August 1946, Mariano Ospina Pérez, was compared by one Colombian social scientist to a prominent U.S. contemporary: he was "the Colombian Eisenhower."[1] That is, he was not a man of genius, much less an intellectual, but he had decent instincts and was moderate and well meaning, a born conciliator. He thus appeared to be just the person to preside over a transition from the rule of one party to another; and—like the Liberal Enrique Olaya Herrera, who had been the last Colombian to fulfill the same role—he started out by forming a coalition government, in which Liberals were represented at all levels. As in 1930, this action did in fact help to ease the political transition. Nevertheless, following the change of administration in Bogotá, the same bad things began to happen in much of the back country as on the previous occasion. There were violent outbreaks here and there, and for the same reasons; only this time it was Conservatives who were out to settle old scores and grievances that they had been accumulating during the years of Liberal rule and Liberals who were sometimes unprepared to accept defeat gracefully and hand over power to the victors. A more critical difference than the mere reversal of party labels was the fact that in 1946 the wave of violence did not, as in 1930, soon peter out. Instead, it eventually engulfed most of the country.

EL NUEVE DE ABRIL

Under the shock of election defeat, the Liberals finally began to heal their divisions and close ranks, and they had little choice but to close them around Gaitán. Although he was cordially disliked by most of the party establishment, Gaitán was easily the party's most magnetic personality and was also less affected than others by the general erosion of prestige of the Liberal leadership. Already in 1947 it seemed clear that next time around he would be the presidential candidate of a united Liberal Party. He was rather less well suited to lead his party in the meantime, on a basis of power sharing with the adversary, since he distrusted most of the other leaders of both parties and, whether out of principle or mere stubbornness, was temperamentally not much given to compromise. In due course he pulled the Liberals out of the coalition with Ospina. Gaitán and other Liberals did not lack grievances by which to justify their break with the Conservative regime, but the inevitable result was to leave rank-and-file Liberals wholly at the mercy of Conservative officialdom. Violent incidents continued and tensions mounted, as Colombia prepared to host the inter-American conference of April 1948, at which the present Organization of American States was destined to be born. But all hell did not break loose until April 9, the day that Gaitán was shot and fatally wounded on the street in Bogotá as he left his office to go to lunch.

What immediately followed was an outburst of mass rioting in protest often referred to, especially outside of Colombia, as the *Bogotazo*. Colombians themselves more commonly speak just of *El nueve de abril*. The latter term is preferable, because *Bogotazo* focuses attention strictly on disturbances in the national capital, whereas in actuality what happened was a nationwide outburst, with scenes of violence repeated not only in other large cities but also in many small towns of heavy Liberal majority. The *Puerto Tejadazo* is illustrative. In Puerto Tejada, on the Cauca River south of Cali, enraged Liberals murdered some leading Conservatives, decapitated them, and then played soccer in the main plaza with the severed heads.[2]

The greatest destruction did occur, however, in Bogotá itself, where much of the downtown section was gutted in the course of the rioting. Stores were broken into and robbed, for many people who joined the crowd had no special interest in avenging Gaitán but saw a good chance to increase their material possessions—much as happened, say, in the *Washingtonazo* of 1968 after the death of Martin Luther King, Jr. Even those who did look upon themselves as political avengers were often willing to help themselves to the ill-gotten goods of wealthy oligarchs. There was also, it seems, an element of destruction for destruction's sake, by people who felt no stake in the existing social order but instead felt alienated from it and turned against it in a rage. The

government of President Ospina seemed very close to being overthrown. It survived because the army remained loyal, and perhaps
also because the remaining Liberal leaders after the death of Gaitán
had too many hesitations and/or legal scruples to seize the opportunity. Liberal looters and demonstrators still in the streets were left
without leadership, and little by little the military restored order,
though not before several hundred people had been killed in Bogotá
and elsewhere in the country.

It was all particularly embarrassing since the inter-American conference was in progress in Bogotá at the time, with foreign dignitaries,
including U.S. secretary of state George Marshall, in attendance. Thus,
Colombian official and semiofficial spokesmen—to save face with
world opinion, among other reasons—were at great pains to make
clear that the trouble was somehow caused by outside Communist
instigation. The Communists, possibly in league with left-wing Liberals or other coconspirators (even Venezuela's social democratic
Acción Democrática party was mentioned),[3] were supposed to have
had Gaitán assassinated so that the ensuing rioting would serve as
cover for a leftist takeover of government. The theory of a leftist conspiracy subsequently gained even wider acceptance when it came to
light that Fidel Castro had been in Bogotá on April 9, 1948! In actual
fact, Fidel's way to Bogotá had been paid not by Stalin in Moscow but
by the regime of Juan D. Perón in Buenos Aires, so that he could
attend a Latin American student conference also scheduled to meet in
the Colombian capital. There is no evidence that Castro (who was not
yet a Communist in 1948) played a significant role in events. As for the
Colombian Communists themselves, along with other left-wing activists they tried to influence the course of the protest once it started,
though without much success. Again, there was never a shred of evidence linking them to the assassination itself, the event that got things
started. Nonetheless, the notion of Communist responsibility remains
an article of faith among great numbers of right-wing Colombians to
the present day.

Still more widely held is the notion that the Conservative administration was behind the assassination, to rid itself of a potentially
dangerous rival. This was firmly believed by the rioters at the time,
and the theory continues to be routinely repeated by Colombian leftists and many rank-and-file Liberals. It is thoroughly implausible. If

President Ospina or the Conservative Party's high command had decided to murder the head of the Liberal Party, they would scarcely have chosen to do so in the midst of an international conference.

In reality, there is little doubt that Gaitán was killed by a slightly unbalanced free-lance assassin, and that the rioting that followed was essentially unplanned and spontaneous. Nevertheless, the various conspiracy theories that have been offered to explain the events are important in themselves, because those beliefs—whether right or wrong (and they were mainly wrong)—critically influenced the course of events on April 9 and afterward. The fact that many Liberals truly thought the Conservatives had killed their leader, and that many Conservatives honestly believed Colombia was threatened by an international leftist conspiracy, helps explain much of the seemingly irrational, even pathological, behavior that Colombians were to exhibit over the next few years. It bears repeating, though, that the wave of violence in Colombia—what became known as *La Violencia* ("The Violence")—did not begin on April 9, 1948. It had begun already, following the change of administration in 1946. In fact, the immediate aftermath of the *Bogotazo* was a tapering off of violence—a sort of temporary respite—because around noon on April 10 the Liberal Party agreed to reenter the government on a coalition basis. But the coalition lasted only about a year, after which the rate of violent incidents increased again until large portions of the country were caught up in an undeclared civil war between adherents of the two parties. The conflict was to last until the early 1960s.

POLITICAL MAYHEM
AND ECONOMIC GROWTH

The further deterioration of public order was closely related to the onset of another round of election campaigning, to choose both Congress and the next president. Congressional elections in June 1949 resulted in another Liberal victory, though with a reduced majority. But the presidential election held in November of the same year was won by Laureano Gómez, running as the Conservative candidate. He won unopposed; the Liberals withdrew from the race shortly before election day, claiming that in the reigning climate of violence it was unsafe for them to come forth and cast their votes. The claim was not wholly unfounded, because Conservatives, having had the scare of their lives on April 9, were determined to take no chances in keeping control of the government. When Gómez was formally inaugurated the following year, most Liberals refused to look upon him as a legitimate ruler. This argument provided a legal rationalization for any acts of violence that might be taken against the new administration—while in the minds of Conservatives it was reason enough for regarding any Liberal as disloyal.

The political violence between Liberals and Conservatives, which had kept getting worse as the presidential election neared, became worse still after the election was over; and it continued without much letup all through Gómez's presidency, from 1950 to 1953. No part of the country was wholly spared, although the phenomenon was primarily rural, not urban (with the notable exception of *El nueve de abril* itself); and some regions, such as the Caribbean coastal plain and the department of Nariño immediately adjoining Ecuador, suffered relatively less than others. Isolated incidents of the sort that had been occurring since 1946 set off chain reactions of reprisals and counter-reprisals, while in the eastern *llanos* and a number of other places organized Liberal guerrilla bands arose to harass government agents and sympathizers and, ostensibly, protect beleaguered Liberals. On the opposing side, groups of progovernment vigilantes with such picturesque names as "Chulavitas" (from a town in Boyacá) and "Pájaros" ("Birds") committed a steady stream of murders and assaults with seeming impunity. All in all, it makes a gruesome story, in which eventually between 100,000 and 200,000 Colombians died, often in quite unpleasant ways. The effort to account for the wave of violence has spawned a vast and still growing historical and social science literature[4]—alongside an equally impressive body of works of fiction set in the era of the *Violencia*.

The explanations that have been offered range from fairly simplistic versions of class conflict to abstruse psychological interpretations of the cultural impact of "modernization." Some of the violence, of course, was little more than sheer banditry, practiced either by professional outlaws or by Liberals and Conservatives who had initially been run off their farms by adherents of the other party and took to a life of criminality as the most practical way to eat under the circumstances. In some instances political motives were used as a screen to conceal crass economic motives. A grasping landlord or a band of downtrodden peasants might harass other peasants who were members of the opposite party, ostensibly to avenge some heinous political act but actually to usurp the victims' land for themselves. Other forms of economic motivation masquerading as something else are easy to imagine; and the fact is that many of the hardest-hit areas had previously been the scene of agrarian unrest or were recently settled areas where there was competition for good coffee land and where property titles were often unclear. Nevertheless, one almost never heard of cases of Liberal peasant fighting against Liberal landlord (or Conservative against Conservative, on class lines). Usually, the violence pitched Liberal peasant against Conservative peasant, while the larger landowners of either party, to say nothing of business and professional people and politicians, stayed in the relative safety of the cities.

There is, then, good reason to regard the inherited partisan rivalry of Liberals and Conservatives as the most important single cause of the *Violencia*. Political events had triggered the process, and political rivalries kept it going. But the sheer intensity of traditional partisan competition in Colombia would have been unthinkable if the level of rural social and economic development had been higher. Only a semiliterate peasantry with the vaguest notions about what was happening at the national level could be made to believe that members of the other party were somehow in league with the devil; and only in small towns of utterly grinding poverty would control of the local government, with a yearly budget amounting to something under a thousand dollars, be sufficient motive to go out and kill people (although, admittedly, municipal offices could help determine the outcome of land disputes and offer various kinds of protection). The fact remains that *La Violencia* was, as noted, a predominantly rural phenomenon. The cities, in which educational levels were higher and a greater variety of means of livelihood available, were largely spared.

Political killing was not the only thing taking place in Colombia in the late 1940s and early 1950s. There was also, for example, a flurry of charges and countercharges about alleged persecution of Protestants. The Protestants had first established themselves in Colombia in the nineteenth century, and they had not made many converts. By 1950 they still made up less than 1 percent of the population. But as the *Violencia* spread, more and more incidents arose involving the Protestant community—churches stoned, preachers beaten up, and so forth. There is no evidence whatever that such attacks were carried out on direct orders of the government in Bogotá, much less the Vatican;

but local Conservative officials and Catholic priests were often involved. From the Protestant standpoint, including that of Protestants
abroad, it added up to a veritable wave of religious persecution.[5]

The official Colombian answer to such charges was twofold. First,
government spokesmen pointed out, correctly, that all Colombian
Protestants were Liberals (as a natural reaction to the historical association between the Roman Catholic church and the Conservatives);
therefore, supposedly, any attacks made on them were just unfortunate by-products of the political struggle raging in the country: they
were being attacked not because they were Protestants but because
they were Liberals. Second, the government argued that some
Protestants—by the vehemence of their attacks on Catholic beliefs and
practices—had so antagonized local Catholics that they simply could
not contain their indignation and came to blows. Again there was an
element of truth in the argument, for not all missionaries or their converts were tactful in their proselytizing activity. Members of long-
established denominations such as the Presbyterians (the first to begin
work in Colombia on a regular basis) were not usually getting beaten
up; the brunt of the violence fell on members of more outspokenly
anti-Catholic groups, often of the Pentecostal variety, which for the
most part had become active only in the last few years. (World War II,
which temporarily closed off mission fields for U.S. Protestants in
East Asia, had led to a sharp upsurge of activity in such places as
Colombia.)

Nonetheless, Conservatives generally believed that Protestant activities ought to be restricted. They did not aim to abolish the constitutional guarantee of religious toleration, but they did take a very narrow interpretation of it, claiming that it meant freedom of conscience
and the right to hold non-Catholic services but not the right to engage
in public proselytizing, seeking to win over the Catholic population.
The Ospina Pérez administration did not seriously implement this particular interpretation of religious freedom; but when Laureano Gómez
came to power, the authorities began taking positive measures to curb
Protestant activities. They would deny use of the radio for Protestant
religious programs, and in many places they prohibited the distribution of Protestant literature on the streets. They also blamed Protestants themselves for the continuing incidents of violence against
individual Protestants.

Still another, and somewhat paradoxical, phenomenon of these years was a surge of economic growth. The death rate was going up, but so was the gross domestic product, at a rate of 5 percent annually between 1945 and 1955. Industrial output showed even sharper growth during the period, at a yearly rate of 9 percent. There was some increase in foreign investment in manufacturing, although the industrial sector was still predominantly Colombian-owned. And the proportion of the population living in towns and cities, which had been a mere 31 percent as late as 1938, rose to 39 percent in the census year 1951 and had reached 52 percent by 1964.[6] The advance of urbanization was no doubt spurred to some extent, as commonly alleged, by the influx to the cities of rural refugees from the *Violencia*, but that factor is easily exaggerated. Increased urbanization was in fact a general trend throughout Latin America, where it owed as much to the sheer poverty and lack of opportunities of the countryside as to the specific jobs in manufacturing or otherwise that were available in the cities—or to the relatively greater safety (as in the Colombian case) of the urban environment.

The economic growth rate, though it may have been close to a record for Colombia, was less spectacular in worldwide perspective, since the developed economies in the same years were posting even sharper increases. It was about average for Latin America, and it was clearly influenced by external conditions. In the postwar era Colombia's terms of trade were generally favorable. The prices of the nation's exports rose faster than those of imports, including the price of capital goods needed for industrialization. The process reached its culmination in the early 1950s, during the Korean War, when among other things the price of coffee set a great new record by piercing the dollar-a-pound barrier. The policies of the Colombian government itself, however, were generally favorable to economic growth, even if not always to political tranquility or to equal sharing of the benefits of growth. President Ospina Pérez, as a wealthy businessman educated in the United States, could inspire the confidence of the business community, both foreign and domestic; and Laureano Gómez, though he had fewer personal ties to that community, was certainly no dangerous leftist. Gómez was unimpeachably orthodox, too, in his handling of government finance, keeping a tight check on expenditures and even achieving a slight reduction in the national debt. The prevailing commitment to respect and work closely with the forces of private enterprise (while holding labor and leftist agitation in check) was well exemplified by the sale to private banks, in 1953, of the government's own shares in the Banco de la República, the Colombian central bank. In such a business climate investors were perhaps less disturbed by rural violence than might have been expected.

Conservative economic policy was at the same time at least slightly more nationalist than that of the previous Liberal regime, even taking into account the impetus given to import substitution during the depression. Since then, there had been a gradual deterioration in the effective level of tariff protection, because the rates charged were not readjusted adequately to keep pace with changes in prices or other conditions; but during the administration of Ospina Pérez, the trend was finally reversed, with a new increase in tariff levels. The move was at first opposed by the president himself. His long association with coffee-export interests, as a leader of the Federación Nacional de Cafeteros (FEDECAFE), had made him leery of moves that might hamper the free flow of trade. It was also opposed, prior to his assassination, by Gaitán, who feared that manufacturers would take advantage of official protectionism to gouge the consuming public. But political pressures exerted by the manufacturers' association, Asociación Nacional de Industriales (ANDI), eventually carried the day. The fact that a disproportionate number of the nation's large-scale industrialists were Antioqueño Conservatives naturally helped; so did ANDI's skill in putting together an intensive lobbying campaign. At any rate, as Eduardo Sáenz Rovner has shown in a trail-blazing study of industrial policy, it was really the Conservatives in the late 1940s and early 1950s—not the Liberals of the 1930s, as conventional wisdom had maintained—who definitively committed Colombia to the import-substitution path.[7]

Another sign of official commitment to industrialization was the creation of a Colombian national steel industry—more specifically, the Paz de Río complex in Boyacá department, about 200 kilometers northeast of Bogotá. The first steps toward this objective were taken in the early 1940s, in the government of Eduardo Santos, but the scheme finally was brought to fruition by the Conservatives. Private enterprise, domestic or foreign, was not interested in establishing a Colombian steel industry, on the ground that the local market was not adequate to support the undertaking. Convinced that Colombia needed a national steel industry if it was to take its rightful place among the nations of the world, the government therefore launched the project on its own initiative. Financing involved a measure of forced savings by the general public, whereby 2.5 percent of Colombians' income tax liability was satisfied by the purchase of Paz de Río stock. Many years later, the steel industry actually became a viable, intermittently profitable—and now privately controlled—operation.

An element of nationalism was also reflected in petroleum policy. The concession granted to the most important of the international oil companies, the Tropical Oil subsidiary of Jersey Standard, was due to expire in 1951. The company was prepared to negotiate a renewal, but Colombia instead allowed the Tropical concession (and the refinery built at Barrancabermeja on the middle Magdalena River to handle its production) to revert to the government itself, which proceeded to create its own state oil corporation, ECOPETROL. Tropical continued to have a role in marketing the petroleum from its former wells, but Colombia—like Mexico and Argentina and ahead of Venezuela— now had its own national oil firm, which would assume a directing role in the industry.

There was, to be sure, no official hostility toward private foreign investment as such. On the contrary, the Conservative regime went out of its way to make foreign investors feel welcome. Even in the oil industry, outside the ex-Tropical concession, international petroleum firms were encouraged to continue looking for oil deposits to develop, and the entry of foreign capital and technology in the manufacturing sector, working alone or in association with national private enterprise, was seen as a positive development both by the Colombian authorities and by public opinion generally—except in some quarters of the badly weakened Colombian left. The thrust of economic nationalism continued to be more moderate, and less explicitly antiforeign, than was customary in Latin America.

Such economic growth as occurred in the period did little to correct the maldistribution of wealth in Colombia, and the most conspicuous benefits went, not surprisingly, to the owners of the means of production—but not quite all the benefits; and in this connection the Conservatives' labor policy is worth a few words. Strikes were definitely frowned upon, and the CTC was practically broken as an effective force under the impact of governmental repression. The CTC was weakened also by the advent of the cold war, which brought a final break between its Liberal and Communist sectors. Moved by their own anticommunism and by an obvious desire to stay in the good graces of the U.S. Embassy, Liberal Party leaders insisted that Communist elements be purged; and in 1950 they were purged—but without seriously lessening the hostility of the Conservative administration. Meanwhile, a new national labor organization—the Unión de Trabajadores de Colombia (UTC), founded in 1946—enjoyed government favor and expanded rapidly. It had Jesuit spiritual advisers, and its original leaders tended to be Conservative rather than Liberal (much less Communist), but it had no formal connection with either the church or the Conservative Party and adopted a policy of concentrating on bread-and-butter issues while criticizing the CTC for its involvement in partisan politics. Its hard-core strength was in Antioquia and in manufacturing industry, whereas the CTC, which had tended to neglect factory workers, had its principal strength in transportation and services. The Conservative government and even employers did not mind if the UTC won some benefits for its members, if only to demonstrate that this new union, and not the CTC, had found the correct approach.

Although the Conservatives distrusted any kind of labor militancy, they did practice a certain amount of condescending paternalism toward the working class. Under Ospina Pérez, Colombia acquired a system of industrial profit sharing by means of annual workers' bonuses. The measure was adopted in 1948, by a frightened national leadership in the aftermath of the *Nueve de abril,* but it inevitably brought to mind the similar benefits being introduced in Argentina in the same period by Juan D. Perón. A rudimentary system of social security, initially limited to providing sickness and maternity benefits for select groups of workers, also went into operation by the end of the decade. At the same time, there is disagreement as to the tendency of real wages. Probably the most common view is that postwar inflation, though fairly moderate in Colombia, still outdistanced wage increases. The arrival in the cities of rural refugees from the *Violencia* had to be an aggravating circumstance, since it created new competition for unskilled jobs that were notoriously poorly paid to begin with. Statistical indicators, on the other hand, do not show any general decline in real wage levels. And workers in the modern factory sector, especially if covered by a UTC collective bargaining agreement, were doing appreciably better than the working population as a whole.[8]

If economic growth was one paradoxical feature of the *Violencia* years, another was the participation of Colombian forces in a military conflict waged on the opposite side of the globe, in Korea. Colombia was the only Latin American country to participate, and it did so by decision of Laureano Gómez as president. Colombia's participation consisted at any given time of one batallion of army troops plus the services of a Colombian naval vessel in Korean waters, and the government recognized that its importance was primarily symbolic—an expression of solidarity. Nevertheless, the Colombian batallion made one of the best combat records of any of the units participating, suffered a full quota of casualties, and won the sincere praise of United Nations commanders. There had never, of course, been any reason to doubt the Colombians' fighting qualities. It did seem odd, though, that just when they were locked in virtual civil war at home, they should be fighting in Korea, especially when no other Latin American country was doing the same. Some other countries had offered to send token forces to help out, but only Colombia had offered a force sufficiently large to be worth the trouble of incorporating it alongside the Korean, U.S., and other foreign contingents.[9]

Critics of Laureano Gómez wondered why this man, who had appeared so unfriendly to the United States during World War II, should now come rushing to fight alongside the United States in Korea. Various complicated explanations were put forward. One widely accepted thesis at the time was that Gómez wanted to get army officers suspected of Liberal sympathies out of the country by sending them off to fight (maybe even to die) in East Asia. But this notion, apart from being wholly unsupported by concrete evidence, is somewhat implausible. Such Liberal officers might have covered themselves with glory on foreign battlefields and then returned home to try to unseat Gómez. Moreover, the Colombian detachment to Korea was primarily a volunteer force: if only for the extra pay involved, more officers and men wanted to serve in Korea than there was room for, and professional qualities were the main criteria for deciding who would go.

It has also been argued (and became the preferred explanation of the Colombian left) that the United States had pressured Colombian authorities to send young men to fight and die overseas. The United States did not make any secret of its keen desire at the time to have Latin American participation in the Korean struggle; but again there is no concrete evidence to support the thesis. Even if it could be shown that direct pressure was exerted, one would still have to ask why

Colombia—of all the Latin American countries presumably exposed to similar tactics—was the only one that responded positively. More plausibly, it was suggested then and has been repeated since that Laureano Gómez wished to erase any lingering bad impressions caused among U.S. policymakers by his previous attitude, and thereby assure himself of a continued flow of U.S. economic and military aid. This explanation does seem perfectly reasonable, and it underscores the way in which, even without an application of overt pressure on a Latin American government, the United States always exerts an amount of indirect pressure simply because its decisions in matters of aid and trade and much else affect the well-being of Latin America. Any Latin American ruler could logically hope that his country would receive more favorable treatment in other respects if it did something manifestly pleasing to the United States—such as sending troops to Korea. Quite apart from Gómez's personal interests, there are indications that the leaders of the Colombian armed forces, unhappy with the budgetary and other priorities assigned to them and eager to obtain rapid upgrading of training and equipment with U.S. help and largely at U.S. expense, lobbied strongly in favor of the move.

Not least, one has to remember that whatever Laureano Gómez may have previously thought of the United States, his credentials as a militant anti-Communist were unimpeachable. This, too, had something to do with the Colombian decision. It also had much to do with Gómez's continuing interest in modifying Colombian institutions in a way that would curb those excesses of liberal democracy that in his estimation opened the door to Marxist influences among other evils. Since 1949, with the spreading Violencia as ample pretext, the country had operated under a state of siege that gave the government the right to suspend a broad range of guarantees. The press was regularly censored even though opposition newspapers still existed, and individuals were exposed to arbitrary infringement of their civil rights. There was no systematic suppression of all dissent, and the restrictions inherent in the state of siege were often applied erratically; but it is not unfair to say that, from the last stage of the Ospina Pérez administration and then continuously under Gómez, Colombia was under at least a mild civilian dictatorship. This was, however, in principle a transitory situation. For the longer term Gómez had other things in mind, which he outlined to a special national convention that he convoked for the purpose of amending the Colombian constitution.

Despite charges to the contrary, Laureano Gómez was still no convert to outright totalitarianism, but he did propose to strengthen the powers of the executive as against Congress. He was prepared to have the president still chosen in popular election by majority vote, despite his past criticisms of the majority principle. He also accepted popular election for the lower house of Congress; but he asked to have the Senate chosen by organized groups, such as the labor unions, the manufacturers' association, and also the church, which would name one senator to represent just itself. This was the most striking innovation of all that he proposed, and it clearly showed the influence of the so-called "corporate state" of European fascism. Another change proposed by Gómez was to allow only heads of families to vote in municipal elections; such a provision was borrowed from the institutions of the Franco dictatorship in Spain, where Gómez had spent time in exile following the *Nueve de abril*.

Gómez's recommendations, though falling considerably short of a wholesale embrace of European fascism (even in its Spanish variant under Franco), aroused widespread opposition in Colombia—not simply from the Liberals but among rival factions of his own Conservative Party. Most important of the dissidents were those grouped around ex-president Ospina Pérez. The Ospinista Conservatives did not share Gómez's doctrinaire distaste for conventional democratic procedures, even though Ospina himself had imposed the state of siege whereby democratic procedures were in large part suspended. These Conservatives also believed that Gómez's partisan rigidity was largely responsible for the continuation and even worsening of the *Violencia*. And they regarded Gómez's insistence on an unpopular constitutional reform as a sign that he and his close supporters intended to monopolize power at their expense.

Already facing the adamant hostility of the Liberal majority, Gómez could not long survive the drift of the Ospinistas as well into opposition, particularly since they had close ties with many leaders of the Colombian army, including the chief of the armed forces, General Gustavo Rojas Pinilla. Convinced (incorrectly it would seem) that Rojas Pinilla was plotting against him with the connivance of his civilian opponents, Gómez tried first to send Rojas Pinilla into diplomatic exile and then, on June 13, 1953, to dismiss him from his command. Instead, Rojas Pinilla dismissed Gómez. He was prepared to offer the presidency to another civilian Conservative, but when the offer was not accepted, he agreed to be president himself.

Laureano Gómez thus became the first Colombian president to be toppled in a coup since Manuel Antonio Sanclemente in 1900. It was certainly an unusual event, but the two cases did have certain points in common: in 1900 as in 1953 there was both a deep split in the governing party itself and a seemingly intolerable situation of national turmoil—the War of a Thousand Days in the first instance, the *Violencia* in the second—that the victim of the coup had been unable to halt. Rojas Pinilla, accordingly, took power amid almost universal acclaim, hailed by the Liberal opposition and all but the hard-core Gómez wing of Conservatives as the one who could finally stanch the blood flow of the *Violencia* and put the country back together.

GUSTAVO ROJAS PINILLA AND THE FAILURE OF MILITARY POPULISM

General Rojas Pinilla might actually have been a better president if (as Gómez believed) he had seized power as the result of a carefully matured conspiracy, rather than having power suddenly thrust upon him. He was quite unprepared for the position and in fact seems to have had no true program to offer the country except generalities about the need for moral regeneration of Colombia and strict adherence to the ideals of Jesus Christ and Simón Bolívar. Creation of an "Estado Cristiano y Bolivariano," as he put it[10]—the "Christian and Bolivarian State"—soon emerged as his basic political philosophy, but just what it meant was far from clear.

To be sure, as far as the "Christian" part was concerned, Rojas Pinilla was a fairly conventional Roman Catholic, who sincerely felt that close collaboration between church and state was essential for the moral regeneration he had in mind. Thus, the small minority of Colombian Protestants was perhaps the first group to discover that the change from Gómez to Rojas was no unmixed blessing. The prohibition of their proselytizing activities, under cover of an exceedingly narrow interpretation of the constitutional guarantee of religious toleration, was made if anything more severe under Rojas Pinilla. There were further restrictions on such things as Protestant schools. But at the same time actual instances of violence against Protestants did fall off, largely because the climate of violence generally declined, even if it did not disappear, under the new regime.

The "Bolivarian" part of the Rojas Pinilla formula was even vaguer. "Bolivarian" meant patriotic, brave, loyal, and true, which no one could be against. It also meant, in Rojas Pinilla's view, the subordination of narrow partisan interests to the higher ideals of national union and reconciliation—another aim that almost everyone gave at least lip service to. The new president gave expression to this spirit of concord by offering amnesty to Liberal guerrilla groups in return for the laying down of arms. Many accepted the offer, with the result that Rojas Pinilla was able to pacify most of eastern Colombia. The amnesty strategy proved effective precisely because Rojas Pinilla was a military man and as such technically nonpartisan. Liberal guerrilla fighters, who would never have trusted an offer of amnesty from a Conservative civilian like Laureano Gómez, were prepared to give Rojas Pinilla the benefit of the doubt.

Rojas Pinilla did not, however, establish another bipartisan coalition government, as many people expected him to do. Though military men loomed larger in high positions than before, the administration was still essentially civilian and 100 percent Conservative at the upper levels. A few Liberals received diplomatic assignments and the like, but never a cabinet post or a governorship. The principal change, perhaps, was that confirmed Laureanistas, or supporters of the deposed Laureano Gómez, had been replaced by members of other Conservative factions. Rojas Pinilla also did not lift the state of siege that had been in existence continually since 1949. Nevertheless, the vast majority of Colombians gladly supported him at first; and most political figures of both parties, except for die-hard Laureanistas, gave Rojas Pinilla their support when a largely hand-picked assembly—which included a smattering of Liberals—elected him for a full four-year term beginning in 1954.

The assembly was supposed to finish the job, left unfinished at the fall of Gómez, of revising the constitution. That it never did, but it managed to give a veneer of legality to Rojas Pinilla's personal continuation in office; and it enacted some miscellaneous reforms, including the official establishment of woman suffrage—a long-overdue measure that by now aroused little opposition. The catch was that Rojas Pinilla never got around to holding a popular election in which Colombian women might have exercised their newly acquired right to vote. Thus, practical implementation came only after his fall, Colombia barely escaping the dishonor (which went to Paraguay) of being the last Latin American nation in which women were able to vote.

In any case, the first or honeymoon stage of the regime did not last much beyond Rojas Pinilla's installation as president for the new term. Soon afterward, the story breaks down into several contrasting themes: the increasingly heavy-handed nature of the regime itself; the hardening of opposition from the traditional parties; Rojas Pinilla's unveiling of a social and economic reform program; and, as a troubling backdrop to it all, an eventual recrudescence of the *Violencia* itself. These themes are interrelated, but the exact relationship has been a matter of controversy. According to the general's critics, then and later, his own arbitrary measures caused the hardening of opposition and delayed the full achievement of pacification, while his reform measures were nothing but insincere attempts to appeal for popular support over the heads of the country's established political leadership. To Rojas Pinilla's admirers, then and later, the order of causation was exactly the reverse: it was his adoption of a far-sighted reform program that aroused the bitter hostility of the politicians, and his allegedly arbitrary actions were an unfortunate necessity, intended to restrain his opponents' irresponsible behavior, which was particularly dangerous in view of the continuing violence in much of the country. No doubt the wisest course is to think of all these developments as occurring more or less simultaneously. Needless to say, they were mutually reinforcing.[11]

Under the heading of arbitrary actions by the government—and without implying that these come first in the order of causation simply because they are discussed first—the most obvious concerned a further decline of press freedom, culminating in August 1955, when the leading newspaper of the country, the Liberal *El Tiempo* of Bogotá, was forced to suspend publication. Curiously, it was soon allowed to reappear, using the same equipment and the same staff, but with a clever new name: *Intermedio*. In effect, the "Times" of Bogotá had become the "Intermission." The new title itself was an implied rebuke, suggesting that the current situation was a passing phase, after which things would and should return to normal. Thus, Rojas Pinilla's treatment of the press was much the same as Gómez's had been: erratic, rather than directed at the absolute suppression of dissent. Other arbitrary actions were the instances of strong-arm tactics against members of the opposition—not just in outlying areas but in the cities. The classic example was the "bullring massacre" in Bogotá in February 1956, when squads of Rojas supporters took offense at the crowd's refusal to join in "vivas" for the government and retaliated by such means as dragging people feet first down the steps, heads banging on the way. At least eight died. That was, however, an extreme case, and there is no reason to suppose it was done at the president's orders. All things considered, the Rojas Pinilla dictatorship was a mild one, again demonstrating that Colombian soil was somewhat inhospitable to dictatorship per se, however much blood it may have soaked up over the years in political battles.

With regard to the growth of political opposition, it is hard to pinpoint exactly when any one group that originally supported Rojas Pinilla turned against him. What happened was a gradual disenchantment; and the Liberals became disenchanted first. As the principal victims of the political violence in recent years, they were delighted to see it initially winding down under Rojas Pinilla. Yet as the "out" party, and the majority party as well, the Liberals were the ones most anxious to restore normal constitutional procedures whereby they might hope to regain power. They were accordingly the ones most disappointed when it became clearer and clearer that Rojas Pinilla was in no hurry to do anything of the sort. Though he had the excuse that the country still had not really settled down, it was no less true that he enjoyed power once he had tasted it.

As for the Conservatives, some of them stayed with Rojas Pinilla to the very end, if only to keep their jobs, because civilian officeholders, as mentioned, were always predominantly Conservative. But practically all the big names of the party ultimately turned against him. Their motives (except those of determined Laureanistas) were less obvious than the Liberal leaders' motives, since Rojas Pinilla was in most respects—in family background and associations—a fellow Conservative. But from the standpoint of the civilian party hierarchy, he was definitely an upstart. He was someone who, instead of working his way up through service to the party, had started right out in the country's top position—and merely because he was a general! A general as stopgap between civilian presidents would have been acceptable, but only if he showed a clear commitment to the prompt restoration of civilian rule. For the Conservatives, too, would have liked to see a faster return to constitutional normalcy, with elections and the rest. That was the kind of game they knew how to play and enjoyed playing.

In addition to their political complaints against Rojas Pinilla, the leaders of both parties had reservations about his socioeconomic policy, in which he sought to stand forth—almost in the manner of Gaitán—as the true defender of the popular masses against selfish oligarchs. Of all the dimensions of his rule, this is the hardest to evaluate. It involved, for one thing, the raising of taxes on wealthy citizens (as in the taxation, for the first time, of stock dividends), with at least part of the proceeds to be invested in welfare activities. The suffering and dislocation resulting from the *Violencia* offered ample opportunities to carry out such programs, which Rojas Pinilla placed under the general supervision of a newly created Secretariado Nacional de Asistencia Social (SENDAS). The government also undertook several ambitious public works projects—including road construction; work on the Atlantic Railroad, which finally linked Bogotá with the coast at Santa Marta (although it was completed only in 1961 after the fall of Rojas); and the construction of tourist hotels and Bogotá's El Dorado airport. The high price of coffee during the first part of the regime helped provide funding for these efforts. On the other hand, Rojas Pinilla had no structural reforms to promote; and certainly he did not pick up the banner of agrarian reform, which had been rather too quickly abandoned by the earlier Liberal Republic. Indeed, Rojas Pinilla, a man of provincial middle-class origin, was in the process of acquiring extensive landed properties himself, whether as a safe investment or as a source of greater social prestige or both.

In the end, probably the most controversial aspect of Rojas Pinilla's socioeconomic policy was his frank attempt to build up organized labor as one of the two main props of his regime, alongside the armed forces. Such a policy looked suspiciously like that of Argentina's Juan D. Perón, another military man who tried to appeal to the people over the heads of civilian party leaders. Perón also proclaimed an ambitious socioeconomic reform program and, with his particular brand of authoritarian populism, was still in power at Buenos Aires at the time Rojas Pinilla took command in Bogotá. The Perón parallel was also suggested by the creation of SENDAS, which inevitably brought to mind the Fundación Eva Perón in Argentina—above all, when Rojas put his daughter, María Eugenia, in charge of it. She was no beauty like the famous Evita Perón, but she became an increasingly effective advocate of her father's policies. (By contrast, Rojas Pinilla's wife kept resolutely in the background; and his personal life did not give rise to the same whispering and scandalmongering as that of the Argentine dictator, particularly after Evita's death.)

More striking still was the *kind* of labor movement favored by Rojas Pinilla. When he came to power, the largest labor organization in Colombia was the Roman Catholic–oriented UTC, which formally rejected a policy of political engagement; the older CTC, now much weakened, had been the labor arm of the Liberal Party, though initially with some Communist participation. Neither one seemed likely to become a trusted partner of the regime, so that Rojas Pinilla gave encouragement instead to still another organization, the small Confederación Nacional de Trabajadores (CNT), which he felt he would be better able to control. The CNT was affiliated with the Latin America–wide labor confederation that went under the acronym ATLAS and was in turn sponsored by the Perón regime in Argentina. To the extent that it had an official ideology, the CNT espoused a version of the Peronistas' "justicialism," which purported to be a third position, avoiding the extremes of both communism and capitalism.

Rojas Pinilla was not, of course, trying to create in Colombia a mere copy of the Perón regime in Argentina, but there were parallels, and no doubt to some extent he was influenced by the example of Perón. Not surprisingly, however, all this worked out less successfully in Colombia because of obvious differences between the two countries. Argentina was then a much richer country to begin with, and one in which a postwar economic bonanza far exceeding any surge in coffee prices for Colombia allowed Perón to shower benefits on the poor without taking an equivalent amount of resources from anyone else. Moreover, although Colombia's urban population increased substantially during the 1950s, the urban labor force was neither as large nor as well organized as in Argentina. And rural labor in Colombia, apart from the banana enclave and other special cases, had never been amenable to union organization. The all-important coffee industry was built around a mass of small producers (peasant proprietors or tenants or sharecroppers) who were independent operators—and as such did not think of themselves as mere wage laborers.

Another problem for Rojas Pinilla was the role of the church. It had originally been a warm supporter of Rojas and of Perón, but it eventually fell out with Perón in Argentina. After that, any seeming ties between Rojas and the Argentine dictator could only arouse the suspicion of the church in Colombia. The church was also protective of the UTC, as against the government-favored CNT, in the field of labor; and a pastoral letter of the Colombian bishops condemning that Argentine-connected labor confederation was one clear sign of displeasure with the way the regime was heading. Consequently, since the united voice of the church hierarchy still carried weight with him, Rojas Pinilla gradually withdrew support from the CNT.

Even though Rojas Pinilla's socioeconomic policies came to alarm the ecclesiastical as well as the traditional political and economic leadership blocs, there was clearly something to be said for his general approach. Since the country's political system had brought so much strife and bloodshed, why not sweep it aside and start over—forget the hereditary hatreds of Liberals and Conservatives and get down to work solving the country's basic problems, in a close alliance of people, government, and armed forces? That in a nutshell was Rojas Pinilla's ideology in its final form, and it had appeal to quite a few people. Unfortunately, though, the measures that he took were not always well thought out or consistently applied. He was also hurt by the various charges of corruption that came to be leveled against him. These charges were no doubt grossly exaggerated; but he did, perhaps, show a sometimes excessive willingness to accept gifts from supporters and admirers, and he was engaging in various business transactions—especially cattle and real estate deals—over and above his presidential duties. He may not have done anything technically illegal, but if nothing else his activities laid him open to the suspicion that he was exploiting his high position for personal gain; and in this respect his conduct offered a painful contrast with that of his predecessor, Laureano Gómez, who was fanatically honest (as well as fanatically everything else). Although there had always been bureaucratic corruption of some sort in Colombia, bare-faced, high-level profiteering on, say, the Mexican scale was simply not done. Hence, even the hint of financial misconduct in the Colombian presidency was unusual, and it hurt the standing of Rojas Pinilla. Influence peddling and the handing out or receiving of special favors among other members of the regime further contributed to giving it a slightly shady moral tone.

Among the weak points of Rojas Pinilla's rule, one must similarly include his ultimate failure, despite a promising start, to put an end to the *Violencia*. Just why and where he went wrong in handling this problem is another source of disagreement. However, there always remained a hard core of guerrilla fighters who did not accept Rojas Pinilla's offers of amnesty. Some of the holdouts were members of Communist rural enclaves in the upper Magdalena Valley who had formed their own self-defense forces; and the regime never showed the same interest in conciliating the Communists that it had shown toward Liberals. (It even declared the Communist Party formally illegal, for the first and only time in Colombia.) Other armed groups were made up of men who had already undergone a process of evolution to outright criminal banditry; and still others undoubtedly wanted to wait a little longer to see how things turned out before committing themselves to lay down arms. In any case, the failure of a large number of armed *guerrilleros* to accept his offers of peace and reconciliation seems to have puzzled Rojas Pinilla and in the end angered him to the extent that he unleashed a campaign of all-out military repression against certain of the remaining strongholds—a campaign that hurt innocent bystanders as well and on balance was probably counterproductive.

Rojas Pinilla's inability to end the *Violencia* inevitably eroded the support that he had received when he first took power. A decline in the price of coffee after the middle of the decade added to the climate of dissatisfaction. Rojas Pinilla might still have managed to serve out the four-year term to which he had been elected by the constitutional assembly he himself convened; but when he began making preparations to be chosen for a second such term, his enemies decided to wait no longer. As a preliminary step, the traditional parties agreed—by the terms of a pact negotiated between Liberal ex-president Alberto Lleras Camargo and Laureano Gómez in his place of Spanish exile— to work together to overthrow the dictatorship and to share power peacefully thereafter. The country's business and professional establishment did its part by calling a "general strike" against Rojas Pinilla in May of 1957. It was not a strike by workers so much as a lockout, whereby businesses and factories simply closed their doors. Many rank-and-file Colombians undoubtedly continued to sympathize with Rojas, but nobody chose to set up barricades and fight in his support. Instead, the working masses in effect agreed to sit this out; and when the rest of the military high command suggested to Rojas Pinilla that he quietly withdraw for the good of the country, he made his way to exile.

The National Front:
Achievements and Failures
(1958–1978)

The overthrow of Rojas Pinilla was meant to usher in a new era of political reconciliation and domestic peace, which in turn would favor rapid social and economic development for Colombia. To a large extent these objectives were achieved, even though, as things turned out, the more progress was made in one area, it seemed, the more problems came to light in others. The forces that overthrew the dictatorship did remain united—so successfully that national politics became almost boring; yet Liberal and Conservative leaders were less successful in coping with the new phenomenon of leftist guerrilla insurgency. Significant economic growth occurred, as well as notable improvements in public education, but there was not much change in overall patterns of inequality. Meanwhile, advances in transportation and communications infrastructure and in the development of mass media served to lessen the differences among regions—bringing a common national culture closer to realization than ever before—but made the problems that were still unsolved more difficult to ignore.

THE INSTITUTIONALIZATION
OF BIPARTISAN RULE

The military junta that replaced Gustavo Rojas Pinilla in May 1957 never aspired to anything more than a caretaker role, and it stayed in power just long enough for a civilian government to be elected under a new set of rules drawn up for the express purpose of preventing a recurrence of the interparty bloodshed the country had just experienced. These rules, devised by the top leaders of the two traditional parties and then approved by the voters in a popular plebiscite, laid the basis for the peculiar bipartisan coalition regime, known as the

National Front, that remained in control of the country until the 1970s. It brought to mind other coalitions that had come to the fore in times of national crisis (most recently in 1946); but this coalition—unlike the others—followed a set of mathematical guidelines written into the constitution itself, so that everyone might know the exact rules of the game and would also know that these rules could not be casually changed from one day to the next. They specified two things primarily: the compulsory sharing of all elective and appointive positions on an equal basis between the Liberal and Conservative parties, and the alternation of the two parties in possession of the Colombian presidency. A natural corollary was the formal exclusion of third parties from any share of political power.

To some outside observers, as well as to a disgruntled minority of Colombians, the new rules represented by their very nature a denial of democratic principles. They certainly did restrict democratic politics—but less than appeared on the surface. To begin with, though by this time the Liberal Party clearly had a permanent edge over the Conservative in popular strength, it was not so great that enforced equality between the two did major violence to the will of the inhabitants—at least, not as far as the nation as a whole was concerned. In some municipalities, to be sure, one party might be so overwhelmingly predominant that it was difficult to find enough members of the other to fill its guaranteed 50 percent share of local positions. Nor did the National Front system put an end to electoral competition. Though each party reserved in advance 50 percent of the seats in the national Congress, departmental assemblies, and municipal councils, elections still took place for all these bodies, and the competition was often heated; it merely was a competition between different slates of either Liberal or Conservative candidates for their own party's guaranteed share of positions. Even the legal exclusion of third parties was less important than it seemed. Quite apart from the general insignificance of third parties in Colombian politics, there was no regulation stating the requirements for party membership. Thus, anyone who so desired could call himself (or herself, since the political rights of women were now at last truly operational) a Liberal or Conservative on election day and compete for one of that party's quota of positions. The Communists, for example, ran candidates as members of a dissident Liberal faction improvised for this very purpose; and they did about as badly as they might have done if running under their own colors.

The institutional mechanisms of the National Front were originally to remain in effect for exactly sixteen years, corresponding to two presidential periods for each of the two parties. But another constitutional amendment, adopted in 1968, provided for the system to be gradually phased out; unrestricted electoral competition was to be fully restored by 1974, and the required equal sharing of executive positions would come to an end in 1978. Yet the constitution, as revised, stipulated that even after 1978 the runner-up party should be given its "equitable" share of positions (without defining "equitable"). As a result, coalition rule was further prolonged, in practice, until 1986, when President Virgilio Barco, having offered the Conservatives a share of power that they spurned as unsatisfactory, reverted to a single-party (Liberal) administration.

The first of the National Front presidents was a Liberal, Alberto Lleras Camargo, who had occupied the presidency from 1945 to 1946, after Alfonso López Pumarejo resigned from office. Lleras Camargo had been absent from Colombia during the worst of the *Violencia*, enhancing his personal and political prestige as secretary general of the Organization of American States; later he was one of the architects of the Liberal-Conservative alliance that overthrew Rojas Pinilla. Known as a successful conciliator and highly esteemed in the United States, from which Colombia hoped to receive help in national rehabilitation, he was a logical person to inaugurate the new system. His Conservative successor from 1962 to 1966 was Guillermo León Valencia, an old-style politician best remembered for such picturesque gaffes as greeting Charles de Gaulle in Bogotá with a rousing "Viva España!" At least he was a man of general tolerance and good will, who administered his office in the spirit of the National Front until turning it over to its third chief executive, the Liberal Carlos Lleras Restrepo, a not very close cousin of Lleras Camargo.

Among all the National Front presidents, the second Lleras was easily the most vigorous administrator and the one responsible for the greatest number of policy innovations, which he carried out with the help of a coterie of young technocrats, trained as often as not at foreign universities. He bequeathed power in 1970 to the Conservative Misael Pastrana, who had been his minister of government but on whom his characteristic hyperactivism seemingly had not rubbed off. After presiding over a largely do-nothing administration, Pastrana transmitted the presidency in turn to Alfonso López Michelsen, son of López Pumarejo, whose opponents in the election of 1974 were the offspring of two other past presidents: Laureano Gómez's son Álvaro, running for the Conservatives, and María Eugenia Rojas as candidate of a new third party. It almost seemed that this election was fought out among the ghosts of the parents, and Colombian voters clearly had the most favorable memories of the earlier López, giving his son a comfortable majority of the votes cast. However, anyone who expected to repeat the exhilaration of the "Revolución en Marcha" was destined to be disappointed. The second López made his chief innovations in foreign affairs rather than in domestic policy. In particular, he sought to take a line more independent of the United States—e.g., restoring the relations with revolutionary Cuba that Colombia, along with all the other Latin American countries except Mexico, had broken in the 1960s.

Even if it did not satisfy all the hopes raised, the National Front successfully accomplished the one thing above all else that it was designed to do: end the *Violencia*. For this purpose it employed the same combination of techniques that Rojas Pinilla had used: offers of amnesty and the select application of military force against holdouts. It also developed ambitious programs of "civic military action," whereby military detachments were deployed to build needed roads and schools and clinics in violence-afflicted areas—and army dentists to fill cavities free of charge in peasant mouths—all with a view to gaining the confidence of the rural population, without which true pacification would not come. The National Front further benefited from a national mood of sheer exhaustion and revulsion against the use of violence. Above all, though, its very structure had a powerful calming effect on the traditional political rivalries that had set off the *Violencia* in the first place. Over and above the messages of interparty fraternity now emanating from party headquarters in the national and departmental capitals, the National Front system vastly reduced the incentives to indulge in violent action. After all, why should members of one party shoot up a neighboring village of opposite political persuasion when each party was guaranteed 50 percent of the patronage jobs no matter what, without even taking risks?

Pacification did not come overnight, but the political death rate fell sharply, and by the midpoint of the second National Front administration—that of Guillermo Valencia—the yearly toll was in only three digits.[1] The *Violencia* was for all practical purposes at an end. Or, to be more precise, the *Violencia* as a Liberal-Conservative feud, with eddies of banditry thrown in, was now over. New forms of violence would gradually take its place, but they never equaled the levels of ferocity seen in the late 1940s and early 1950s.

Partly as a by-product of this achievement, the religious question in Colombia disappeared even more rapidly and completely than the *Violencia*. Protestants were no longer mishandled for either political or religious reasons, and the various restrictions that had been imposed on Protestant activities were lifted. Most striking was the spread of a genuine tolerance between Catholics and Protestants themselves, to the point that Protestant ministers and Roman Catholic priests could be seen sharing the platform at public functions. Naturally, the winds of renewal blowing through the church at large, of which the reforms of John XXIII and the Second Vatican Council were the clearest expression, also had something to do with this transformation. Indeed, the Roman Catholic church in Colombia began a rapid evolution away from its previous doctrinaire rigidity and close alliance with political Conservatism. And, while the church leadership came to assume a position of moderate progressivism in political and social matters, a growing minority of priests—strongly influenced by the new movements of liberation theology and Third World activism prevalent among the clergy elsewhere in Latin America—began dabbling in leftist causes and thereby giving aid and comfort to Marxist revolutionaries, who became one of the new forces of violence on the Colombian scene.

The return of religious freedom was one aspect of a more general restoration of Colombia's once proud record as a country of free speech and press and other basic liberties. Even after the fall of Rojas Pinilla, the country remained much of the time under a state of siege, often loosely interpreted by foreign observers as a kind of martial law. Yet in practice the state of siege seldom made much difference. It allowed the authorities to limit public assemblies, censor the press, and restrict other basic liberties, but most of the time these emergency powers were not used. Under the state of siege, small leftist weeklies or monthlies openly sympathized with guerrillas who were trying to overthrow the existing regime by force, and nobody bothered to interfere. Of course, if such publications had enjoyed a mass circulation, which they did not, the response might have been different. When in the early 1970s a nonrevolutionary but strongly antiestablishment Bogotá newspaper, called simply *El Periódico*, was launched by dissident Liberals and proved an almost instant success, it was quickly starved by the systematic denial of advertising revenues—but this was essentially the doing of the private sector, not any official censor.[2] The one emergency procedure under the state of siege that came into play with some regularity was the use of summary military courts to deal with those accused of public-order crimes. There were charges of arbitrary treatment and even torture of individuals being held under this provision, but at least the charges were publicly aired, and they did not become pervasive until the aggravation of the guerrilla and terrorist problem in the early 1980s.

A revealing example is the treatment accorded to General Rojas Pinilla, when in October 1958, to the annoyance of both Liberal and Conservative leaders, he came home from exile. If he expected a mass uprising in his favor at his arrival, he was disappointed. Instead, he was brought before the Colombian Senate, acting as a special jury for ex-presidents, to be tried for assorted misdeeds committed in office. But he got off very lightly, with nothing more than deprivation of his political rights, meaning his right to vote, to hold office, and to engage in partisan activities; and even this sentence was later overturned by the Colombian Supreme Court, which thus once again demonstrated its independence vis-à-vis the other branches. It was all a bit odd in view of the terrible accusations of corruption and worse that had been made against him; but quite apart from the exaggeration in those charges to begin with, there seems to have been some unwillingness to press matters too far, since many people now high in the councils of the National Front had been collaborators of Rojas Pinilla in the earlier phases of his regime. They could well have been embarrassed if all the dirty linen were exposed in public. Be that as it may, the fallen dictator—alone among the distinguished group of Latin American dictators who were overthrown within a few years of each other in the late 1950s—returned home to live peacefully in his own country and did all he could, until his death in 1974, to make life difficult for the people who overthrew him. It makes one wonder what might have happened to Fulgencio Batista if he had suddenly turned up in Havana. And Perón did not return to Buenos Aires until he received full assurances that he would not be brought to trial.

Rojas Pinilla proceeded to organize a new political movement of strongly populist flavor, similar to what he had tried to launch even while dictator but considerably more successful. It took the name of

Alianza Nacional Popular (ANAPO). Like the National Front that it was formed to combat, it was bipartisan in makeup, with Liberal and Conservative wings, which on election day fielded candidates under their respective labels just like any mainstream factions of the traditional parties. ANAPO's colors were red, white, and blue—not in imitation of gringo symbolism but in token of peaceful coexistence between Colombia's own "reds" and "blues," for those were the colors historically used by the Liberal and Conservative Parties. The ex-dictator thus urged Colombians once more to rise above the old party hatreds, but not in the manner of the ruling National Front, which he dismissed as an alliance of oligarchs fighting to defend their selfish privileges against the common people. Much of his appeal was again reminiscent of Gaitán's, although his specific program was even harder to characterize. On the one hand, he took a nationalist line, accusing the oligarchs of being too beholden to the United States, but his nationalism was one that emphasized the traditional values of fatherland, family, religion, and community—just as one might have expected from someone of his personal background. On the other hand, his sweeping condemnation of the oligarchs and their system of socioeconomic and political privilege had a vaguely leftist ring. A witticism that gained wide currency at the time had it that the ANAPO program was nothing more nor less than a mixture of "vodka and holy water."

ANAPO quickly established itself as a force to be reckoned with. In some small towns one of the traditional party bosses might decide to throw in his lot with it and then would deliver his own collection of captive votes to its candidates on election day. Yet it struck the most responsive chord among the lower-class and lower-middle-class urban population, whose inherited Liberal or Conservative loyalties were weaker. These people found in Rojas Pinilla, as earlier in Gaitán, a figure who seemed to understand the problems of unemployment and high prices that afflicted them and who was prepared to take a stand against the obscure forces that were to blame for it all. In the congressional elections of 1966, the two wings of ANAPO won between them almost 20 percent of the seats. The high point for the movement came, though, in 1970, when Rojas Pinilla presented himself as a candidate for president. He did so under the Conservative label, because the 1970–1974 term was reserved to the Conservatives by the alternation agreement. The election was complicated by the presence of two other dissident Conservative candidates who did not flatly oppose the National Front per se as did Rojas Pinilla. As a result, no one received an outright majority; and Rojas Pinilla trailed the official National Front candidate, Misael Pastrana, by only 1.6 percent.

To be precise, Rojas Pinilla received 39.0 percent of the vote against Pastrana's 40.6 percent. Since the election rules contained no provision for a runoff, Pastrana's edge was enough to make him Colombia's next president. ANAPO loyalists, however, were convinced that their candidate had really won, only to be cheated out of victory by official fraud. They pointed out that early returns had shown Rojas Pinilla enjoying a comfortable lead but that, as soon as they took to the streets to begin celebrating their victory, the government of President Lleras Restrepo clamped a state of siege on the country and interrupted the announcement of election results. When reporting was resumed the next morning, Pastrana was suspiciously moving ahead. The election-night scenario convinced even many non-Anapistas and foreign observers that the election must have been stolen. Yet the final returns did not reveal any grossly suspicious vote totals, and the overall pattern was exactly what one could have predicted: the cities went predominantly for Rojas Pinilla, while small towns and rural areas, where the traditional parties remained strong and from which returns were reported more slowly because of the difficulties of transportation and communication, generally backed Pastrana. If, then, the election was "stolen," it was only in the sense that any Colombian election was bound to be marred by miscellaneous irregularities committed on all sides—a few false credentials here, a touch of intimidation there—with government supporters having an obvious advantage in getting away with their abuses. The net balance of petty frauds might well have amounted to more than the slim margin of Pastrana's victory, but that would be impossible to prove. In any event, the disputed presidential contest of 1970 does not change the fact that, all in all, the conduct of elections under the National Front was marked by far fewer irregularities than Colombia had known up to that point.

THE DEVELOPMENT AGENDA
OF THE 1960s

Colombia's implementation of a unique form of constitutional democracy went hand in hand with a series of social and economic programs designed both to rehabilitate *Violencia*-stricken areas of the country and to speed the pace of development generally as one way of preventing the recurrence of the same disasters. In a hemispheric context these programs fitted in admirably with what came to be known as the Alliance for Progress, the U.S.-sponsored effort to undercut the appeal of the Cuban Revolution by demonstrating that progressive capitalism rather than communism was the most effective means of improving Latin America's material conditions of life. Colombia would in fact become, with Chile, one of the two most touted "show-cases" of the Alliance. Unlike Chile, it did not repay the United States for aid received by choosing a Marxist as president—the victory of Salvador Allende in the Chilean election of 1970—although the near victory of Rojas Pinilla in that same year, running on a populist anti-establishment platform, did raise questions about the adequacy of the formulas adopted for Colombia.

The efforts to promote socioeconomic development inevitably entailed a further expansion of the activity of the state, or—more precisely—of the national executive and assorted quasi-autonomous administrative agencies. The increasing use of technocratic specialists in official positions (a trend given particular impetus by Carlos Lleras Restrepo) led to at least some increase in governmental efficiency and thus helped to offset the intrinsic cumbersomeness of a coalition regime, with its requirement always to seek out consensus among the parties and factions. Moreover, the constitutional reform of 1968, in addition to setting guidelines for the gradual dismantling of the National Front's political mechanisms, provided the executive with new tools to use in implementing economic policy—notably, the ability to declare a "state of national economic and social emergency" as a means of bypassing Congress in the adoption of needed reforms or adjustments. Congress also lost its right of initiative in social and economic legislation, except for local pork-barrel projects needed to reward constituents. While the legislature lost ground, however, private producers' associations retained a key role in all matters that concerned their interests. The prime example was always the Federación Nacional de Cafeteros (FEDECAFE), to which the state had in effect delegated most of the responsibility for managing the nation's single most important industry. But the Asociación Nacional de Industriales (ANDI) had a major role in setting industrial policy (or for that matter economic policy generally); and the Sociedad de Agricultores de Colombia (SAC), which represented mainly large-scale agriculturalists, was successful in keeping the National Front's agrarian reform program within very moderate limits.

Agrarian reform had languished in Colombia since the abortive start made by the first López administration in the 1930s. There was no major upsurge of grass-roots demand for it now from the Colombian peasantry, which had no strong national organizations to press the issue in any case; and the Communists and other leftist groups that talked about the need for land redistribution were weak, not to mention technically excluded from political participation under National Front rules. However, the *Violencia* had amply revealed the pathology of much of rural life in Colombia, including the conflicts over land in certain areas and the general state of deprivation and lack of education of the rural masses, which had made them susceptible to murderous political manipulation. Hence, agrarian reform seemed to offer a means of repairing some of the damage done in recent years and creating a sturdy, prosperous peasant class that would resist future calls to partisan insanity. The possibility that such a peasant class would be a better market for Colombian manufactures recommended the idea to enlightened industrialists, while social engineers of various persuasions hoped that agrarian reform would stem the tide of rural-to-urban migration that was placing impossible demands on urban services.

There was thus widespread support for the concept of agrarian reform, and it became a top priority of the first National Front administration of Alberto Lleras Camargo. But the SAC in the name of the landowners, plus the cattle raisers' association and less enlightened political leaders, mounted a campaign of obstruction that delayed enactment of the measure until 1961 and then made sure that it was thoroughly limited in scope. The 1961 law set up an agrarian reform agency—Instituto Colombiano de Reforma Agraria, or INCORA—and authorized the outright expropriation of privately owned estates, if necessary, for redistribution to those who had insufficient land or no land. But the terms of the law made clear that expropriation was a last resort. The major emphasis would be on resettling peasants on lands reclaimed for agriculture through irrigation works and the like, or on the existing public domain.

Most of the law's backers saw no need to carry out a wholesale restructuring of land tenure. Small peasant plots already constituted the great majority of landholdings. In 1960 some 86 percent of holdings measured less than 20 hectares. Although these holdings accounted for only 15 percent of total agricultural property, small-holders supplied most of such widely consumed traditional food-stuffs as plantains and potatoes. Large estates were predominant in the production of cotton, rice, and cane sugar for refining. In coffee the family farm was the basic unit of production; but larger properties, which were introducing new varieties of coffee and making greater use of technical innovations, were beginning to increase their share of total production once again.[3] In any case, the aim of the legislation was to help peasants whose plots, through repeated subdivision among family members, were no longer sufficient to offer a decent livelihood, as well as to give land to an indeterminate number of land-less farmworkers, provided all this could be done without seriously disrupting existing patterns of production. The purpose of the reform was as much social and political—to defuse actual or potential rural unrest—as economic.

For a few years the measure was implemented at snail's pace. The pace picked up after Lleras Restrepo took office; for among the leaders of the two dominant parties, he was clearly the one most committed to agrarian reform. His reasons were not entirely agrarian. He also hoped to check, at its rural source, the rise of urban unemployment—a problem that Rojas Pinilla's new political movement could exploit. But the result was a sharp increase in the rate of land distribution by INCORA, the reform agency. In addition, and most interestingly, Lleras Restrepo sponsored the creation of the Asociación Nacional de Usuarios Campesinos (ANUC), or National Association of Peasant Users, as a countrywide organization of peasant farmers. Its members were "users" of state agrarian services, not merely the service of land reform per se but other governmental credit and agricultural extension programs; they were even to have a part in administration of the services in question. It was also assumed that they would give valuable political support to the reform objectives and thus help counter the continued foot-dragging and outright opposition of the landed interests and party leaders associated with them.

With active government assistance, ANUC branches were rapidly organized throughout the country. By early 1970 over three-fourths of a million peasants were listed as members, almost as many as the nation's labor unions had managed to enroll in a half century of struggle.

Heartened by the administration's commitment to the reform, ANUC branches began demanding even faster land distribution, and they did not hesitate to bring pressure by staging "invasions" of large private estates.

In April 1970 the peasant vote, much of it orchestrated by ANUC, provided the slim margin of victory for the official National Front candidate, Pastrana, against the populist challenge of Rojas Pinilla with his massive urban support. Yet Pastrana did not share Lleras Restrepo's enthusiasm for agrarian reform. Even if land redistribution did not come to a halt, progress made under the new administration was largely the result of the momentum built up under its predecessor and the continuing wave of land invasions, which repeatedly forced the hand of officials. But the invasions greatly hardened the attitude of the reform's opponents, and at a time when many industrialists were beginning to have second thoughts on the issue, among other reasons because of the advantage they derived from rural-urban migration in the form of cheap labor. The slowdown of agrarian reform became even more noticeable during the administration of Alfonso López Michelsen, who had never been a strong supporter of land redistribution although he did push other efforts designed to help smallholders modernize their production. In much of the country, meanwhile, ANUC was taken over by ultraleftists whose absorbing interest was to promote revolution. This development alienated many peasants who were more interested in concrete incremental gains, and it evoked ever harsher state repression.

The reform nevertheless remained on the statute books, and if progress was less than spectacular, neither was it wholly negligible. From 1962 to 1979 over 250,000 families gained land under INCORA's auspices. Seven-eighths of these families benefited merely by the allocation of titles to public land—often land on which they previously had been squatters, though in some instances it was formerly private land to which the owner's title was officially declared to have lapsed. But the overall pattern of land distribution in the country was virtually the same at the end of the period as at the beginning, so that the creation of new peasant landholdings was roughly equivalent to the number of small farms that meanwhile disappeared through the expansion of large-scale commercial agriculture or migration to the cities or for any other reason.[4] Perhaps, in the final analysis, Colombia's agrarian reform should be credited simply with helping to ward off the dissolution of the independent peasantry that Marx had predicted and some proponents of unmitigated agrarian capitalism have frankly favored. To be sure, the continuing vitality of the smallholding producers themselves had even more to do with their survival.

National Front programs in the industrial area were both less controversial and less novel. The drive for import substitution was intensified, by the use of tariffs and import quotas, tax incentives, and more direct forms of official involvement, including help with financing from the government's industrial development institute, Instituto de Fomento Industrial (IFI). A landmark of sorts was the definitive launching of automobile production in Colombia. After a few false starts and some more limited assembly operations, a contract was signed in 1969 between IFI and Renault of France to establish a full-scale passenger-car production plant near Medellín. As part of the arrangement, an engine plant was created in the department of Boyacá, close to the Paz de Río steel complex but linked to the main Renault operation by rather inconvenient transport over mountain roads. Boyacá's status as a vote-rich depressed area certainly influenced the siting of engine production; but Colombia's approach was more rational than that of other Latin American countries, such as Peru and Venezuela, which from an early date had allowed the proliferation of an excessive number of separate automobile assembly plants. Colombia waited longer than any other of the larger countries to get started, and it consciously tried to scale the size of the industry to that of the potential national market. There would be subsequent changes in the lineup of vehicle manufacturing firms in Colombia, but as of 1992 there were still only three—and despite a declining market share Renault remained stereotypically *el carro colombiano*.

Both consumer durables and capital goods manufacturing increased their respective shares of industrial output, and they both represented import substitution. Yet they remained heavily dependent on inputs of foreign capital and technology. Foreign companies accounted for roughly three times as large a share of industrial employment in 1970 as in 1955; and remittance of profits and transfer payments for the use of technology naturally limited the balance-of-payments relief and other net benefits to Colombia from this industrial expansion. Naturally, too, the more capital-intensive an industry— and on the whole the fastest-growing industries were capital-intensive—the fewer jobs were created for a population that was growing rapidly. For all these reasons the Colombian government it-self, without abandoning the cause of import substitution, began to show renewed interest in export promotion as well in its economic planning. As in many other aspects of economic policy, it was the Lleras Restrepo administration that took the decisive steps, by creat-ing a special agency to provide credit, market information, and other help to exporters and by offering extensive tax rebates to the exporters of "nontraditional" products. The program was conspicuously suc-cessful, the value of "nontraditional" exports nearly doubling from 1967 to 1971. Without doubt, the outstanding success story was that of Colombian flower sales, which today are second in the world only to Holland's. Based mainly in the suburbs of Bogotá, the flower indus-try took advantage of a fertile soil, a year-round growing climate, and a hub of dense air traffic to carry freshly cut flowers to foreign mar-kets. But the initial impetus came from those official incentives.

A somewhat special case was the recovery of Colombian banana exporting, which had virtually collapsed during World War II, briefly recovered in the mid-1950s, but languished again until the early 1960s. Then a new area for banana plantations began to be opened up around the port of Turbó, near the border with Panama in western Colombia, which soon overshadowed the original Santa Marta ba-nana zone. The United Fruit Company was involved in developing this area too, but only as an exporter, not a grower, and in association with Colombian private investors and government agencies. The new banana zone attracted a steady stream of job seekers and speculators; it became notorious for its rough frontier atmosphere and for the myriad social problems that would, by the 1980s, make it a fertile ground for both labor activists and leftist guerrillas. It also became an important new source of wealth for the Colombian economy.

Lleras Restrepo again had export promotion in mind when he signed the Andean Pact of 1969, which created a limited common market comprised of the countries of western South America from Colombia to Chile. Chile subsequently dropped out, and though Venezuela came to take its place, the venture never lived up to ex-pectations; but Colombian trade with its immediate neighbors did increase somewhat. Of considerably greater importance, in both the short and the long term, was Lleras Restrepo's new departure in man-aging the exchange rate. Since the 1950s Colombia had experienced a succession of foreign exchange crises, caused primarily by a persistent weakness of export earnings and of coffee prices in particular. From the bonanza of the Korean War period, when coffee was selling at over a dollar a pound, the price fell to less than half as much in the early 1960s; and the OPEC-style price support scheme adopted under the auspices of the 1962 International Coffee Agreement (with market quotas assigned to the producing countries) only gradually helped the coffee industry regain lost ground. The result was a series of balance-of-payments crises in Colombia, leading to abrupt devaluations of the peso. Lleras Restrepo was facing one such exchange crisis after he assumed the presidency; and international lending agencies insisted, as was their custom, that another major devaluation was essential. The Colombian president rejected the advice. Instead, he struck a pose of gallantly rejecting foreign dictation—and then proceeded to devalue the peso, but in a manner that was relatively painless and ultimately more effective than the previous sudden, sharp changes in the value of the currency.

To be exact, in 1967 Lleras Restrepo instituted a system of continuous mini-devaluations, which aimed to keep the exchange value of the peso always in line with its intrinsic worth in the world market. The system has remained in effect since then, and though at times the pace of devaluation has fallen slightly behind the difference between internal inflation and world price levels—and the peso has thus become moderately overvalued—the basic exchange mechanism rendered such problems easy to correct. After 1967 Colombia was wholly spared the massive devaluations that have scarred the economies of other Latin American countries. The maintenance of a realistic exchange rate, furthermore, was an indispensable condition for success of the export-promotion campaign.

A number of advances occurred also in aspects of social policy. The system of Cajas de Compensación Familiar (literally "family compensation funds"), introduced in 1962, provided a wide array of fringe benefits, from education subsidies to health care to inexpensive vacations, for employees of affiliated organizations. This program benefited mainly white-collar workers and the better-paid factory workers, but coverage did gradually expand. Basic social security coverage also expanded, although it still reached only about one-third of Colombian workers in the private sector.

Progress was more striking in the field of education, seen as a critical ingredient for economic development and a greater degree of social equality. At the fall of Rojas Pinilla, between 60 and 65 percent of primary-age children were actually enrolled in school, and some 15 percent of Colombian children, mainly rural, had no access at all to formal schooling. The literacy rate as of 1960 stood at 63 percent. These were thoroughly unimpressive figures, even if close to the Latin American norm, and they reflected the fact that popular education had seldom been a top priority of the nation's rulers. However, education was placed high on the country's agenda by the same 1957 plebiscite that created the National Front regime, for it specified that henceforth not less than 10 percent of the national government's budget should be devoted to educational expenditures. This goal was not much more than the average level of educational spending in recent years, but it was comfortably exceeded in practice, with some of the funds coming from Alliance for Progress aid. In 1964 the budget allocated 14 percent of expenditures to education—and by 1978 the figure was almost 20 percent (reflecting in part the assumption by the national government of responsibilities previously left to the departments). The result was a significant increase in school attendance. As of 1975, total enrollments among seven- to thirteen-year-old children came to more than 77 percent. By 1981 adult illiteracy was less than 15 percent.[5]

These and other statistical indicators attest to the degree of emphasis being placed on public primary education, which had not yet achieved universal coverage but was not far from it. At the secondary level the rate of increase was even greater, with enrollments more than doubling just in the 1960s. In the following decade, although postprimary education was still reaching considerably fewer than half of Colombian children, the number attending state secondary schools actually came to surpass private secondary enrollments. The change was a significant one, because Colombia, like most of Latin America, had long tended to rely on private institutions to provide most secondary schooling; and, since they charged tuition, the great majority of the population was automatically excluded. This educational bottleneck in the way of upward mobility was now at last in the process of being removed.

Progress toward overcoming the nation's educational deficiencies might have been faster if the educational system had not been burdened by the rapid growth in population, especially among the lower age groups. When the National Front came to power, Colombia was facing the phenomenon commonly defined as "demographic explosion," when advances in medicine and public health have significantly lowered death rates but the birthrate, governed by social and cultural forces that change more slowly, remains high. In the 1960s Colombia experienced an overall increase in population at a rate of something like 3.2 percent a year. The rate would have been higher still except for the steady drain of legal and illegal migration to Colombia's more prosperous neighbor, Venezuela. The rapidity of population growth created other challenges besides the burden on the school system, from provision of all kinds of services to the creation of needed employment opportunities.

The country's rulers were aware of the demographic problem, and they moved to attack it directly through systematic official support to family-planning agencies. In reality, they were promoting wider use of artificial birth-control methods, although this self-evident fact was purposely downplayed because of the Roman Catholic church's stated opposition to such practices. Thanks to the discretion shown in talking about the program, and the fact that the church as a whole was highly supportive of the National Front regime, ecclesiastical opposition did not become a major problem. There was also criticism from the ANAPO of Rojas Pinilla, and from the left, which alleged that population control was something foisted on Latin America by the United States and its allies in international development agencies out of fear that the growing numerical superiority of Latin Americans over North Americans endangered imperialist domination. But leftist criticism was even more easily ignored.

The nation's vital statistics soon showed that Colombians were receptive to the idea of limiting family size. By 1980 the population growth rate had fallen to about 2 percent a year—one of the fastest declines recorded anywhere in the contemporary world. To be sure, the decline could not be attributed solely to the accessibility of birth-control clinics and pills; it reflected as well the overall process of social and economic development. A population that was becoming increasingly urban had less need for extra children as farm laborers than did a traditional peasant society. Economic growth in and of itself likewise brought women more opportunities for outside employment, and they were beginning to assert their preference for fewer children.

The fall in the birthrate was not the only circumstance that affected the situation of women (and vice versa). Colombia had been one of the last countries in Latin America to grant women even the right to vote, but they were soon being elected as well as electing. The proportion of women in Congress, though hovering in the vicinity of 3 percent, was not much different from that in the United States, where their legal enfranchisement had come much sooner. Women were also being appointed to high executive positions—starting actually under the dictatorship of Rojas Pinilla, when woman suffrage was first enacted even if not yet put into practice. In addition to putting his daughter María Eugenia in charge of administering social welfare programs, Rojas had named the first woman governor and the first woman cabinet minister. As often happened in Latin America, education was the first ministry entrusted to a female appointee, but women steadily expanded their foothold after the dictatorship fell, even if they did not receive such key positions as minister of government (interior) or finance, or the governorships of such major departments as Cundinamarca and Antioquia. (Only in 1989 did President Virgilio Barco finally name a woman to administer Antioquia, in the midst of a violent crackdown on the illegal drug traffic centered in Medellín.)

Colombian women received more than just a growing share of official positions. They also won a battle for formal legal equality that had begun, in the face of vehement opposition, under Enrique Olaya Herrera in the 1930s. Married women had then won control over their own property. Now, under the National Front, they gained equal authority over minor children, and in general, whether married or single, women obtained the same rights under civil law as male citizens. This legal reform made less difference in the actual conditions of women than did the emergence of greater economic opportunities; but it well exemplifies the effort being made to promote social and cultural as well as economic and infrastructural modernization.

THE LIMITS OF PROGRESS AND THE CHALLENGE FROM THE LEFT

In the late 1960s, with Carlos Lleras Restrepo and his crew of highly trained young technocrats guiding the nation along the path of a thoroughly moderate, supposedly scientific, path of social and economic development, there were those who spoke of a "Colombian miracle," reminiscent of the postwar German *Wirtschaftswunder*. The economy was growing at an annual rate of around 6 percent, and the nation was at peace except for a few guerrilla-infested zones that were mostly out of sight and out of mind. Then, in April 1970, on the basis of a seemingly incoherent populist message, Gustavo Rojas Pinilla nearly defeated the National Front candidate for president—*did* defeat him, in the view of many. How could this near disaster be reconciled with the picture of smooth and steady progress?

A large part of the answer is that net economic growth had outpaced the progress made toward lessening social inequality. Income distribution, long highly unequal, became more so during the 1960s, at least in the rural sector. In that sector a number of developments—notably, the displacement of tenant farmers by the advance of large-scale commercial production, the forced migrations resulting from the *Violencia*, and the continuing concentration of the best land in relatively few hands—tended to increase the supply of manual labor in relation to demand and thus hold down wages. Depressed coffee prices were an aggravating condition. There may have been some improvement in the share of urban income going to the working class, but not enough to offset the contrary trend in rural areas, and not enough, certainly, to satisfy aspirations raised by the initial euphoria of the National Front period. When Colombians went to the polls in 1970, the poorest half of the urban population was receiving not quite 16 percent of total urban income, and the highest tenth over 43 percent. The disparity in the countryside was appreciably greater; almost two-thirds of rural Colombians were living in what has been defined as "absolute poverty."[6]

In some cases the very achievements of the regime led to increased dissatisfaction. Advances in secondary education produced more applicants for white-collar and service jobs than the economy could accommodate, and the rapid growth in the number of teachers—many of them only minimally qualified and almost all of them very poorly paid—created in itself another potential focus of unrest. Meanwhile, too, the physical isolation of mountain valleys and lowland plains was breaking down, thanks to gradual improvement of the road network and other infrastructure (again with considerable Alliance for Progress help); and intellectual isolation declined with the rise in literacy and the greater general awareness that accompanied it.

Closer national integration and the rise of hard-to-fulfill expectations were two phenomena that went hand in hand. Emblematic in this regard was the spread of television. When it was first introduced in 1954 under Rojas Pinilla, there were only 1000 sets to receive the programs,[7] so that the impact was minimal. Yet by the mid-1970s most Colombians were exposed to this pervasive molder of opinions and attitudes—if not through their own sets, through sets owned by neighbors or local stores or bars. No one had yet mastered the art of exploiting the medium politically, but it was already broadening horizons and was graphically portraying to many the comforts of a lifestyle that remained far beyond their grasp. Increasing numbers of others were directly experiencing a more affluent society by moving to Venezuela, whose oil prosperity was now at its peak (just before the crash of the 1980s), or even to the United States. Remittances from either destination made life better for those who stayed home but inevitably made them wonder why Colombia, despite the progress that its rulers boasted about, seemed to lag so far behind.

It was just such nagging dissatisfaction with the overall performance of the society, combined with countless individual hardships and disappointments, that carried Rojas Pinilla to his near victory. His ANAPO did not, however, succeed in permanently channeling unrest. Some Anapistas became disillusioned when the ex-dictator in the end meekly accepted his defeat. Still others drifted away when, in preparation for the return of unrestricted electoral competition, the movement reconstituted itself as a separate party, dropping the pretense that it was an alliance of dissident Liberals and dissident Conservatives. Rojas Pinilla's final illness and death completed ANAPO's decline. María Eugenia, as the party candidate in 1974, received 9.4 percent of the votes cast, which was a creditable showing for the first woman to make a serious run for the presidency, but it represented a major falling off from her father's record.

No new populist party strove to take the place of ANAPO. Its heir instead was a growing apathy and cynicism concerning the political process generally, although the actual rate of abstention from voting in elections did not change much. Fortunately for the ruling Liberal-Conservative alliance, the same apathy limited the appeal of the various leftist movements that were combating it by either legal or illegal means or a combination of both. Nevertheless, this challenge—which had flared up in the mid-1960s and then appeared to recede, if only because it was overshadowed by that of Rojas Pinilla—was becoming troublesome again roughly a decade later.

Historically, the left had always been weaker in Colombia than in other Latin American countries at a comparable stage of development.

Both the structure of the coffee economy (as discussed in chapter 7) and the general phenomenon of a deep emotional identification with one or the other of the historic parties contributed to this weakness. The parties' success in manipulating the labor movement—converting the CTC into a virtual appendage of the Liberal Party, while the UTC initially was close to the church, which in turn was aligned with the Conservatives—prevented the unions from becoming a focus of militant left-wing politics. These circumstances, however, were rapidly changing. Industrialization and urbanization lessened the relative importance of coffee growers and other rural constituencies and at the same time weakened the simplistic appeal of the ancient party allegiances. The pull of those loyalties was further weakened by the very success of the National Front in forging a bipartisan consensus; and that in turn worked against the CTC and the UTC, with their ties to the political establishment and essentially moderate approaches to socioeconomic development.

The advent of the National Front was at first favorable to organized labor, because it provided a greater freedom for union activity to take place. The percentage of workers enrolled in unions more than doubled from 1959 to 1965. Though union membership was still only a modest 13.4 percent in 1965, that was probably close to the high point of unionization in Colombia; for even if total membership continued for some time to grow, the proportion of workers who belonged to unions was declining. And, significantly, the older confederations lost ground more and more to the new Confederación Sindical de Trabajadores de Colombia (CSTC), created in 1964 under primarily Communist auspices, and to still other "independent" unions that were affiliated with no national confederation but were generally Marxist in leadership.[8] The various branches of organized labor did not usually work closely together, but there were exceptions. The most notable occurred in 1977, when the UTC and the CTC joined with the CSTC and other unions in a nationwide "civic strike," called because of economic and other grievances at a time when inflation was rising and, for many workers, wages were not keeping pace. The protest briefly paralyzed many economic activities and led to violent clashes with the police in some places. Any effect it may have had on government policy is hard to discern.

Although the Communist Party as a strictly political force remained inconsequential, it won a larger voice on the labor front through the

CSTC. The Communists had still another voice, and arms, in the Fuerzas Armadas Revolucionarias de Colombia (FARC), or self-styled Revolutionary Armed Forces of Colombia. The oldest of the nation's leftist guerrilla groups, the FARC was an outgrowth of self-defense forces established during the *Violencia* in the Communists' rural enclaves of the upper Magdalena Valley; its supreme figure was the legendary Tirofijo ("Sure Shot"), a man who was pronounced dead more than once but always reappeared. From its original strongholds the FARC eventually extended operations to other areas, in particular to regions of recent settlement east and south of the Cordillera Oriental, where it served as the protector of peasant squatters and frontier colonists. These people's overriding desire for land of their own was logically incompatible with the guerrillas' theoretical collectivism, but in the short run they often found the guerrillas more helpful than the distant or venal government officials. The FARC, with its own highly experienced leadership, was no mere military wing of the Communist Party. The two organizations did, however, cooperate when occasion arose, and in principle they shared similar ultimate objectives.

A different guerrilla front was opened up by the Ejército de Liberación Nacional (ELN), or Army of National Liberation, whose initial base was in thinly populated stretches of the middle Magdalena Valley, in the department of Santander. Its inspiration was the Cuban Revolution of Fidel Castro, who helped it with training and material support. Lacking the roots that the FARC had in a genuine peasants' movement, the ELN conformed to a more common Latin American model of left-wing guerrilla/terrorist activity by drawing its combatants typically from disaffected middle-class youth. Its most famous recruit was Father Camilo Torres, scion of a distinguished Colombian family and European-trained, who sharpened his social conscience and became involved in student politics while serving as a university chaplain in Bogotá in the early 1960s. With a cadre of enthusiastic student followers, he first launched his own political movement, called Frente Unido del Pueblo (United People's Front), in Colombian cities, but he quickly came to the conclusion that peaceful protest was of no use against the entrenched oligarchy and the traditional parties that served its interests. He therefore decided to throw in his lot with the ELN—and was killed in combat early in 1966, just weeks after joining the guerrilla forces.

Camilo Torres exemplified the convergence of new currents in the Roman Catholic church (drawing inspiration from the reforms of the Second Vatican Council and from what was loosely termed liberation theology) with Marxist-oriented secular revolutionary action. Though he abandoned the active priesthood, he did not abandon his faith, which meant to him that as a Christian he must struggle to bring about justice for the poor and outcasts of society, to whom Jesus himself had reached out in his ministry—scandalizing the oligarchy of his own day by so doing. It is hard to imagine Jesus Christ grabbing a rifle with which to slay the Pharisees and Sadducees, but Torres was not the only priest in Colombia or other Latin American countries to join an active guerrilla struggle; and the ELN itself, after being almost wiped out by military repression in the early 1970s, eventually rose to prominence again under the supreme command of a renegade Spanish priest, *el cura Pérez*. More commonly, priests who felt a deep commitment to transform society were content to participate in symposia on social problems while working to "raise the consciousness" of their parishioners, and even such nonviolent activism was less prevalent among the clergy in Colombia than in such countries as Brazil or Peru or El Salvador. Inevitably, though, it did encourage a critical reappraisal of the existing order that led others to embrace revolutionary action or at least to sympathize with it from a safe distance.

The presence of radicalized priests and ideological affinity with Fidel Castro set the ELN apart from the FARC and from the orthodox pro-Moscow Colombian Communist Party with which the FARC was loosely allied. It was nevertheless a rigidly doctrinaire organization as compared to a third major revolutionary force, the M-19, which burst on the scene in 1973. Its full name was Movimiento 19 de Abril, recalling the date of the 1970 election in which Rojas Pinilla narrowly lost the presidency. Among the M-19's principal founders were embittered Anapistas who were convinced not only that the election had been stolen but that the lesson it taught was the impossibility of bringing needed changes to Colombia except by violent revolutionary action. As with ANAPO itself, the precise changes sought by the M-19 were never very clear. It was strongly nationalist, hostile to U.S. investment and influence generally; it espoused greater social equality, and it decried the lack of bona fide popular participation in the political system. If the ANAPO program was a mixture of "vodka and holy water," M-19 was heavier on the vodka, but it never called for socializing all the means of production. Its objectives remained generally pragmatic and more than a little vague.

The M-19 made its mark, in any case, through its leadership style and methods, which were strongly reminiscent of Uruguay's famous urban guerrillas, the Tupamaros. Like them, it cultivated a Robin Hood image by thefts of food and other merchandise to be distributed in poor neighborhoods. It also had a gift for the spectacular. In the first of many publicity coups, for instance, it stole the sword of Simón Bolívar from its museum case, pledging to return it only when the Liberator's ideals were finally realized. It thus associated itself with, and shrewdly exploited, an emerging leftist cult of Bolívar, which emphasized his support of slave emancipation and any other socially progressive causes and attributed his ultimate failure to liberate the masses from socioeconomic oppression to the selfish opposition of local elites supported by the United States.

Not least, the M-19 employed armed violence, but it was slow to develop a rural guerrilla presence and never very successful when it made the attempt. Instead, its specialty was urban terrorism, which would have its disastrous culmination in 1985, when an M-19 detachment seized the Supreme Court building in Bogotá and was exterminated when the army took it back. This penchant for urban violence was clear almost from the start, taking the form of kidnappings (for ransom or political concessions), bank robberies, and even symbolic assassination. One victim was José Raquel Mercado, who had worked his way up from stevedore on the docks of Cartagena to the status of head of the CTC and as such was a key figure in Liberal Party politics. He was the most highly placed Afro-Colombian in public life, but to the leaders of the M-19—all of them from a higher social background—he had sold out to the establishment, and sold out for crassly material as well as other kinds of rewards. He was therefore "executed" in 1976.

This by no means exhausts the roster of leftist groups that seemed to proliferate on the political landscape. Some of these groups were frankly dedicated to the violent overthrow of the existing order; some (like the M-19) advocated violent action as a means of exerting pressure for a faster pace of change; still others confined themselves to nonviolent agitation despite the use of revolutionary rhetoric. At least one other, the Ejército Popular de Liberación (EPL), or Popular Lib-

eration Army, which claimed to find inspiration in the Maoist variant
of communism, succeeded in fielding a guerrilla force of some importance, concentrated in the lowland region to the north of Antioquia.
The Quintín Lame movement (named for an Indian leader of the early
twentieth century), which sprang up among the indigenous communities of the southern Cordillera Central, was a rural self-defense force
much like the original FARC. Its immediate targets were usurpers of
Indian land and repressive government agents, but it also found itself
struggling from time to time against leftist guerrilla bands that sought
to take advantage of the Indians' militancy on behalf of non-Indian
causes. Ad hoc cooperation among the various revolutionary groups
was not unknown, but neither was bitter feuding over questions of
doctrine and tactics. Similar dissensions often wracked the groups internally, even to the point of bloody purges carried out by one faction
against another.

The splintered Colombian left was perfectly correct in arguing that
the rules of the political game—referring not merely to the mechanics
of the National Front but to all the built-in advantages enjoyed by the
government in power and by the economic owners of the means of
production—were stacked against the proponents of radical structural
transformation. Left-wing groups also were correct in charging that
the nation's rulers went through the motions of consulting labor
unions and other popular organizations on policy issues but paid
much more attention to such powerful vested interests as the industrialists' ANDI and large landowners' SAC, to say nothing of FEDE-
CAFE. But in concluding that peaceful protest was not worth the
trouble, these groups failed to recognize that violence was not likely
to be any more effective in the end than the slow, hard work of mo-
bilizing opinion and competing legally within the system. Moreover,
the tendency of the left itself to dissipate its strength in factional
disputes made the revolutionary strategy for Colombia even more
problematical.

The revolutionary left did succeed in establishing a series of mostly
isolated, though fairly large, rural zones where different guerrilla
organizations exercised control or at least prevented the state from
establishing full authority. Often, of course, these were zones where
state authority had been little more than nominal in the first place.
The M-19, on its part, demonstrated that it could stage incidents of
urban direct action with relative impunity. These developments,

although they had little impact on most Colombians' daily lives, represented a drain of some importance on the Colombian economy. There was, for one thing, the expense of government countermeasures, which amounted basically to a policy of containment; an all-out effort to destroy the revolutionary left would have entailed both fiscal and political costs that no Colombian government was prepared to assume. There was also the added cost of doing business in guerrilla-infested zones, where landowners had to pay off the leftists or run the risk of being kidnapped or worse; and naturally they passed on the expense as far as possible to consumers in the form of higher prices.

Finally, and really more serious, there was the political cost: first, the gradual erosion of governmental legitimacy because of the government's inability to crush the revolutionary threat by force or to remove the underlying sources of societal discontent that had given rise to the threat; second, the growing political polarization as the objects of the leftists' wrath hardened their own positions and often came to regard legitimate peaceful protest as an expression of guerrilla terrorism. In the mid-to-late 1970s all this was overshadowed by another spurt of rapid economic growth, fueled by a combination of high world coffee prices and the beginnings of the Colombian drug bonanza; but the challenge of the violent left, and corresponding overreaction of sectors on the right, would shortly become a source of greater concern, just as the economy itself entered a phase of diminished growth.

I I

The Latest Era:
Confounding the Predictions (1978–   )

The seeming contradictions in the Colombian pattern of development during the heyday of the National Front did not disappear in subsequent years. If anything, they became starker. A noticeable increase in political violence was suddenly complemented by violence resulting from a massive illegal drug trade. Meanwhile, the traditional parties continued to practice the usual political game—showing more interest in controlling rural bloc votes on a basis of sheer clientelism than in offering fresh policies and programs. Colombia also was affected by the general economic crisis that afflicted Latin America in the 1980s— a crisis prompted by deteriorating external economic relations and varying degrees of internal mismanagement. At different times sensationalist voices were predicting for Colombia everything from a military coup to the outbreak of generalized civil war. The "social fabric," some said, was coming unraveled. Happily, none of the more dire predictions came true. Colombia continued to demonstrate a remarkable ability to adapt to disconcerting levels of violence, which still did not equal those of *La Violencia* proper, despite exaggerated claims that its carnage had even been surpassed. Meanwhile, the performance of the Colombian economy was consistently one of the most satisfactory, or at any rate least unsatisfactory, to be found in Latin America.

The demise of the National Front as a political system was actually a gradual process. The elections of 1978 brought to the presidency the Liberal Julio César Turbay Ayala, a slightly corpulent professional politician whose trademark bow tie was no less anachronistic than his political style, that of the skilled manipulator whose loyalty was to the party organization rather than to any set of theoretical principles. Turbay interpreted the continuing constitutional requirement to give the runner-up party an "equitable" share of official positions in such a way that the Conservatives received a patronage quota equal to their share of elected congressmen, which was roughly 40 percent. At the same time, Turbay as president had the misfortune to face both the recrudescence of guerrilla activity and the onset of economic difficulties that he did little to ward off. The resulting deterioration of his image played into the hands of the dissident Liberal Luis Carlos Galán, who condemned the machine politics at which Turbay was past master while articulating a program that sounded vaguely reformist without offering radical innovations. But the eventual beneficiary of the administration's loss of prestige was a maverick Conservative, Belisario Betancur, who won the presidential election of 1982 by a narrow margin.

Betancur's campaign slogan, "Sí se puede" ("Yes, it can be done"), sought to capitalize on his reputation as a typically hard-working, practical-minded Antioqueño, and he did in fact embody many of the traits stereotypically associated with his native Antioquia. Born to a lower-middle-class family of over twenty children, most of whom died young, he had become wealthy strictly through his own efforts. Betancur was at one time a die-hard follower of Laureano Gómez, but by the time of his election he was known as a progressive who cultivated contacts with a wide spectrum of cultural and intellectual figures, in part through his work in the publishing business. Because of the minority status of his own party, he had to appeal to disgruntled Liberals to win the election, and once in office he reverted to the 50–50 power sharing of the classic National Front system. When he left office, the Liberals reasserted their nationwide majority by electing their own candidate, Virgilio Barco, for the 1986–1990 presidential term; and when Conservatives declined to accept the share of offices that Barco chose to offer them, he set up the first strictly one-party administration since the deposition of Laureano Gómez in 1953.

Barco—an M.I.T.-trained engineer and the consummate technocratic politician—had come to the conclusion that National Front power sharing, by diluting responsibility for government actions, had contributed to a decline of public confidence in the political system; in addition, by seeming to enshrine forever a Liberal-Conservative monopoly, it had convinced many on the left that peaceful participation in politics was a fruitless exercise. He therefore did not try very hard to obtain Conservative collaboration. But the return to one-party responsibility, with the other party reduced to the role of loyal opposition, did not produce the results that he had hoped. It would therefore be abandoned by his immediate successor, César Augusto Gaviria, another Liberal. In putting together a government of national union, Gaviria did not even limit himself to members of the two historic parties (or of the military initially for the Ministry of Defense) in choosing his collaborators.

A greater departure from past procedures was Gaviria's sponsorship of a new constitution, formally adopted in 1991, to replace the 1886 constitution designed by Rafael Núñez and Miguel Antonio Caro. It included numerous provisions designed to make Congress and the judicial system more responsible and more efficient; for example, the upper house of Congress was now to be elected by proportional representation on a nationwide basis, so as to lessen the influence of party bosses whose power base was essentially regional and to make it easier for new political and social movements to gain at least some representation. Even more striking was the reintroduction of the popular election of governors, although the new charter still was not truly federalist; in this respect it resembled that of 1853 (as originally adopted), in which elected provincial governors had served as agents of the national executive. Then there were miscellaneous changes affecting individual rights and civil law and much else.

No specific provisions quite explain the euphoria with which the new constitution was greeted by broad segments of Colombian opinion. The problems lately afflicting the country could not fairly be blamed (with rare exceptions) on the written text of the previous constitution; however, there had been a consistent perception that somehow the nation's institutions were proving inadequate to the challenges they faced. If a new constitution could help remove that perception and thereby contribute to a rebirth of national confidence, Gaviria was happy to oblige. He had therefore urged his predecessor to hold a referendum authorizing the election of a constituent convention; and after taking office himself, he drafted the guidelines for it and conducted the election. The convention turned out to be a bewilderingly pluralistic body, containing representatives of the indigenous movement and of the Protestant churches along with those of the traditional parties and of the left; no one group held a majority. But Gaviria worked closely with it, and in the end the Constitution of 1991 contained nothing that he (and in his view Colombia) could not live with.

VIOLENCE AMID NORMALCY

The demand for constitutional reform was a consequence, above all, of the severe problems of public order that Colombia had been facing. Even as presidents and congressmen rotated regularly in office by electoral means and the majority of public services continued to function in more or less normal fashion, commentators with ever greater frequency were bemoaning the spread of "insecurity," a term that covered both pervasive criminality and a resurgence of political violence. The most alarming data concerned the incidence of homicide, in which Colombia by the mid-1980s was one of the world leaders. In 1986 homicide was the leading cause of death, whereas in 1973 it had been only the seventh leading cause.[1] The homicide rate was swollen by political factors and by the flowering of an illegal drug traffic; but there was also a long-term increase in almost all forms of criminal activity, reflecting among other things the rapid expansion of cities and the growing complexity and frustrations of modern life, not to mention the unfortunate incapacity of the Colombian state to do much about them. One result of the ineffectiveness of official crime prevention was a proliferation of strictly private protection services— or, as it was sometimes put, the quasi-privatization of the police and criminal justice systems. Despite the growing enthusiasm in Latin America for "privatization" as an economic policy, it proved a poor solution on the public-order front.

Although the distinction between "criminal" and "political" violence was often fuzzy in practice, it was the latter that chiefly absorbed the practitioners of Colombia's burgeoning social science subdiscipline of "violentology." In round tables and symposia and published works, these specialists joined in decrying the phenomenon they studied, even if they tended to argue that in Colombian terms political violence was something historically "normal."[2] Any such analysis, of course, encountered serious difficulty in explaining away the outward tranquility of the pre-1930 Conservative hegemony and probably took most nineteenth-century civil conflicts too seriously. Moreover, the problem now was at least in part another matter of perception, since the sharpest rise was in urban terrorism, a relatively new problem that Colombians had not learned to live with, as they had learned to live with the back-country guerrilla fighting that had been going on since the late 1940s. The increase in the rate of political violence generally was therefore a bit less than many people thought. Yet, exactly as with nonpolitical violence, there was appreciably more political violence than there had been in the mid-1970s.

The reasons for the upsurge were not instantly apparent. There is no indication whatever that everything was being orchestrated from Moscow and Havana, as angry members of the middle class often insisted. Nor could the deterioration of public order be reasonably attributed to increasing immiseration of the masses, because the masses had little part in the groups perpetrating violence, and also because the Colombian economy (as discussed at greater length below) was spared the worst of the Latin America–wide economic downturn that marked the 1980s. There was, though, an increase in urban unemployment, along with continuing inflation and other social and economic difficulties that the existing regime seemed unable to solve, thus fueling discontent. And the nature of the regime continued to be a problem. The constitutional straitjacket of the National Front system had been removed, but its spirit lived on, and President Turbay, in particular, seemed to exemplify its worst features. After 1978 the ruling parties were in a position to introduce real changes in the way politics was conducted, and they failed to do so, inevitably confirming the beliefs of all who had insisted that only armed force could make a difference.

Insofar as urban terrorism was the problem, one principal reason was that the M-19 had consolidated its own organization and tactics, which were always oriented more to urban than to rural action. The group did at various times mount rural guerrilla fronts, but its most spectacular operations were reserved for the urban theater. Early in 1979 it inflicted major humiliation on the Colombian armed forces by a daring theft of arms from a military installation in Bogotá itself. The army succeeded in recapturing the arms and seizing a large number of M-19 activists and left-wing sympathizers, many of whom were very roughly handled in the crackdown. Yet the M-19 went on to stage an even more sensational coup the next year, taking over the Dominican Embassy in Bogotá in the midst of a diplomatic reception and holding hostage some fourteen ambassadors, including the U.S. envoy. The embassy occupation ultimately came to an end, with all hostages safely released, in return for a safe conduct out of the country for the guerrillas who staged the operation and payment of a large ransom, which was widely assumed to have come from West European sources.

The most sensational of all M-19 operations—and in many ways the group's undoing—was its seizure in November 1985 of the Palacio de Justicia, on the north side of Bogotá's central Plaza Bolívar, directly opposite the Colombian capitol. This was the seat of the Supreme Court and other judicial offices, none of which were in any sense the real targets of the action. The objective, rather, was to compel President Betancur to answer a list of charges and in effect resume negotiations with the M-19 that had been broken off some time before. It was a hare-brained scheme doomed to failure—though sure to bring the M-19 at the very least the kind of high-profile publicity that always formed part of its strategy.

An M-19 commando seized the Palacio without much difficulty; it merely had to kill two guards on the way in. Almost immediately, however, and apparently without waiting to get the president's concurrence, the army launched a military assault on the building. The most dramatic moment of the assault came when a Brazilian-made light tank was driven through the front entrance. Though some occupants had managed to escape or were rescued by the military, half of the Supreme Court judges died in the affair, along with every one of the M-19 terrorists. The leftist group lost some of its most valuable members; it also lost prestige and much of whatever popular sympathy it had managed to acquire. The government lost badly, too, and not just in terms of judicial lives. Many who decried the M-19's tactics were unconvinced that a strictly military response had been the correct one; in fact, the operation fostered the impression—justified or not—that on matters of public security the president was taking orders from the military, not giving them.[3] (The incident did not, on the other hand, interrupt the annual Miss Colombia pageant under way at the same moment in Cartagena, although the news coming over the radio from Bogotá did cast a certain pall on the proceedings.)

Even if the M-19 received most attention abroad, the Communist-aligned FARC remained much the largest of the leftist revolutionary organizations. Its chief strongholds were in the upper Magdalena Valley and adjacent areas of the eastern plains, but in the course of the 1980s it opened new "fronts" in various other sections of the country. The presence of the state was usually weak in these areas, so that the

FARC could offer protection to peasant farmers and a rudimentary kind of frontier justice, at the same time squeezing forced contributions out of larger landowners. Its forces grew in the mid-1980s to perhaps 4,000 armed men, which in turn was close to half the total guerrilla forces in the field.[4]

The Castroite ELN grew also, never rivaling the FARC in total strength but in its own way posing just as serious a challenge for authorities to deal with. Badly battered by the military in the early 1970s, it never wholly lost its regional foothold in northeastern Colombia, and this location fortuitously helped it become the wealthiest of the guerrilla groups. In the next decade new oilfields were brought into production in the Arauca region of the Colombian *llanos* along the Venezuelan border and connected with the Caribbean coast by a pipeline passing through the very part of the country where the ELN was strongest. The oil companies and the German firm constructing the pipeline were vulnerable to extortion and were prepared to pay sums much greater than could be demanded from some back-country rancher. The Germans were especially cooperative because their only interest was to complete the pipeline and move on to projects elsewhere. After collecting millions of dollars in return for letting the pipeline be completed, the ELN adopted a policy of periodically blowing holes in it as a way of protesting against "overgenerous" contractual arrangements between the Colombian government and the multinational oil companies that were sharing with the state oil company, ECOPETROL, in the exploitation of the new fields. These tactics polluted fields and streams with spilled petroleum and cut into the funds that ECOPETROL was ceding to communities in its areas of operation to help with social projects. Thus did the Spanish ex-priest who commanded the ELN succeed in making a statement on behalf of Colombian nationalism.

Still other leftist guerrilla organizations were active, including some—such as the EPL—held over from the pre-1978 period and some that were new. A number of them carried out urban exploits à la M-19 (though never with the same flair), but most of their operations were in rural Colombia. One of the groups might turn up at any time to attack a small-town police station, seize funds in the local office of the government's agrarian credit bank, and subject the local inhabitants to a harangue on the justice of the revolutionary cause before disappearing once again to its base camp. Guerrillas conspicuously failed to operate, on the other hand, in such long-established areas of peasant family farming as the highlands of Boyacá and the northwestern coffee zone, appearing instead in areas of recent colonization or of relative land concentration.

Not even all the groups working together (which they sometimes did and more often did not) could have mounted a credible threat to overthrow the government. The FARC, which might once have fancied itself in Leninist terms as forming the vanguard of the proletariat, was becoming instead, in the words of one Colombian Liberal, simply "the rearguard of the *colono* [peasant settler]."[5] The ELN still spoke of taking power but in practice ended up engaged essentially in armed lobbying for such pet causes as a change in petroleum policy. And the M-19 was—well, the M-19. Despite the lack of a coherent project to offer the country, however, the revolutionary left succeeded in winning rather widespread sympathy at various times, not just among disgruntled middle-class intellectuals but among the urban poor and landless peasants and the inhabitants of many small towns that had been left behind in the steady expansion of basic services (roads, potable water, and so forth). A striking feature of the 1980s was the number of protest marches and demonstrations over precisely these deficiencies in government services. Some were orchestrated or infiltrated by subversive groups, but the indignation of the protesters was genuine. A parallel sign of radicalization in some sectors of the working class was the formation, in 1985, of the Central Unitaria de Trabajadores (CUT), representing an amalgamation of the Communist-leaning CSTC, the once Catholic-oriented UTC, and a number of independent labor unions. The CUT was intent on pressing labor demands more vigorously, through joint action, upon a system perceived as indifferent to workers' interests. It did not live up to expectations; yet the pervasive discontent and decline of confidence in the nation's formal political institutions gave at least a veneer of legitimacy, in the minds of many, to those struggling against the established order.

The seeming inability of government forces to flush the guerrillas out of their strongholds led inevitably to feelings of frustration among officials and supporters of the Colombian regime and to a continuing debate over the proper solution to the problem. Perceptions of the problem itself, moreover, had been permanently altered by the appearance of an urban component alongside the all-too-familiar phenomenon of rural guerrilla activity. This new component was more threatening because it seemed harder to contain, and because the members of the Colombian establishment—socioeconomic as well as political—themselves lived in the cities. Except on the *Nueve de abril*, the cities had been generally safe through the worst of the earlier *Violencia*, but apparently they were no longer. It is thus hardly surprising that one now began hearing of the use of torture against political detainees and of unexplained "disappearances" of supposed guerrilla activists or sympathizers. Under the Turbay administration, particularly in the wake of the great M-19 arms robbery, top officials at least tacitly accepted the use of illegal methods to combat left-wing violence. The following administrations were more forthright in condemning human rights abuses but did not always control middle- and lower-level military and police agents. Even under Turbay abuses were hardly on the same scale as under the military governments of Chile and Argentina in the 1970s, and in Colombia they were openly denounced in Congress, the press, and public forums (though not without danger at times to the denouncer). Nonetheless, by the early 1980s Colombia was receiving much unfavorable attention from international human rights organizations such as Amnesty International.

In addition to meting out harsh treatment to those arrested for public-order offenses, the Turbay administration had some success in military action against the rural guerrilla fronts. Its generally hard-line approach was further reflected in the decision to break relations with Castro's Cuba (relations only recently reestablished by López Michelsen) because of continued Cuban assistance to Colombian revolutionary leftists—a decision viewed with warm approval by Washington. But the violent left was still not defeated, and some of the methods used against it—notably, the torture of suspects—were simply counterproductive, generating new sympathy for the cause of the victims.

Belisario Betancur therefore took a radically different approach. He attempted to seek a peaceful settlement of the problem by means of negotiations. The task was made difficult because influential leaders in the political parties and the armed services lacked enthusiasm for the president's policy and because the guerrilla organizations were divided on the response to take. But Betancur was determined and resourceful. He enlisted the good offices of the novelist Gabriel García Márquez, and at one point he met personally in Spain with representatives of the M-19. In the end he achieved agreements not just with the M-19 but with the FARC and the EPL.

. In each case the agreement provided for a truce between the guerrillas and government forces, during which hostilities would be suspended by both sides and a process of "dialogue" undertaken to determine the further steps to be taken before the cease-fire could become a permanent peace, with the revolutionary groups actually laying down arms. Betancur in addition made a liberal grant of amnesty. However, the guerrillas wanted not only further guarantees of personal safety but also a series of structural reforms that were ill defined to begin with and generally beyond the power of the president to deliver: at most he could press Congress to act. Meanwhile, the various truces were being violated on all sides, since neither Betancur nor the revolutionary chieftains had full control over their respective subordinates. Before long, the M-19 denounced its agreement, claiming betrayal, and reembarked on the course of open hostilities that would ultimately lead to its attack on the Palacio de Justicia.

The FARC never formally withdrew its acceptance of the truce, despite the wave of violations, in considerable part because it hoped to launch a new political party that would unite ex-guerrillas with members of the existing Communist Party and other leftists and engage in legal political activity. Dubbed Unión Patriótica (UP), the party was created in 1985, in time to field a candidate in the next year's presidential election. Although the candidate, Jaime Pardo, gained only 4.5 percent of the votes, that was a respectable showing by the standards of the Colombian left. Furthermore, one key structural reform did get adopted at this point. It was a constitutional amendment, finally enacted at the end of 1985 (and later incorporated in the new Constitution of 1991), that provided for mayors to be popularly elected rather than appointed by the department governors as in the past. The reform in question had been under discussion for some time and did not lack support within the traditional parties. However, it almost certainly would not have passed when it did except for the need to produce some tangible evidence of a "democratic opening," as the revolutionary left had been vaguely but insistently demanding. It could be readily accepted because it did not really endanger the dominance of Liberals and Conservatives. In fact, the Conservatives, frozen out at the national level with the return of single-party Liberal government under Virgilio Barco, were the most obvious beneficiaries. The new UP picked up 16 mayoralties (out of 1,009) when the first mayoral elections took place in 1988, but the Conservatives collected almost half the total and, thanks to Liberal factional divisions, walked off with the two biggest prizes of all: Medellín and Bogotá.[6]

Because the truce agreements did not work out as planned, many Colombians were quick to condemn the Betancur negotiation policy as a dismal failure. It was, though, something that needed to be tried. Almost no one seriously questioned the president's own good faith, and even most of those who found both sides to blame for violations concluded that the guerrillas had not tried as hard as he had to make the policy work. They had therefore wasted their best opportunity to gain broad acceptance as legitimate actors; and in any future negotiations they would be even less able to impose their conditions. The M-19, at least, came to realize that the left generally had lost ground, even as it sought to recover from its own disastrous assault on the Palacio de Justicia. Early in 1990, near the end of the Barco administration, it simply laid down its arms and agreed to take its chances in legal political competition. It soon proved far more successful at the polls than the UP or than it had ever been in the use of violent methods. The settlement with the M-19, however, was Barco's only clear-cut success in dealing with the revolutionary left. And during his government, even more than that of his predecessors, the whole problem of public order became intertwined with and vastly complicated by new types of violence spawned by the country's illegal drug industry.

FROM DRUG BONANZA TO DRUG WAR

During the 1980s Colombia was best known around the world for its involvement in the production and export of illicit drugs. The phenomenon gave rise to many wildly exaggerated reports about the importance of the drug business to the Colombian economy and its political and social ramifications. One heard or read that cocaine had displaced coffee as Colombia's number-one industry and that the drug lords "controlled" the entire country. Common sense might have cautioned that the drug lords were not interested in "controlling" the country (what did they care about school budgets or the minimum wage?), only in making money and staying out of jail; but common sense was all too often absent from the discussions.

The true economic importance of the drug traffic, as well as many of the noneconomic side effects, was difficult to measure precisely because, by its nature, this new growth industry was illegal. Scholars had to learn to study the Colombian balance of payments in new ways, to detect the inflow of narcodollars in the form of unrealistically high "tourist expenditures" or other such rubrics. And possibly more difficult even than reaching some estimate of the scale of the business was the task of distinguishing and weighing the positive and negative effects on the general economy.

The difficulty of analyzing the drug bonanza, and eventually curbing at least its more negative consequences, was compounded by the fact that most Colombians initially did not pay much attention to it. Indeed, whatever its relative importance as a generator of export income, it never came close to coffee as a direct employer, while its very illegality made it less visible. It began, moreover, in a thinly populated and somewhat isolated area, on the slopes of the Sierra Nevada de Santa Marta and adjoining portions of the northeastern coastal region, where small cultivators in the 1970s discovered that growing marijuana for export to the United States was far more lucrative than the production of other crops. Santa Marta and other coastal cities became centers for the commercialization of this commodity, with new-rich dealers and their squads of bodyguards much in evidence. The economic impact was mainly regional, but by the middle of the decade the inflow of illicit dollars was enough (coming on top of other irregular exchange transactions) to push the value of the "black" dollar slightly below that of legally traded U.S. currency.

The marijuana boom was short-lived. At the urging of the United States, the Turbay administration undertook eradication efforts in the main marijuana-growing zone. The effectiveness of these efforts is not entirely clear, but a more serious blow to Colombian export sales was expanded production of high-quality marijuana in the United States itself, which did not eliminate but greatly reduced demand for the Colombian product. The growers could then, if necessary, go back to raising subsistence crops. But the bodyguards and assorted criminal elements that had been earning a livelihood from the marijuana business could not readily find (if they even sought) legitimate alternatives; as a result, the coastal cities experienced an upsurge of burglaries, holdups, and car thefts, as these people turned to prey on their fellow citizens. These crimes, too, gradually subsided. At the same time, the center of gravity of the illegal drug trade and related activities now shifted to Medellín—and cocaine displaced marijuana as the principal trade item.

The new narcotics industry was eventually quite different both in structure and in scale from the old. Marijuana had been grown in Colombia and then exported; distribution in the United States was largely in the hands of North Americans. Colombia was not, however, a major producer of the coca plant, from which cocaine is ultimately derived. The main producers were Bolivia and Peru, from which a semiprocessed coca paste was then brought to laboratories located in and around the Antioqueño capital (in due course elsewhere too) for final processing. Colombians likewise took charge of shipping the finished product to foreign markets, and they even came to control much of the distribution within those markets, of which the United States was far and away the most important. As processors and distributors, Colombian cocaine producers were receiving a much larger share of the ultimate sales price than the Bolivian or Peruvian raw material producers—or than the Colombian growers of marijuana. The market, after all, tends to reward manufacturing value added and skill in commercialization more liberally than it does mere primary production.

The cocaine industry did not at first attract much attention either. However, it grew rapidly, until by the mid-1980s one often heard that cocaine meant more to the Colombian economy than coffee. That statement was almost certainly never true in any strict sense, even though there may have been years when net illegal earnings of foreign exchange from cocaine—for which the best estimates ranged between 2 percent and 3 percent of Colombia's gross domestic product[7]—were greater than the total export sales of coffee. But coffee employed far more people, both in the growing and, because of its bulk, in handling and transportation. Moreover, there was always appreciable coffee production for domestic consumption as well, whereas virtually all the cocaine produced was intended for foreign users. Though domestic use of *bazuco*, roughly comparable to crack cocaine, became great enough in the end to worry Colombian authorities, it was never as widespread as cocaine consumption in the principal foreign markets.

Regardless of its precise weight in the overall economy vis-à-vis coffee, the drug business had significant socioeconomic impact. In macroeconomic terms, the most evident indicator of its importance for Colombia was the fact that dollars continued to be available on the black market, often for less than the rate established for legal exchange transactions; and the ready availability of illicit dollars helped to buffer the official rate against the crises that produced sharp currency devaluations almost everywhere else in Latin America during the 1980s. For a number of years the peso was overvalued, in that the official depreciation of the exchange rate came to less than the difference between Colombian and U.S. levels of inflation. The high price of coffee in the late 1970s had first given rise to this phenomenon, but cocaine prolonged it until the Betancur administration took steps to speed up the pace of devaluation.

Even when overvaluation was corrected, the peso still enjoyed a higher quotation than would have existed in the absence of massive inflows of cocaine earnings. This relatively high valuation helped Colombia maintain service on its foreign debt and purchase needed capital equipment. It also made vacations to Disney World more accessible for the Colombian middle class. On the other hand, legitimate exporters found it harder to compete with producers of neighboring countries that had undergone massive devaluations, and Colombian manufacturers were hurt because imported consumer goods (including contraband) were correspondingly cheaper in peso terms. The textile industry of Medellín itself was one of those most adversely affected, both through the loss of export markets that it had been cultivating with some success in the early 1970s and by an influx of competing foreign textiles and clothing.

Among the social consequences, most obvious was the emergence of a corps of new-rich traffickers, whose top figures were loosely referred to as the "Medellín cartel" even though not all were actually from the Medellín area. The most powerful of them, Pablo Escobar, was singled out by *Forbes* business magazine as the wealthiest man in all of Latin America and indeed a world-class billionaire.[8] Like most of the drug entrepreneurs, he came from an undistinguished social background and so exemplified what Colombians referred to as the *clase emergente* (emerging class), made up of people who had risen rapidly in economic status, not necessarily through legitimate means. By constructing low-cost housing and giving lavishly to worthy causes, he gained the sincere admiration of many in the Antioqueño capital, to the point that he even won election as a Liberal Party alternate to the national Chamber of Representatives. For himself, he acquired urban and rural real estate and a private zoo stocked with animals imported from Africa. He was not the only drug lord to develop a zoo, but most of them settled for less—e.g., indulging in original artworks to hang on their walls and thus contributing to a small boom in the price of Colombian paintings.

If Colombian artists had no reason to complain about the Medellín cartel, the same could not be said of judges and police officers and others involved in law enforcement—unless, of course, they were among the many at the lower and middle levels who happily accepted bribes to look the other way when illegal activities took place. As long as the highest authorities in the land were not overconcerned, the growth of the drug industry was accompanied by spreading corruption but not much outright violence. Ultimately, however, the phenomenon could no longer be simply ignored, both because of the corruption of official personnel and because of the unfavorable attention attracted abroad—above all, in the United States, whose government repeatedly called for firmer action. In Colombia itself the dissident Liberal movement headed by Luis Carlos Galán, who liked to strike a moralistic pose in denouncing the tactics of party bosses, was particularly uncomfortable with the burgeoning drug economy; and Justice Minister Rodrigo Lara Bonilla, representing the Galán faction in the government of Belisario Betancur, brought matters to a head in the first half of 1984. Lara Bonilla increased pressure on the drug industry and brought about the destruction of the largest clandestine laboratory to date; then he was himself assassinated, apparently by a contract gunman commissioned by the Medellín cartel.

The death of Lara Bonilla was followed by a spectacular crackdown on the drug industry, with seizure of much equipment and vehicles and the arrest of mostly minor figures. A number of these figures (plus one major figure) were eventually extradited to the United States on drug charges. The extradition procedure brought indignant denunciations from the traffickers and others on nationalist grounds but was defended with the argument that the Colombian justice system was simply too exposed to bribery and intimidation to mete out sentences. Indeed, the cold-blooded assassination of judges and law enforcement officials who took their duties too seriously now became a common occurrence.

In the latter part of 1989, the "drug war" (as it came to be known) was fanned to new heights by the assassination of Luis Carlos Galán, who had seemed assured of the Liberal nomination as successor to Virgilio Barco and, in the absence of some unforeseen catastrophe, was almost certain to be the next Colombian president. The Medellín cartel provided the catastrophe and thereby spurred Barco to launch the most spectacular crackdown ever. In it, the number-two figure of the so-called cartel, Gonzalo Rodríguez Gacha ("el Mexicano" as he was known because of his infatuation with Mexican popular culture), was gunned down by police, though not before he and/or some of his colleagues had caused an Avianca airliner to be blown out of the sky between Bogotá and Cali in order to destroy police informants supposedly on board. The fact that the explosion killed over a hundred ordinary passengers nicely illustrated the single-minded determination of the cocaine traffickers to achieve their ends.

Public officials and innocent passengers were not the only victims of drug-related violence. Official actions and factional quarrels among the dealers themselves and their teams of armed enforcers also took a heavy toll. Particularly notorious was the feud between the Medellín-based organization headed by Escobar and what came to be known as the "Cali cartel." The Cali group had managed to garner a growing share of the market while generally eschewing violent attacks on government agents in favor of bribery or the use of political influence. Thereby it deflected the brunt of official crackdowns from itself onto the Medellín cartel, but it was not immune to armed retaliation from the Antioqueños when they felt it was infringing on business rightfully theirs. Both groups of traffickers, however, became involved in shadowy campaigns to "cleanse" their respective environments of petty thieves, prostitutes, homosexuals, and other undesirables. Such people would be killed by nighttime death squads, apparently assisted by off-duty police and right-wing vigilantes. Similar sweeps occurred in other cities, among them Bogotá, though always on a lesser scale.

The first of the death squads to win notice was the MAS, or Muerte a Secuestradores (Death to Kidnappers), formed in Medellín after M-19 terrorists foolishly seized the daughter of a leading cartel family and tried to hold her for ransom. Kidnapping, a not uncommon crime in Colombia, was practiced by professional bands as well as by leftists seeking to make a political statement or to replenish their treasuries. The families of kidnap victims normally agreed to pay. The drug families preferred not to; and by the threat of extreme countermeasures, they gained virtual immunity. In due course, however, confrontations between the cocaine entrepreneurs and the revolutionary left—two elements that in the beginning had seemed poised to cooperate, on the basis of their common illegality—turned increasingly violent.

For a time, producers and distributers of cocaine, as well as growers of the coca leaf, in those parts of the country where cultivation of the raw material also became widespread, routinely paid for the protection offered by revolutionary organizations. In the growing areas of the eastern lowlands, the FARC usually did the protecting, but for reasons that were never completely clear, this business relationship in the end turned sour. Elsewhere—above all, in the guerrilla-infested middle Magdalena Valley and northwestern coastal plains—the reasons for ultimate confrontation were more obvious. People who made fortunes in the drug trade began to buy up landed estates, which ordinary landowners, tired of guerrilla extortions, were eager to sell. The new purchasers, moreover, were less inclined to put up with demands for "revolutionary taxes" and the like, and they had the sophisticated weaponry and the organization to resist. Specifically, they worked with legitimate farmers and ranchers and regional police or military to form rural self-defense forces. Before long, large areas were again made safe for ranching and farming operations; but they also were made increasingly unsafe for anyone even suspected, on the flimsiest ground, of being a guerrilla sympathizer or collaborator. One notorious case involved Fabio Castaño ("Rambo"), who had acquired rural property with drug profits and swore his own war to the death against guerrillas after some of them kidnapped his father in a rural section of northeastern Antioquia. Ransom was paid; the father never reappeared. The son, infatuated with the Rambo character of North American cinema, much as Rodríguez Gacha was with things Mexican, launched a violent anti-Communist crusade in which his armed men massacred whole groups of peasant suspects, often after torturing them in the hope of gaining information about the hated guerrillas.[9]

The vendetta against leftists by drug-traffickers-turned-hacendados and their nontrafficking collaborators took a special toll among members of the Unión Patriótica, the party formed in 1985 by (among others) former members of the FARC. They had founded the party to test the waters of legal political competition. But in the view of hard-line antileftists, UP members were still committed to the violent over-throw of the existing system and had formed the party to undermine that system from within—a strategy whereby UP elected officials would be defending the interests of those still under arms in the back country. Within five years, more than one thousand UP militants were assassinated, including Jaime Pardo, its presidential candidate in 1986, and Bernardo Jaramillo, its nominee for the election of 1990 (slain before the election took place). Even more UP candidates for mayoral and city council posts were killed—which undoubtedly con-tributed to the party's poor showing in the first mayoralty elections.

Still another candidate assassinated in 1990 was Carlos Pizarro, former head of the M-19 guerrillas. Since the M-19 had just laid down arms in an agreement worked out with the government of Virgilio Barco, thereby demonstrating that they were truly abandoning violent action, something the FARC had never done, the M-19 people were less vulnerable than the UP to the charge of playing a double game. Pizarro was nevertheless caught (in some still unexplained way) in the cross-fire of the running battle among the drug traffickers, right- and left-wing terrorists, and the nation's political institutions. While no new UP candidate stepped forward, another former M-19 guerrilla leader, Antonio Navarro Wolf, did agree to pick up Pizarro's banner and, with just a few weeks to campaign, took almost 13 percent of the votes cast. He actually came in ahead of the official candidate of the Conservative Party (or Social Conservative, as it now formally called itself)—though only because the Conservatives' most prominent fig-ure, Álvaro Gómez Hurtado, son of ex-president Laureano Gómez and twice before the party standard-bearer himself, broke with the party machine and ran as an independent under the auspices of a so-called Movimiento de Salvación Nacional. Even so, Navarro's per-formance demonstrated the potential that had long existed for a left-ist movement that was prepared to make a clear break with revolu-tionary violence.

The winner in the same election was the Liberals' César Augusto Gaviria, an ex-minister of Barco and the candidate who was perceived as likely to take the hardest line against the narcotics industry. With many people tiring of the struggle, that perception probably lost him more votes than it won him; but not many Colombians based their choice solely on the drug issue. Once in office, moreover, Gaviria unveiled a program of negotiation for dealing with the drug problem that might well be compared to Betancur's overtures to the guerrilla left but produced more concrete results. The new president proposed that any trafficker who voluntarily surrendered to the Colombian authorities and pleaded guilty to one or more charges would not be extradited to the United States but instead tried in Colombia, where sentences were both lighter and more predictable than in the U.S. judicial system. One by one, figures associated with the Medellín cartel began taking advantage of the government's offer, and in June 1991 they were joined by Pablo Escobar himself. He had waited until it became clear that the extradition of Colombian citizens would be explicitly forbidden by the new national constitution. Nevertheless, with Colombia's most wanted criminal safely behind bars, the "drug war" was, for all practical purposes, finally over.

Critics of Gaviria's solution—including the U.S. government and media, as well as friends and families of the Colombian victims of Escobar and his associates—felt that the government had in effect surrendered to its adversaries. It placed them in special detention facilities equipped with amenities not available to ordinary prisoners and with extraordinary security arrangements designed more to protect the prisoners than to prevent their possible escape. Certainly, the production and export of cocaine did not come to an end just because Escobar was in jail. In Medellín and elsewhere, clandestine laboratories continued their operations, and there have been disturbing signs that Colombians were beginning to branch out into the growing heroin trade. On the other hand, there really were some important changes. Above all, drug-related violence fell off sharply and now consisted mainly of fighting within the industry itself, not assassination of government figures or innocent bystanders; and from the standpoint of the average Colombian, this one consideration far outweighed all others. The cocaine business, Colombians assumed, would continue in some fashion just as long as the United States remained addicted; so why should they meanwhile be getting killed in trying to stop it? Yet the trade itself had also undergone changes. Thanks in part to the Colombian government's efforts at repression, Colombia's relative share of the business had been slipping vis-à-vis neighboring Latin American countries (where, of course, experienced Colombians were leading participants). Within Colombia, moreover, Cali had finally displaced Medellín, and by a substantial margin, as the leading center of cocaine sales. In the final analysis, just as the transformation of the M-19 had demonstrated that peaceful competition in politics was more effective than armed confrontation, the eclipse of Medellín by Cali underscored the same lesson in the narcotics trade.

THE PACE OF ECONOMIC GROWTH

The violence spawned by the new drug industry, like that from political causes, meant both the outright destruction of wealth and property and a wasteful diversion of resources in order to combat it. Nor did the continual round of violence that afflicted Colombia contribute to a climate of confidence for either domestic or foreign investors. Nevertheless, exactly as during the earlier *Violencia*, the overall performance of the economy was distinctly superior to that of the political system. Though the rate of economic growth was generally unspectacular, Colombia was in fact the only Latin American country that did not experience a negative rate of growth at any time during the 1980s, which for the Latin American economy as a whole was a dismal period. And while Colombia could not escape the inflation and debt problems that plagued neighboring countries, it was plagued to a conspicuously lesser extent than most.

In 1978 Colombia posted its all-time record rate of increase in gross domestic product: 8.8 percent (see table). This statistic reflected the lucrative state of the world coffee market in the mid-to-late 1970s, when prices were at new highs. The coffee bonanza spread its benefits more widely, and with fewer negative side effects, than the subsequent drug bonanza. It could well be compared to the petroleum bonanzas that Mexico and Venezuela were experiencing during the same years—just before the price of oil collapsed. In the peak year, 1978, Colombia's domestic product grew at almost twice the Latin American average. The following year Colombia's growth rate fell below average, and in the 1980s it seldom rose above 5 percent; but in 1983, for example, the paltry 1.9 percent increase contrasted with a Latin America—wide *decrease* of 2.5 percent. During 1982 and 1983 Colombia also experienced negative growth in per capita terms, but on the basis the record for the region as a whole would also be even starker.

Yearly Increase in Gross Domestic Product, 1975–1990

	Latin America	*Colombia*
1975	3.2	4.3
1976	4.6	4.2
1977	4.6	4.7
1978	4.7	8.8
1979	6.4	4.3
1980	5.7	5.5
1981	.5	2.3
1982	−1.2	1.1
1983	−2.5	1.9
1984	3.7	3.8
1985	3.6	3.8
1986	3.8	5.9
1987	2.6	5.5
1988		4.1
1989		3.2
1990		4.2

Sources: Figures for Latin America (which do not include Cuba) and for Colombia through 1987 are from *Statistical Abstract of Latin America*, 28 (1990), 1,023, 1,042. Those for Colombia 1988–1990 are from *Colombia Today*, 25, no. 8 (1991).

There were, of course, differences in performance from one economic sector to the next, although changes in the relative importance of the principal sectors themselves were only gradual. Agriculture and manufacturing contributed between a fifth and a quarter each to the total national production of goods and services, with no other single activity coming close. Within the agricultural sector itself, coffee maintained its leadership—even after the coffee bonanza of the late 1970s faded away. The coffee industry was steadily modernizing, moreover, as the Federación Nacional de Cafeteros energetically promoted the use of improved farming techniques and new varieties of coffee—in particular the so-called *caturra*, which gave higher yields and lent itself to higher-density planting. The growing "technification" of coffee farming was accompanied by a continued increase in the share of total production coming from large holdings that used extensive wage labor, as against the stereotypical family farm of Juan Valdez. Even so, the latter was by no means out of the picture; and what passed for a large estate in the coffee zones might not have been so regarded in areas devoted to commercial production of rice or cotton or sugar-cane.

Whatever the size of their holdings, coffee growers were vulnerable to world market fluctuations, but these were mitigated to some extent by a system of support prices and by an official policy of putting away some of the proceeds from good years in a fund to help tide the growers over in lean years. When in 1989 the International Coffee Agreement suddenly collapsed (the victim of disagreements among the producing nations and of the United States' lack of enthusiasm for the principle of market quotas), a calamitous price decline ensued. Nevertheless, Colombian growers were able, for a time, to continue receiving payments for their coffee in excess of its international market value.

Except for the coffee industry in years of favorable world prices, the performance of the agricultural sector was on the whole sluggish. Guerrilla violence continued to discourage investment in some areas, though without seriously impinging on either the coffee zones or regions of traditional peasant *minifundios*. Manufacturing, meanwhile, was little affected—at least directly—by the problem of violence, but it faced other problems. It was even more sluggish in its performance; and it actually declined as a percentage of gross domestic product in the late 1970s and early 1980s.

Colombian manufacturers continued to enjoy, at least on paper, a high level of effective tariff protection, which was supplemented by a system of import licensing that further discouraged the entry of industrial goods competing with national products. The degree of protection had diminished, however, in the course of the 1970s, in part as a matter of explicit government policy. On the grounds that easy advances in import substitution had been exhausted, and that excessive protection discouraged industrial efficiency, Colombia adopted a slightly more liberal approach to the granting of import licenses and simultaneously reduced import tariffs. This move was still far from a radical "opening" of the economy to world market forces, such as the dictatorship of Augusto Pinochet undertook after the 1973 coup in Chile; but in conjunction with the influx of dollars from high coffee prices (while they lasted) and from the growing sales of illegal narcotics—all of which, as noted before, strengthened the exchange value of the peso—it created serious problems for domestic manufacturers.

For a variety of reasons, then, the growth of the industrial sector lagged behind that of the economy generally. Indeed, during the early 1980s, when the world economy entered a period of recession, the Colombian manufacturing sector actually contracted. Between 1979 and 1983, for the first time in half a century, industrial employment fell substantially, from 517,000 to 472,000, or almost 6 percent.[10] To be sure, the decline was primarily in the "formal" manufacturing sector, of established firms whose operations were covered in government statistics and whose workers received, for the most part, whatever fringe benefits and pay standards were legally mandated. As such firms cut back, the "informal" sector—of unregistered small firms and individual workers taking piecework to do at home—correspondingly expanded. Often the larger firms themselves were cutting costs by subcontracting parts of the production process to home workers (women especially), who did not receive fringe benefits and were recompensed for long hours of labor at the equivalent of even less than the national minimum wage, which hovered in the area of three dollars (U.S.) a day.

The industrial recession began to abate in 1984, when the Betancur administration adjusted its exchange-rate policy, so as to correct the existing overvaluation of the peso, and again heightened official protectionism. Colombian industry nevertheless continued to operate under severe constraints, of which the most serious was an internal market limited by the continuing low income levels of the popular majority. The problem was compounded by the preference of many Colombian industrialists to maintain a high profit margin on low volumes of sales rather than cutting prices to reach a larger pool of customers. Some manufacturers, as well as government economists, at different times proposed to get around the deficiencies of the internal market by adopting an industrial export strategy, and efforts to do so had some success. Garment makers, for example, made inroads in the U.S. market with various lines of products, including garments that were simply assembled in Colombia from cloth precut in Miami.[11] And Colombia unexpectedly emerged as the leading book exporter of Latin America, though less as a printer of Colombian or other Latin American works of literature than as mass producer of more specialized publications. One notable export success story was that of the Cali printing and publishing firm Carvajal, which became the world's largest producer of animated (or "pop-up") children's books, assembled by nimble-fingered women workers for the world market in any language desired.

As with garment exports, foreign sales of picture books were made possible in part by Colombia's relatively low wage costs, though cheap labor alone clearly was not sufficient to make Colombia a major industrial exporter. Carvajal also happened to be one of the country's most advanced firms technologically; and in the last analysis improved productivity standards were needed simply to supply the domestic market without unduly burdening consumers. By the end of the 1980s, in Colombia as in most of Latin America, there was ever more talk of "opening" the economy to the world market as the best way to compel manufacturers to become more cost-efficient while weeding out those that could not adapt. Such a policy was embraced in principle by the government of Virgilio Barco, even as it battled the drug cartels. Implementation was left for Barco's successor, César Gaviria, who was even more committed to the goal in question and lost no time in starting the dismantling of Colombia's relatively high levels of commercial protection. (The Gólgotas and Radicals would have felt vindicated at last.)

Another economic success story turned out to be petroleum. Although it had once been a strong second to coffee among Colombian exports, its production had failed to keep pace with the growth of domestic demand, so that by 1976 Colombia became an importer of crude petroleum. At virtually the same time, however, the Colombian government adopted a policy of aggressively exploring for new oil reserves, offering more attractive terms to the multinational companies that entered into "association" contracts with the state oil firm, ECOPETROL. The results exceeded most expectations, mainly because of the discovery of major new reserves in the eastern *llanos*. As of the mid-1980s Colombia had not only ceased to be a net importer but was again exporting petroleum to the world market. The world price for oil was depressed during this period, yet the additional foreign exchange earnings (over $700 million in 1988),[12] not to mention the share of ECOPETROL's profits that went to cover other government expenditures, were a little-noticed but highly significant factor in helping Colombia weather the economic problems afflicting Latin America as a whole in the same years. The prospects for the oil industry were sufficiently favorable for the multinational firms to continue active in Colombia even in the face of the ELN's sabotage campaign directed against them.

Petroleum developments were only one, though admittedly the most important, of the reasons why the mining sector of the economy expanded from a meager 1 percent share of gross domestic product in 1975 to 3.8 percent in 1988.[13] Offshore gas deposits along the Caribbean coast began to be exploited, too, and major coal and nickel enterprises were launched as joint ventures of Colombian state enterprises and foreign companies. Coal mining was nothing new for Colombia, as the Muiscas had first made use of coal for fuel, but the numerous deposits scattered through the interior highlands were exploited mainly by small firms, sometimes on an almost artisanal basis. The largest deposits by far were at El Cerrejón in the northeastern Guajira Peninsula. Thanks to these, Colombia had probably Latin America's greatest coal reserves, but they were far removed from population and industrial centers and were still undeveloped in the mid-1970s, when in collaboration with EXXON and other foreign firms the government set out to create an enormous open-pit mining operation for the extraction of high-quality (i.e., low-sulfur) coal, to be exported through a specially constructed port facility. The project had its formal inauguration early in 1985, and coal rapidly became an important export product—though at a time when coal prices, partly as a result of the depressed international oil market, were low. They more than covered the actual costs of operation, but Colombia was carrying a heavy load of interest on funds the government had borrowed to pay for its own participation in the project; and this debt burden raised doubts about the long-term profitability of the Cerrejón complex if prices did not improve.

Nickel mining, finally, was something entirely new for the Colombian economy, made possible by the development of an extensive strip-mining operation in the northwestern department of Córdoba. This, too, was a collaborative undertaking of the Colombian government and a foreign consortium. It went into operation in 1982, and though it faced fluctuations in world market conditions, nickel became one of the more important of the country's "minor exports."

It is easier, of course, to point to the development of new exports and to changes in the size and composition of gross domestic product than to ascertain just who was benefiting from the progress made. The oil companies benefited handsomely, as did the leaders of the drug cartels; and profit levels were generally acceptable in other fields, for both foreign and domestic firms. (If little new foreign investment flowed into Colombia save in the mining and energy fields, the reason was a feeling of physical insecurity more than anything else.) The great majority of Colombians, however, were not living from profits on investment but from salaries and wages or from the yields of their own rural or urban microenterprises; and the estimation of trends in real income for different segments of the population, a hazardous exercise anywhere, is particularly so in Latin American countries such as Colombia, where serious gaps exist in the statistical coverage. The late 1970s, it is true, clearly did bring some improvement in the relative position of the rural population, thanks in good part to the coffee bonanza. On the other hand, the first part of the 1980s, when rates of open unemployment in the major cities rose to around 15 percent, was clearly difficult for urban workers. Overall, a highly uneven distribution of income remained the rule in both rural and urban areas, and if there was some net improvement in this matter (as there does appear to have been),[14] it was not very great. But at least Colombians were spared the sudden falls in real income that people in many other parts of Latin America were experiencing. Even if the distribution of income had not become significantly more egalitarian, the total amount to be distributed was increasing year after year.

A factor that worked against major improvements in either real income or income distribution was a rate of inflation that came to average in the neighborhood of 25 percent a year. Despite occasional bursts of inflationary pressure in earlier years, inflation had not been a critical problem for the Colombian economy until the mid-1970s; but once it developed, it seemed impossible to eradicate. Nor did it result simply from uncontrolled public spending, though fiscal deficits bore part of the blame. The primary "structural" reason for Colombian inflation was the inability of domestic production to keep up with the growth of a consumer demand fueled by increasing legal (and also illegal) export sales. Wages and salaries were regularly adjusted in line with the cost of living, but generally with a time lag that put wage earners at a disadvantage vis-à-vis those whose income derived from capital, particularly financial speculation. At least Colombia also was spared the hyperinflation that periodically devastated Argentina, Brazil, and a number of other Latin American countries.

Similarly, Colombia stood out in Latin America for its relative success in handling the problem of foreign indebtedness. Colombia's official foreign debt (including private loans guaranteed by the government) rose from three and a half billion dollars in 1974 to nearly seven billion in 1980 and by 1987 had more than doubled again to around sixteen billion. Interest alone in the mid-1980s was equal to approximately one-fifth the total of legal exports, and this was an obvious burden on the Colombia economy.[15] Compared with neighboring countries, though, Colombia was well off. It became the only Latin American country to maintain service on the debt as contracted, without moratoria or skipped payments or special restructuring. Venezuela and Peru, each having something like two-thirds of Colombia's population, had larger foreign debts—Venezuela over twice as much. Venezuela also had nearly twice the gross domestic product of Colombia; but Peru, which in the 1970s had a higher product per capita, fell steadily behind Colombia in the 1980s. The country's relative advantage in foreign indebtedness consisted further in the fact that an unusually high portion of the total was made up of long-term financing from international agencies rather than commercial banks. And, though some of the borrowed money had without doubt been unwisely used, certain economically questionable investments at least resulted in tangible new production facilities and infrastructure. Two cases in point are the borrowing of money for El Cerrejón (originally justified on the assumption that coal would bring a higher price than it actually did) and for a series of mammoth hydroelectric plants that cost too much and encountered many construction delays (even while encouraging the neglect of older generating facilities). But gradually they did get built.

All things considered, it is safe to conclude that successive Colombian administrations directed economic policy with relative moderation and technical skill. It would be less safe to conclude that they did so because Colombians are more intelligent than other Latin Americans, given their conspicuous lack of success in solving public-order problems. On the other hand, the nature of the political system, with all its shortcomings, clearly did influence the management of the economy. Precisely because the system was dominated by two long-established middle-of-the-road parties, economic policy was reasonably consistent over the years, with none of the wild swings that other countries experienced. Indeed, seldom could anything be done without extensive consultation among party factions and with the private-sector interest groups that are closely tied in with them. This pattern typically meant cumbersome decision making, but it helped avoid egregious errors. Thus, it has even been suggested that one reason Colombia did not get itself dangerously in debt was that the Colombians took so long to draw up their borrowing schemes that by the time they might have done something really foolish, the lenders were no longer as free with their money.

A related factor to be taken into account has been the general weakness of populism in Colombian politics. To what extent things might have been different if Jorge E. Gaitán had lived or if Gustavo Rojas Pinilla had won the election of 1970 is a matter of speculation, but one can perhaps assume that a "populist" regime in Colombia as elsewhere would have sought to reward its supporters with hefty wage increases and would have greatly increased the extent of the state's social spending. Such policies would have delivered immediate benefits, though at the risk of unleashing inflationary pressures that would wipe them out in the end. In Colombia, instead, one government after another has discouraged large wage increases, for fear of inflationary effects, and has been a little stingy with social spending, even where social improvements would in the long term enhance economic productivity. The Barco administration, for example, proclaimed as one of its chief goals the eradication of "absolute poverty," but the proportion of government spending that it devoted to social programs actually fell.

As a result of such neglect, there has been a noticeable lag in some aspects of social welfare, including the all-important matter of health care. Life expectancy rose to a very respectable sixty-seven years, but the infant mortality rate was still over twice that of Costa Rica. Some 80 percent or more of Colombian homes now have electricity, but less than two-thirds have potable water. And in education, where access to rudimentary primary schooling has become almost universal, there remains a glaring contrast at the secondary level between urban and rural areas: only 7 percent of the rural population has access to post-primary schooling.[16] Hence, the currency remains stable, the economy keeps growing, but it has not been easy to convince the poorer Colombians that they are truly getting their fair share. The very virtues of the Colombian system—whereby it has promoted sound economic management—helped create a climate of latent discontent that never threatened the basic stability of the regime but lessened its legitimacy in the eyes of many.

A NEW SOCIETY COMING OF AGE

Just as the economic record is a useful reminder that there is more than political or drug-related violence to recent Colombian history, there is also more to the country's experience than prices and production trends and foreign debt. Scholars and casual observers often failed to notice that the Colombian population itself was changing in ways not always readily susceptible to political or economic analysis (and seldom consciously planned by any official agency).

The Colombian 1985 census clearly depicted a number of longer-term changes in process. The pace of urbanization continued, with 67 percent of the population classified urban, as compared to 52 percent in 1964 (and just 30 percent in 1938); urban growth was not concentrated in Bogotá, Medellín, and Cali, since intermediate cities were growing faster than the major metropolitan areas. The growth rate for the population as a whole had fallen to 1.8 percent annually in the 1973–1985 period, though the natural rate of increase had not declined quite so far: the net growth data took account of continuing out-migration, chiefly to Venezuela and the United States, totaling perhaps a million persons over the twelve years. Because of the fall in births, the median age of the Colombian population was now twenty years, as against fifteen and a half in 1964. There was thus a sharp drop in the proportion of dependent children, but not yet a troublesome increase in the number of dependent aged.[17]

The census results reaffirmed the nation's recent progress in education, revealing not just the advance of basic literacy training but the fact that one-tenth of Colombians of university age were now enrolled in higher education, as against a mere 1 percent in 1950. They also reflected the changing role of women, whose participation in the registered work force had risen from 15.4 percent in 1964 to almost one-third. Much of this increase was in low-paid manufacturing and service jobs, though by no means all; just a few years later, women were heading anywhere from 70 percent to 89 percent of the Bogotá branch offices of the nation's largest savings and loan associations.[18] Domestic service still represented one major source of women's employment;

but, as anyone who listened casually to the conversation of the urban middle class would quickly discover, maids no longer were prepared to accept any type of drudgery for a purely nominal wage. They were now asking for paid vacations, guaranteed TV-watching time, and other benefits; and in major cities at least, they were probably getting most of what they asked for. Even when they did, they were likely to consider domestic service just a stepping-stone to some more remunerative or ostensibly higher-status employment.

The growing disinclination of women to enter what they perceived as a dead-end line of work reflected a greater assertiveness among men and women of lower-class origin; they were less willing than before to accept automatically an inferior social status for themselves and their children. Rising to a higher social class was still not easy, but the prominence of the *clase emergente* (consisting not solely of illegal drug dealers) in both business and politics did attest to an increasing fluidity of Colombian society. By the same token, power, political or otherwise, was more and more diffuse. The families conventionally described as "oligarchic" (e.g., the Ospina clan) still had wealth and prestige, but they shared political influence with countless newcomers. Economically, it is true, the controlling interest in Colombian industrial and commercial enterprises was highly concentrated in the hands of a few great holding companies and financial "groups," and the private professional and trade associations (as repeatedly noted) almost always had a major role in the formulation of government economic policy—more so than, say, the labor unions. Yet the economy had grown to the point where no one vested interest could be said to control it, and the Colombian state, though hardly autonomous from the wielders of economic power, was too big and too amorphous to be a fully reliable servant of anyone.

The decline of social deference was paralleled by a decline of confidence in all national institutions—most notably, the state itself. Not even the church was immune to this general phenomenon. Scant attention was paid, for example, to its strictures against artificial birth control; and priests complained that nobody seemed to make personal confession any more, whereas a generation earlier, at least in Holy Week, long lines formed outside the confessionals. To be sure, Colombians still went to mass more than most Latin Americans, and in opinion surveys the church consistently scored higher in public trust than the civil authorities or armed forces. The influence of the institutional church was still pervasive, even if not all-powerful: barriers to pornography in print or in film had either disappeared or lost their effectiveness through lax enforcement, but Colombia was a country where *The Last Temptation of Christ* could not be shown in movie theaters because of its seeming disrespect for the central beliefs of the Christian religion.

The status of divorce reflected as well as anything the ambiguities in the position of the church and of traditional religious values. Legal divorce was reintroduced into Colombia only in 1976, and then with a glaring exception: marriages carried out by the rites of the Roman Catholic church could be dissolved only by ecclesiastical annulment, not by the state. But pressure for annulments steadily increased, and so did the social acceptability of foreign divorces (generally without legal standing in Colombia) and of purely de facto separations. At least in the urban areas, where most people lived, the changing of partners via divorce and remarriage or otherwise no longer aroused much comment. It was wholly symptomatic that for the presidential election of 1990 the Conservative Party, once the archdefender of Catholic values, nominated a divorced man who was remarried to a previously divorced woman. The final step in this matter was taken by the 1991 constituent assembly, which made all marriages fully subject to civil law and thus to legal termination. The same assembly underscored the growing secularization and pluralism of society by eliminating any reference to Roman Catholicism as the religion of the nation and specifically placing all denominations on a footing of equality. Yet at the same time it restored the name of Santa Fe (Holy Faith) to the Colombian capital, and it decisively rejected a proposition that would have allowed the legalization of abortion.

Changing sexual mores, no less than the proliferation of salad bars in restaurants and the appearance of "Gracias Por No Fumar" ("Thanks For Not Smoking") signs in taxicabs, were a reminder that Colombia in the last analysis formed part of Western civilization and experienced the same fads and fancies as any other part. It experienced them with steadily decreasing time lag. In its turn, Colombia was contributing more than coffee and cocaine to the rest of the world. Here the most obvious example is the work of the novelist Gabriel García Márquez, who—starting with his classic *One Hundred Years of Solitude* in 1967—produced one international best-seller after another and in 1982 became the first Colombian to win a Nobel prize. As one who also kept a residence in Mexico and boasted of close friendship with Fidel Castro, García Márquez was not universally admired at home; but thanks to his Nobel prize in literature, he became one of the few living persons ever to be honored with a portrait on Colombian postage stamps. And his writing is distinctively Colombian, or, more precisely, it is deeply influenced by the popular culture of the Caribbean coastal region where he was born. His particular style was that dubbed "magic realism," whereby the most improbable occurrences are narrated in a matter-of-fact manner; but the setting is almost always his native part of Colombia, and the action is often patterned after coastal folk tradition or real historical events. His writings also contain an undercurrent of pejorative comment on Bogotá and more generally the people and places of the Colombian highlands; yet the appeal of García Márquez is truly national (indeed international). Despite his regionalism, he thus contributed to the final emergence of a Colombian national literature in place of the fragmented regional literary traditions that with a few exceptions predominated until the mid-twentieth century.

It is unfortunate that the fame of García Márquez has overshadowed the work of other contemporary writers, such as Manuel Mejía Vallejo and Álvaro Mutis, who won lesser international prizes but still are leading Colombian contributors to the "boom of the Latin American novel" in the last third of the twentieth century. In much the same way, the attention lavished on the painter Fernando Botero has obscured the work of other figures—especially Alejandro Obregón and Enrique Grau—who were helping to place Colombia suddenly in the forefront of Latin American painting. Botero's trademark is the ironic depiction of grossly obese figures ranging from small boys to nuns to bemedaled generals. When, in 1989, a new magazine, *Latin American Art*, was launched in the United States, one of Botero's figures—a properly obese armored angel with Colombian village scenery as background—graced the cover of the inaugural issue.[19]

No symphonic work of a Colombian composer has won fame comparable to that of the novelists and painters; instead, in the area of classical music, the country became best known around the world for the performances and recordings of its great harpsichordist Rafael Puyana. At the level of popular music, the Afro-Colombian rhythm of the cumbia swept through the rest of Latin America in the 1960s and 1970s but never became widely known outside the region. It is significant, though, that the cumbia and other varieties of Caribbean coastal music have since midcentury largely displaced the traditional music of the Colombian interior, except in those settings where an ambience of Andean folklore is artificially re-created. The only serious rival of *música costeña* today consists of imported sounds, rock or otherwise. Thus, a common culture of popular music was taking shape spontaneously, even as Colombians kept killing each other over other issues.

In Colombia as in other countries of the modern world, the strongest popular emotions of all seem to be associated with sports competition. Colombia has never truly starred in the Olympic Games or other pseudoamateur sporting events, although a Barranquillero with the unlikely name of Helmut Bellingrodt has garnered Olympic medals in trapshooting. Other Colombians have won notice in world boxing. But the nation's first conspicuous successes in international competition came in bicycle racing. The rugged Andean topography provided a superb training ground for developing the skills and stamina necessary in uphill cycling, which proved to be the forte of Colombian cyclists when, starting in the 1980s, they regularly took part in world cycling events. In 1987 Colombia's Luis Herrera won the Vuelta a España. Though the Tour de France has more often produced frustrations, the Colombians have at least established themselves as a factor to be reckoned with in the cycling world.

Then, as everywhere in Latin America, there is soccer (or *fútbol*). Though Colombia is one of the former Spanish colonies where bullfighting is still regularly practiced, on any Sunday afternoon far more spectators will be found in the soccer stadiums than in the bullrings. As a professional sport, soccer in Colombia became really established only in the late 1940s and early 1950s, at a time when labor problems in Argentine soccer allowed Colombian sports entrepreneurs to hire significant numbers of Argentine coaches and players and thus quickly raise the quality of play to international standards. By 1960 Colombia qualified to field a team in the World Cup competition that was played in Chile. The same did not happen again until 1990, when Colombia made a respectable showing in another World Cup in Italy. By that time, while the Colombian leagues still had foreign players, they were no longer dependent on them, and in fact Colombian players were being sought after for European leagues.

To many Colombians, the most important event of the year 1989 was not the assassination of Luis Carlos Galán or President Barco's all-out war on the drug lords but their national soccer team's qualifying to play for the 1990 World Cup. The world press, in contrast, barely took notice of anything happening in Colombia except the upsurge of drug-related and political violence—all of which was of major concern to Colombians as well. Yet the euphoria that greeted the achievements of national athletes was more than sheer escapism. It was also another reminder that Colombia is a country of over thirty million people who for the most part earn their livelihood and seek their recreation in ways that are perfectly legal and not unlike those of people in neighboring countries, except for the relatively greater success of Colombia in managing its economy. The cyclists and novelists and Juan Valdez and his family tending their coffee farm will still be around after the sheer anachronism of guerrilla warfare is finally set aside and world narcotics fashions move on to some new substance for which Colombia is less favorably situated.

Epilogue

As Colombia entered the last decade of the twentieth century, the phenomena of guerrilla warfare and drug-related violence seemed to be winding down. The record of steady if unspectacular economic growth, under conditions of moderate annual inflation, continued, as did the country's unusual (for Latin America) degree of financial stability. Meanwhile, on the political scene, a first post-*Violencia* generation was rising to the top, led by César Augusto Gaviria. In 1990, at age forty-three, Gaviria became the youngest chief executive of the century, and he filled his government with many figures even younger than himself; one of them was the former M-19 commandant Antonio Navarro Wolf, appointed minister of health. Gaviria's youth and personal lifestyle, including a much-touted addiction to rock music, seemed to exemplify a general changing of the guard in Colombia that could be only for the better.

There were nevertheless important continuities: problems of severe inequality in the distribution of income and provision of essential services; the relative inefficiency of much of the productive structure; and the vulnerability of coffee, still the major industry, to world market fluctuations. The state itself was still dangerously weak in many respects, and its legitimacy continued to be questioned by many Colombians—not just the small minority of active resisters. To a people who in the last analysis measured their country's performance by the standards of the so-called First World (and who yearned to win themselves a place in that world), the condition of Colombia left much to be desired.

Another striking continuity was the survival of political parties founded in the first half of the nineteenth century. Gaviria was a young president, but no ruler anywhere in the hemisphere could claim membership in as venerable a political organization as the Colombian Liberal Party to which he belonged. He had attained the highest office, moreover, by skillfully putting together a coalition of reform-minded followers of the martyred Luis Carlos Galán and hard-bitten party bosses of the old school. His style was different; yet beneath the veneer of rock culture and youthful vitality, he was clearly no radical but, rather, an efficiency-seeking technocrat who had much in common with Virgilio Barco and Carlos Lleras Restrepo. Actually, in ideological terms, he was somewhat to the right of both of them, being a firm believer in the neoliberalism—with its emphasis on privatization and deregulation—that seemed to be sweeping even such former Latin American bastions of statist populism as Venezuela and Argentina.

Unlike his Venezuelan counterpart Carlos Andrés Pérez or the Argentine Carlos Menem, Colombia's Gaviria did not have a populist past to live down. His country, in fact, had somehow avoided the perils of populism, just as it had avoided the outright socialism that was now equally discredited and the sudden economic retrenchments that in various other countries of Latin America were carried out at the expense of massive unemployment and income loss for the working population. Politically, with certain brief exceptions, it had avoided dictatorships of either right or left (or for that matter center) and had remained faithful to the formulas of constitutional government as implanted in the immediate aftermath of independence. The political scientist and Barco brain truster Fernando Cepeda thus extolled "moderation" as one of his nation's quintessential characteristics.[1] It is not entirely clear how this "moderation" can be squared with the horrors of *La Violencia* or the many other instances of immoderate conduct of Colombians toward one another; but surely nations can sometimes display incompatible character traits just as individuals can.

Still another continuity, which underlies the others, has been social. The picture of Colombia as a country controlled from its birth by a narrow "oligarchy" or "elite" is much overdrawn, even though it is accepted and propagated by most of the Colombians themselves. The dominant groups—large-scale owners of the means of production and the main political power brokers, who might or might not be the same people—have always been open to new blood from outside or from below, and they have been steadily growing in size, especially over the last half century. They have often been content to leave the immediate conduct of affairs, whether in government or in the private sector, to the ever-growing class of middle-sector professionals. Nevertheless, their position has never been successfully challenged, and because of this fact any gains made by the rural or urban working classes have necessarily been limited. At the same time, constitutional government in Colombia has endured at least partly because it has suited the interests of the wealthy and powerful. It is a political system that they can easily participate in themselves and, through the parties and other devices, ultimately control, whereas any sort of autocracy is in danger of sometimes getting out of hand. Happily, Colombian oligarchs did not *need* to call on crude military dictators to save them from social revolution, except perhaps for Rojas Pinilla in 1953; and, in their view, his performance served only to underscore the all-round superiority of civilian constitutional rule.

Though Colombia may not have experienced social revolution, it has not lacked violence of many kinds. The same parties by which the masses until recently were successfully co-opted have over the years contributed their full share, and recurring violence represents the most obvious failure of the political system. In the world today, however, there is no intrinsic connection between constitutional democracy and political bloodshed, and the Colombian system, which in many ways has demonstrated a high degree of adaptability and resiliency, should be able to overcome the burden in question. The two traditional parties have finally outgrown their own mutual feuding, and now that the head of the M-19 has served in the national cabinet (which he then left only to play a key role in the 1991 constitutional assembly), it becomes harder than ever to sustain the thesis that guerrilla violence arises simply because those parties adamantly refuse to share political space with anyone else. True, the M-19 was never as radical as it sounded or acted, and Antonio Navarro Wolf, as its leader in legality, incorporated even a dash of economic neoliberalism into its program; he also returned Bolívar's sword. But neither was the Colombian system ever as rigid as Navarro, for one, had once believed. The Colombian establishment will not consent to be violently overthrown; pretty much anything else is subject to negotiation and indeed *was* negotiated in the recent assembly.

Appendix A

Population

National Population Data

Census Year	National Total	Annual Growth from Previous Census (%)
1825	1,223,598[a]	
1835	1,686,038	[b]
1843	1,955,264	1.9
1851	2,243,054	1.7
1871	2,951,111	1.4
1912	5,072,604[c]	1.4
1918	5,855,077	2.2
1938	8,701,816	2.0
1951	11,548,172	2.2
1964	17,482,420	3.2
1973	22,915,229	2.7
1985	29,265,499	1.8

[a]This first census, conducted during the Gran Colombian period, represented a decided underenumeration and is of little use for comparison with other censuses.

[b]No rate of increase calculated, for reason indicated in note (a).

[c]Panama is no longer included.

Sources: Fernando Gómez, "Los censos en Colombia antes de 1905," in Compendio de estadísticas históricas de Colombia, ed. Miguel Urrutia and Mario Arrubla (Bogotá, 1970), 9–30; Departamento Administrativo Nacional de Estadística, Colombia estadística (Bogotá, 1987), 1:51.

Population of Major Cities[a]

City	1851	1870	1912	1928	1938	1951	1964	1973	1985
Bogotá	29,649	40,833	121,257	235,421	330,312	648,324	1,697,311	2,995,556	4,207,657
Medellín	13,755	29,765	71,004	120,044	168,266	358,189	772,887	1,613,910	2,095,147
Cali	11,848	12,743	27,747	122,847	101,038	284,186	637,929	1,316,808	1,741,969
Barranquilla	6,114	NA[b]	48,907	139,974	152,348	279,627	498,301	799,011	1,137,150
Bucaramanga	10,008	11,255	19,735	44,083	51,283	112,252	229,748	361,799	544,567
Cartagena	9,896	NA[c]	36,632	92,491	84,937	128,877	242,085	312,557	491,368

[a]The figures through 1964 give the population of entire *municipios*, which especially in the earlier censuses could include some outlying rural districts; later figures are for metropolitan areas.

[b]Not available. Population in 1874 was 11,595.

[c]Not available. Population in 1874 was 8,603.

Sources: William Paul McGreevey, *An Economic History of Colombia, 1845–1930* (Cambridge, England, 1971), 110 (table); "Colombian Census of 1985," *Colombia Today,* 21, no. 8 (1986).

Appendix B

Presidential Elections, 1826–1990

Note: Figures in italics are the totals of electoral votes cast under a system of indirect elections, as practiced up to 1853 and again from 1892 to 1904, or of state unit votes, as practiced under the Constitution of 1863; an asterisk indicates that the candidate was finally named president by Congress, when no one received the required majority. The year is that in which the official scrutiny of votes was completed, not necessarily the year in which votes were cast. Starting in 1841, party designations are included with the names of principal candidates, "L." standing for Liberal and "C." for Conservative (including Ministerial under the latter heading). Valid blank votes are sometimes included with "Others," and sometimes not included, but are seldom numerous. Those who occupied the presidential office by other than popular election are listed in brackets.

Year	Candidates	Votes Received
1826	Simón Bolívar	*582*
	Others	*26*
[1830	Joaquín Mosquera, elected by Congress.	
1830–1831	Rafael Urdaneta, president-dictator by military coup.	
1831–1832	A succession of vice-presidents as acting chief executives.]	
1833	Francisco de Paula Santander	*1,012*
	Joaquín Mosquera	*121*
	Others	*130*
1837	José Ignacio de Márquez	*616**
	José María Obando	*536*
	Vicente Azuero	*164*
	Others	*281*

Year	Candidates	Votes Received
1841	Pedro Alcántara Herrán (C.)	*581**
	Vicente Azuero (L.)	*596*
	Eusebio Borrero (C.)	*377*
	Others	*70*
1845	Tomás Cipriano de Mosquera (C.)	*762**
	Eusebio Borrero (C.)	*475*
	Rufino Cuervo (C.)	*250*
	Others	*177*
1849	José Hilario López (L.)	*725**
	José Joaquín Gori (C.)	*384*
	Rufino Cuervo (C.)	*304*
	Others	*276*
1853	José María Obando (L.)	*1,548*
	Tomás Herrera (L.)	*329*
	Others	*131*
[1854–1855	José de Obaldía (L.), vice-president, acting chief executive.	
1855–1857	Manuel María Mallarino (C.), vice-president, acting chief executive.]	
1857	Mariano Ospina Rodríguez (C.)	97,407
	Manuel Murillo Toro (L.)	80,170
	Tomás Cipriano de Mosquera (National)	33,038
	Others	75
1860[a]	Julio Arboleda (C.)	58,506
	Pedro Alcántara Herrán (C.)	21,390
[1861–1864	Tomás Cipriano de Mosquera (L.), president by civil war.]	
1864	Manuel Murillo Toro (L.)	6
	Santos Gutiérrez (L.)	2
	Tomás Cipriano de Mosquera (L.)	1
1866	Tomás Cipriano de Mosquera (L.)	7
	José Hilario López (L.)	1
	Pedro J. Berrío (C.)	1
[1867–1868	Santos Acosta (L.), presidential designate, takes office at deposition of Mosquera.]	
1868	Santos Gutiérrez (L.)	5
	Pedro J. Berrío (C.)	2
	Eustorgio Salgar (L.)	1
1870	Eustorgio Salgar (L.)	6
	Tomás Cipriano de Mosquera (L.)	2
	Pedro A. Herrán (C.)	1

Year	Candidates	Votes Received
1872	Manuel Murillo Toro (L.)	6
	Manuel María Mallarino (C.)	2
	Julián Trujillo (L.)	1
1874	Santiago Pérez (L.)	6
	Julián Trujillo (L.)	3
1876	Aquileo Parra (L.)	5
	Bartolomé Calvo (C.)	2
	Rafael Núñez (L.)	1
1878	Julián Trujillo (L.)	9
1880	Rafael Núñez (L.)	7
	Tomás Rengifo (L.)	2
1882	Francisco J. Zaldúa (L.)	8
	Solón Wilches (L.)	1
[1882–1884	José Eusebio Otálora (L.), presidential designate, takes office at death of Zaldúa.]	
1884	Rafael Núñez (L.)	6
	Solón Wilches (L.)	3
1892	Rafael Núñez (National)	*2,075*
	Marceliano Vélez (National-C.)	*509*
[1894–1898	Miguel Antonio Caro (National), vice-president, completes term interrupted by death of Núñez.]	
1898	Manuel Antonio Sanclemente (National)	*1,606*
	Miguel Samper (L.)	*318*
	Rafael Reyes (C.)	*121*
[1900–1904	José Manuel Marroquín (C.), vice-president, takes power by coup.]	
1904	Rafael Reyes (C.)	*994*
	Marceliano Vélez (C.)	*982*
[1909–1910	Ramón González Valencia (C.), elected by Congress following resignation of Reyes.	
1910–1914	Carlos E. Restrepo (Republican), elected by National Assembly for full term.]	
1914	José Vicente Concha (C.)	300,735
	Nicolás Esguerra (L.)	36,764
1918	Marco Fidel Suárez (C.)	216,595
	Guillermo Valencia (C.)	166,498
	José María Lombana (L.)	24,041
	Others	42

Year	Candidates	Votes Received
[1921–1922	Jorge Holguín (C.), presidential designate, completes term at resignation of Suárez.]	
1922	Pedro Nel Ospina (C.)	413,619
	Benjamín Herrera (L.)	256,231
	Others	203
1926	Miguel Abadía Méndez (C.)	370,492
	Others	431
1930	Enrique Olaya Herrera (L.)	369,934
	Guillermo Valencia (C.)	240,360
	Alfredo Vásquez Cobo (C.)	213,583
	Others	577
1934	Alfonso López Pumarejo (L.)	938,808
	Others	3,401
1938	Eduardo Santos (L.)	511,947
	Others	1,573
1942	Alfonso López Pumarejo (L.)	673,169
	Carlos Arango Vélez (L.-C.)	474,637
1946	Mariano Ospina Pérez (C.)	565,939
	Gabriel Turbay (L.)	441,199
	Jorge Eliécer Gaitán (L.)	358,957
1950	Laureano Gómez (C.)	1,140,122
	Others	23
[1953–1957	Gustavo Rojas Pinilla, president by military coup.	
1957–1958	Military junta.]	
1958	Alberto Lleras Camargo (L.)	2,482,948
	Jorge Leyva (C.)	614,861
	Others	290
1962	Guillermo León Valencia (C.)	1,633,873
	Jorge Leyva (C.)	308,814
	Alfonso López Michelsen (L.)	624,863[b]
	Gustavo Rojas Pinilla (C.-ANAPO)	54,557[b]
	Others	494
1966	Carlos Lleras Restrepo (L.)	1,881,502
	José Jaramillo Giraldo (L.-ANAPO)	741,203
	Others	589
1970	Misael Pastrana (C.)	1,625,025
	Gustavo Rojas Pinilla (C.-ANAPO)	1,561,468
	Belisario Betancur (C.)	471,350
	Evaristo Sourdis (C.)	336,286

Year	Candidates	Votes Received
1974	Alfonso López Michelsen (L.)	2,929,719
	Álvaro Gómez Hurtado (C.)	1,634,879
	María Eugenia Rojas (ANAPO)	492,166
	Others	142,778
1978	Julio César Turbay Ayala (L.)	2,503,681
	Belisario Betancur (C.)	2,366,620
	Others	187,624
1982	Belisario Betancur (C.)	3,189,587
	Alfonso López Michelsen (L.)	2,797,786
	Luis Carlos Galán (L.)	746,024
	Others	83,368
1986	Virgilio Barco (L.)	4,214,510
	Álvaro Gómez Hurtado (C.)	2,588,050
	Jaime Pardo (Unión Patriótica)	328,752
	Others	90,506
1990	César Augusto Gaviria (L.)	2,834,118
	Álvaro Gómez Hurtado (Salvación Nacional)	1,401,128
	Antonio Navarro Wolf (M-19)	739,320
	Rodrigo Lloreda (C.)	702,043

[a] The election was held in the midst of national civil war. Liberal-held areas (and the Liberal Party) did not participate.

[b] The votes for López Michelsen were annulled on the ground that it was the Conservatives' turn to hold the presidency under the National Front alternation plan, and those for Rojas Pinilla were annulled on the ground that his political rights had been canceled.

Sources: David Bushnell, "Elecciones presidenciales colombianas, 1825–1856," in *Compendio de estadísticas históricas de Colombia*, ed. Miguel Urrutia and Mario Arrubla (Bogotá, 1970), 219–310, and "Elecciones presidenciales, 1863–1883," *Revista de Extensión Cultural* (Universidad Nacional de Colombia, Sede de Medellín), 18 (Dec. 1984): 44–50; Oscar Delgado, *Colombia elige* (Bogotá, 1986), 38; Jesús María Henao and Gerardo Arrubla, *Historia de Colombia*, 8th ed. (Bogotá, 1967), 885 (for 1930), 898 (for 1936); *El Nuevo Tiempo*, Apr. 8, 1914; Ministerio del Interior, *Memoria* (Bogotá, 1918), xxvi–xxvii, and *Memoria* (Bogotá, 1922), 193; *Diario Oficial* (Bogotá, July 21, 1926); Departamento Administrativo Nacional de Estadística, *Colombia política* (Bogotá, 1972), 154–155, 282; Departamento Administrativo Nacional de Estadística, *Colombia estadística* (Bogotá, 1987), 1:769 (for 1986); *Revista Javeriana* (July 1990), 82.

Notes

INTRODUCTION

1. Jesús María Henao and Gerardo Arrubla, *A History of Colombia*, trans. and ed. J. Fred Rippy (Chapel Hill, N.C., 1938).

2. Personal communication, of date long since forgotten, on which is partly based the discussion of the relative neglect of Colombia in David Bushnell, "South America," *Hispanic American Historical Review*, 65, no. 4 (Nov. 1985): 783–785.

CHAPTER I

1. Hermes Tovar Pinzón, *La formación social chibcha*, 2d ed. (Bogotá, 1980), 18.

2. In Spanish, "retinte de sabor a los oídos." Juan de Castellanos, *Elegías de varones ilustres de Indias*, 4 vols. (Bogotá, 1955), 4: 231.

3. José Antonio Ocampo, ed., *Historia económica de Colombia* (Bogotá, 1987), 20. For a broad discussion of the problems involved in measuring the preconquest population and its subsequent decline, see Germán Colmenares, *Historia económica y social de Colombia*, 2 vols. (Cali and Medellín, 1973–1979), 1: 47–71.

4. Total population figures are from José Manuel Restrepo, *Historia de la Revolución de la República de Colombia*, 3d ed., 8 vols. (Bogotá, 1942–1950), 1: xx. Restrepo, however, lumps whites and mestizos into a single category. For the population growth rate, see *Manual de historia de Colombia*, 2d ed., 3 vols. (Bogotá, 1982), 2: 139.

5. José Toribio Medina, *Historia del tribunal del Santo Oficio de la Inquisición de Cartagena de las Indias* (Santiago, 1899), 417.

6. Jane M. Rausch, *A Tropical Plains Frontier: The Llanos of Colombia, 1731–1831* (Albuquerque, 1984), chaps. 3 and 9 and passim.

7. Restrepo, *Historia de la Revolución*, 1: xxxviii.

8. The figure of 5 percent given in the text is an inference based on the analysis of properties seized from the church in the 1860s. See Jorge Villegas, *Colombia: Enfrentamiento iglesia-estado, 1819–1887* (Medellín, 1977), 82.

9. Consulado de Cádiz to Ministro de Real Tesoro, Sept. 27, 1773, in Archivo General de Indias (Seville), Indiferente General, legajo 2411. This gem was discovered by Allan Kuethe.

CHAPTER 2

1. José Manuel Restrepo, *Historia de la Revolución de la República de Colombia*, 3d ed., 8 vols. (Bogotá, 1942–1950), 1: xlvii.
2. John Leddy Phelan, *The People and the King: The Comunero Revolution in Colombia, 1781* (Madison, Wis., 1978), 143.
3. José María Pérez Ayala, *Antonio Caballero y Góngora Virrey y Arzobispo de Santa Fe, 1723–1796* (Bogotá, 1951), 380.
4. Indalecio Liévano Aguirre, *Los grandes conflictos sociales y económicos de nuestra historia* (Bogotá, 1964), chaps. 16–17.
5. Guillermo Hernández de Alba, *El proceso de Nariño a la luz de documentos inéditos* (Bogotá, 1958), 160.
6. Camilo Torres, *Memorial de agravios*, facsimile of 1832 ed. (Bogotá, 1960), 21.
7. Gabriel Camargo Pérez, "Etiología y metamorfosis de la voz 'Cundinamarca,'" *Boletín de Historia y Antigüedades*, 73, no. 754 (July–Sept. 1986): 665–688.
8. Horacio Rodríguez Plata, *La antigua provincia del Socorro y la independencia* (Bogotá, 1963), 47.
9. William Frederick Sharp, *Slavery on the Spanish Frontier: The Colombian Chocó, 1680–1810* (Norman, Okla., 1976), 125–126. Though the work cited refers specifically to the Chocó, in this matter it is unlikely that Antioquia presented a different picture.
10. David Bushnell, ed., *Simón Bolívar: Man and Image* (New York, 1970), 127.
11. José Antonio Ocampo, ed., *Historia económica de Colombia* (Bogotá, 1987), 104.

CHAPTER 3

1. David Bushnell, *The Santander Regime in Gran Colombia* (Newark, Del., 1954), 37. Most of the data in this chapter are ultimately derived from the same work.
2. Santander's principal biographer, Pilar Moreno de Ángel, in *Santander: Biografía* (Bogotá, 1989), does her best to make him an attractive figure, both as a human being and as a political leader, but the lack of strictly personal details in her 752 pages of text is striking. As Laureano García Ortiz observed in a famous essay of 1918, reproduced in *Algunos estudios sobre el general Santander* (Bogotá, 1946), 20, Santander lacked "true sensibility" or "tenderness" and was "only a statesman"—though a thoroughly admirable one in his view.
3. Bushnell, *Santander Regime*, 320 (table).
4. Bolívar to Carlos Soublette, Mar. 16, 1827, in *Cartas del Libertador*, ed. Vicente Lecuna, 11 vols. (Caracas and New York, 1919–1948), 6: 230–232.
5. Indalecio Liévano Aguirre, *Bolívar* (Medellín, 1971). Much the same interpretation is followed more recently by Gabriel García Márquez in his

fictionalized account of Bolívar's final days, *The General in His Labyrinth* (New York, 1990).

6. Santander to Alejandro Vélez, Mar. 17, 1828, in *Cartas y mensajes del general Francisco de Paula Santander*, ed. Roberto Cortázar, 10 vols. (Bogotá, 1953–1956), 7: 399.

7. Quoted in David Bushnell, "The Last Dictatorship: Betrayal or Consummation?" *Hispanic American Historical Review*, 63, no. 1 (Feb. 1983): 67.

8. José Manuel Restrepo, *Historia de la Revolución de la República de Colombia*, 3d ed., 8 vols. (Bogotá, 1942–1950), 6: 495.

9. Letter to Juan José Flores, Nov. 8, 1830, in David Bushnell, ed., *Simón Bolívar: Man and Image* (New York, 1970), 86.

CHAPTER 4

1. On freight rates see the table in William Paul McGreevey, *An Economic History of Colombia, 1845–1930* (Cambridge, England, 1971), 43–45; for times see José Orlando Melo, "La evolución económica de Colombia, 1830–1900," in *Nueva historia de Colombia*, 8 vols. (Bogotá, 1989), 2: 74.

2. Eduardo Posada Carbó, "Bongos, champanes y vapores en la navegación fluvial colombiana del siglo XIX," *Boletín Cultural y Bibliográfico*, 21 (1989): 3–5.

3. José Antonio Ocampo, *Colombia y la economía mundial, 1830–1910* (Bogotá, 1984), 84, 89, 100, 141–142, and passim.

4. John V. Lombardi, *The Decline and Abolition of Negro Slavery in Venezuela* (Westport, Conn., 1971), 164–172; David Bushnell and Neill Macaulay, *The Emergence of Latin America in the Nineteenth Century* (New York, 1988), 301 (table, in which the per capita amounts are given in 1880 U.S. dollars).

5. Melo, "La evolución económica," 2: 87, 90; for a revealing overview see Malcolm Deas, "The Fiscal Problems of Nineteenth-Century Colombia," *Journal of Latin American Studies*, 14, no. 2 (Nov. 1982): 287–328.

6. Quoted by Germán Colmenares, "Formas de la conciencia de clase en la Nueva Granada de 1848 (1848–1854)," *Boletín Cultural y Bibliográfico*, 9, no. 3 (1966): 399.

7. See table in Melo, "La evolución económica," 2: 67.

8. Vicente Restrepo, *Estudio sobre las minas de oro y plata en Colombia*, 5th ed. (Medellín, 1979), 175.

9. Mercedes Chen Daley, "The Watermelon Riot: Cultural Encounters in Panama City, April 15, 1856," *Hispanic American Historical Review*, 70, no. 1 (Feb. 1990): 95–108.

10. Departamento Administrativo Nacional de Estadística (DANE), *Estadísticas históricas* (Bogotá, 1975), 110.

11. Pilar Moreno de Ángel, *Santander: Biografía* (Bogotá, 1989), 588–608.

12. Fabio Zambrano Pantoja, "Aspectos de la agricultura colombiana a

comienzos del siglo xix," *Anuario Colombiano de Historia Social y de la Cultura*, 10 (1982): 188.

13. James L. Payne, *Patterns of Conflict in Colombia* (New Haven, Conn., 1968), 120.

14. Anthony P. Maingot, "Social Structure, Social Status, and Civil-Military Conflict in Urban Colombia, 1810–1858," in *Nineteenth-Century Cities: Essays in the New Urban History*, ed. Stephan Thermstrom and Richard Sennett (New Haven, Conn., 1969), 297–342.

15. Jean Batou, *Cent ans de résistance au sous-développement: La industrialisation de l'Amérique latine et du Moyen-Orient face au défi européen, 1770–1870* (Geneva, 1990), 335.

16. Ramón J. Velásquez, "Pórtico," in *Libro de decretos del Poder Ejecutivo de Venezuela por el Despacho del Interior y Justicia, 1831–1842* (Caracas, 1973), xxv.

17. Vol. 3 of Luis Martínez Delgado and Sergio Elías Ortiz, eds., *Epistolario y documentos oficiales del general José María Obando*, 4 vols. (Bogotá, 1973–1975), contains an assortment of writings in defense of Obando. One U.S. historian was also drawn to examine the dispute; see Thomas F. McGann, "The Assassination of Sucre and Its Significance in Colombian History, 1828–1848," *Hispanic American Historical Review*, 30, no. 3 (Aug. 1950): 269–289, which upholds the thesis of Obando's guilt, contrary to what is today the accepted version among Colombian historians.

18. Moreno de Ángel, *Santander*, 691–692.

19. Jesús María Henao and Gerardo Arrubla, *Historia de Colombia*, 8th ed. (Bogotá, 1967), 642.

20. Frank Safford, "Social Aspects of Politics in Nineteenth-Century Spanish America: New Granada, 1825–1850," *Journal of Social History*, 5, no. 3 (Spring 1972): 344–370. This is just one of several versions of the same essay, which has also appeared in Colombia in Spanish.

21. David Lee Sowell, "The Early Latin American Labor Movement: Artisans and Politics in Bogotá, Colombia, 1832–1919," 2 vols., Ph.D. diss., University of Florida, 1986, 1: 78–82 and passim.

22. Manuel Antonio Pombo and José Joaquín Guerra, *Constituciones de Colombia*, 4 vols. (Bogotá, 1951), 3: 259 and 329.

23. Frank Safford, *The Ideal of the Practical: Colombia's Struggle to Form a Technical Elite* (Austin, Tex., 1976), 114–123 and chap. 6.

24. John W. Kitchens and J. León Helguera, "Los vecinos de Popayán y la esclavitud en la Nueva Granada," and John W. Kitchens and Lynne B. Kitchens, "La exportación de esclavos neogranadinos en 1846 y las reclamaciones británicas," *Boletín de Historia y Antigüedades*, 63, no. 713 (Apr.–June 1976): 219–239, 239–293.

CHAPTER 5

1. Luis Eduardo Nieto Arteta, *Economía y cultura en la historia de Colombia*. 5th ed. (Bogotá, 1975), 247.

2. Antonio Cacua Prada, *Don Mariano Ospina Rodríguez fundador del conservatismo colombiano* (Bogotá, 1985), 23.

3. José Antonio Ocampo, *Colombia y la economía mundial, 1830–1910* (Bogotá, 1984), 100, 203–254.

4. René de la Pedraja Toman, "Los cosecheros de Ambalema: Un esbozo preliminar," *Anuario Colombiano de Historia Social y de la Cultura*, 9 (1979): 39–61, stresses the negative effects of changes in the tobacco industry for the farmers themselves. A more positive assessment is given by Miguel Samper, one of the apostles of classical economic liberalism in nineteenth-century Colombia, in *Escritos político-económicos*, 3 vols. (Bogotá, 1925–1926), 1: 35–36.

5. See William Paul McGreevey, *An Economic History of Colombia, 1845–1930* (Cambridge, England, 1971), 123–127, and Glenn Thomas Curry, "The Disappearance of the Resguardos Indígenas of Cundinamarca, Colombia, 1800–1863," Ph.D. diss., Vanderbilt University, 1981, 205–206 and passim.

6. Margarita González, *Ensayos de historia colombiana* (Bogotá, 1977), 330.

7. *El Eco de los Andes* (Bogotá), Aug. 10, 1852; Carlos Restrepo Piedrahita, *Constituciones de la primera república liberal, 1853–1866*, 2 vols. (Bogotá, 1979), 1: 173–178; *Informe que presenta el gobernador provincial de Vélez, en sus sesiones de 1855*, 2, 8.

8. *El Sur-americano* (Bogotá), Sept. 27, 1849.

9. James L. Payne, *Patterns of Conflict in Colombia* (New Haven, Conn., 1968), 120 (table).

10. David Lee Sowell, "The Early Latin American Labor Movement: Artisans and Politics in Bogotá, Colombia, 1832–1919," 2 vols., Ph.D. diss., University of Florida, 1986, 1: 161 and passim.

11. David Bushnell, "Voter Participation in the Colombian Election of 1856," *Hispanic American Historical Review*, 51, no. 2 (May 1971): 242.

12. It must be assumed that at least some of the votes for "others" were simply not tabulated, but clearly they still came to an insignificant total.

13. Payne, *Patterns of Conflict*, 146–152. Payne's discussion centers on the twentieth century but is equally applicable to the nineteenth.

14. Frank Safford, "Politics, Ideology and Society in Post-independence Spanish America," in *The Cambridge History of Latin America*, ed. Leslie Bethell (Cambridge, England, 1984–   ), 3: 413.

15. David Church Johnson, *Santander siglo xix: Cambios socioeconómicos* (Bogotá, 1984), 47–114.

16. Robert J. Knowlton, "Expropriation of Church Property in Nineteenth Century Mexico and Colombia: A Comparison," *The Americas*, 25, no. 4 (Apr. 1969): 387–401.

17. Jorge Villegas, *Colombia: Enfrentamiento iglesia-estado, 1819–1887* (Medellín, 1977), 82. The available records do not by any means allow greater precision. The figure of twelve million pesos found elsewhere in Villegas's book (29–31) as well as in other works includes certain nonecclesiastical

properties also seized by virtue of the same decree.

18. Patricia Londoño, "Mosaico de antioqueñas del siglo xix," *Revista de Estudios Colombianos*, 5 (1988): 31.

19. David Bushnell, "Elecciones presidenciales, 1863–1883," *Revista de Extensión Cultural* (Universidad Nacional de Colombia, Sede de Medellín), 18 (Dec. 1984): 48.

20. Malcolm Deas, "The Fiscal Problems of Nineteenth-Century Colombia," *Journal of Latin American Studies*, 14, no. 2 (Nov. 1982): 305.

21. Indalecio Liévano Aguirre, *El proceso de Mosquera ante el Senado* (Bogotá, 1966).

22. Marco Palacios, *Estado y clases sociales en Colombia* (Bogotá, 1986), 116.

23. Quoted in Antonio García Isaza, "Reflexiones sobre nuestro radicalismo y tradicionalismo en el siglo xix," *Boletín de Historia y Antigüedades*, 75, no. 760 (Jan.–Mar. 1988): 105.

24. Jaime Jaramillo Uribe, "El proceso de la educación en la República (1830–1886)," in *Nueva historia de Colombia*, 8 vols. (Bogotá, 1989), 2: 232. These figures are for 1870 specifically.

25. José Antonio Ocampo, ed., *Historia económica de Colombia* (Bogotá, 1987), 125–126. The official statistics are, of course, not to be taken as wholly accurate. Slightly different figures, but also reflecting a sharp increase in enrollments, are given by Jane M. Loy, "Primary Education during the Colombian Federation: The School Reform of 1870," *Hispanic American Historical Review*, 51, no. 2 (May 1971): 288.

26. Ocampo, *Historia económica*, 141–143, and *Colombia y la economía mundial*, 84, 89.

27. Ocampo, *Colombia y la economía mundial*, 63.

28. David Bushnell and Neill Macaulay, *The Emergence of Latin America in the Nineteenth Century* (New York, 1988), 301. The values are given as dollars of 1880.

29. Ocampo, *Colombia y la economía mundial*, 113.

CHAPTER 6

1. On the varying interpretations of Núñez—which mainly reflect widely divergent assessments of his political motives—see the article by Helen Delpar, "Renegade or Regenerator? Rafael Núñez as Seen by Colombian Historians," *Revista Interamericana de Bibliografía*, 35, no. 1 (1985): 25–37.

2. Jesús María Henao and Gerardo Arrubla, *Historia de Colombia*, 8th ed. (Bogotá, 1967), 781.

3. José Antonio Ocampo, *Colombia y la economía mundial, 1830–1910* (Bogotá, 1984), 326–334, discusses evidence both for and against the thesis.

4. David Lee Sowell, "The 1893 *bogotazo*: Artisans and Public Violence in Late Nineteenth-Century Bogotá," *Journal of Latin American Studies*, 21, no. 2 (Nov. 1989): 267–282.

5. Charles W. Bergquist, *Coffee and Conflict in Colombia, 1886–1910* (Durham, N.C., 1978), 51–99 passim.
6. Malcolm Deas, "The Fiscal Problems of Nineteenth-Century Colombia," *Journal of Latin American Studies*, 14, no. 2 (Nov. 1982): 325.
7. Bergquist, *Coffee and Conflict*, 145 (table).

CHAPTER 7

1. As quoted in, among many others and in slightly different translation, Charles W. Bergquist, *Coffee and Conflict in Colombia, 1886–1910* (Durham, N.C., 1978), 221.
2. William Paul McGreevey, *An Economic History of Colombia, 1845–1930* (Cambridge, England, 1971), 256 (table).
3. Bergquist, *Coffee and Conflict*, 242.
4. David Bushnell, *Política y sociedad en el siglo xix* (Tunja, Colombia, 1975), 35–36.
5. Quoted in Darío Mesa, "La vida política después de Panamá," *Manual de historia de Colombia*, 2d ed., 3 vols. (Bogotá, 1982), 3: 148.
6. Mauricio Archila Neira, "La formación de la clase obrera colombiana (1910–1945)," paper presented to Latin American Studies Association, New Orleans, March 1988, 1; see also Miguel Urrutia, *The Development of the Colombian Labor Movement* (New Haven, Conn., 1969), 63–64.
7. Lucy Cohen, *Las colombianas ante la renovación universitaria* (Bogotá, 1971), 51, n.40; interview with Lucy Cohen, May 1991; Jaime Jaramillo Uribe, "El proceso de la educación del virreinato a la época contemporánea," in *Manual de historia de Colombia*, 3: 288.
8. Miguel Urrutia, *Cincuenta años de desarrollo económico colombiano* (Bogotá, 1979), 35.
9. Bernardo Tovar Zambrano, *La intervención económica del estado en Colombia, 1914–1936* (Bogotá, 1984), 79, 167 (tables).
10. Christopher Abel, *Política, iglesia y partidos en Colombia* (Bogotá, 1987), 83.
11. Ibid.
12. McGreevey, *Economic History*, 202 (table); José Chalarca and Héctor H. Hernández Salazar, *El café* (Bogotá, 1974), 210, 257 (tables). Charles W. Bergquist, *Labor in Latin America: Comparative Essays on Chile, Argentina, Venezuela, and Colombia* (Stanford, Calif., 1986), chap. 5, discusses the rise of coffee primarily from the perspective of the peasant producers themselves.
13. José Antonio Ocampo, ed., *Historia económica de Colombia* (Bogotá, 1987), 187.
14. On the "Jewish myth," see the study of Antioquia by Ann Twinam, *Miners, Merchants, and Farmers in Colonial Colombia* (Austin, Tex., 1982), 8–13.
15. Ambassador Lane to Secretary of State, Bogotá, Sept. 3, 1943, U.S. National Archives, State Dept. decimal files, 821.6363/1498.
16. Roberto Herrera Soto and Rafael Romero Castañeda, *La zona bananera del Magdalena: Historia y léxico* (Bogotá, 1979), 79.

CHAPTER 8

1. Robert H. Dix, *Colombia: The Political Dimensions of Change* (New Haven, Conn., 1967), 211, attributes the term to Miguel Antonio Caro.

2. David Bushnell, *Eduardo Santos and the Good Neighbor* (Gainesville, Fla., 1967), 3.

3. Lucy Cohen, *Las colombianas ante la renovación universitaria* (Bogotá, 1971), 43. The *bachillerato* requirement was not an obstacle for the first woman doctor mentioned in the previous chapter, since she had earned the equivalent (and more) abroad.

4. *La política oficial: Mensajes, cartas y discursos del presidente López*, 4 vols. (Bogotá, 1936–1938), 1: 141.

5. José Antonio Ocampo, ed., *Historia económica de Colombia* (Bogotá, 1987), 239, 244 (table).

6. The characterization of López's economic policy given here owes much to Richard J. Stoller, "Alfonso López Pumarejo and Liberal Radicalism in 1930s Colombia," unpublished paper presented to the Latin American Studies Association, Miami, December 1989.

7. *Revista del Consejo Administrativo de los FF. CC. Nacionales*, 55 (Feb. 1937): 74, referring specifically to the change as carried out on the Ferrocarril del Norte between Bogotá and Barbosa.

8. Eduardo Zuleta Ángel, in *El Espectador* (Bogotá), May 24, 1964.

9. *La gran pausa de Eduardo Santos*, fascicle 16 of *Historia de Colombia*, ed. Oveja Negra (Bogotá, 1985).

10. Spencer S. Dickson to Anthony Eden, Mar. 4, 1936, in Public Record Office (London), FO 3712-1977/280.

11. Herbert Braun, *The Assassination of Gaitán: Public Life and Urban Violence in Colombia* (Madison, Wis., 1985), 54–55 and passim.

CHAPTER 9

1. Miguel Urrutia Montoya, personal conversation, ca. 1970.

2. Germán Guzmán Campos, Orlando Fals Borda, and Eduardo Umaña Luna, *La Violencia en Colombia*, 2d ed., 2 vols. (Bogotá, 1962–1964), 2: 370.

3. Vernon Lee Fluharty, *Dance of the Millions: Military Rule and the Social Revolution in Colombia, 1930–1956* (Pittsburgh, 1957), 96–98, 100–106. By far the best account is that in Herbert Braun, *The Assassination of Gaitán: Public Life and Urban Violence in Colombia* (Madison, Wis., 1985), chaps. 6–7. But see also, on events outside Bogotá, Gonzalo Sánchez, *Los días de la revolución: Gaitanismo y el 9 de abril en provincia* (Bogotá, 1983).

4. See, e.g., Russell W. Ramsey, "Critical Bibliography on La Violencia in Colombia," *Latin American Research Review*, 8, no. 1 (Spring 1973): 3–44, whose annotated list of 250 titles consists mainly of items published in the 1960s. The outpouring has continued since then.

5. Eduardo Ospina, S.J., *The Protestant Denominations in Colombia: A Historical Sketch with a Particular Study of the So Called "Religious Persecu-*

tion" (Bogotá, 1954), presents the official reply to the allegations and in so doing also cites the sources of the allegations themselves.

6. José Antonio Ocampo, ed., *Historia económica de Colombia* (Bogotá, 1987), 259 (table).

7. Eduardo Sáenz Rovner, "Industriales, proteccionismo y política en Colombia: Intereses, conflictos y violencia," *Historia Crítica*, 3 (Jan.–June 1990): 85–105.

8. The pessimistic view on wages and living standards is well exemplified by Fluharty, *Dance of the Millions*, 91–93, 127, 193–194. Miguel Urrutia, by contrast, suggests that it was precisely during the *Violencia* that "the situation of the proletariat begins to improve"; see, e.g., his "El desarrollo del movimiento sindical y la situación de la clase obrera," in *Manual de historia de Colombia*, 2d ed., 3 vols. (Bogotá, 1982), 3: 199. For some series on real wages, see the data compiled by Urrutia and Albert Berry for the *Compendio de estadísticas históricas de Colombia* (Bogotá, 1970), 76–82.

9. Russell W. Ramsey, "The Colombian Batallion in Korea and Suez," *Journal of Inter-American Studies*, 9, no. 4 (Oct. 1967): 541–560. This article covers the highlights of Colombian participation but does not present a full discussion of conflicting interpretations.

10. For a compilation of Rojaspinillista ideology, see Gonzalo Canal Ramírez, *El estado cristiano y bolivariano del 13 de junio* (Bogotá, 1955).

11. The standard defense of Rojas Pinilla in English is the Fluharty volume cited above. A more critical appraisal is found in John Martz, *Colombia: A Contemporary Political Survey* (Chapel Hill, N.C., 1962). See also the more recent, not very complimentary, account by two Colombian journalists, Silvia Galvis and Alberto Donadío, *El jefe supremo: Rojas Pinilla en la violencia y en el poder* (Bogotá, 1988).

CHAPTER 10

1. Paul Oquist, *Violencia, conflicto y política en Colombia* (Bogotá, 1978), 322 (table).

2. When the newspaper was acquired by a new management that changed the editorial policy, advertising immediately increased, but circulation plummeted. The paper soon folded.

3. Leon Zamosc, *The Agrarian Question and the Peasant Movement in Colombia: Struggles of the National Peasant Association, 1967–1981* (Cambridge, England, 1986), 21–30 and passim.

4. Ibid., 146–149 and passim.

5. Hernán Peñaloza Castro, *Educación y población en Colombia* (Bogotá, 1974), 17; *Statistical Abstract of Latin America*, 21 (1981): 7, 32; and 28 (1990): 196.

6. Nola Reinhardt, *Our Daily Bread: The Peasant Question and Family Farming in the Colombian Andes* (Berkeley and Los Angeles, 1988), 130. See also the tables in José Antonio Ocampo, ed., *Historia económica de Colombia* (Bogotá, 1987), 331.

7. *El Tiempo* (Bogotá), June 14, 1954.

8. Ocampo, *Historia económica*, 322–323.

CHAPTER 11

1. "Indicadores sociales," *Coyuntura Social*, 1 (Dec. 1989): 51.

2. See, for example, Gonzalo Sánchez, "La Violencia in Colombia: New Research, New Questions," *Hispanic American Historical Review*, 65, no. 4 (Nov. 1985): 789. Sánchez describes Colombia as "a country of *permanent and endemic warfare*" (his emphasis).

3. A controversy arose over whether the military took any prisoners in their recapture of the Palacio, something the army denied but others claimed to have seen. The one thing certain is that none of the attackers survived. There is a substantial and often polemical literature on the subject, but the main facts are clearly set forth in the news story in *Semana*, "28 horas de terror," Nov. 18, 1985, 26–41.

4. Jorge P. Osterling, *Democracy in Colombia: Clientelist Politics and Guerrilla Warfare* (New Brunswick, N.J., 1989), 266 and passim.

5. Quoted in Malcolm Deas, "Homicide in Colombia," *London Review of Books*, 12, no. 6 (Mar. 22, 1990): 6.

6. Jonathan Hartlyn, *The Politics of Coalition Rule in Colombia* (Cambridge, England, 1988), 226–227; Pilar Gaitán, "Primera elección popular de alcaldes: Expectativas y frustraciones," *Análisis Político*, 4 (May–Aug. 1988): 63–83. The Conservatives retained control of the two largest cities for only two years.

7. See *La cuestión de las drogas: Una problemática, tres perspectivas*, Serie Documentos Ocasionales, no. 3, Universidad de los Andes (Bogotá, 1988), 32 and passim.

8. "The World's Billionaires," *Forbes*, Oct. 5, 1987, 153.

9. "Rambo," *Semana*, Apr. 24, 1990, 26–32.

10. José Antonio Ocampo, ed., *Historia económica de Colombia* (Bogotá, 1987), 278.

11. Kathleen Ann Gladden, "Hanging by a Thread: Industrial Restructuring and Social Reproduction in a Colombian City," Ph.D. diss., University of Florida, 1991, esp. chaps. 3 and 4.

12. "Petroleum Discoveries in Colombia," *Colombia Today*, 24, no. 3 (1989).

13. *Colombia Today*, 12, no. 2 (1977), and 24, no. 5 (1989).

14. Juan Luis Londoño de la C., "Distribución nacional del ingreso en 1988: Una mirada en perspectiva," *Coyuntura Social*, 1 (Dec. 1989): 103–111.

15. José Antonio Ocampo and Eduardo Lora, *Colombia y la deuda externa: De la moratoria de los treinta a la encrucijada de los ochenta* (Bogotá, 1989), 13, 68, and passim.

16. John W. Sloan, "The Policy Capabilities of Democratic Regimes in Latin America," *Latin American Research Review*, 24, no. 2 (1989): 120

(table); "La nueva Colombia," *Semana*, Sept. 27, 1988, 27–28; "Indicadores sociales," *Coyuntura Social*, 1 (Dec. 1989): 31–32.

17. "Colombian Census of 1985," *Colombia Today*, 21, no. 8 (1986).

18. "Sólo para ellas," *Semana*, Apr. 24, 1990, 108.

19. *Latin American Art*, 1 (Spring 1989).

EPILOGUE

1. Fernando Cepeda Ulloa, "Pensamiento político colombiano contemporáneo," paper presented at Congreso sobre el Pensamiento Político Latinoamericano, Caracas, 1983.

Bibliographical Essay

For a nation that has often prided itself on its intellectual accomplishments, Colombia has produced a remarkably uneven historical literature, and it has in this matter received little foreign aid from scholars in other countries. In Colombia itself the emergence of history as a modern professional discipline dates only from the 1960s. In the quarter century since then, much has been accomplished; but a large number of topics in Colombian history still have not been treated or have received only the attention of the more traditional historians, writing without benefit of much scholarly apparatus or conceptual sophistication. There are, of course, honorable exceptions: self-trained historians of an older generation who produced works of genuine and lasting value. But the traditionalists have by and large been content to write chronological narratives of political and military events. The more recent "scientific" historians, by contrast, have generally concentrated on socioeconomic themes.

GENERAL WORKS

With rare exceptions, historians have not attempted to write a comprehensive general history of even a single period, much less of the entire national experience. Even the genre of collaborative general histories has not attained the development in Colombia that it has in other Latin American countries.

In English the only synthesis of Colombian history is J. Fred Rippy's translation of the outdated Colombian secondary text by Jesús María Henao and Gerardo Arrubla. In Spanish the most convenient general references are the multiauthor, multivolume (and overlapping) *Manual de historia de Colombia* and *Nueva historia de Colombia*. These volumes have contributions from some of the best-known scholars in Colombia, including Jaime Jaramillo Uribe, dean of present-day Colombian historians, whose collected essays, mainly on social and cultural topics, are worth consulting in their own right. Also helpful, and lavishly illustrated, is the *Historia de Colombia*, issued by the Spanish publishing firm Salvat Editores. Largest of all is the *Historia extensa de Colombia*, published by the Academia Colombiana de Historia, which offers some of the best (and worst) of the traditional-style history. Several of its volumes are listed separately by author in this bibliography.

There are in addition a number of general works on particular aspects of Colombian history. Economic history has been best served, with the fine collection of essays compiled by José Antonio Ocampo; an introduction to economic history by Álvaro Tirado Mejía; the more detailed survey (and covering more than just the economy) by Salomón Kalmanovitz; and the study of public finance prepared by Abel Cruz Santos for the *Historia extensa*. A short monograph by Juan Friede, first published in the 1940s, is still essential reading on the history of Indian communities. Rural society in the eastern cordillera specifically is the subject of a trail-blazing study by the sociologist Orlando Fals Borda, who is also the author of a highly stimulating if idiosyncratic four-volume history of social conflict and popular culture in the Caribbean coastal region. For literature the four-volume survey by Antonio Gómez Restrepo is still useful; on the history of art there is another multivolume, beautifully illustrated set published by Salvat Editores. On foreign relations the student may turn to the studies of the all-important U.S.-Colombian relationship by E. Taylor Parks and Stephen Randall and the more general works of the Colombian scholars Germán Cavelier and Raimundo Rivas. Of these only Randall takes the story up to the latest era. Finally, the student has the benefit of two historical dictionaries, one in English and one in Spanish, by Robert Davis and Horacio Gómez Aristizábal, and for that matter the all-about-Colombia introductory volume (of mostly contemporary content, admittedly) by Harvey Kline.

To be sure, neither in the first, or general, section of the bibliography nor in those that follow is an effort made to provide an exhaustive inventory of available sources. Readers will find most of the English-language books on Colombian history, as well as some important articles that have appeared in English. They will find a less complete sampling of the more abundant writings in Spanish; but the intent has been to include all those that are truly essential and that any major U.S. library ought to possess.

Cavelier, Germán. *La política internacional de Colombia.* 2d ed. 4 vols. Bogotá, 1959.

Cruz Santos, Abel. *Economía y hacienda pública.* 2 vols. Bogotá, 1965–1966.

Davis, Robert H. *Historical Dictionary of Colombia.* Metuchen, N.J., 1977.

Fals Borda, Orlando. *El hombre y la tierra en Boyacá: Desarrollo histórico de una sociedad minifundista.* 2d ed. Bogotá, 1973.

———. *Historia doble de la costa.* 4 vols. Bogotá, 1979–1984.

Friede, Juan. *El indio en lucha por la tierra.* 3d ed. Bogotá, 1974.

Gómez Aristizábal, Horacio. *Diccionario de la historia de Colombia.* 2d ed. Bogotá, 1985.

Gómez Restrepo, Antonio. *Historia de la literatura colombiana.* 3d ed. 4 vols. Bogotá, 1953–1954.

Henao, Jesús María, and Gerardo Arrubla. *Historia de Colombia.* 8th ed. Bogotá, 1967. An earlier edition appeared as *A History of Colombia*, trans. and ed. J. Fred Rippy. Chapel Hill, N.C., 1938.

Historia de Colombia. Ed. Salvat Editores. 8 vols. Bogotá and Barcelona, 1985–1987.

Historia del arte colombiano. Ed. Salvat Editores. 7 vols. Barcelona, 1977–1982.

Historia extensa de Colombia. 41 vols. (to date). Bogotá, 1964–.

Jaramillo Uribe, Jaime. *Ensayos sobre historia social colombiana*. Bogotá, 1969.

———. *Ensayos de historia social*. Bogotá, 1989.

Kalmanovitz, Salomón. *Economía y nación: Una breve historia de Colombia*. 3d ed. Bogotá, 1988.

Kline, Harvey. *Colombia: Portrait of Unity and Diversity*. Boulder, Colo., 1983.

Manual de historia de Colombia. 2d ed. Ed. Jaime Jaramillo Uribe. 3 vols. Bogotá, 1982.

Nueva historia de Colombia. 8 vols. (the first two vols. largely duplicate portions of the *Manual*). Bogotá, 1989.

Ocampo, José Antonio, ed. *Historia económica de Colombia*. Bogotá, 1987.

Parks, E. Taylor. *Colombia and the United States, 1765–1934*. Durham, N.C., 1935.

Randall, Stephen J. *Colombia and the United States: Hegemony and Interdependence*. Athens, Ga., 1992.

Rivas, Raimundo. *Historia diplomática de Colombia, 1810–1934*. Bogotá, 1961.

Tirado Mejía, Álvaro. *Introducción a la historia económica de Colombia*. 6th ed. Medellín, 1976.

PREINDEPENDENCE HISTORY (CHAPTER 1)

Colombia's pre-Columbian past has received less attention than the comparable period of Mexican or Peruvian history, both because the achievements of the original inhabitants were less spectacular than those of the Incas or Aztecs and because the present inhabitants are simply not as conscious of their Native American forebears. The works available are mostly by amateur historians or anthropologists; and the best general survey in English, by Gerardo Reichel-Dolmatoff, is not exactly current. But a more recent work, by Armand Labbé, while placing some relative emphasis on ceramics, incorporates later findings of Reichel-Dolmatoff himself as well as of other scholars. In Spanish the works of Luis Duque Gómez and Carl Langebaek are also highly valuable.

The story of conquest and colonization was first told by Spanish chroniclers such as Juan de Castellanos, Pedro de Aguado, and Pedro Simón, and the pertinent literature is ably discussed in the historiographical survey by Bernardo Tovar Zambrano. In English there are two rather dated works, by Clements Markham and by R. B. Cunninghame-Graham, and the translation of a popularized account by the Colombian author Germán Arciniegas. Nicolás Del Castillo Mathieu has provided a convenient recent overview. But the most important recent work is that by José Ignacio Avellaneda Navas, based on meticulous research and applying the methodology of prosopography, or collective biography. Nor can one ignore the extensive writings of Juan Friede, the first Colombian historian to combine rigorous investigation with a profound sympathy for the indigenous victims of the conquest.

For the study of colonial institutions and society, the chroniclers are again worth reading, and so is the English version of Juan Rodríguez Freile's vignettes of life in early Bogotá (misleadingly titled *The Conquest of New Granada*). Also worthwhile are two quite different nineteenth-century accounts by José Antonio Plaza and José Manuel Groot. Plaza's is perhaps mainly important for establishing the broad lines of a liberal critique of the colonial heritage, whereas Groot, on the basis of good research and with a sprightly prose, offers a conservative traditionalist's apologia. In the present century, members of the Academia Colombiana de Historia and similar institutions at the regional level have produced an abundance of chronological narratives dealing with the colonial period, generally with an institutional or a biographical emphasis; these are well represented in the *Historia extensa*. The revisionist author Indalecio Liévano Aguiree, in *Los grandes conflictos sociales y económicos*, presented a provocative but undocumented reinterpretation from colonial origins to the independence era, in which he sought to vindicate the Jesuits and early Hapsburg monarchs at the expense of later Bourbon rulers and creole oligarchs. However, Juan Friede—who has also written a detailed account of Gonzalo Jiménez de Quesada—was for many years almost alone in his effort to do historiographical justice to the Indian population.

Despite the early efforts of Friede, socioeconomic history came fully into its own only with the professionalization of the historical discipline in Colombia over the past thirty years. Its principal exponent was Germán Colmenares, author of seminal works on the Indian population and the hacienda system, but he did not labor alone. Hermes Tovar Pinzón, Jorge Palacios Preciado, Jorge Orlando Melo, and Margarita González must be mentioned also. Foreign scholars have made their principal contributions on social and economic aspects: Robert West on gold mining; Peter Marzahl on provincial urban society; David Chandler and William Sharp on the slave population (concerning which there is also an English version of Ángel Valtierra's life of the slaves' champion Pedro Claver); Jane Rausch on the *llanos* frontier; and Ann Twinam on the formation of a distinctive society in Antioquia.

Aguado, Pedro de. *Recopilación historial*. 4 vols. Bogotá, 1956.
Arciniegas, Germán. *The Knight of El Dorado: The Tale of Don Gonzalo Jiménez de Quesada and His Conquest of New Granada*. New York, 1942.
Avellaneda Navas, José Ignacio. *Los compañeros de Féderman: Cofundadores de Santa Fe de Bogotá*. Bogotá, 1990.
Castellanos, Juan de. *Elejías de varones ilustres de Indias*. 4 vols. Bogotá, 1955.
Chandler, David L. *Health and Slavery in Colonial Colombia*. New York, 1981.
Colmenares, Germán. *La provincia de Tunja en el Nuevo Reino de Granada: Ensayo de historia social, 1539–1800*. Bogotá, 1970.
———. *Historia económica y social de Colombia*. 2 vols. Cali and Medellín, 1973–1979.
Cunninghame-Graham, R. B. *The Conquest of New Granada*. New York,

1967. (Originally published 1922.)

Del Castillo Mathieu, Nicolás. *Descubrimiento y conquista de Colombia.* Bogotá, 1988.

Duque Gómez, Luis. *Prehistoria.* 2 vols. Bogotá, 1965–1967.

Friede, Juan. *Vida y luchas de Juan del Valle, primer obispo de Popayán y protector de indios.* Popayán, Colombia, 1961.

————. *Los chibchas bajo la dominación española.* Bogotá, 1974.

————. *El adelantado don Gonzalo Jiménez de Quesada.* 2 vols. Bogotá, 1979.

González, Margarita. *El resguardo en el Nuevo Reino de Granada.* Bogotá, 1970.

Groot, José Manuel. *Historia eclesiástica y civil de Nueva Granada.* 2d ed. 5 vols. Bogotá, 1889–1893.

Labbé, Armand J. *Colombia before Columbus: The People, Culture, and Ceramic Art of Prehispanic Colombia.* New York, 1986.

Langebaek, Carl Henrik. *Mercados, poblamiento e integración étnica entre los muiscas: Siglo xvi.* Bogotá, 1987.

Liévano Aguirre, Indalecio. *Los grandes conflictos sociales y económicos de nuestra historia.* Bogotá, 1964.

Markham, Clements. *The Conquest of New Granada.* London, 1912.

Marzahl, Peter. *Town in the Empire: Government, Politics, and Society in Seventeenth-Century Popayán.* Austin, Tex., 1978.

Melo, Jorge Orlando. *Historia de Colombia.* Vol. 1: *El establecimiento de la dominación española.* Medellín, 1977.

Palacios Preciado, Jorge. *La trata de negros por Cartagena de Indias.* Tunja, Colombia, 1973.

Plaza, José Antonio. *Memorias para la historia de la Nueva Granada desde su descubrimiento hasta el 20 de julio de 1810.* Bogotá, 1850.

Rausch, Jane M. *A Tropical Plains Frontier: The Llanos of Colombia, 1731–1831.* Albuquerque, 1984.

Reichel-Dolmatoff, Gerardo. *Colombia.* New York, 1965.

————. *San Agustín: A Culture of Colombia.* New York, 1972.

Rodríguez Freile, Juan. *The Conquest of New Granada.* London, 1961.

Sharp, William F. *Slavery on the Spanish Frontier: The Colombian Chocó, 1680–1810.* Norman, Okla., 1976.

Simón, Pedro. *Noticias historiales de las conquistas de Tierra Firme en las Indias Occidentales.* 9 vols. Bogotá, 1953.

Tovar Pinzón, Hermes. *La formación social chibcha.* 2d ed. Bogotá, 1980.

————. *Hacienda colonial y formación social.* Barcelona, 1988.

Tovar Zambrano, Bernardo. *La colonia en la historiografía colombiana.* Medellín, 1984.

Twinam, Ann. *Miners, Merchants, and Farmers in Colonial Colombia.* Austin, Tex., 1982.

Valtierra, Ángel. *Peter Claver: Saint of the Slaves.* Westminster, Md., 1980.

West, Robert C. *Colonial Placer Mining in Colombia.* Baton Rouge, La., 1952.

THE INDEPENDENCE ERA (CHAPTERS 2-3)

The independence movement has always held a special attraction for Colombian historians of the old school, who produce mainly political-military chronological narratives, paying retrospective homage to the founders of the nation. At their best such works are competent if unimaginative; at their worst they are blatantly uncritical. It is still necessary to consult them, if only because the topic has not proved equally attractive to the newer, professionally trained historians or to foreign scholars. The most important single work on independence thus continues to be the very first that was published, the classic multivolume survey by José Manuel Restrepo, written while its author was secretary of interior of Gran Colombia. Unfortunately, there simply is no standard modern survey.

On the revolt of the Comuneros, the best work is that by John Leddy Phelan, an obvious convenience for readers who are limited to English. Anthony McFarlane surveys other late colonial disorders. New Granada on the eve of independence is also covered by Allan Kuethe's fine study of the military. As for biographies in English, there are Thomas Blossom's somewhat pedestrian life of Nariño and numerous biographies of Bolívar (as there are in almost any language). None of the Bolívar biographies approaches definitive status, but those by Gerhard Masur and Augusto Mijares are quite serviceable. On the internal history of Gran Colombia, one may consult the work by David Bushnell.

In Colombia itself the most popular life of Bolívar is that by Indalecio Liévano Aguirre, whose interpretation is briefly mentioned in chapter 3. Liévano had covered the antecedents of independence and the Patria Boba in *Los grandes conflictos*, projecting contemporary issues back onto an earlier period in an analysis that is always suggestive though often tendentious. Innovative interpretations by the guild of university-trained historians in Colombia have been few and focus mainly on social aspects. But the slim volume by Germán Colmenares and his colleagues is an essential source. Zamira Díaz de Zuluaga, one of the contributors to that volume, has separately examined the socioeconomic context in the southwestern region; and Hermes Tovar Pinzón has contributed an important article on the 1810–1820 period. More recently, Pilar Moreno de Ángel has restated the traditional, highly positive, liberal interpretation of Santander in a massive biography. The military struggle in New Granada is well covered by the works of Camilo Riaño, Guillermo Plazas Olarte, and Oswaldo Díaz Díaz, all forming part of the Academia's *Historia extensa*.

The student of independence can benefit from the numerous collections of printed sources that have appeared in honor of Bolívar, Santander, and other heroes, or in commemoration of particular anniversaries. Two of the more important are the *Memorias del General O'Leary*, by Simón B. O'Leary (actually a collection of documents from the archive of Bolívar), and the *Gaceta de Colombia*, official organ of the Gran Colombian government, which has been reprinted. But one should not neglect the accounts of foreign travelers, which began to appear in the 1820s and provide numerous insights (from a perspective at the same time prejudiced and detached) into social customs and material conditions, topics that the formal historical literature has barely begun to explore. The original editions tend to be scarce, but the major ones (including those listed here) have mostly been reissued later in Spanish translation. The diary and journal of the first U.S. minister, Richard C. Anderson, is of particular importance for early relations with the United States.

Anderson, Richard Clough. *Diary and Journal, 1814–1826.* Ed. Alfred Tischendorf and E. Taylor Parks. Durham, N.C., 1964.

Blossom, Thomas. *Nariño: Hero of Colombian Independence.* Tucson, Ariz., 1967.

Bushnell, David. *The Santander Regime in Gran Colombia.* Westport, Conn., 1970. (Originally published 1954.)

Cochrane, Charles Stuart. *Journal of a Residence and Travels in Colombia.* 2 vols. London, 1825.

Colmenares, Germán, et al. *La independencia: Ensayos de historia social.* Bogotá, 1986.

Díaz de Zuluaga, Zamira. *Guerra y economía en las haciendas: Popayán, 1780–1830.* Bogotá, 1983.

Díaz Díaz, Oswaldo. *La reconquista española.* 2 vols. Bogotá, 1964–1967.

Duane, William. *A Visit to Colombia in the Years 1822 and 1823, by Laguayra and Caracas, over the Cordillera to Bogotá, and Thence by the Magdalena to Cartagena.* Philadelphia, 1826.

Fisher, John R., Allan J. Kuethe, and Anthony McFarlane, eds. *Reform and Insurrection in Bourbon New Granada and Peru.* Baton Rouge, La., 1990.

Gaceta de Colombia. 6 vols. Bogotá, 1973–1975. (Originally published 1822–1831.)

Groot, José Manuel. *Historia de la Gran Colombia.* Caracas, 1941. (Last part of his *Historia eclesiástica y civil de Nueva Granada.*)

Hamilton, John P. *Travels through the Interior Provinces of Colombia.* 2 vols. London, 1827.

Kuethe, Allan J. *Military Reform and Society in New Granada, 1773–1808.* Gainesville, Fla., 1978.

Liévano Aguirre, Indalecio. *Bolívar.* Medellín, 1971 (and many later editions).

McFarlane, Anthony. "Civil Disorders and Popular Protests in Late Colonial New Granada." *Hispanic American Historical Review,* 64, no. 1 (Feb. 1984): 17–54.

Masur, Gerhard. *Simon Bolivar.* Rev. ed. Albuquerque, 1969.

Mijares, Augusto. *The Liberator.* Trans. John Fisher. Caracas, 1983.

Mollien, Gaspar Théodore. *Voyage dans la République de Colombie en 1823.* 2 vols. Paris, 1824.

Moreno de Ángel, Pilar. *Santander: Biografía.* Bogotá, 1989.

O'Leary, Simón B., ed. *Memorias del General O'Leary.* 32 vols. Caracas, 1879–1888.

Phelan, John Leddy. *The People and the King: The Comunero Revolution in Colombia, 1781.* Madison, Wis., 1978.

Plazas Olarte, Guillermo. *Historia militar: La independencia, 1819–1828.* Bogotá, 1971.

Restrepo, José Manuel. *Historia de la Revolución de la República de Colombia.* 3d ed. 8 vols. Bogotá, 1942–1950.

Riaño, Camilo. *Historia militar: La independencia, 1810–1819.* 2 vols. Bogotá, 1971.

Tovar Pinzón, Hermes. "Guerras de opinión y represión en Colombia durante la independencia (1810–1820)." *Anuario Colombiano de Historia Social y de la Cultura,* 11 (1983), 187–233.

THE FIRST CENTURY OF INDEPENDENCE
(CHAPTERS 4–7)

To a greater extent than the history of the colonial and independence periods or of the more recent past, the history of nineteenth-century "nation building" can be studied with the help of an extensive literature bequeathed by participants and direct observers. José Manuel Restrepo is again one of the key sources, with both a general history that takes the story to the 1850s and a fact-crammed four-volume diary. Almost equally valuable are the memoirs of Joaquín Posada Gutiérrez, José María Samper, Salvador Camacho Roldán, and Aquileo Parra—all deeply involved in the politics and government of the period; the last two were strong Liberals, and Samper was an early Gólgota who turned increasingly Conservative. In his reminiscences José María Cordovez Moure presents picturesque episodes and vignettes of daily life. To these can be added some noteworthy travel accounts, especially the Colombian Manuel Ancízar's description of the northern provinces (a by-product of his service on a midcentury scientific survey), Isaac Holton's *Twenty Months in the Andes,* and John Steuart's *Bogotá in 1836–7.*

Historians of the political-military narrative school also have left some valuable works. Outstanding in this regard is the detailed chronicle by Gustavo Arboleda, which reached 1859 before it was interrupted by the author's death. Also useful are the works by Miguel Aguilera, Antonio Pérez Aguirre, Eduardo Rodríguez Piñeres, Luis Martínez Delgado, and Eduardo Lemaitre. Lemaitre provides both a biography of Rafael Reyes and an account of the separation of Panama from the Colombian perspective. Indalecio Liévano Aguirre finds another outlet for his revisionist bent in a biography of Núñez that is probably the best available whether or not one accepts Liévano's thesis that the Regenerator was a precursor of contemporary social democracy. Socialist intellectual Gerardo Molina's *Las ideas liberales en Colombia* is more a general history of liberalism than a history of "ideas" in a strict sense; for the intellectual history of the period, there is no substitute for the classic treatment by Jaime Jaramillo Uribe.

The current generation of professional historians in Colombia has shown little interest in nineteenth- or early-twentieth-century political history. One of the few exceptions is Germán Colmenares, whose earliest published work concerned the origins of the parties and who returned to political themes in one of his last studies, of the early-twentieth-century caricaturist Ricardo Rendón. Foreign scholars have partly made up for this neglect. Unfortunately, J. León Helguera's fundamental study of the first Mosquera administration remains unpublished (though constantly cited in dissertation form), and his intriguing study of *indigenismo* is available only as a published working paper. Helen Delpar, however, in her book *Red against Blue*, has given a sound overview of the development of bipartisan politics, with emphasis on the Liberals. Her article "Renegade or Regenerator?" is a helpful introduction to the historiography of Núñez and the Regeneration. An article by Robert Gilmore provides suggestive commentary on midcentury ideological currents; and one by Malcolm Deas, focusing on the Liberal political-military figure Ricardo Gaitán Obeso, gives insight into the texture and style of nineteenth-century politics. James Park analyzes regional rivalries as antecedents of the Regeneration, and David Johnson offers an excellent regional study that is as much a work of political economy as strictly socioeconomic in focus.

Charles Bergquist's *Coffee and Conflict in Colombia* is the best account to date of the Thousand Days' War. In this work Bergquist also presents his thesis that Colombian political divisions were determined in large part by differences in the relationship of Colombian elite sectors to the world economy. This interpretation has given rise to a friendly polemic with another North American Colombianist, Frank Safford, who takes issue with Bergquist in an article, "Acerca de las interpretaciones socioeconómicas de la política," in which he reviews a range of contrasting interpretations of nineteenth-century political economy. Safford has presented his own interpretation of political alignments in a highly influential essay, "Social Aspects of Politics in Nineteenth-Century Spanish America." But his work—for instance, *The Ideal of the Practical*, a trail-blazing study of technical education—has concentrated on economic history and on the material constraints conditioning social and cultural attitudes.

Other foreign scholars working on economic questions include William McGreevey, whose general economic history is insightful but sometimes careless in details, and Catherine Legrand, who has written a broad analysis of the process of frontier settlement. The specifically Antioqueño variant of agrarian settlement was the subject of an earlier classic study by the geographer James Parsons (which goes back to colonial origins) and an article by Keith Christie. The development of the Antioqueño economy generally is the topic of a major work by Roger Brew, and Richard Hyland has written on credit and land tenure in the Valle del Cauca; neither work has appeared in English, though Hyland's main findings are available in an English-language article. J. Fred Rippy and Paul Drake have written on U.S.-Colombian economic relations in the early twentieth century, and René De la Pedraja has discussed energy production and policy. Malcolm Deas produced a truly seminal article on nineteenth-century public finance. An article by Eugene Huck briefly addresses economic policy in the first decades after independence. Robert Gilmore and

John Harrison treat river navigation; Hernán Horna covers railroad building; and Theodore Nichols traces the changing importance of the major ports.

Still another article by Deas and one by Michael Jiménez discuss the rise of coffee production in Cundinamarca. In economic history, however, the Colombians themselves (economists as well as historians) have led the way. A half century ago the essays of Luis Eduardo Nieto Arteta established a framework for the interpretation of liberal economic reforms. The subsequent work by Luis Ospina Vásquez, which despite its title is a general economic history of the period, quickly became and still remains an obligatory point of reference for its solid research base and dispassionate analysis. The recent study by José Antonio Ocampo promises to become another standard reference, analyzing the external sector of the economy from a moderate and highly nuanced "dependency" perspective. Bernardo Tovar Zambrano has approached the problem of the state's role in economic affairs during the early twentieth century. Then, too, we have significant studies of particular economic sectors by Marco Palacios (coffee) and Luis Sierra (tobacco); a study of slave emancipation by Margarita González; and a regional study of society, politics, and economics in the Valle del Cauca by José Escorcia.

In view of the critical importance of the religious question, it is regrettable that more has not been written on the church. Juan P. Restrepo's comprehensive recital of injuries received by the clergy, published over a century ago, thus remains essential reading. However, Lars Schoultz has written a brief overview of the topic, and Fernando Díaz Díaz, Robert Knowlton, and Jorge Villegas have at least begun a serious examination of the conflict over church property. Fernán González surveys other aspects of church-state relations in the Radical era, and Christopher Abel has perceptively treated the post-Regeneration alliance between church and state.

In foreign relations (other than the works on economic relations already noted), the primary focus of interest has been the events leading to the loss of Panama and the subsequent efforts to heal Colombian relations with the United States. The English-language literature is too vast to discuss here, but David McCullough's popularly written book and the older work by Dwight C. Miner give satisfactory coverage. From a Colombian perspective, the principal work is that of Eduardo Lemaitre. The Colombian domestic repercussions of the affair are suggestively treated by Joseph Arbena, and the process of negotiating a settlement with the United States is covered in the recent work of Richard Lael.

On modern and contemporary literary history, a good starting point is Raymond Williams's history of the Colombian novel from 1849 to 1989. The current vogue of social history was to some extent anticipated years ago by the sociologist Anthony Maingot with his shrewd analysis of attitudes toward the military during the last century; and both Jane Loy and Aline Helg have treated the subject of education. For the history of the artisans and of labor more generally, one should consult the writings of David Sowell and Miguel Urrutia; Charles Bergquist analyzes labor in the coffee industry in one chapter of his comparative study of Latin American labor history. Álvaro Tirado Mejía has compiled, with introduction, a collection of texts illustrating "social" aspects of Colombian civil warfare. And Carlos Uribe Celis has produced a fascinating miscellany of data concerning fads and fashions of the 1920s. But the "new social history" is best represented by articles on scattered topics that have appeared over the last few years in Colombian journals and by certain of the chapters in the *Nueva historia de Colombia* (cited under "General Works").

Abel, Christopher. *Política, iglesia y partidos en Colombia*. Bogotá, 1987.

Aguilera, Miguel. *Visión política del arzobispo Mosquera*. Bogotá, 1954.

Ancízar, Manuel. *Peregrinación de Alpha por las provincias del norte de la Nueva Granada*. Bogotá, 1856.

Arbena, Joseph. "Colombian Reactions to the Independence of Panama, 1903–1904." *The Americas*, 33, no. 1 (July 1976): 130–148.

Arboleda, Gustavo. *Historia contemporánea de Colombia*. 6 vols. Bogotá, 1918–1932.

Bergquist, Charles W. *Coffee and Conflict in Colombia, 1886–1910*. Durham, N.C., 1978.

———. *Labor in Latin America: Comparative Essays on Chile, Argentina, Venezuela, and Colombia*. Stanford, Calif., 1986.

Brew, Roger. *El desarrollo económico de Antioquia desde la independencia hasta 1920*. Bogotá, 1977.

Camacho Roldán, Salvador. *Memorias*. 3d ed. 2 vols. Bogotá, 1946.

Christie, Keith H. "Antioqueño Colonization in Western Colombia: A Reappraisal." *Hispanic American Historical Review*, 58, no. 2 (May 1978): 260–283.

Colmenares, Germán. *Partidos políticos y clases sociales*. Bogotá, 1968.

———. *Rendón: Una fuente para la historia de la opinión pública*. Bogotá, 1984.

Cordovez Moure, José María. *Reminiscencias, Santafé y Bogotá*. 6th ed. 6 vols. Bogotá, 1942.

Deas, Malcolm. "A Colombian Coffee Estate: Santa Bárbara, Cundinamarca, 1870–1912." In *Land and Labour in Latin America*, ed. Kenneth Duncan and Ian Rutledge, 269–298. Cambridge, England, 1977.

———. "Poverty, Civil War and Politics: Ricardo Gaitán Obeso and His Magdalena River Campaign in Colombia, 1885." *Nova Americana* (Turin), 2 (1979): 264–303.

———. "The Fiscal Problems of Nineteenth-Century Colombia." *Journal of Latin American Studies*, 14, no. 2 (Nov. 1982): 287–328.

De la Pedraja, René. *Energy Policy in Colombia*. Boulder, Colo., 1989.

Delpar, Helen. *Red against Blue: The Liberal Party in Colombian Politics, 1863–1899*. University, Ala., 1981.

———. "Renegade or Regenerator? Rafael Núñez as Seen by Colombian Historians." *Revista Interamericana de Bibliografía*, 35, no. 1 (1985): 25–37.

Díaz Díaz, Fernando. *La desamortización de bienes eclesiásticos en Boyacá.* Tunja, Colombia, 1977.

Drake, Paul. *The Money Doctor in the Andes: The Kemmerer Missions, 1923–1933.* Durham, N.C., 1989.

Escorcia, José. *Desarrollo político, social y económico, 1800–1854.* Bogotá, 1983.

Gilmore, Robert L. "Nueva Granada's Socialist Mirage." *Hispanic American Historical Review,* 36, no. 2 (May 1956): 190–210.

———, and John P. Harrison. "Juan Bernardo Elbers and the Introduction of Steam Navigation on the Magdalena River." *Hispanic American Historical Review,* 28, no. 3 (Aug. 1948): 335–359.

González, Fernán. "Iglesia y estado desde la Convención de Rionegro hasta el Olimpo Radical, 1863–1878." *Anuario Colombiano de Historia Social y de la Cultura,* 15 (1987): 91–163.

González, Margarita. "El proceso de manumisión en Colombia." In her *Ensayos de historia colombiana,* 182–333. Bogotá, 1977.

Helg, Aline. *Civiliser le peuple et former les élites: L'éducation en Colombie, 1918–1957.* Paris, 1984. (Spanish trans., Bogotá, 1987.)

Helguera, J. León. "The First Mosquera Administration in New Granada, 1845–1849." Ph.D. diss., University of North Carolina, 1958.

———. *Indigenismo in Colombia: A Facet of the National Identity Search, 1821–1973.* Buffalo, N.Y., 1974.

Holton, Isaac. *New Granada: Twenty Months in the Andes.* New York, 1857.

Horna, Hernán. "Francisco Javier Cisneros: A Pioneer in Transportation and Economic Development in Latin America, 1857–1898." *The Americas,* 30, no. 1 (July 1973): 54–82.

Huck, Eugene R. "Economic Experimentation in a Newly Independent Nation: Colombia under Francisco de Paula Santander, 1821–1840." *The Americas,* 29, no. 1 (July 1972): 17–29.

Hyland, Richard. "A Fragile Prosperity: Credit and Agrarian Structure in the Cauca Valley, Colombia, 1851–87." *Hispanic American Historical Review,* 62, no. 3 (Aug. 1982): 362–406.

———. *El crédito y la economía, 1851–1880.* Bogotá, 1983.

Jaramillo Uribe, Jaime. *El pensamiento colombiano en el siglo xix.* Bogotá, 1964.

Jiménez, Michael. "Traveling Far in Grandfather's Car: The Life Cycle of Central Colombian Coffee Estates, the Case of Viotá, Cundinamarca (1900–30)." *Hispanic American Historical Review,* 69, no. 2 (May 1989): 185–219.

Johnson, David Church. *Santander siglo xix: Cambios socioeconómicos.* Bogotá, 1984.

Knowlton, Robert J. "Expropriation of Church Property in Nineteenth-Century Mexico and Colombia: A Comparison." *The Americas,* 24, no. 4 (Apr. 1969): 387–401.

Lael, Richard. *Arrogant Diplomacy: U.S. Policy toward Colombia, 1903–1922.* Wilmington, Del., 1987.

Legrand, Catherine. *Frontier Expansion and Peasant Protest in Colombia, 1850–1936*. Albuquerque, 1986.

Lemaitre, Eduardo. *Rafael Reyes: Biografía de un gran colombiano*. 3d ed. Bogotá, 1967.

———. *Panamá y su separación de Colombia*. 2d ed. Bogotá, 1972.

Liévano Aguirre, Indalecio. *Rafael Núñez*. 3d ed. Bogotá, 1967.

Loy, Jane M. "Primary Education during the Colombian Federation: The School Reform of 1870." *Hispanic American Historical Review*, 51, no. 2 (May 1971): 275–94.

McCullough, David. *The Path between the Seas: The Creation of the Panama Canal, 1870–1914*. New York, 1977.

McGreevey, William Paul. *An Economic History of Colombia, 1845–1930*. Cambridge, England, 1971.

Maingot, Anthony P. "Social Structure, Social Status, and Civil-Military Conflict in Urban Colombia, 1810–1858." In *Nineteenth Century Cities: Essays in the New Urban History*, ed. Stephan Thermstrom and Richard Sennett, 297–342. New Haven, Conn., 1969.

Martínez Delgado, Luis. *República de Colombia, 1885–1910*. 2 vols. Bogotá, 1970.

Miner, Dwight C. *The Fight for the Panama Route: The Story of the Spooner Act and the Hay-Herrán Treaty*. New York, 1940.

Molina, Gerardo. *Las ideas liberales en Colombia*. 3 vols. Bogotá, 1970–1977.

Nichols, Theodore E. "The Rise of Barranquilla." *Hispanic American Historical Review*, 34, no. 2 (May 1954): 158–174.

———. *Tres puertos de Colombia*. Bogotá, 1973.

Nieto Arteta, Luis Eduardo. *Economía y cultura en la historia de Colombia*. 5th ed. Bogotá, 1975.

Ocampo, José Antonio. *Colombia y la economía mundial, 1830–1910*. Bogotá, 1984.

Ospina Vásquez, Luis. *Industria y protección en Colombia, 1810–1930*. Medellín, 1955.

Palacios, Marco. *Coffee in Colombia, 1850–1970: An Economic, Social and Political History*. Cambridge, England, 1980.

Park, James. *Rafael Núñez and the Politics of Colombian Regionalism, 1863–1886*. Baton Rouge, La., 1985.

Parra, Aquileo. *Memorias de Aquileo Parra*. Bogotá, 1912.

Parsons, James J. *Antioqueño Colonization in Western Colombia*. Berkeley, 1949.

Pérez Aguirre, Antonio. *25 años de historia colombiana, 1853 a 1878: Del centralismo a la federación*. Bogotá, 1959.

Posada Gutiérrez, Joaquín. *Memorias histórico-políticas*. 4 vols. Bogotá, 1929.

Restrepo, José Manuel. *Diario político y militar*. 4 vols. Bogotá, 1954–1955.

———. *Historia de la Nueva Granada*. 2 vols. Bogotá, 1952–1963.

Restrepo, Juan Pablo. *La iglesia y el estado en Colombia*. London, 1885.

Rippy, J. Fred. *The Capitalists and Colombia*. New York, 1931.

Rodríguez Piñeres, Eduardo. *El Olimpo Radical*. Bogotá, 1950.

Safford, Frank. "Foreign and National Enterprise in Nineteenth-Century Colombia." *Business History Review*, 39, no. 4 (Winter 1965): 503–526.

———. "Social Aspects of Politics in Nineteenth Century Spanish America: New Granada, 1825–1850." *Journal of Social History*, 5, no. 3 (Spring 1972): 344–370.

———. *The Ideal of the Practical: Colombia's Struggle to Form a Technical Elite*. Austin, Tex., 1976.

———. "Acerca de las interpretaciones socioeconómicas de la política en la Colombia del siglo xix: Variaciones sobre un tema." *Anuario Colombiano de Historia Social y de la Cultura*, 13–14 (1985–86): 91–151.

———. "Race, Integration, and Progress: Elite Attitudes and the Indian in Colombia, 1750–1870." *Hispanic American Historical Review*, 71, no. 1 (Feb. 1991): 1–33.

Samper, José María. *Historia de un alma*. Medellín, 1971.

Schoultz, Lars. "Reform and Reaction in the Colombian Catholic Church." *The Americas*, 30, no. 2 (Oct. 1973): 229–250.

Sierra, Luis F. *El tabaco en la economía colombiana del siglo xix*. Bogotá, 1971.

Sowell, David L. "The 1893 *bogotazo*: Artisans and Public Violence in Late Nineteenth-Century Bogotá." *Journal of Latin American Studies*, 21, no. 2 (Nov. 1989): 267–282.

———. *The Early Latin American Labor Movement: Artisans and Politics in Bogotá, 1832–1919*. Philadelphia, 1992.

Steuart, John. *Bogotá in 1836–7: Being a Narrative of an Expedition to the Capital of New-Grenada and a Residence There of Eleven Months*. New York, 1838.

Tirado Mejía, Álvaro. *Aspectos sociales de las guerras civiles en Colombia*. Bogotá, 1976.

Tovar Zambrano, Bernardo. *La intervención económica del estado en Colombia, 1914–1936*. Bogotá, 1984.

Uribe Celis, Carlos. *Los años veinte en Colombia: Ideología y cultura*. Bogotá, 1985.

Urrutia, Miguel. *The Development of the Colombian Labor Movement*. New Haven, Conn., 1969.

Villegas, Jorge. *Colombia: Enfrentamiento iglesia-estado, 1819–1887*. Medellín, 1977.

Williams, Raymond L. *The Colombian Novel, 1844–1987*. Austin, Tex., 1991.

CONTEMPORARY COLOMBIA (CHAPTERS 8–11)

For the most recent period, the specifically historical literature is thin. Professional historians in Colombia have tended to neglect the contemporary period, and foreign historians show less interest than in the nineteenth century, although at least some of the works noted in the previous section also cover a greater or lesser part of the period since 1930. Among the Colombians, Álvaro Tirado Mejía has produced an important study of Alfonso López Pumarejo; and a number of others, to be noted below, have examined aspects of the *Violencia*. Eduardo Sáenz Rovner has looked at industrial policy. There is not much else, although the journalists Silvia Galvis and Alberto Donadío offer a documented if far from definitive history of the Rojas Pinilla dictatorship; and Carlos Lleras Restrepo has been grinding out a detailed set of memoirs, which is almost the only thing of its kind for the present century.

Among historical studies in English dealing primarily with the years since 1930, the most noteworthy is that of Herbert Braun on Gaitán and the political culture of his time. Gaitán is also the subject of a more conventional biography by Richard Sharpless; and Laureano Gómez is the subject of an idiosyncratically favorable treatment by James Henderson. Both Stephen Randall and David Bushnell have written on U.S.-Colombian relations. One must also note the work of Vernon Fluharty, technically a political scientist but writing more in the vein of political history; his *Dance of the Millions* is the one overview of the whole period from the 1920s to Rojas Pinilla, whom Fluharty much admired. The last part of the same period, to the start of the National Front, is covered by John Martz, another political scientist writing in historical vein (who is less admiring of Rojas Pinilla).

The *Violencia* is the subject of an extensive literature by historians, social scientists, and others. Here the most fundamental work is also one of the first: the brutally realistic collaborative treatment by Germán Guzmán Campos and his associates, which became a historical event in its own right because of the polemic it unleashed when first published. Among the principal later works by Colombian scholars on the topic are those of Gonzalo Sánchez and Carlos Miguel Ortiz Sarmiento. In English the best work is that of James Henderson, despite its emphasis (not really exclusive) on a single region. The U.S. historian Russell Ramsey and the Canadian Keith Christie have also written on the *Violencia* period, although their principal works have appeared only in Spanish, and Christie takes his point of departure well before 1946.

Several foreign political scientists have made important contributions on twentieth-century Colombia that deal with the *Violencia* but are not limited to that phenomenon. These include the North Americans Robert Dix, James Payne, Paul Oquist, and Jonathan Hartlyn, and the Peruvian Jorge Osterling. Dix and Payne trace the political system back to its nineteenth-century origins, although they emphasize the recent period. Hartlyn deals essentially with the last thirty years, and Oquist and Osterling take the story of political violence beyond the years of the *Violencia* proper. The French scholar Daniel Pécaut has also written a major work on politics and violence in Colombia. Unlike Oquist and numerous others, Pécaut believes that the loss of state autonomy to economic interest groups, rather than the hypertrophy of partisan competition, was largely responsible for "the collapse of the state" that made the *Violencia* possible. Still another political scientist, Daniel Premo, has produced a balanced account of the Alianza Nacional Popular (ANAPO) in his dissertation on that movement; unfortunately, the dissertation remains unpublished.

Economists have written widely on Colombian developments since 1930 but mainly in highly specialized monographs and scattered articles; no handy synthesis is available in English. However, on agrarian questions there are excellent works by economist Nola Reinhardt, sociologist Leon Zamosc, and the French scholar Pierre Gilhodès. José Antonio Ocampo must be mentioned again here as coauthor of a survey of the debt problem since the 1930s, and likewise Miguel Urrutia for a provocative analysis of income distribution.

Two more items by foreign social scientists—*The Church and Labor*, by Kenneth Medhurst, and *Religion and Politics*, by Daniel Levine—deal with the church. Yet there is still much ground not covered in the monographic literature or in scholarly journals. Fortunately, those interested in contemporary Colombia can fill some of these gaps with the help of periodical publications such as the newsmagazine *Semana*, the general-interest weekly *Cromos*, and the Bogotá daily *El Tiempo*, all three widely available at U.S. libraries (the latter normally in microfilm), not to mention the monthly *Colombia Today*, which is published in New York by the Colombian government itself.

Braun, Herbert. *The Assassination of Gaitán: Public Life and Urban Violence in Colombia.* Madison, Wis., 1985.

Bushnell, David. *Eduardo Santos and the Good Neighbor, 1938–1942.* Gainesville, Fla., 1967.

Christie, Keith H. *Oligarcas, campesinos y política en Colombia: Aspectos de la historia socio-política de la frontera antioqueña.* Bogotá, 1986.

Dix, Robert H. *Colombia: The Political Dimensions of Change.* New Haven, Conn., 1967.

———. *The Politics of Colombia.* New Haven, Conn., 1986.

Fluharty, Vernon Lee. *Dance of the Millions: Military Rule and the Social Revolution in Colombia, 1930–1956.* Pittsburgh, 1957.

Galvis, Silvia, and Alberto Donadío. *El jefe supremo: Rojas Pinilla en la violencia y el poder.* Bogotá, 1988.

Gilhodès, Pierre. *La question agraire en Colombie.* Paris, 1974.

Guzmán Campos, Germán, Orlando Fals Borda, and Eduardo Umaña Luna. *La Violencia en Colombia.* 2d ed. 2 vols. Bogotá, 1962–1964.

Hartlyn, Jonathan. *The Politics of Coalition Rule in Colombia.* Cambridge, England, 1988.

Henderson, James. *When Colombia Bled: A History of the* Violencia *in Tolima.* University, Ala., 1985.

———. *Conservative Thought in Twentieth Century Latin America: The Ideas of Laureano Gómez.* Athens, Ohio, 1988.

Levine, Daniel H. *Religion and Politics in Latin America: The Catholic Church in Venezuela and Colombia.* Princeton, N.J., 1981.

Lleras Restrepo, Carlos. *Crónica de mi propia vida.* Bogotá, 1983– .

Martz, John. *Colombia: A Contemporary Political Survey.* Chapel Hill, N.C., 1962.

Medhurst, Kenneth N. *The Church and Labor in Colombia.* Manchester, England, 1984.

Ocampo, José Antonio, and Eduardo Lora Torres. *Colombia y la deuda externa: De la moratoria de los treinta a la encrucijada de los ochenta.* Bogotá, 1989.

Oquist, Paul. *Violence, Conflict, and Politics in Colombia.* New York, 1980.

Ortiz Sarmiento, Carlos Miguel. *Estado y subversión en Colombia (La Violencia en el Quindío años 50).* Bogotá, 1985.

Osterling, Jorge P. *Democracy in Colombia: Clientelist Politics and Guerrilla Warfare.* New Brunswick, N.J., 1989.

Payne, James L. *Patterns of Conflict in Colombia.* New Haven, Conn., 1968.

Pécaut, Daniel. *Orden y violencia: Colombia, 1930–1954.* 2 vols. Bogotá, 1987.

Premo, Daniel. "Alianza Nacional Popular: Populism and the Politics of Social Class in Colombia, 1961–1974." Ph.D. diss., University of Texas at Austin, 1972.

Ramsey, Russell W. "The Colombian Batallion in Korea and Suez." *Journal of Inter-American Studies,* 9, no. 4 (Oct. 1967): 541–560.

———. *Guerrilleros y soldados.* Bogotá, 1981.

Randall, Stephen. *The Diplomacy of Modernization: Colombian-American Relations, 1920–1940.* Toronto, 1976.

Reinhardt, Nola. *Our Daily Bread: The Peasant Question and Family Farming in the Colombian Andes.* Berkeley and Los Angeles, 1988.

Sáenz Rovner, Eduardo. *Industriales, política y violencia en Colombia, 1945–1952.* Bogotá, 1992.

Sánchez, Gonzalo. *Los días de la revolución: Gaitanismo y el 9 de abril en provincia.* Bogotá, 1983.

———. *Ensayos de historia social y política del siglo xx.* Bogotá, 1985.

———. "La Violencia in Colombia: New Research, New Questions." *Hispanic American Historical Review,* 65, no. 4 (Nov. 1985): 789–807.

———, and Donny Meertens. *Bandoleros, gamonales y campesinos: El caso de La Violencia en Colombia.* Bogotá, 1983.

Sharpless, Richard E. *Gaitán of Colombia: A Political Biography.* Pittsburgh, 1978.

Tirado Mejía, Álvaro. *Aspectos políticos del primer gobierno de Alfonso López Pumarejo, 1934–1938.* Bogotá, 1981.

Urrutia, Miguel. *Winners and Losers in Colombia's Economic Growth of the 1970s.* New York, 1985.

Zamosc, Leon. *The Agrarian Question and the Peasant Movement in Colombia: Struggles of the National Peasant Association, 1967–1981.* Cambridge, England, 1986.

Index